POVERTY IN CANADA

POVERTY IN CANADA

edited by

JOHN HARP

Department of Sociology, Carleton University

and

JOHN R. HOFLEY

Department of Sociology, University of Winnipeg

p

PRENTICE-HALL OF CANADA, LTD.

h

Scarborough, Ontario

PRENTICE-HALL, INC., ENGLEWOOD CLIFFS, NEW JERSEY
PRENTICE-HALL INTERNATIONAL, INC., LONDON
PRENTICE-HALL OF AUSTRALIA, PTY., LTD., SYDNEY
PRENTICE-HALL OF INDIA PVT., LTD., NEW DELHI
PRENTICE-HALL OF JAPAN, INC., TOKYO

Library of Congress Catalog Card No. 72-160257

ISBN
0-13-686550-X (pa.)
0-13-686568-2 (cl.)
1 2 3 4 5 75 74 73 72 71

PRINTED IN CANADA

Table of Contents

III • OPPORTUNITY STRUCTURES AND THE CULTURE OF POVERTY

POVERTY IN CANADA

Section I
Introductory Articles

The anomaly of poverty amid affluence was recognized in Canada at about the same time as in the United States. However, there are some notable differences in approaches to the problem. There has been no sustained war on poverty in Canada, although several official government statements testify to the seriousness of the problem. This is not to suggest that research on the topic is non-existent. Various agencies of the federal government have sponsored and/or carried out research on selected aspects of Canada's poverty problem. Investigators who have reviewed the literature on poverty in both the United States and Canada report that in Canada unpublished material, much of which is buried or hidden in government research libraries, makes up a sizeable proportion of poverty references. Reports from a variety of studies comprise the present collection and represent discussions of poverty by Canadian social scientists. The articles illustrate the complexity, extent and immediacy of poverty in Canada.

Apart from the general need for a volume that brings together Canadian studies on poverty, the more ambitious task of explicating the concept of poverty within a sociological perspective is also undertaken by the editors. Many discussions of poverty lack any reconciliation between fact and theory. Some are heavily theoretical in approach, and often quite philosophical, but they are totally devoid of empirical evidence. Others are highly empirical accounts, employing only operational definitions. To be sure, sociology, with its wide range of methodology, contributes to this array of apparently disparate studies. We have decided to combine both approaches to the problem and to identify several important themes that appear in the literature.

Contemporary discussions of poverty often begin with the search for an appropriate definition. Students of the subject and especially those concerned with ameliorative programs, agree that a comprehensive definition is needed to facilitate the identification of specific sub-populations and/or types of poverty, and thereby to enhance the effectiveness of social programs. But first a basic operational definition is required, if we are to make judgements about the scope and character of poverty in Canada. In other words, we must identify the poor. Most of the recent literature regard the "poor" as those whose income is low, who are unable to cope with their poverty, and who present problems to society.

Drawing heavily on the Weberian tradition, Kasper Naegele describes the salient social characteristics of a modern industrial society such as Canada. He examines the processes of differentiation and integration which have occupied sociologists since the founding of the discipline and reveals that the dilemmas of our age have their origin in the nature and direction of social change. Naegele's comments provide a description of the social context in which poverty must be analyzed if it is to be understood.

Excerpts from the Fifth and Sixth Annual Reviews of the Economic Council of Canada give the reader an overview of the scope of the problem of poverty in Canada. The first report deals with the relative character of poverty, and the second emphasizes its economic significance for Canada.

Poverty is a many-faceted social phenomenon defined as the social and economic state of possessing fewer resources than required for providing oneself with the physical and conventional necessities of life. It is a social rather than a physical concept, changing with time and place; in other words, the concept of poverty derives from its societal context. In a democratic society questions arise as to equality of access to society's rewards, as well as equality of distributions of rewards for various groups.

In speaking of access to society's rewards within the context of an industrial society, one must discuss both economic and occupational structures. The question of employability of various groups in society can be more broadly interpreted through use of the concept of opportunity structure. More explicitly, opportunity structures include both the physical and normative dimensions of any social structure. One must consider not only the availability of resources (material and social) and occupations (physical), but the individual's access to them as well. The former involves assessing the way in which a structure "blocks" access to fuller social participation by means of certain economic and political strata or "classes". The latter involves some understanding of the values, attitudes and complex motivations of individuals. Furthermore, when one speaks of the availability of occupations, ecological or locational dimensions must also be considered. In Canada this gives rise to an analysis of regional disparities. Consequently, we are concerned with three dimensions of poverty: occupational, ecological and sociocultural. All three are important to any understanding of the social origins of poverty. It is seldom, however, that one finds all three dimensions treated in the same empirical research.

Studies of lower socio-economic groups have not been given a high priority within Canadian sociology. Consequently there is a paucity of sociological data on these groups. Nevertheless, one finds some agreement among writers as to specific characteristics of the lower stratum in the total society. One must be cautious in generalizing to all segments of the lower class, but these are generally regarded as critical features of lower-lowers in North American society:

1) *Occupational history*: Intermittent employment with public assistance (transfer payments) as a major source of income. Employment is at the lowest skill level in the occupational hierarchy.

2) *Community characteristics*: A deficiency of local organizations, inadequate service agencies, and low levels of social participation. In rural areas one finds small communities with large dependency ratios.

3) *Family and interpersonal relations*: A high incidence of family instability, a greater number of households headed by females. Unstable and superficial inter-personal relations coupled with little knowledge of or involvement in activities of the larger society.

4) *Value orientations*: A sense of powerlessness, dogmatism and authoritarianism in political ideology, fundamentalist religious views with some strong inclinations towards belief in magic, low fulfilment of needs and low levels of aspiration for the self.[1]

The applicability of these characteristics to the Canadian scene is largely a matter of conjecture, for we lack research in several crucial areas — for example, regional differences, the efficacy of our welfare and manpower programs, the relationship between our economic system and the perpetuation of poverty. There are also major points of disagreement among researchers, and these show up in the present volume. A recurrent question is whether the differences between the poor and the more affluent groups in society are a matter of degree or kind. Those who accept

[1] Peter H. Rossi and Zahava D. Blum, *Social Stratification and Poverty*. An excellent review of the literature presented at the annual meeting of the Sociological Research Association, San Francisco, California, August 1967.

the latter position are searching for evidence of a contraculture and the rejection of certain core values of society by the poor. Of course, isolation or the degree to which individuals are cut off from the mainstream of society would facilitate the development of a unique subculture.

A derived issue concerns whether the characteristics of the poor are transmitted from generation to generation. The subculture idea is consistent with this position. On balance, the evidence is far from conclusive on this point, and the problem is compounded by the lack of comparability among studies employing different methodological approaches and measurement devices. Obviously, differences of kind do exist among groups in a complex and diversified society, but the nature and significance of these differences for social mobility (access to society's rewards) within the system remain a moot question.

Certain general themes appear in the literature on poverty. First, there is the relationship between fact and theory, or between operational definitions of poverty and an overall theoretical perspective of the problem. Recognizing this theme, we have selected readings to represent both points of view. Second, the approach which views the poor as those at the bottom of the socio-economic continuum is contrasted with a culture of poverty approach. Finally, issues of social policy are reviewed in several articles on programs and strategies.

The articles are organized within three main sections; theoretical perspectives, the nature of the opportunity structure, and programs and strategies. Brief introductory comments are included for each section, as well as a bibliography of suggested readings. It is hoped that the collection will aid in clarifying significant issues associated with the study of poverty in Canada, and that it will fill the void for a needed overview of representative Canadian research on this important social issue.

1. *Modern National Societies*[*]

Kaspar Naegele

One of the main features of an industrial and modern society . . . is the separation of such domains as those of kinship and of the economy, or of the polity (in the form of a formally organized state), from various forms of "private life," including private economic enterprise. This separation and differentiation is always a matter of degree and of complexity. It cannot ever be an absolute matter. Besides, there are *kinds* of industrial societies. We can distinguish them precisely on the basis of the mode of their inner differentiation.

Some — from the point of view of Canadian society — we would call "totalitarian." In these the polity and the private life are by no means strongly divided. This particular kind of inner wall is thin. Besides, the polity takes a particular shape in that it does without the republican or monarchical-parliamentarian form that is familiar to any Canadian by participation or observation.

The differentiation of domains implies other social arrangements. It is not only constituted in the fact that a majority of the population in an industrial society live in one place, go to school or work in another, and think of a holiday as yet another form of journey. The differentiation of the domains of social activity — be it familial, economic, political, recreational, or, for that matter, religious — tends to be associated with two facts. These can mark any of the domains. They are: (1) the growth of complex and impersonal social organizations, and (2) the development of fluid but serious patterns of social stratification.

Admittedly the kinship system of an industrial society seems to be different in this regard from the other domains. It tends to take on a rather specific pattern. This pattern consists of relatively small families

*Reprinted from *Canadian Society* (3rd. edition), by B.R. Blishen et al, by permission of the author and the Macmillan Company of Canada Limited (Toronto 1968).

which stress closeness among people of similar age rather than among members of a given line of continuity. Families are not marked by bureaucratic arrangement. Outside of kinship, however, Max Weber pointed again and again to the development of bureaucratic patterns and of social organizations as a mark of modern society.

Essentially, bureaucracy implies a network of definable positions that are constituted by a definite sphere of competence and responsibility. These positions are arranged in a hierarchical order. Ideally they are filled by people with appropriate qualifications rather than with right connections. Bureaucracy, therefore, implies standards of technical competence, considerations of efficiency, and the just dispatch of diverse business. It tends to depend on a money economy. It thrives on the general notion, taken for granted in a modern society, that work can be done with means and facilities which are not owned by those who use them.

Stratification is even more diversified a phenomenon than bureaucracy. It has been the subject of ideological debate, sociological analysis and controversy, and an almost endless array of large and small empirical investigations. Marx and Veblen, as well as Weber and a series of contemporary theorists, have made the phenomenon of stratification, of class and caste, of status and mobility, the object of considerable interest and thought.

Whatever one's definition of class or status and whatever one's view of the possibility, on this earth, of a classless society, this would seem agreed: when societies are prominently involved in industrialism and in the use of technical expertise for medical, military and economic purposes, all have a ranked occupational system. All, moreover, use a man's job for far more purposes than as just a source of income. The occupational system, under these circumstances, becomes a complex division of labour. In this division a majority work within organizations, many of which are large. The family firm becomes the exception. A majority, too, work within urban contexts and rural work becomes itself increasingly mechanized. But a *division* of labour also raises the issue of the *co-ordination* of it. Two facts arise in this connection.

An industrial society creates many positions which primarily involve the responsibilities and skills of administration. An industrial society requires managers and executives. These can be found within industry and within education, within the religious organizations and within government, within the armed services and within various philanthropies and foundations. They are also found, of course, in the domain of entertainment and of advertising. As a result, our world of work is populated by a series of pyramids or diamonds – hierarchies involving a variety of workers and managers, foremen and technical experts, professionals and administrators. Besides, any one enterprise – be it a factory or an industry, a university or a hospital, a television network or a government department – is never an island unto itself. It also stands at the point of intersection of various other organizations. These may be unions and professional organizations, the presumed aggregate of buyers or the visible chain of clients, widely distributed audiences or half-known groupings of voters.

The occupational system, then, is constituted through very different kinds of work – ranging from the direct production of specific commodities or the personal entertainment of a night club audience to the administration of research grants, the arrangement of railway timetables, or the formulation of defence policy. It is also ordered into a stratified – and stratifying – domain by associating unequal worth with different kinds of work. There is no single evaluative principle by which two lines of work are arranged into claims for unequal honour, privilege, or respect. Still, work that implies more responsibility or more educated competence, or both, tends to be ranked above work implying less of these.

Modern industrial societies tend to rank certain categories of work – such as those of doctors, journalists, ministers of religion, executives, skilled workers, judges – in broadly similar ways despite their ideological differences. Rewards, in the form of honour, would then have to be available for these, especially if they involved as well either risk or long (and expensive) previous training. To what extent money alone can be used to provide a sufficient supply of persons to accept the necessary array of jobs and undertakings remains an open question. In North America, income not only takes different forms (wages, salaries, returns on investments, fringe benefits, gratuities, expense accounts, and the like); it is also used in a double way: to express the rank of a job or to compensate for the lack of it.

Finally, another pattern is implied by these facts: an industrial society requires the distinction between position and person and the cultivation of a far-flung web of impersonal human relations. In other words, an emphasis on loyalty, family ties, religiosity, or any other personal attribute or inherited quality is not enough for choosing among people when filling the positions that constitute the domains of society outside the domain of kinship. No society does without these. They are part of the consensus and of the structure of industrial societies as they have been of previous societies. But today they are insufficient. Increasingly, personal ties and concerns are complemented by impersonal considerations and by the cultivation of impersonal social relations.

An industrial society must give prominence to "universalistic" values and relations. It must prize efficiency and competence. It must also maintain a relatively high order of mobility. Mobility tends to be incompatible with intense personal relations except when intensity is confined to limited and private circles. Consequently, industrial societies tend to be much concerned with standards of performance, with measureable rates of change, and with the matching of individual accomplishments against general norms that are impersonally applicable to diverse situations and undertakings.

One means for accomplishing this is to develop codified bodies of rules, regulations, and laws, which require systems of courts and of various administrative tribunals. The legal domain, in other words, is an essential aspect of an industrial society. Typically that domain, for all its connections with the polity and the economy, is a fairly autonomous structure regulating the settlement of the conflicts that arise in such a society.

THE CONTINUITY OF SOCIETY

The differentiation of kinship, the economy, the polity, the legal system, and religion (and their respective involvement in the patterns of formal organization and of stratification) proceeds from the general consensus of active mastery and affects that consensus. The same is true for technology and science. Together, as we have seen, these structures are anti-traditional; at least they stand for a collective impatience with accepting as good enough any present standard of living, of health, of efficiency. Nor are these matters considered unimportant. Quite the reverse. Together with other values, Western industrial societies are much concerned with the standard of living and with its relatively equal distribution amid quite heterogeneous populations. No society, however, can in fact do without tradition and without paying some attention to certain continuities, both in the lives of individuals and in the arrangements that link one generation to the previous and to the following one. This makes of education, and its social arrangement, an especially strategic feature of industrial society. Indeed, especially in a politically free industrial society, education is likely to be subject to intense debate. The reasons for this are revealing of the structure of such a society:

1) All human accomplishments, including the persistence of society itself, depend on some appropriation of past accomplishments.

2) Education, especially formal education, is a necessary condition for many of those positions which provide esteem or prestige.

3) Through education, inequalities of birth can cease to be handicaps.

4) The maintenance of technology, science, and the professional management of human affairs depends on a continuous supply of appropriately trained people.

5) A society that has institutionalized science and technology engenders continuous social change which demands solutions that cannot be provided by mentalities rooted in tradition and committed to the maintenance of a *status quo*.

6) An industrial society not only "chooses" between different degrees of political or social freedom, it also inherits a non-industrial past. As a result, it is likely to engender various debates. These debates concern the relative importance of public and private enterprise, of social security

and individual scope, of the cultivation of excellence and the maintenance of relatively equal chances for all, of local autonomy and uniformly high standards. These are only some examples. Such debates inevitably become imported into the educational domain. There they are compounded by other issues, endemic to the domain itself. Among the latter, for instance, is the question of the professional status of the teacher, especially when teachers are subject to lay control. The educational debate is likely to raise the questions of the relative importance of technical expertise as against a state of general cultivation, of traditional and intellectual subject matter as against concern with the wider conditions of social and personal life (including driving a car), of the right of all to an education as against notions of selection.

Education is likely to be widely and publicly institutionalized in an industrial society, especially one that strives toward equality. As such, education becomes associated with the previously mentioned patterns of bureaucracy and professionalization. Weber also suggested that modern education is ineluctably committed to producing technical experts, at least in fairly considerable numbers. The alternative — the generally cultivated man or gentleman — is essentially dependent on a more rigid system of stratification and on a less technological economy. Clearly, education is at once a means of social continuity and of social change, and is likely to have to carry many of the burdens of a society that depends heavily on the literacy of its citizens.

THE SERIOUSNESS OF SOCIETY

The genesis of modern capitalism and its development into industrial forms has been helped by the combination of subjective consequences that flow from a general Protestant orientation to the world. Such an orientation tends to emphasize individual self-reliance, self-control, and the devotion to hard work and effort. This is especially true for Calvinist Protestantism, which can be characterized as calling for "inner-worldly asceticism." The latter attitude, in turn, is congruous with an emphasis on "calling," an emphasis that can easily be translated into notions of career, discipline, planning. Such individual notions are, of course, shared. Protestant beliefs, no less than Catholic ones, imply a consensus and have consequences for social organization. The disparate Protestant individual, who may also be desperate, arrives at his autonomy as a result of beliefs shared with those to whom he is also distant.

In general the Jewish-Christian tradition, more than that of any of the other world religions, has been associated with the development and structure of Western societies. The Protestant variant of this tradition has, as we have argued, played a special part in the genesis of the modern industrial form of these societies. It is worth remembering, however, that the constellation of institutions, motives, and values necessary for the genesis of social developments is not necessarily the same as the constellation of these necessary for the maintenance or subsequent transformation of such developments. Nor, once developed, do those who now adopt these patterns have to be characterized by intentions and involvements similar to those of the originators of these patterns. Nearly one-half of Canada, after all, is Roman Catholic; it is nevertheless an industrial society.

Religious beliefs and organizations have contributed to the consensus and tradition of modern societies. They have done so while also losing much of the kind of power and influence they exerted under feudal and medieval conditions. Religion has clearly become a rather separate realm. In North America this realm tends to be jealously separated from the polity. This separation is uneven. Nor should it be mistaken for the insulation of religious beliefs and activities from all other beliefs and activities. Rather, the connections have become more indirect. Direct connections, especially in the realms of education, health, and welfare, also persist. Sometimes the ties between religious and other social patterns become visible in the private or public conflicts between older and newer values or in the tensions between religious teachings, especially in their fundamentalist forms, and the claims of science. Clearly certain forms of religiosity are antithetical to some of the main features of modern societies, especially those forms which would be content with the acceptance of received forms of belief and theology and which would demand a *comprehensive* form of austerity that would reject an enjoyment of the (luxurious) fruits of hard work. Whatever the degree of discipline necessary in a modern society, one would hardly be able to imagine such a society utterly rejecting the notions of pleasure, fun, or happiness in the here and now.

Yet Weber showed — and we certainly had to be shown — that it is not religiosity as such that is a barrier to modernity. Rather, modernity depends on the cultivation of a certain kind of religiosity. All societies, after all, raise ultimate questions, face the facts of individual death, and have to formulate purposes and directions.

By definition, the concern with ultimate matters, especially when it is more than an individual, private quest, is part of the constitution of a religion. However, Weber also proposed that modern societies are subject to a process of "rationalization." Sometimes he used the term first proposed by the German dramatist Schiller: "the disenchantment of the world."

As with all the other suggestions in this general outline of industrial societies, we cannot now stop to debate and qualify this proposal. Clearly, contemporary society is a hugely rationalized, organized, and even frequently planned affair. It is thoroughly dependent on mathematics, physics, chemistry, and engineering. It goes as far as it can with dissolving all the puzzles, natural and human. Abstract thought and calculation, in the head or with machines, are continually cultivated. Yet modernity also includes Fascist and Communist movements and régimes. In part they are a form of religiosity representing protests against the present in the name of the past or the future. The fanaticism of these protests can stand in rather incongruous contrast to at least one meaning of the word "rational."

Weber allowed for such paradoxes. He distinguished between substantive and formal rationality. The first concerns the nature of the specific ends people seek. To the extent that one can speak of rational ends, these would include the pursuit of scientific knowledge. Formal rationality concerns one's choice of means. It represents a concern with efficiency and control as against the cultivation of traditional continuity. Bureaucracy is a form of formal rationality. It may be the instrument of quite irrational or non-rational ends.

In introducing these and other contrasts, Weber sought to make possible a more systematic analysis of social change. He was interested in the causes and directions of such change. His concern with the structure of societies was part of this interest. His notion of the rationalization of the world indicates part of his general conclusion. His concern with the rise of Western capitalism and with the social consequences of the world religions became the focus of this interest.

STRAIN AND CHANGE

Industrial societies are internally heterogeneous. They consist of diverse groupings, aggregates, and styles of life. Besides, for all the emergence of mass society and totalitarian regimentation, modern societies have become the context for the development of individualism. In addition, they have provided opportunities on an unprecedented scale for diverse groups and individuals within one society to participate in the enjoyment and even management of that society. Such claims are, of course, subject to much debate.

Social arrangements do not stay put under any circumstance. Modern societies, however, are marked by fairly rapid and comprehensive transformations in relatively short periods of time. They value change and exhibit it. They also generate movements and institutions that counter social change in the name of various traditions. Progress and improvement, as well as stability and the preservation of certain cultural resources, belong to the values that govern modern social arrangements. Indeed, as Weber especially suggested, modern societies contain a series of dichotomies and strains that engender change, and are the product of it.

For Weber, one of the pervasive tensions in modern society arises from the contrast between personal and impersonal bases of social coherence, especially when such coherence takes the form of leader and follower, or authority and subordinate. Weber distinguishes three kinds of authority: charismatic, traditional, and rational-legal. He arrived at this distinction by asking: What are the main ways in which people justify that others obey their authority?

Charismatic authority demands obedience because of the special gifts and qualities of the person exacting obedience. It stands for personal devotion and discipleship. Rational-legal authority, as embodied in bureaucracy, stands for the opposite. In that case one does not obey the person, but follows the rules enunciated by persons holding office: one salutes the uniform, not the man. Traditional authority (as represented, for instance, in a hereditary monarch) is handed down along lines of ascribed social relations. Rational-legal authority can be assumed by anyone who qualifies for office. To qualify for office can be a matter of previous education and attainment. Traditional authority is more closed: it is ascribed. It is also less likely to be codified. Kings and fathers rule, if and when they do, on the basis of rights and through the agency of demands that are not specifically listed in written documents. Charismatic authority — be it that of a Christ or of a Hitler — is the least socially stable of the three. It is likely to be transformed into one of the other two forms. In one respect the Roman Catholic Church represents the transformation of charismatic authority into a hierarchical and partly bureaucratic form. The office of the Pope bestows rights and obligations on its incumbent.

Weber's analysis of authority is an essay on social change, as well. This is so not only because of his concern with the transformation of charismatic authority but also because the contrast between charismatic and rational-legal attitudes turns out to be one of the basic conflicts in modern societies. This conflict embraces other dilemmas. We want just and equal treatment of "each case" before the law but we are also concerned to see the person behind the case. We want efficient and productive industrial enterprises, but we also want "human relations in industry." We want to apply impersonal and scientific knowledge to human plights, but we also want patients to be considered as persons. We want to go far in maintaining general standards of merit for employing or promoting people, but we also want work situations in which people are congenial with one another. We want an increasing number of our economic, political, and social patterns to be informed by rational calculation, foresight, and systematic knowledge, but we also want to cultivate intense ideals of romantic attachments. Admittedly, these conflicts are mitigated through the very differentiation of society. The particular norms of one domain need not be those of another. Nor are different sectors of the population of one society subject to the same expectations. Still, this heterogeneity, whether it creates conflict or not provides the citizen of a modern nation with a sense of diversity and inconsistency. When in addition he is, to some degree at least, possessed of a need for consistency, contrast and conflict are likely to give rise to attempts at social change, either on the plane of values or on the plane of social institutions.

2. *The Basis for Concern*

A. THE PROBLEM OF POVERTY*

Poverty in Canada is real. Its numbers are not in the thousands, but the millions. There is more of it than our society can tolerate, more than our economy can afford, and far more than existing measures and efforts can cope with. Its persistence, at a time when the bulk of Canadians enjoy one of the highest standards of living in the world, is a disgrace.

What is poverty in Canada? Those who have seen it, felt it, experienced it – whether as its victims or as those trying to do something about it – can supply some telling descriptions. But one of the notable characteristics of poverty in modern times is that it is so located in both city and country, and often so disguised (it does not, for example, invariably go about in rags), that it can pass largely unnoticed by those in happier circumstances. An occasional glimpse from a car window; a television show or Saturday supplement article – these may be the only manifestations of it which touch many a middle-class consciousness. Yet the figures – even the conservative, rather tentative estimates in this [article] – show indisputably that it is there, almost everywhere in Canada, on a larger scale than most Canadians probably suspect.

One reason for poverty's partial invisibility is that the poor tend to be collectively inarticulate. Many of them lack the education and the organization to make themselves heard. For example, most of them are outside the ambit of the trade union movement. They have few spokesmen and groups to represent them and give voice to their needs.

Another difficulty is that it is all too easy, in Canada, to file poverty away under the heading of certain other long-standing national problems, and in this way to lose sight of it as a major problem in its own

*Reproduced with the permission of the Queen's Printer for Canada, from the Economic Council of Canada, *Fifth Annual Review* (Ottawa: Queen's Printer, 1968), pp. 103-121.

right. Thus many Canadians may assume that the problem of poverty is close to identical with the problem of low average incomes in the Atlantic Provinces and Eastern Quebec (especially their rural areas) and among the Indian and Eskimo populations. But this is an inaccurate impression. The *incidence* of poverty – the chance of a given person being poor – is certainly much higher in the areas and among the groups just mentioned. But in terms of absolute numbers, between a third and a half of the total poverty in Canada is to be found among the white population of cities and towns west of Three Rivers. The resident of Montreal or Toronto need not travel far to see poverty first-hand; a subway fare will suffice. Much rural poverty, too, is to be found dispersed through areas where *average* income, by rural standards, is relatively high.[1]

There are two major problems in defining poverty. First, it is a *relative* concept. Second, while the availability of relevant statistics compels it to be discussed here largely in terms of low incomes, it means something more than simple income deficiency.

Let us deal first with the problem of relativity. It is of course true that generally-agreed-upon concepts of poverty alter through space and time. Thus, the situation of those Canadians whom the majority of their fellow citizens would deem to be suffering from poverty is hardly to be compared with that of the street-sleepers of Calcutta. And if a typical 1968 "poverty line," defined in terms of real income, were extended back through time, most Canadians during the Depression of the 1930's, and perhaps even most Canadians of the 1920's, would be found to have been living below that line.

But neither of these facts makes poverty in Canada in 1968 any less real or painful. To feel poverty is, among other things, to feel oneself an unwilling outsider – a virtual non-participant in the society in which one lives. The problems of poverty in developed industrial societies is increasingly viewed not as a sheer lack of essentials to sustain life, but as an insufficient access to certain goods, services, and conditions of life which are available to everyone else and have come to be accepted as basic to a decent, minimum standard of living.

Poverty, thus defined, is not quite the same thing as low income. A statistician would say there is a very strong association between the two, to the extent that one can often be used as a rough-and-ready substitute for the other. They are not, however, identical. For example, the low-income population of Canada includes a small proportion of people such as the university student who gets by on $1,500 a year, but does not feel himself irrevocably poverty-stricken, first, because he has a family to fall back on if necessary, and second, because much better income prospects lie a short distance ahead of him. Much more serious and more widespread is the kind of low-income situation that carries with it a sense of entrapment and hopelessness. Even the best statistics can only hint at this. They cannot capture the sour atmosphere of poor health and bad housing – the accumulated defeat, alienation and despair which often so tragically are inherited by the next and succeeding generations.

We believe that serious poverty should be eliminated in Canada, and that this should be designated as a major national goal. We believe this for two reasons. The first is that one of the wealthiest societies in world history, if it also aspires to be a just society, cannot avoid setting itself such a goal. Secondly, poverty is costly. Its most grievous costs are those felt directly by the poor themselves, but it also imposes very large costs on the rest of society. These include the costs of crime, disease, and poor education. They include the costs of low productivity and lost output, of controlling the social tensions and unrest associated with gross inequality, and of that part of total welfare expenditure which is essentially a pallative made necessary by the failure to find more fundamental solutions. It has been estimated in the United States that one poor man can cost the public purse as much as $140,000 between the ages of 17 and 57.

It should also be noted that in recent years there has been a burst of improvement in the available weaponry against poverty. Not only have new weapons been devised or proposed; but there has also been a development of techniques of evaluation by which the effectiveness of both old and new weapons can be assessed and enhanced. Much of this improvement has occurred since the U.S. Government declared formal war on poverty with its Economic Opportunity Act of 1964. (The term "war on poverty" is appropriate in more than one sense, for, ironically enough, some of the techniques of policy planning and evaluation now being applied in the field of poverty originated within the military and defence planning establishments.) There have also been some extremely promising developments in Canada and some overseas countries. We would not wish to paint an overoptimistic picture, nor to suggest that much further experimentation and improvement are not required. But it is undoubtedly the case that the prospects for mounting a powerfully renewed offensive against poverty, with clear performance criteria and appropriate feedbacks of information on actual results obtained, and with a greater sense of involvement on the part of the poor themselves, are considerably better today than they would have been ten years ago.

In the remainder of this [article], some income statistics are first presented in order to give the reader some sense of the over-all magnitude of the problem of poverty in Canada. Some broad characteristics of low-income families and individuals are also examined — characteristics significant for the planning of anti-poverty programs.

[1] "...the problem of low rural incomes can be associated to a degree with the problem of poor regions, but if this association is overemphasized, attention may be unduly diverted from the dispersed, but in absolute numbers still very substantial, poverty problem in prosperous regions. Although one third of the 'poor' farms in Canada were located in areas where their proportion was so high that the areas themselves could be classified as poor, almost another third of the poor farms were located in areas where the opposite was true." Helen Buckley and Eva Tihanyi, *Canadian Policies for Rural Adjustment*. A Study of the Economic Impact of ARDA, PFRA and MMRA, Special Study No. 7, Economic Council of Canada, Ottawa, Queen's Printer, 1967.

The Extent of Low Incomes in Canada

In popular discussion of the problem of poverty, a traditional opening question has been, "Are the rich getting richer while the poor get poorer?" In other words, poverty has been viewed in terms of trends in the distribution of income through society as a whole. This is not a particularly useful way of coming to grips with poverty as it is defined here. Nevertheless, recent trends in the distribution of income are taken as a starting point in order to clear the ground for what we regard as a more fruitful approach.

As may be seen from Table 1, there has been relatively little change in the distribution of family income in Canada over the last 15 years. In particular the share of total income received by the bottom fifth of families has altered only fractionally. Breaks in the statistics make it difficult to extend these comparisons further back in time, but it appears that there may have been a trend towards greater income equality between 1931 and 1951, with the share received by the bottom fifth showing an appreciable increase. Between 1951 and 1965, however – a period over which average family income increased very rapidly – little shift in percentage shares was apparent. (It should be noted that the distribution of family income in Table 1 is *before tax;* exactly corresponding figures of income *after tax* are not available, but Table 2 gives some idea of the effective rates of income tax applying to various income groups in 1961.)

The lower fifth, or lower third, or any other fraction of an income distribution, makes a poor statistical substitute for poverty as we have defined it. It bears no necessary relation to the needs of the poor – to their degree of access to certain goods and services regarded as basic to a decent standard of life at any point in time. The proper object of an attack on poverty should be the careful identification and aiding of those whose circumstances do not permit them to achieve such a standard. Ultimately, the object should be the elimination of poverty.

. . . Here . . . we . . . feel it necessary to give the reader some general notion of the size and character of the poverty problem which proper estimates would be likely to reveal. The tentative and broadly illustrative character of the figures should be strongly emphasized. It would be most distressing to see them taken up as fixed, precise and authoritative measures of poverty in Canada: rather, they should be superseded as soon as possible by better and more informative figures. To underline this point, two alternative estimates of "total poverty" are presented.

The two estimates are derived from a special study of the low-income population of Canada, carried out by the Dominion Bureau of Statistics on the basis of the 1961 Census.[2] Low-income families were defined as families with incomes insufficient to purchase much more than the basic essentials of food, clothing and shelter. An examination of data on family expenditures, collected from a sample of about 2,000 families living in urban centres with populations of 15,000 or more, showed that, on aver-

Table 1

Distribution of Nonfarm Family Income Before Tax

	DISTRIBUTION OF TOTAL INCOME			AVERAGE INCOME PER FAMILY
	1951	1961	1965	1965
	(Percentage)			(Dollars)
Lowest-income fifth of families	6.1	6.6	6.7	2,263
Second fifth	12.9	13.4	13.4	4,542
Third fifth	17.4	18.2	18.0	6,102
Fourth fifth	22.5	23.4	23.5	7,942
Top fifth	41.1	38.4	38.4	13,016
All families	100.0	100.0	100.0	6,669

Source: Based on data from Dominion Bureau of Statistics.

Table 2

Classification of Nonfarm Families and Persons Not in Families, by Income Group, 1961

INCOME GROUP	NUMBER OF FAMILIES	NUMBER OF PERSONS NOT LIVING IN FAMILIES	AVERAGE INCOME TAX AS A PERCENTAGE OF INCOME*
	(000)	(000)	
Under $1,000	137	306	—
$1,000–$1,999	275	192	1.5
$2,000–$2,999	356	157	3.2
$3,000–$3,999	524	150	4.6
$4,000–$4,999	583	71	6.0
$5,000–$5,999	500	35	6.5
$6,000–$6,999	365	17	7.1
$7,000–$7,999	260	9	7.4
$8,000–$9,999	296	8	8.5
$10,000 and over	331	10	16.5
Total	3,627	955	8.1

*Applies to families and persons not living in families.
Source: Based on data from Dominion Bureau of Statistics.

[2] J.R. Podoluk, *Incomes of Canadians,* Dominion Bureau of Statistics Census Monograph, 1968.

age, families allocated about half of their income to these needs. It might therefore be concluded that where a family was using up a good deal more than half its income on essentials, that family was likely to be in straitened circumstances, having little money left over for such things as drugs, medical care, education of children, recreation, savings, etc.

For purposes of the first estimate, low-income families and individuals were defined as those using 70 per cent or more of their incomes for food, clothing and shelter. On this basis, low-income families and individuals would include single persons with incomes below $1,500, families of two with less than $2,500, and families of three, four, and five or more with incomes of less than $3,000, $3,500, and $4,000 respectively.

As of 1961, some 916,000 nonfarm families plus 416,000 individuals were living below these levels.[3] The total number of persons involved was about 4.2 million, including 1.7 million children under 16 years of age. In all, they accounted for some 27 per cent of the total nonfarm population of Canada.

There are a number of special difficulties in defining and estimating the incomes of farm families, and the figures in this area are not much more than educated guesses. It would appear that, in 1961, roughly 150,000 farm families,[4] comprising perhaps 55,000 persons, may have been living below the income levels set forth above. The addition of these people to the nonfarm group would have brought the low-income percentage for all of Canada, including farms, to just under 29 per cent on the basis of the definition employed.

The Canadian economy has of course undergone a vigorous expansion since 1961, sufficient to lift the incomes of a good many families and individuals above the low-income lines we have specified. No comparative figures are available for farm families or for nonfarm individuals, but it would appear that by 1965 the percentage of nonfarm families living below the specified levels (their incomes being expressed in 1961 dollars) had declined from 25 per cent to 20 per cent. This probably gives an exaggerated impression of the longer-term trend of improvement, inasmuch as in 1961 the economy was at a low point of the business cycle, with the ranks of the poor temporarily swollen by unusually large numbers of unemployed.

The above estimate is the more conservative of the two presented. Most readers who care to reflect on the income cut-offs on which the estimate is based, and to compare these cut-offs with their own personal income situations, will agree that living standards at or just above the cut-offs are likely to be modest indeed.

In the second estimate, the cut-offs are raised somewhat by the device of assuming that the expenditures of 60 per cent or more (instead of 70 per cent or more) of income on food, clothing and shelter by an individual or family indicates straitened circumstances. This brings the cut-offs up to $2,000 for a single person, $3,500 for a family of two, $4,000 for families of three and four, and $5,000 for families of five or more.

Applied to the 1961 nonfarm population, these changes raise the low-income percentage from 27 per cent to 41 per cent.

At the beginning of this series of estimates, their "tentative and broadly illustrative character" was emphasized. They are not fully adequate measures of poverty. Such measures require among other things a thorough-going analysis of the needs and expenditure patterns of different types of families, and a consideration of assets, borrowing power, and income in kind as well as money income. It is useful also to distinguish between temporary and long-term poverty, and to allow for differences in living costs between different cities, towns, and rural areas.

But for all their shortcomings, the estimates presented here – particularly the first, more conservative set – suggest very strongly the existence of a major poverty problem in Canada. The statement that at least one Canadian in every five suffers from poverty does not appear to be a wild exaggeration. It is almost certainly close enough to the truth to be taken as one of the most serious challenges facing economic and social policy over the next few years.

Some Statistical Characteristics of Low-Income Families and Individuals

Statistics cannot adequately describe poverty. But used with care they are capable of furnishing important clues to types of policies likely to be effective against poverty. With this end in view, some further information is set forth here concerning the nonfarm low-income families and individuals included in the *first* of our estimates of the extent of poverty in Canada.

Two important warnings must be issued at the outset. Statistically, low-income families and individuals differ noticeably from the total Canadian population in respect of a number of things besides income. Certain characteristics of age, family size, place of residence, education, relationship to the labour force, and occupation, are more commonly found among them than among the population at large. Put another way, where these characteristics are present, the chance of a family or individual having a low income (the *incidence* of low income) is high. These high rates of incidence are often significant as policy guides to particular kinds of poverty problems.

This can be demonstrated in terms of some of the characteristics covered in Table 3. It is evident from the incidence figures that income

[3] Average incomes of low-income families in 1961 were:

Two persons in family	$1,427
Three persons in family	$1,851
Four persons in family	$2,347
Five or more persons	$2,707

[4] The *total* number of families primarily dependent on farming for a livelihood in 1961 was in the order of 275,000. Thus more than half these families were below the income levels used here.

Table 3

Selected Characteristics of All Nonfarm Families and Low-income Nonfarm Families Year Ending May 31, 1961

	(1) NUMBER OF NONFARM FAMILIES	(2)	(3) INCIDENCE OF LOW INCOME
	ALL FAMILIES	LOW-INCOME FAMILIES	(2) AS A PERCENTAGE OF (1)
	(000)	(000)	
Nonfarm Families	3,627	916	25
Place of Residence:			
Metropolitan	1,901	314	17
Other Urban	959	250	26
Rural	767	352	46
Region:			
Atlantic	349	158	45
Quebec	988	276	28
Ontario	1,363	254	19
Prairies	556	150	27
British Columbia	368	78	21
Sex of Head:			
Male	3,344	795	24
Female	283	121	43
Age of Head:			
Under 25	149	43	29
25–54	2,509	554	22
55–64	491	109	22
65 or over	478	210	44
Size of Family:			
Two	960	280	29
Three	734	148	20
Four	758	157	21
Five or more	1,175	331	28
Number of Children under 16:			
None	1,383	330	24
One	699	143	21
Two	679	156	23
Three or more	866	287	33
Labour Force Status of Head:			
In current labour force	2,996	573	19
Not in current labour force but worked during year	100	49	49
Did not work	531	294	55

continued . . .

Table 3

Selected Characteristics of All Nonfarm Families and Low-income Nonfarm Families Year Ending May 31, 1961 — concluded

	(1)	(2)	(3)
	NUMBER OF NONFARM FAMILIES		INCIDENCE OF LOW INCOME
	ALL FAMILIES	LOW-INCOME FAMILIES	(2) AS A PERCENTAGE OF (1)
	(000)	(000)	
Nonfarm Families	3,627	916	25
Education of Head:			
No schooling or elementary only	1,681	625	37
Secondary, 1–3 years	1,068	208	20
Secondary, 4–5 years	551	62	11
Some university	137	13	9
University degree	190	8	4
Number of Earners in Family:			
No earners	268	217	81
One earner	1,870	529	28
Two earners	1,114	142	13
Three or more earners	375	28	7
Major Source of Income:			
Wages and salaries	2,909	533	18
Self-employment	306	76	25
Transfer payments	271	245	90
Investment income	75	26	35
Other income	55	25	45
No income*	11	11	100

*This relatively small group includes such people as recent immigrants and recently widowed women who had received no income in Canada over the period covered.

Source: Based on data from Dominion Bureau of Statistics.

is more likely to be low when one or more of the following characteristics are present:

1) The head of the family had no formal education beyond elementary school.

2) The family lives in a rural area.

3) The family lives in the Atlantic Provinces.

4) The head of the family is not a member of the labour force.

5) No member of the family worked during the year.

6) The head of the family is 65 years of age or over.

7) The head of the family is a woman.

Chart 1
Percentage Distribution of Low-income Nonfarm Families, 1961

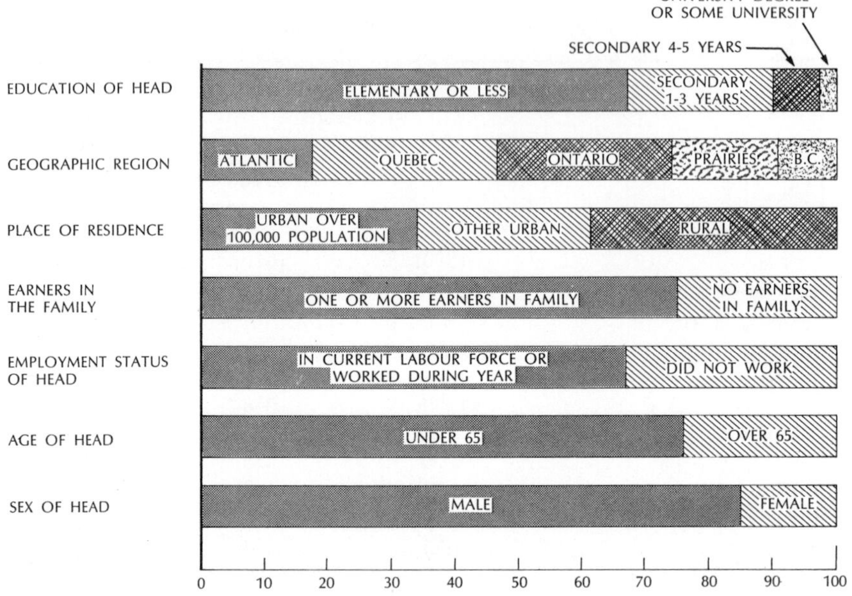

From this list, it is all too easy to form a picture of poverty in Canada that consists of a relatively few stereotyped categories, most of them involving high dependence on government pensions and welfare payments. There are indeed many people in such situations, but a more balanced picture of the total low-income population of Canada is necessary. It is vital, in framing policy, not to be overinfluenced by rates of incidence, and in this way to form too simple and stereotyped a picture of poverty. Chart 1 points out the following facts:

1) 62 per cent of low-income nonfarm families in 1961 lived in urban areas, and of this group more than half lived in metropolitan areas. (If the rough estimate of 150,000 low-income *farm* families in 1961 were included in the Charts, the proportion of all low-income families living in urban areas would still have been more than 50 per cent.)

2) 83 per cent of low-income nonfarm families lived elsewhere than in the Atlantic Provinces. 53 per cent of them lived in Ontario and the Western Provinces.

3) 68 per cent of the same group of families had heads who were in the labour force for at least part of the year.

4) 76 per cent of the group had one or more earners in the family, and (see Table 3) 66 per cent of families obtained most of their income from wage, salary and self-employment earnings.

5) 77 per cent of family heads in the group were under 65 years of age.

6) 87 per cent of families in the group were headed by men.

It can thus be seen that a set of anti-poverty policies directed towards major groups or geographical areas showing a very high *incidence* of low incomes would almost certainly fail to deal adequately with poverty. It would, for example, have a tendency to neglect unduly the very considerable group whose poverty problems are associated not with an absence of earnings, but with an insufficiency of earnings. It would tend to miss the many pockets of poverty that are scattered through relatively high-income regions – pockets which, in the aggregate, account for a large proportion of total poverty in Canada.

So much for the first warning concerning the interpretation of these statistics. The second warning is to avoid confusing characteristics with causes, and to bear in mind constantly how the total amount of poverty can be affected by broad, economy-wide forces such as the rate of economic growth in relation to potential. If the economy falls well below its potential, the incomes of many people will drop because they become unemployed. It is highly likely under these circumstances that unemployment will tend to strike hardest at those with least education; but to say simply that these persons' low incomes are *caused* by lack of education is not an adequate analysis of the situation.

With these two important cautions stated, we may now proceed to look at some further policy implications suggested by the low-income statistics.

Sources of Income

The principal source of income for most families, including low-income families, is earnings in the form of wages, salaries and income from self-employment. Any factors that adversely affect the market value of labour services, or which prevent the services from being offered, may result in income falling below poverty lines. Among the more notable factors of this kind are lack of job skills (often associated with low levels of formal education), old age, disablement, ill health and participation in low-paying occupations. The necessity of caring for young children may also prevent labour services from being offered. A small percentage of families are able to offset deficient labour income with returns from wealth holdings. But most must rely on some form of government transfer payment, such as pensions, unemployment insurance, or family allowances; hence the higher degree of reliance on such payments among low-income families, who, as a group, received 27 per cent of their income from this source in 1961, compared with a figure of 8 per cent for all families.

Where a low-income family is for one reason or another incapable of offering labour services, and is therefore largely dependent on government payments, the policy problem of how to aid that family is in one sense relatively simple: the major issue is the size of the income to be provided. But where there are earnings, but on an insufficient scale, or where there is an unexploited potential for earnings, the policy choices are less simple. Other things being equal, it is far better to help people to help themselves — to put them in a position to upgrade their earnings permanently through such measures as training and manpower mobility programs, and to exploit unused earnings potential (provided this does not involve a sacrifice of future to present earnings, as in the case of the youth who drops out of high school to augment family income). But self-help takes time, and meanwhile income support in the form of government payments may be needed. It seems a fair generalization that in the past Canadian social policy has tended to emphasize various forms of income maintenance, and has only recently moved strongly into the more difficult area of promoting self-help among low-income people.

Low-Income Occupations

Where the head of a family is in the labour force, his chances of having a low income are very much greater in certain occupations than in others. This statement is a well-worn commonplace, but the extent of the differences revealed in Table 4 is nevertheless striking. The incidence of low incomes in 1961 was more than twice the over-all average in four occupational groups: farm workers; loggers and related workers; fishermen, trappers and hunters; and labourers.

Once again, it is necessary to draw a careful distinction between incidence and total numbers, and to note that the four occupations named accounted for only 22 per cent of all the low-income family heads in the Table. Nevertheless, it is worth remarking that the four occupations tend to be characterized by much seasonality and other irregularity of employment and earnings. This cross-checks with other information suggesting that, across the whole occupational spectrum, insufficiency of wage and salary earnings is often associated with intermittent and part-time work.

Education, Location and Occupation

The association between low income and lack of education beyond the elementary level is particularly strong. Not only did families whose heads had less than secondary education show a high incidence of low income in 1961 (37 per cent), they also accounted for more than two-thirds of all low-income families.

However, in addition to education there are other factors such as occupation, region, and place of residence (urban or rural).[5] In addition, there is some interaction between education and income, rather than a purely one-way casual connection. Thus the education levels of family heads were very likely influenced by the income and related circumstances of *their* parents; and their circumstances in turn are likely to influence the education levels achieved by their children.

In the cross-classifications of Charts 2, 3, and 4, low educational achievement continues to exhibit a strong association with low income, but does not wipe out the influence of other factors. Thus, even where

Table 4

Occupational Distribution of Male Nonfarm Family Heads, 1961

	(1) NUMBER OF NONFARM FAMILY HEADS	(2)	(3) INCIDENCE OF LOW INCOME
	TOTAL	LOW INCOME	(2) AS A PERCENTAGE OF (1)
	(000)	(000)	
Managerial*	419	42	10
Professional and technical	256	12	5
Clerical	200	21	11
Sales	182	24	13
Service and recreation	246	50	20
Transport and communications	256	61	24
Farm workers†	34	19	56
Loggers and related workers	35	20	57
Fishermen, trappers, hunters	20	14	70
Miners, quarrymen, related workers	44	8	18
Craftsmen, production process and related workers	991	183	19
Labourers	149	60	40
Not stated	39	10	26
Total of male nonfarm family heads in current labour force	2,871	524	18

*Includes self-employed, as do other occupational classifications.
†Includes farm *workers* not living on farms.
Source: Based on data from Dominion Bureau of Statistics.

there is education beyond the elementary level, the incidence of low income continues to be notably higher in the Atlantic Provinces than elsewhere, higher in rural than in urban areas, and considerably higher in some occupations than in others.

It seems clear that provision of adequate education generally, plus deliberate special efforts to help those whose family circumstances tend to discourage persistence in education, must form a highly important part of policy against poverty. As some of the other work of the Council has shown, the performance of the educational system has very long-range effects. To the extent that it fails to perform well in helping the

[5] A regression analysis of the low-income data has suggested that many of the factors associated with a high incidence of low income tend to occur together. The explanatory variables used in the analysis were education, place of residence (urban or rural), age, religion and occupation. As a general rule, the partial effect of each variable was smaller than the corresponding incidences given in Table 3.

Chart 2
Education and Low Incomes by Region, 1961

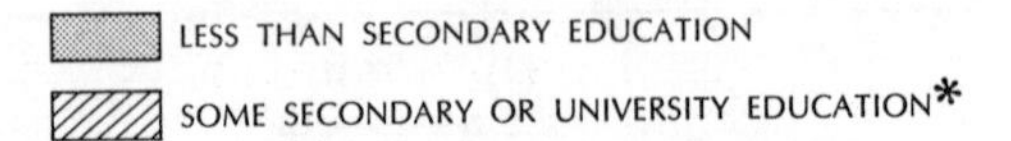

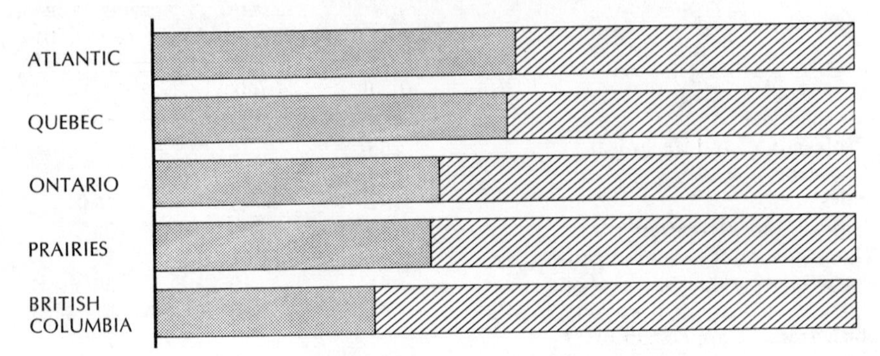

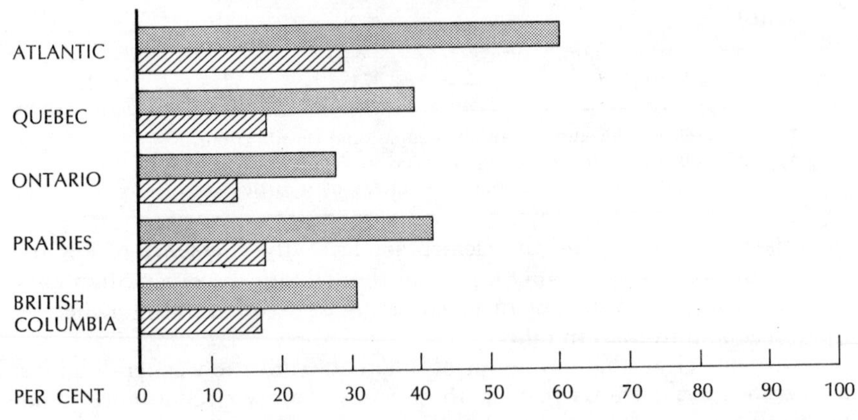

Source: Based on data from Dominion Bureau of Statistics and estimates by Economic Council of Canada.

*EDITOR'S NOTE: It should be noted that those people classified as having some secondary or university education in Ontario probably have a higher educational level than those persons so classified in the Atlantic provinces.

children of low-income parents to break out of the poverty cycle, there are likely to be distressing social and economic costs for one and perhaps more generations.

Chart 3
Education and Low Incomes by Place of Residence, 1961

EDUCATION OF ALL NONFARM FAMILY HEADS AND NONFAMILY INDIVIDUALS

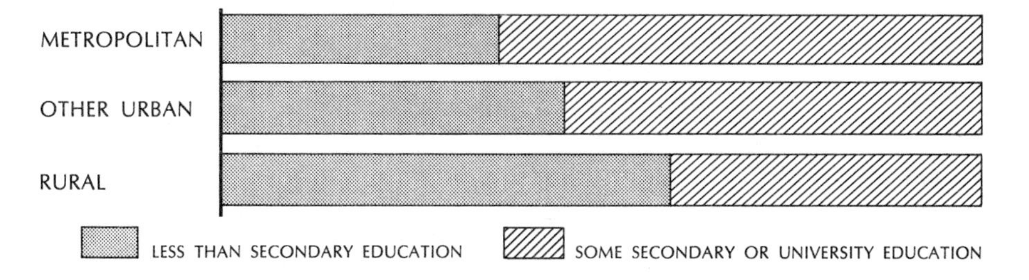

INCIDENCE OF LOW INCOMES BY EDUCATION

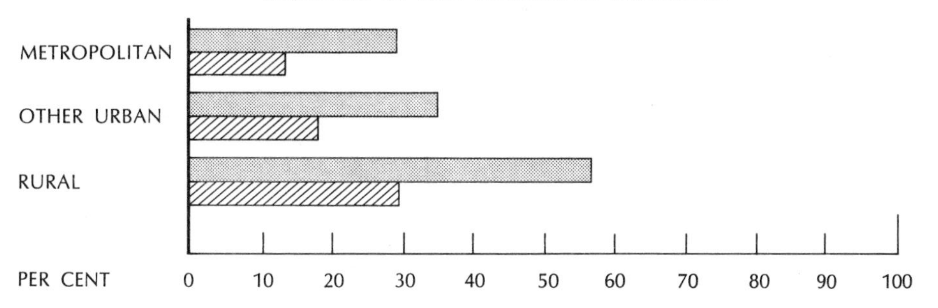

Source: Based on data from Dominion Bureau of Statistics and estimates by Economic Council of Canada.

It is also clear, however, that the upgrading of human resources involved in combatting poverty calls for a good deal more than strong improvement in the formal educational system. There must also be many other elements, such as adult retraining and manpower mobility programs, to help families and individuals escape from the low-income circumstances which entrap them.

Families Headed by Women

The high incidence of low income among families headed by women is strongly related to the presence of dependent children. Most low-income families headed by women under 65 are families where there are two or more children under 16. For all such families, the incidence of low income is close to 50 per cent.

The presence of dependent children often prevents a woman who is head of a family from entering the labour market, or restricts her to low-paid, part-time jobs. While transfer payments such as mothers' allowances will probably always play an important role in relieving this type

Chart 4

*Occupational Groups and Incidence of Low Incomes by Education, 1961**

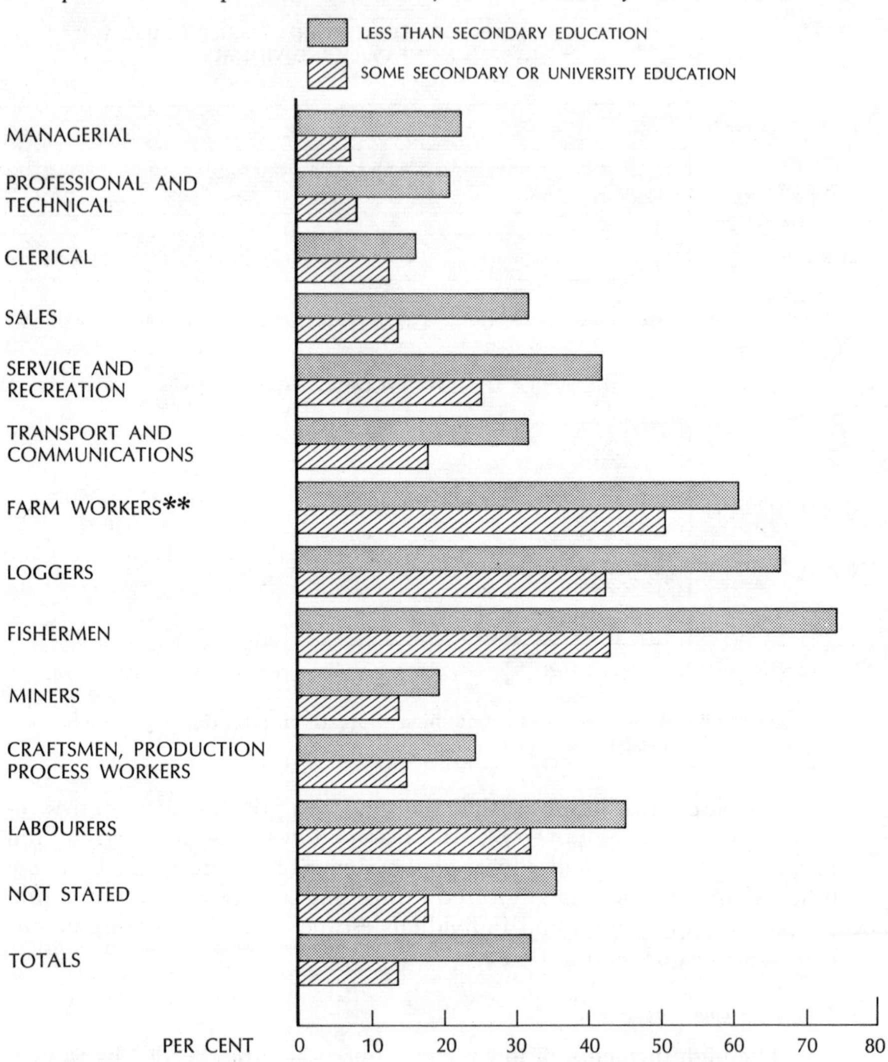

*Includes all nonfarm family heads and nonfamily individuals under 65 years of age.

**See Notes to Table 4.

Source: Based on data from Dominion Bureau of Statistics and estimates by Economic Council of Canada.

of situation, it is evident that much improved day-care facilities for young children could also make a major contribution. Such facilities would also improve the situation of low-income families headed by men whose wives would be glad to seek paid work if given the opportunity.

Some Family Income Trends

The concept of low incomes changes with time. What may have been regarded in an earlier period as an adequate family income comes to be regarded later as inadequate, even after taking account of price changes. It is, nevertheless, useful to examine income trends to see what changes have taken place in the proportion of Canadian families in certain income brackets over a period of time. Consistent statistical data on family incomes go back to 1951. It is, therefore, possible to get some idea of how the distribution of family income evolved over the period from 1951 to 1965. With a substantial rise in the real income of the nation as a whole, it is only to be expected that there would have been a decline in the proportion of families in low-income brackets. For example, in 1951, nearly two-fifths of all nonfarm families received incomes of $3,000 or less. After making the necessary adjustments for changes in the value of the dollar, this proportion had dropped to slightly more than one-fifth in 1961, and by 1965 it had declined still further to less than one-fifth.

However, the growth in real incomes over this period was not shared equally by all family groups. The sharpest decline in the proportion of low-income families was among those whose major source of income was earnings. On the other hand, there was only a modest decline in the proportion of low-income families who were dependent upon income from sources other than earnings, or among families whose heads were not in the labour force.

Whether the head of the family was a man or a woman made a considerable difference in terms of income improvement over this 15-year period. The proportion of families with incomes under $3,000 and headed by women declined by only 24 per cent. This contrasted with a drop of 58 per cent in the case of families headed by men.

Another important characteristic associated with income improvements was age. The younger the age of the family head, the greater was the increase in income. For example, while average family income in real terms was 55 per cent higher in 1965 than in 1951, families whose heads were under 35 had real incomes about 63 per cent higher. On the other hand, the average family whose head was 65 and over had real income averaging only 34 per cent higher. The obvious conclusion is that the young benefited more from economic growth over this period than the middle-aged and elderly.

Above-average increases in the incomes of families with younger heads probably reflect a number of factors. Younger age groups have higher levels of education and are thus generally more mobile, both occupationally and geographically. Their incomes are more likely to rise as a result of their own increasing productivity as well as productivity increases in the economy as a whole.

While family heads aged 55 to 64 are still employed, their earnings usually level off or start to decline relative to younger age groups. Furthermore, this age group is more vulnerable to unemployment than workers between the ages of 25 and 54. The contraction of employment opportunities, especially for older workers with limited education and training, often results in a withdrawal from the labour force. Employment statistics show that on the average the less educated is the worker, the earlier is his departure from the labour force.

Age is also an important characteristic of low-income individuals who are not living in families. For example, 60 per cent of such low-income individuals in 1961 were 55 or older, and nearly one-third of these were over the age of 70. On the other hand, less than 25 per cent of low-income individuals were between 25 and 55. To a large extent older persons who are not part of a family are outside the labour force and thus primarily dependent upon government payments for income maintenance.

There is much further statistical material available concerning the characteristics of low-income Canadians.[6] Some of this material confirms tendencies already fairly well-known – e.g., the poorer health of low-income people, and the crowded and otherwise substandard housing conditions which many of them face. No attempt is made here to give a well-filled-out picture of the low-income population; the object has been only to identify a limited number of characteristics which will begin to suggest the range of policies required to mount a truly comprehensive and effective attack on poverty.

B. THE COSTS AND ECONOMIC IMPLICATIONS OF POVERTY*

From now until at least the mid-1970's there are exciting possibilities for economic growth and development that could bring great benefits to most Canadians. But rapid growth in the national economy will not automatically assure either an adequate participation in the benefits of economic growth among *all* Canadians, or an adequate participation in the process of growth by all those who could play some part in it. Special attention therefore should be focused on the need to achieve a *broad basis of participation* in the future economic development of our country. Among other things, this means that we must move to deal more effectively with the problem of poverty.

Our last Review described the seriousness of poverty in Canada – its large dimensions and its widespread prevalence in all parts of the country. We called for a national commitment to move towards the elimina-

[6] Much of this material is to be found in the series of 1961 *Census Monographs* being issued by the Dominion Bureau of Statistics. A useful general compendium of statistics relating to the low-income population is to be found in the document, *Profile of Poverty in Canada,* issued by the Special Planning Secretariat of the Privy Council, Ottawa.

*Reproduced with the permission of the Queen's Printer for Canada, from the Economic Council of Canada, *Sixth Annual Review* (Ottawa: Queen's Printer, 1969) pp. 107-115.

tion of poverty. At the same time, we stressed the complex nature of the underlying factors involved in poverty, and hence the need to develop much better information and analysis as a basis for a really effective longer-term strategy for eliminating it. We also indicated that we intended to continue our work in this field; this [article] is a reflection of our continuing interest in this field.

The main purpose of this [article] is to persuade Canadians to think about poverty in a new way — a way which reflects its *economic* significance. Historically, the predominant view of poverty has been that it is primarily a human and social problem — a problem of how the fruits of the economic system should be shared and human misery alleviated. When poverty has manifested itself as a lack of income, the typical solution has been to transfer income to the poor. When it has manifested itself as a lack of access to particular services, the typical solution has been to provide access to certain services for the poor. This view of poverty appears to be predominant in the present complex of public and private efforts to minimize poverty in Canada, and has resulted in *social welfare* policies being the primary approach to alleviation. However, poverty is an economic problem to a much greater extent than most people have realized in the past. This is not to denigrate the human and social aspects of poverty. These are of vital importance. But there are also important economic aspects to poverty which have been generally overlooked, or at least underemphasized. We therefore attempt here to focus attention on the *economic costs of poverty* . . .

Our approach starts from the premise that the greatest assets of a nation are its people and that the most important resources of an economy are its human resources. Our society and our economy are significantly weakened by the widespread poverty that exists in Canada today. To the degree that poverty contributes to the exclusion of individuals and families from the mainstream of society, it contributes to potential social tensions and unrest. To the degree that poverty places an economic burden on the society, it acts as a brake on Canada's economic growth and detracts from the well-being of all Canadians.

The adult poor fall basically into two categories. In one group are those who cannot, or should not be expected to, earn incomes (for example, the aged and the chronically sick and disabled) and those who can and do work but whose income-earning capacity is essentially static (because they are near retirement, or for other reasons). On the other hand, there are those who are poor mainly because they have difficulties in finding or holding steady, rewarding jobs — difficulties arising from *remediable disadvantages,* such as lack of education or training, lack of information about job opportunities, inability to move to known job opportunities, poor work habits, and poor physical or mental health stemming from economic deprivation. These are also usually the first to suffer when unemployment rises.

If all the poor were in the first category, the solution to the problem of poverty might be simply to guarantee them a certain income. But only a minority of the adult poor are in this category. These should be ensured a decent minimum standard of living, without qualification; their incomes should be fully protected against inflation; and they should be assured of some participation in the rising average real standards of living which the growing productivity in our economy makes possible.

The majority of the poor in Canada, however, fall into the second category. They represent, in economic terms, unutilized or underutilized resources of human capital. Poverty in Canada can be reduced through measures designed to more fully utilize these resources by providing them with better access to job opportunities and through investments in human capital. The result would be to increase the output of the entire society, with potential benefits not only for the poor themselves, but for all Canadians. Policies that reduce poverty by creating new output, and therefore new incomes, are clearly preferable to policies that simply redistribute existing output and incomes. Poverty could be reduced, if not eliminated, by direct income *transfers* but as long as poverty reflects substantial unused manpower resources in the economy, redistributive schemes by themselves are likely to be second-best choices.

The burden imposed by poverty on the Canadian economy is largely invisible in the usual aggregative economic measures. This partly explains the widespread lack of public appreciation of its existence. Yet the burden is real, and it takes two forms. These might be termed "lost output" and "diverted output."

Lost output is the additional production of goods and services that the poor would have created had their productive potential been better developed and effectively used. This additional production would, among other things, be reflected in higher personal incomes and purchasing power, and hence also in higher business sales volumes and government revenues. But these goods and services do not get produced and purchased. And such incomes do not get generated.

Diverted output, on the other hand, consists of the goods and services that are not produced because productive resources are diverted from other potential uses into activities made necessary by the failure to eliminate remediable poverty. For example, the existence of substantial poverty in Canada leads to the diversion of resources to deal with more sickness than would otherwise occur; it requires substantial resources to administer public welfare and assistance programs (including many hours of skilled manpower on a voluntary basis for fund raising); it requires larger expenditures for protecting persons and property and for administering justice; and in various respects, it places a heavier burden on our educational systems. In these and many other ways, it imposes additional costs on all Canadians in the sense that resources would otherwise have been available for other, more productive and more socially desirable uses.

There is no easy way to measure the total economic costs of lost and diverted output. Nevertheless, these costs are substantial.

Before turning to a further consideration of some of the aspects of these costs and to possible means for reducing them, two popular misconceptions should be laid to rest.

First, the real costs of poverty to the economy as a whole do *not* refer to the large government transfer payments that are used to alleviate poverty, such as the transfers of income involved in family allowances, public assistance payments, old age security, unemployment insurance, payments under the Canada and Quebec Pension Plans and tax exemptions.[7] These transfers are simply a substantial flow of funds passing through the government sector on the way from the "payers" to the recipients of the transfers (many of whom, on examination, turn out to be the same people, and most of whom are nonpoor). The government acts largely as a funnel; apart from the relatively small costs of administration, these flows do not reflect use by governments of the real resources of the economy. The distinction between transfer payments by governments and government programs that actually *consume* resources can be an important one, and one that tends to be obscured when government expenditures are lumped together and regarded as all of a kind. The costs of poverty related to lost and diverted output are *real* costs to the economy, not simply transfer payments.[8] It is also relevant to note that to the extent that shifts in command over goods and services help to make the poor more productive and bring larger numbers of them into employment, they represent a form of investment, essentially similar to business investment, or to increased education and training, or other forms of expenditure yielding longer-term benefits for the whole economy.

The second misconception is an apparently widespread impression that the poor are somehow synonymous with those who don't work or don't want to work. This is simply incorrect. While there may be some voluntary poverty in Canada – for example, in the case of university students who temporarily forgo income in anticipation of later gains – the great bulk of the poor are clearly not voluntarily poor. The analysis of 1961 Census data in the *Fifth Annual Review* revealed that two-thirds

[7] It is perhaps not widely appreciated that tax exemptions constitute, in effect, a form of transfer payment. For example, for families with two young children, who are in receipt of family allowances and have annual gross incomes of $2,700, $6,500 and $18,500, the exemptions in effect transfer to each $0, $114, and $270, respectively, in the form of tax savings. In other words, those whose incomes are too low to pay taxes gain nothing, and other families tend to gain in relation to their incomes. Of course, if tax exemptions were to be altered, any such change would have a significant effect on a relatively large number of lower-income families.

[8] There may, of course, be some *real* cost to the economy if higher transfer payments to the poor from the nonpoor were to blunt incentives among the latter group. But there is little evidence to support the view that any such adverse effects on incentives would be very significant. Moreover, any such effects would perhaps tend to be offset by some accompanying favourable effects on the incentives of the poor.

of the heads of poor families (on the basis of fairly conservative estimates) were in the labour force and over three-quarters of poor families had *at least* one wage-earner.

Lingering beliefs that the poor generally lack motivation are being undermined by a growing range of studies and evidence to the contrary. On the basis of careful investigations, it would appear that most of the poor are ready to seize appropriate job opportunities when these are available. The real sources of poverty among the potentially employable poor are generally to be found among such factors as a high incidence of inadequate skills and education, a lack of knowledge about how to seek out and exploit job opportunities, sickness, and a repeated thwarting of employment aspirations. Furthermore, some recent research suggests that the aspirations of the poor for economic opportunities and a middle-class style of life may be very strong, and that the desire to participate in a productive way in our society is more often frustrated than lacking.

To these aspects of labour force behaviour and aspirations, which give every evidence of embracing a very large fraction of the poor, must be added the relatively new and growing body of evidence about the development of human abilities. Until recently, it has been assumed that ability (such as reflected in IQ tests) was "given" at birth and that not much could be done to alter it. However, at the very least, environment has been found to play a significant role in the degree to which abilities are developed, and there is an emerging body of evidence supporting the proposition that even basic intelligence is modifiable. Thus the poor — apparently to a very substantial degree — may be no less able to participate in the economy than the nonpoor, and their poverty would appear most often to be a reflection of undeveloped abilities or inadequate job opportunities, rather than a lack of abilities.

If the unutilized or undeveloped human resources in Canada are potentially highly productive, why has our economic system failed to seek out and harness the potential of these resources? To some extent, this failure appears to be associated with institutional rigidities and attitudes — in the education system, in industry, in labour unions, in governments — which have become embedded in policies and practices that tend to make the economy function in a way that is pervasively discriminatory against the poor. Such discrimination frequently prevents the poor from fully utilizing their skills in productive jobs and restricts their access to opportunities for improving their skills. Even some of the social welfare policies and programs operate, in some respects, with disincentives that make it difficult for the poor to pull themselves out of poverty. Both the removal of such discrimination — often entirely inadvertent discrimination — and better incentives for the poor to develop and use their income-earning abilities would contribute to higher potential output for the whole economy.

In the labour market, the poor are handicapped relative to the nonpoor. The poor tend to lack the resources to explore the best alternative opportunities. They make fewer informal contacts through social groups which might lead to jobs or information about job opportunities. Often the jobs they might fill are not advertised locally, or they are not advertised outside the area in which the job is located. Lack of resources may also handicap the poor when information is sold, as in newspapers or through other advertising media. Minority groups, in particular, as well as recent migrants, tend to have inadequate channels of information and communication.

The costs of transportation frequently put the poor at a disadvantage when they are looking for a job opening, or when they are required to appear in person before receiving a job offer. To the poor, the cost of moving their family to the location of a new job (or, alternatively, the additional expense and hardship of living away from home) is often prohibitive. The programs of the Department of Manpower and Immigration do not appear to be operating with a high degree of effectiveness in relation to the need for overcoming the barriers faced by the poor in this field. Much remains to be done to make the whole complex of these programs — from information and counselling services through the training and mobility-facilitating services — more adequate to meet the problems of those who are most in need of these services. Moreover, increased co-operation between the Canada Manpower Centres and the growing number of job placement services being developed by voluntary social agencies is needed.

Wage discrimination against the poor is also a problem, especially among women and certain minority groups who may be faced with unfair recruitment and employment practices. Discrimination may also be inherent in recruitment practices based on arbitrary educational qualifications not carefully related to the requirements of the job or which fail to take account of the skills and aptitudes of job applicants. Such practices, again, tend to work to the particular disadvantage of the poor. But they may also work to the disadvantage of employers. A re-examination of hiring practices and job specifications by governments and by business firms — in order to match skill levels of job applicants more closely with the whole spectrum of skill needs — would assist in reducing the economic costs of poverty. Such improved matching would also tend to keep costs and prices more stable. Recent U.S. attempts to develop careers for the poor by redefining job specifications in a number of fields, such as health services, education and social welfare, are particularly worthy of note in this context.*

Other institutional arrangements tend similarly to discriminate — often unconsciously — against the poor in our society. Attitudes, policies

*EDITOR'S NOTE: Attempting to develop careers for the poor by redefining job specifications could open up many new jobs. However, we must realize that those persons who are defined as professionals might resist such changes, resenting a redefinition of their jobs and entrance qualifications.

and decisions made by governments, businesses, labour unions, and farm and other private groups sometimes have the effect of deterring the more efficient use and development of human resources. For example, government subsidies (and perhaps some tax exemptions), along with some tariffs, may have the effect of locking individuals into low-income situations. Inadequate attention to the efficient use of both labour and capital in business firms may have similar effects. Some labour union rules and practices may discriminate against the entry of the poor into employment, and some forms of aid to farmers may, instead of promoting viable income growth and resolving other basic problems in agriculture, have instead the ultimate effect of preserving low-income agricultural activities. In both the government and the private sectors, more attention is needed to the implications of decisions that may adversely affect the poor, and to reducing the discriminatory handicaps which they already suffer in seeking opportunities for more productive employment.

The poor are even more pervasively handicapped with respect to educational and training opportunities. The restricted personal resources of the poor deprive them of the chance of making the same investments in training and education that many of the nonpoor take for granted. The outcome is that the least investment is made by the very groups who need it most if poverty and its costs are to be eliminated. Within our public school systems, the low-income child frequently does not get the compensatory attention which he needs in order to be able to generate an adequate income in later life. Moreover, there is always a tendency for business firms and governments to undertake too little investment in human resources because they cannot be sure they will be able to retain human capital which they create. Workers migrate, and move from province to province or from firm to firm. Too little attention has been devoted to possible means of offsetting this tendency to underinvest and to developing more appropriate levels of investment in human resources, especially among the poor. It is important that this be done in ways that enhance rather than inhibit labour mobility, for in an age of accelerating technological and other change, our economic system will need increasing mobility if it is to function well.

Economic stabilization policies, too, have considerable relevance for the dimensions of poverty. The use of these policies to achieve sustained and balanced economic growth will tend to hold down and reduce the level of poverty over time. At the same time, serious or persistent inflationary pressures may require restriction of the growth of total demand through restraining fiscal and monetary policies in such a way that unemployment increases. In such a case, the poor may be caught in a situation of diminished employment opportunities, rising taxes (the overall tax system in Canada is regressive at low-income levels — that is, the poor are relatively overtaxed),[9] and diminished availability and increased cost of credit. All tend to fall more heavily upon this minority than upon the rest of society.

Having a more marginal attachment to the labour force, whether through their lower levels of skills, more-checkered employment histories, higher incidence of sickness, or for whatever reasons (studies have revealed a whole cluster of variables that may be responsible), the poor feel the impact most heavily when unemployment rises and job opportunities become relatively scarce. Under such conditions, it is low-income families particularly who are faced with difficulties in finding jobs and obtaining credit. Some are compelled to seek welfare assistance, and growing welfare costs typically emerge in this situation. In short, the burden of maintaining price stability may tend to fall particularly heavily on the poor. In this context, a recent study in the United States has concluded that while some of the poor may be seriously hurt by inflation — notably the elderly poor — more of them are hurt by high unemployment.[10]

[9] "The schedule of effective tax incidence for the total tax structure is regressive up to an income level of at least $3,000 and possibly $5,000, and mildly progressive beyond." Irwin Gillespie, *Studies for the Royal Commission on Taxation,* No. 2, Ottawa, Queen's Printer, 1968, p. 72.

[10] R.G. Hollister and J.L. Palmer, "The Impact of Inflation on the Poor", Discussion Papers of the Institute for Research on Poverty, University of Wisconsin, 1969.

Section II
Sociological Perspectives on Poverty

In sociological literature we find two basic types of work on poverty: 1) empirical descriptions of the extent of poverty, intended to show the basis for concern; and 2) examination of some of the empirical information, followed by an attempt to explain why there is poverty, what it is, and sometimes how it can be alleviated. Infrequently do we find sociologists attempting to test hypothesis designed to explain the origins of the social condition we call poverty. The articles included in this section present various perspectives on poverty, some complementary, others contradictory. The authors are all sociologists and, in our view, their writings are representative of the varied approaches to an analysis of poverty within the discipline. Four recurrent themes are found in these four articles: 1) poverty is a social phenomenon; 2) it must be related to a study of the total society; 3) it can be seen as either relative or absolute; and 4) programs to alleviate poverty must take into account its heterogeneity.

Unlike many nineteenth century thinkers, particularly the social Darwinists who saw poverty as the inevitable outcome of the struggle for survival, the authors included in this section perceive poverty as "part of an organic whole," a phenomenon that cannot be divorced from an analysis of the relationship between and among the various institutions – particularly the political and economic institutions – of society. Cooley develops this point by showing that "poverty is unfitness, but in a social and not a biological sense."

From the sociological perspective, then, poverty is normatively defined. Whyte states that "the poor are defined as those considered by others to be poor." Thus the nature, extent and type of poverty will differ not only between rich and poor nations at various stages of development, but within a country. In Canada, for example, a single person earning $3,000 per year but living on a farm may not be defined as poor, but such a person living in Toronto, Montreal or Vancouver would be poor.

Two other closely related themes follow from Cooley's statement that poverty is a social phenomenon: 1) the study of poverty must be related to a study of the total society in which the poverty is found, and 2) poverty can be conceptualized in either relative or absolute terms.

It is clear that poverty is an attribute not simply of the poor, but of the total society – that is, poverty is a collective phenomenon. As Simmel clearly points out, there is an interactive effect between the poor person and poverty in that persons who are defined by the society as poor, for example those receiving assistance, behave as poor people. Simmel states that "what makes one poor is not the lack of means. The poor person sociologically speaking is the individual who receives assistance because of this lack of means."

Whyte picks up this point of the interaction between the person's conception of himself and society's definition of him, and sees poverty as an outgrowth of the structural differentiation that occurs in an industrial society. With an ever increasing division of labour, specialization, and the use of machines, many jobs become obsolete. It is true that new types of jobs are often created – for example, all the various jobs associated with computers – but the men and women who performed these tasks previously as unskilled or semi-skilled labourers, or clerks, may become unemployed and poor.[1]

A further consequence of such structural changes is a further decrease in the power of the poor, already low *vis à vis* the affluent. The poor become relatively deprived. This lack of power enables them to be ignored, manipulated and oppressed by the more affluent members of the society. In short, the poor have no rights. The distribution of society's goods and services is in the hands of the powerful, as John Porter has illustrated so well in *The Vertical Mosaic*. Simmel noted a long time ago that "the fact of taking from the rich to give to the poor does not aim at equalizing their individual positions and is not, even in its orientation, directed at suppressing the social difference between the rich and the poor." This underlines the fact that a study of poverty cannot be done without a study of the distribution of a society's economic surplus – in short, its stratification system.

Both Whyte and Miller address themselves to the second theme mentioned above, which is also found in Simmel, that poverty can be seen as relative or absolute. Simmel had noted that, "He is poor whose means are not sufficient to obtain his ends." If poverty is viewed in a strictly relativistic way and is seen as a logical outgrowth of structural differentiation, the poor will be always with us. Whyte argues that poverty can be seen as a felt discrepancy between need-satisfaction and need-aspiration, although he is aware that relative deprivation can be defined by community standards ("objective poverty") or by individual values ("subjective poverty"). Thus, this definition of poverty as relative deprivation can apply equally to a rich man. Given this deficiency in the concept of relative deprivation, we must attempt to distinguish theoretically, as do Simmel and Miller, between relative poverty and absolute poverty.

Generally, sociologists who see poverty as essentially relative attempt to show that the society must increase social mobility, open its doors by maximizing equality of opportunity through universal education, retraining, and so on. This would change the distribution of individuals and thereby guarantee that the poor would not be a social group that persists over generations. This ignores the point made earlier that poverty is a collective phenomenon and can be overcome only through collective efforts and changes. It also ignores the possibility that an increase in level of education on the part of the total population might not necessarily redistribute individuals but simply elevate the educational level of the total population. The granting of assistance through welfare and manpower programs is not collective but personal, and does little more than meet personal needs.

The concept of absolute poverty suggests that we must theoretically and empirically determine a minimum standard of living (compare the notion of a guaranteed annual income), a "zero-point" below which no one in society should fall. This "floor," to use Miller's term must be sufficient so that the individual or family members can maintain their human, legal rights and have enough means at their disposal to enjoy true "equality of opportunity." For persons to participate minimally in the economic, political and social institutions of our society, they must have minimal access to resources.

No matter what the theoretical or conceptual approach used, the question of alleviation or amelioration always looms large. The

[1] Jacques Ellul in *The Technological Society* sees the extent of such obsolescence increasing as we continually stress the importance of efficiency as a goal in itself and thereby subordinate all aspects of the society to the demands of technique. He defines technique as "the totality of methods rationally arrived at and having absolute efficiency in every field of human activity. Jacques Ellul, *The Technological Society* (New York: Alfred A. Knopf, 1964) p. 25

types of programs will vary according to the goals and values of a society and the theoretical framework within which poverty is defined. Thus, as Miller so clearly illustrates, poverty that is dominant – for example, in India – will necessitate programs quite different from those used in a society such as Canada, where poverty is real for a minority. Poverty is not a unidimensional phenomenon, and programs must take into account its heterogeneity.

The articles included in this section deal directly or indirectly with themes described above. Each views poverty from a sociological perspective, yet each stresses different aspects of the phenomenon, the dominant theme being that poverty is a collective state resulting from structural as well as cultural conditions prevalent in a society. It is the task of the sociologist to delineate these conditions as carefully as he can.

1. *Poverty**

Charles Horton Cooley

The most practical definition of poverty is that now widely adopted which relates it to function, and calls those the poor whose income is not sufficient to keep up their health and working efficiency. This may be vague but is not too much so to be useful, and is capable of becoming quite definite through exact inquiry. At least it indicates roughly a considerable portion of the people who are poor in an obvious and momentous sense of the word.

Being undernourished, the poor lack energy, physical, intellectual and moral. Whatever the original cause of their poverty, they cannot, being poor, work so hard, think so clearly, plan so hopefully, or resist temptation with so much steadfastness as those who have the primary means of keeping themselves in sound condition.

Moreover, the lack of adequate food, clothing and housing commonly implies other lacks, among which are poor early training and education, the absence of contact with elevating and inspiring personalities, a narrow outlook upon the world, and, in short, a general lack of social opportunity.

The poor are not a class in the sense of having a distinct psychical organization. Absorbed in a discouraging material struggle, or perhaps in the sensuality and apathy to which a discouraging outlook is apt to lead, they have no spirit or surplus energy adequate to effectual cooperative endeavour on their own initiative, or even to grasping the benefits of existing organization. As a rule they get far less from the law and its administration, from the church, the schools, the public libraries and the like, than the classes more capable of self-assertion, and this is particularly true in a *laissez-faire* democracy, such as ours, which gives

*Reprinted with the permission of Charles Scribner's Sons from *Social Organization*, pages 290 to 300, by Charles Horton Cooley. Copyright 1909 Charles Scribner's Sons; renewal copyright 1937 Elsie Jones Cooley.

rights pretty much in proportion to the vigor with which they are demanded. It is this lack of common consciousness and purpose that explains the ease with which, in all ages, the poor have been governed, not to say exploited, from above. And if they are getting some consciousness and purpose at the present time, it is largely for the very reason that they are less inveterately and hopelessly poor now than in the past.

The familiar question whether poverty is due to personal or social causes is in itself somewhat fallacious, as smacking of a philosophy that does not see that the personal and social are inseparable. Everything in personality has roots in social conditions, past or present. So personal poverty is part of an organic whole, the effect in one way or another, by heredity or influence, of the general life. The question has significance, however, when we understand it as asking whether or not the cause is so fixed in personality that it cannot be counteracted by social influences. We find that in a community generally prosperous a part of the people – say ten per cent – are poor in the urgent sense indicated above. The practical question is, Are these people poor from causes so established in their characters (however originating) that the rest of the community can do nothing effectual for them, or are they plastic to forces which might raise them to a normal standard of living?

As to this – leaving out the various extreme opinions which attend all such questions – there is a fair measure of agreement among competent observers somewhat to the following effect: There is a considerable number of individuals and families having intrinsic defects of character which must always keep them poor so long as they are left in the ordinary degree of self-dependence. The great majority of the poor, however, have no ineradicable personal weakness but are capable of responding to influences which might raise them to a normal standard of living. In other words, the nine-tenths of the community which is not poor might conceivably bring influences to bear which would – in a healthy manner and without demoralizing alms-giving – remove all but a small part of the poverty of the other tenth. It is only a question of putting into the matter sufficient knowledge and good will. As to the view, still not uncommon, that the laziness, shiftlessness and vice of the poor are the source of their difficulties, it may be said that these traits, so far as they exist, are now generally regarded by competent students as quite as much the effect as the cause of poverty. If a man is undervitalized he will either appear lazy or will exhaust himself in efforts which are beyond his strength – the latter being common with those of a nervous temperament. Shiftlessness, also, is the natural outcome of a confused and discouraging experience, especially if added to poor nutrition. And as to drink and other sensual vices, it is well understood that they are the logical resource of those whose life does not meet the needs of human nature in the way of variety, pleasantness and hope. There are other causes of vice besides poverty, as appears from its prevalence among the unresourceful rich, but there can be no doubt that good nurture, moderate work, wholesome amusement and a hopeful outlook would do away with a great, probably the greater, part of it. There are, no doubt, among the poor, as among the well-to-do, many cases of incurable viciousness and incompetence, but it would be no less unjust and foolish to assume that any individual is of this sort than to give up a scarlet fever patient because some will die of that disease in spite of the best treatment.

I find that the ablest and most experienced workers have generally the most confidence as to what may be done even with the apparently lazy, shiftless or vicious by bringing fresh suggestions, encouragements and opportunities to bear upon them. And it is only a small portion of the poor that are even apparently lazy, shiftless or vicious; the majority comparing not unfavorably with the well-to-do classes in these respects.

Leaving aside general conditions which may depress whole nations or races, the main cause of poverty in a prosperous country like the United States is without doubt some sort of maladjustment between the individual, or the family or neighbourhood group, and the wider community, by reason of which potential capacity does not yield its proper fruit in efficiency and comfort. This is evidently the case, for example, with the sort of poverty most familiar in our American cities; that due to the transplanting of vast numbers of Europeans to a society, not too good for them as we carelessly assume, but out of connection with their habits and traditions. The Italians, Slavs and Russian Jews who just now throng our cities are by no means deficient, on the whole, either in intelligence, industry or thrift; and those who know them best find them prolific in some qualities, such as artistic sensibility of various kinds, in which America is otherwise rather deficient. But the process of adaptation to our industrial conditions is trying and leaves many in poverty and demoralization.

Among the native population also, poverty and the moral degradation which is often found with it is due largely, perhaps chiefly, to various kinds of maladjustment between the working classes and the industrial system — to loss of employment from periodical depressions or from the introduction of new methods, to the lack of provision for industrial education, to the perils attending migration from country to city, and so on.

What shall we say of the doctrine very widely, though perhaps not very clearly, held that the poor are the "unfit" in course of elimination, and are suffering the painful but necessary consequences of an inferiority that society must get rid of at any cost? A notion of this kind may be discovered in the minds of many men of fair intelligence, and is due to remote, obscure and for the most part mistaken impressions of the teaching of Malthus and Darwin.

The unfit, in the sense of Darwin and of biology in general, are those whose hereditary type is so unsuited to the conditions of life that it tends to die out, or at least suffer relative diminution in numbers, under the action of these conditions – as white families tend to die out in the tropics. In other words, they have an inferiority due to heredity, and this inferiority is of such a character that they do not leave as many children to continue their race as do those of a superior or fitter type.

It is very questionable whether any great part of the poor answer the description in either of these respects. As to the first, it is the prevailing opinion with those most familiar with the matter that their inferiority, except possibly where a distinct race is in question, as with the Negroes, is due chiefly to deficient nurture, training and opportunity, and not to heredity. This view is supported by the fact that under the conditions which a country of opportunity, like the United States, affords, great masses of people rise from poverty to comfort, and many of them to opulence, showing that the stock was as capable as any. Something of this sort has taken place with Germans and Irish immigrants, and is likely to take place with Jews, Slavs and Italians.

As to elimination, it is well known that only poverty of the most extreme and destructive kinds avails to restrict propagation, and that the moderately poor have a higher rate of increase than the educated and well-to-do classes. It is, in fact, far more the latter that are the "unfit" in a biological sense than the former.

The truth is that poverty is unfitness, but in a social and not a biological sense. That is to say, it means that feeding, housing, family life, education and opportunity are below the standards that the social type calls for, and that their existence endangers the latter in a manner analogous to that in which the presence of inferior cattle in a herd endangers the biological type. They threaten, and to a greater or less degree actually bring about, a general degradation of the community, through ignorance, inefficiency, disease, vice, bad government, class hatred (or, still worse, class servility and arrogance) and so on.

But since the unfitness is social rather than biological, the method of elimination must also be social, namely, the reform of housing and neighbourhood conditions, improvement of the schools, public teaching of trades, abolition of child-labor and the humanizing of industry.

That there are strains of biological unfitness among the poor – hereditary idiocy, or nervous instability tending toward vice and crime, for example – is not to be denied, and certainly these should be eliminated, but poverty, far from effecting elimination, is perhaps their main cause. This will, no doubt, be duly considered by students of the new science of eugenics, for which those of us who approach social problems from another point of view may yet have the highest regard and expectation. Only a shallow sort of mind will suppose there is any necessary conflict between biological and psychological sociology.

As to the question, who is to blame for poverty, let us remember that the whole question of praise or blame is one of point of view and expediency. Blame the poor if it will do them any good, and sometimes, perhaps, it will, but not so often probably as the well-to-do are apt to imagine. It used to be thought that people must always be held responsible for their condition, and that the main if not the only source of improvement was to prod their sense of this responsibility; but more thoughtful observation shows that it is not always a good thing to urge the will. "Worry," says an experienced worker,[1] "is one of the direct and all-pervading causes of economic dependence," and he asserts that "Take no thought for the morrow" is often the most practical advice. Many indications, among them the spread of "mind-cure" doctrines and practices, point to a widely felt need to escape from the waste and unrest of an over-stimulated sense of responsibility.

The main blame for poverty must rest upon the prosperous, because they have, on the whole, far more power in the premises. However, poverty being due chiefly to conditions of which society is only just beginning to become conscious, we may say that in the past nobody has been to blame. It is an unintended result of the economic struggle, and is "done with the elbows rather than the fists." But consciousness is arising, and with it comes responsibility. We are becoming aware of what makes poverty and how it can in great part be done away with, and if accomplishment does not keep pace with knowledge we shall be to blame indeed.

All parts of society being interdependent, the evils of poverty are not confined to one class, but spread throughout the whole; and the influence of a low standard of living is felt in the corruption of politics, the prevalence of vice and the inefficiency of labor. The cause of the poor is therefore the cause of all, and from this point of view those of them who in spite of weakness, discouragement and neglect keep up the fight for a decent life and shun dependence and degradation, should be regarded as heroic defenders of the general welfare, deserving praise as much as the soldier at the front. If we do not so regard them, it is because of our lack of intelligence and social consciousness.

In a truly organic society the struggles and suffering of a poor class would arouse the same affectionate and helping solicitude as is felt when one member of a family falls ill. In contrast to this, the indifference or somewhat contemptuous pity usually felt toward poverty indicates a low state of community sentiment, a deficient we-feeling. Respect and appreciation would seem to be due to those who sustain the struggle successfully, and sympathetic help to those who are broken down by it. Especially brutal, stupid and inexpedient — when we think of it — is the old way of lumping the poor with the degenerate as "the lower class," and either leaving them to bear their discredited existence as best they may, or dealing out to them a contemptuous and unbrotherly alms. The confusion with the degraded of those who are keeping up the social

[1] An editorial writer in *Charities and the Commons,* presumably Professor Devine, the author of *Principles of Relief,* and other works on rational charity.

standard in the face of exceptional difficulties is as mean and deadly a wrong as could well be.

In so far as there is an effective, self-conscious Christian spirit in the world, thought, feeling and effort must concentrate wherever there is injustice or avoidable suffering. That this takes place so slowly and imperfectly in the matter of poverty is largely owing to a lack of clear perception of what ought to be done. I suppose there is no doubt that if mere gifts could wipe out poverty it would be wiped out at once. But people are now, for the most part, just sufficiently informed to see the futility of ordinary alms, without being instructed in the possibilities of rational philanthropy. Rational philanthropy is coming, however, along with an excellent literature and a body of expert persons who unite humane enthusiasm with a scientific spirit.[2]

The fundamental remedy for poverty is, of course, rational organization having for its aim the control of those conditions, near and remote, which lead people into it and prevent their getting out. The most radical measures are those which are educational and protective in a very broad and searching sense of the words — the humanization of the primary school system, industrial education, facilities for play, physical training and healthy amusement, good housing, the restriction by law of child labor and of all vicious and unwholesome conditions, and, finally, the biological precaution of stopping the propagation of really degenerate types of men.

If we can give the children of the poor the right start in life, they will themselves, in most cases, develop the intelligence, initiative, self-control and power of organization which will enable them to look out for their own interests when they are mature. The more one thinks of these questions the more he will feel that they can only be solved by helping the weaker classes to a position where they can help themselves.

[2] "Our children's children may learn with amazement how we thought it a natural social phenomenon that men should die in their prime, leaving wives and children in terror of want; that accidents should make an army of maimed dependents; that there should not be enough houses for workers; and that epidemics should sweep away multitudes as autumn frost sweeps away summer insects." Simon N. Patten, *The New Basis of Civilization,* 197.

2. The Poor*

Georg Simmel

Translated by Claire Jacobson†

Insofar as man is a social being, to each of his obligations there corresponds a right on the part of others. Perhaps even the more profound conception would be to think that originally only rights existed; that each individual has demands which are of a general human character and the result of his particular condition, and which afterward become the obligations of others. But since every person with obligations in one way or another also possesses rights, a network of rights and obligations is thus formed, where right is always the primary element that sets the tone, and obligation is nothing more than its correlate in the same act and, indeed, an inevitable correlate.

Society in general may be regarded as a reciprocity of beings endowed with moral, legal, conventional, and many other kinds of rights. If these rights imply obligations for others, this is simply, so to speak, a logical or technical consequence; and if the unimaginable should happen — that is to say, if it were possible to satisfy every right in such a way that it would not imply the fulfillment of an obligation — society would in no way need the category of obligation. With a radicalism that certainly does not correspond to psychological reality but which could be developed in the sense of an ethical-ideal construction, one could interpret all the prestations of love and compassion, of generosity and religious impulse, as *rights* of the beneficiary. Ethical rigorism has already asserted, in the fact of all these motivations, that the highest to which a man can aspire is to do his duty and that the fulfillment of duty

*Reprinted with the permission of Arnold Simmel and The Society for the Study of Social Problems, from *Social Problems,* Vol. XII, No. 2, pp. 118-140.

† Translated from Georg Simmel, "Der Arme," Chapter 7 in *Soziologie: Untersuchungen über die Formen der Vergesellschaftung,* Leipzig: Duncker and Humblot, 1908, pp. 454-493. I wish to thank Professor Juan J. Linz for his invaluable assistance in the preparation of this translation.

requires by definition precisely that which a self-adulatory way of thinking considers a merit above duty. One more step from this ethical rigorism, and behind every duty of the person with an obligation, there is the right of the claimant; indeed, this seems to be the ultimate and most rational foundation on which the mutual prestations of men may be based.

A fundamental opposition between the sociological and ethical categories manifests itself here. Inasmuch as all relations of prestation are derived from a *right* — in the widest sense of this concept which includes, among other elements, legal right — the relationship between man and man has totally imbued the moral values of the individual and determined his course. However, in contrast to the undoubted idealism of this point of view, there is the no less deeply based rejection of any interindividual genesis of duty. Our duties (from this standpoint) — it is said — are duties only toward ourselves and there are no others. Their content may be the conduct toward other men, but their form and motivation as duty do not derive from others, but are generated with full autonomy by the self and its own purely internal demands, being independent of anything that lies outside of it. It is only in the case of right that the other is the *terminus a quo* of motivation in our moral actions, but for morality itself he is no more than the *terminus ad quem.* In the final analysis, we ourselves are the only ones responsible for the morality of our acts; we are responsible for them only to our better selves, to our self-esteem, or whatever we wish to call this enigmatic focus which the soul finds in itself as the final judge that decides freely up to what point the rights of others are obligations.

This fundamental dualism in the basic sentiments which govern the course of moral action is exemplified or empirically symbolized by various conceptions that exist in relation to assistance to the poor. The obligations we have toward the poor may appear as a simple correlate of the rights of the poor. Especially in countries where begging is a normal occupation, the beggar believes more or less naively that he has a right to alms and frequently considers that their denial means the withholding of a tribute to which he is entitled. Another and completely different characteristic — in the same category — implies the idea that the right to assistance is based on the group affiliation of the needy. One point of view according to which the individual is merely the product of his social milieu confers upon that individual the right to solicit from the group compensation for every situation of need and every loss. But even if such an extreme dissolution of individual responsibility is not accepted, one may stress, from a social viewpoint, that the rights of the needy are the basis of all assistance to the poor. For only if we assume such rights, at least as a socio-legal fiction, does it appear possible to protect public assistance from arbitrariness and dependence upon a chance financial situation or other uncertain factors. Everywhere the predictability of functions is improved whenever in the correlation between the rights and obligations that underlie them right constitutes the methodological point of departure; for man, in general, is more easily disposed to demand a right than to fulfil an obligation.

To this may be added the humanitarian motive of making it easier for the poor person to request and accept assistance, when by doing so he only exercises his due right; for the humiliation, shame, and *déclassement* that charity implies are overcome for him to the extent that it is not conceded out of compassion or sense of duty or utility, but because he can lay claim to it. Since this right naturally has limits, which must be determined in each individual case, the right to assistance will not modify these motivations in the material quantitative aspect with respect to other motivations. By making it a right, its inner meaning is determined and is raised to a fundamental opinion about the relationship between the individual and other individuals and between the individual and the totality. The right to assistance belongs in the same category as the right to work and the right to life. It is true in this case that the ambiguity of the quantitative limits, which characterizes this as well as other "human rights," reaches its maximum, especially if assistance is in cash; for the purely quantitative and relative character of money makes it much more difficult objectively to de-limit requests than assistance in kind – except in complex or highly individualized cases in which the poor person may make a more useful and fruitful application of money than of assistance in kind, with its providential character.

It is also unclear to whom the rights of the poor ought to be addressed, and the solution of this question reveals very deep sociological differences. The poor person who perceives his condition as an injustice of the cosmic order and who asks for redress, so to speak, from the entire creation will easily consider any individual who is in better circumstances than he jointly liable for his claims against society. This leads to a scale which goes from the delinquent proletarian who sees in any well-dressed person an enemy, a representative of the "exploiting" class who can be robbed in good conscience, to the humble beggar who asks for charity "for the love of God," as though each individual had the obligation of filling the holes of the order which God desired but has not fully implemented. The poor man addresses his demands in this case to the individual; however, not to a specific individual, but to the individual on the basis of the solidarity of mankind. Beyond this correlation which allows any particular individual to appear as a representative of the totality of existence with respect to the demands directed to that totality, there are multiple particular collectivities to which the claims of the poor are addressed. The State, municipality, parish, professional association, circle of friends, family, may, as total entities, maintain a variety of relationships with their members; but each of these relationships appears to include an element which is manifested as the right to assistance in the event of impoverishment of the individual. This characteristic is the common element of such sociological relationships, although in other respects they are of highly heterogeneous character. The rights of the poor which are generated by such ties are curiously mixed under primitive conditions, where the individual is dominated by the tribal customs and religious obligations that constitute an undifferentiated unity. Among the ancient Semites, the right of the poor to participate in a meal is not associated with personal generosity, but rather with social affiliation and with religious custom. Where assistance to the poor has its *raison d'être* in an organic link between elements, the *rights* of the poor are more highly emphasized, whether their religious premise derives from a meta-physical unity or their kinship or tribal basis from a biological unity. We will see, on the contrary, that when assistance to the poor derives teleologically from a goal one hopes to pursue in this way, rather than from the casual basis of a real and effective unity among all the members of the group, the rights of the poor dwindle to nothingness.

In the cases examined so far, a right and an obligation seemed to be two aspects of an absolute relationship. Completely new forms appear, however, when the point of departure is the obligation of the giver rather than the right of the recipient. In the extreme case, the poor disappear completely as legitimate subjects and central foci of the interests involved. The motive for alms then resides exclusively in the significance of giving for the giver. When Jesus told the wealthy young man, "Give your riches to the poor," what apparently mattered to him were not the poor, but rather the soul of the wealthy man for whose salvation this sacrifice was merely a means or symbol. Later on, Christian alms retained the same character; they represent no more than a form of asceticism, of "good works," which improve the chances of salvation of the giver. The rise of begging in the Middle Ages, the senseless distribution of alms, the demoralization of the proletariat through arbitrary donations contrary to all creative work, all these phenomena constitute the revenge, so to speak, that alms take for the purely subjectivistic motive of their concession — a motive which concerns only the giver but not the recipient.

As soon as the welfare of society requires assistance to the poor, the motivation turns away from this focus on the giver without, thereby, turning to the recipient. This assistance then takes place voluntarily or is imposed by law, so that the poor will not become active and dangerous enemies of society, so as to make their reduced energies more productive, and so as to prevent the degeneration of their progeny. The poor man as a person, and the perception of his position in his own mind, are in this case as indifferent as they are to the giver who gives alms for the salvation of his own soul. In this case, the subjective egoism of the latter is overcome not for the sake of the poor, but for the sake of society. The fact that the poor receive alms is not an end-in-itself but merely a means to an end, the same as in the case of the man who gives alms for the sake of his salvation. The predominance of the social point of view with reference to alms is shown in the fact that the giving can be refused from that same social point of view, and this frequently happens when personal compassion or the unpleasantness of refusing would move us strongly to give.

Assistance to the poor, as a public institution, thus has a unique sociological character. It is absolutely personal; it does nothing but alleviate individual needs. In this respect, it differs from other institutions which pursue public welfare and security. These institutions attempt to fulfill the needs of all citizens: the army and police, the schools and public works, the administration of justice and the Church, popular representation and the pursuit of science are not, in principle, directed toward persons considered as differentiated individuals, but rather toward the totality of these individuals; the unity of many or all is the purpose of these institutions. Assistance to the poor, on the other hand, is focused in its concrete activity on the individual and his situation. And indeed this individual, in the abstract modern type of welfare, is the *final* action but in no way the *final purpose,* which consists solely in the protection and furtherance of the community. The poor cannot even be considered as a *means* to this end – which would improve their position – for social action does not make use of them, but only of certain objective material and administrative means aimed at suppressing the dangers and losses which the poor imply for the common good. This formal situation is not only valid for the total collectivity, but also for smaller circles. Even within the family there are many acts of assistance, not for the sake of the recipient himself, but so that the family need not be ashamed and lose its reputation owing to the poverty of one of its members. The aid which English trade unions grant to their unemployed members does not purport so much to alleviate the personal situation of the recipient as to prevent that the unemployed, prompted by necessity, should work more cheaply and that this should result in lower wages for the entire trade.

If we take into consideration this meaning of assistance to the poor, it becomes clear that the fact of taking away from the rich to give to the poor does not aim at equalizing their individual positions and is not, even in its orientation, directed at suppressing the social difference between the rich and the poor. On the contrary, assistance is based on the structure of society, whatever it may be; it is in open contradiction to all socialist and communist aspirations which would abolish this social structure. The goal of assistance is precisely to mitigate certain extreme manifestations of social differentiation, so that the social structure may continue to be based on this differentiation. If assistance were to be based on the interests of the poor person, there would, in principle, be no limit whatsoever on the transmission of property in favor of the poor, a transmission that would lead to the equality of all. But since the focus is the social whole – the political, family, or other sociologically determined circles – there is no reason to aid the person more than is required by the maintenance of the social *status quo.*

When this purely social and centralist teleology prevails, assistance to the poor offers perhaps the greatest sociological tension between the direct and the indirect goals of an action. The alleviation of personal need is emotionally so categorical an end-in-itself, that to deprive it of this ultimate purpose and to convert it into a mere technique for the transsubjective ends of a social unit constitutes a significant triumph for the latter. This distantiation between the individual and the social unit — despite its lack of visibility — is more fundamental and radical in its abstractness and coldness than sacrifices of the individual for the collectivity in which the means and the ends tend to be bound together by a chain of sentiments.

This basic sociological relationship explains the peculiar complications of rights and duties which we find in modern assistance to the poor by the State. Frequently we find the principle according to which the State has the obligation to assist the poor, but to this obligation there is no corresponding right to assistance on the part of the poor. As has been expressly declared in England for example, the poor person has no recourse to action for unjust refusal of assistance, nor can he solicit compensation for illegally refused assistance. All the relations between obligations and rights are located, so to speak, above and beyond the poor. The right which corresponds to the obligation of the State to provide assistance is not the right of the poor, but rather the right of every citizen that the taxes he pays for the poor be of such a size and applied in such a manner that the public goals of assistance to the poor be truly attained. Consequently, in the case of negligence in assistance to the poor, it would not be the poor who are entitled to take action against the State, but rather the other elements indirectly harmed by such negligence. In case it should be possible, for instance, to prove that a thief might not have carried out a robbery if the legal assistance requested by him had been granted, it would in principle be the robbed one who would be entitled to claim compensation from the welfare administration. Assistance to the poor holds, in legal teleology, the same position as the protection of animals. No one is punished in Germany for torturing an animal, except if he does it "publicly or in a manner that results in scandal." It is not, therefore, consideration for the mistreated animal but rather for the witnesses that determines punishment.

This exclusion of the poor, which consists in denying them the status of a final end in the teleological chain and, as we have seen, does not even permit them to stand there as a means, is also manifested in the fact that within the modern relatively democratic State public assistance is perhaps the *only* branch of the administration in which the interested parties have no participation whatsoever. In the conception to which we are referring, assistance to the poor is, in effect, an application of public means to public ends; and, since the poor find themselves excluded from its teleology — something that is not the case for the interested parties in other branches of administration — it is logical that the principle of self-government, which is recognized to a varying degree in other matters, should not be applied to the poor and to their assistance. When the State is obligated by a law to channel a stream to provide irrigation for certain districts, the stream is approximately in the situation of the poor supported by the State: it is the object of obligation but is not entitled to the corresponding right, which is rather that of the adjacent property holders. And every time that this centralist interest prevails, the relationship between right and obligation may be altered for the sake of utilitarian considerations. The projected Poor Law of 1842 in Prussia asserts that the State must organize assistance to the poor in the interest of public prosperity. With this objective, it creates legal public bodies which are obligated to the State to assist needy individuals; but they are not so obligated to the latter since these have no legal claim.

This principle acquires an extreme character when the law imposes upon well-to-do relatives of the poor an obligation of support. It would appear at first sight that in this case the poor hold over their well-to-do relatives a *claim* which the State merely secures and makes effective. The inner meaning is, however, a different one. The political community cares for the poor for utilitarian reasons, and gets compensation from the relatives because the cost of assistance would be excessive, or so it considers it. The law does not take into account any immediate obligation of person to person, for example between a wealthy brother and a poor brother; this obligation is purely moral. The law is concerned only with serving the interests of the community, and it does this in two ways: by assisting the poor and by collecting from relatives the cost of assistance. This is, in effect, the sociological structure of the laws pertaining to support. They do not simply purport to give a legally binding form to moral obligations. This is shown in facts like the following. Undoubtedly, the moral obligation of assistance between brothers is a strong imperative. Nonetheless, when in the first draft of the German Civil Code an attempt was made to give it legal sanction, the explanatory reasons acknowledged the extraordinary harshness of such an obligation, but stated that otherwise the cost of public assistance would be too high. This became manifest in the fact that on occasions the legal quota of maintenance exceeds anything that might be required from an individual and moral point of view. The German Imperial Court of Justice sentenced an old man to give up all his possessions—a few hundred marks—for the maintenance of a disabled son, although he argued on plausible grounds that he too would be disabled and that this money was his sole resource. It is very doubtful that one can speak in this case of a moral right on the part of the son. But such a right does not concern the collectivity; the only thing it asks is whether it may have recourse to the relatives in order to impose upon them its obligation toward the poor, in accordance with the general norms.

This internal meaning of the obligation to provide support is also symbolized by the manner in which it is carried out in practice. First, the poor man at his request is assisted, and then a search is made for a son or a father who, eventually and in accordance with his economic situation, is sentenced to pay not the entire cost of assistance but perhaps one half or one third. The exclusively social meaning of the legal rule appears also in the fact that the obligation to provide maintenance, according to the German Civil Code, only occurs when it does not "jeopardize" the "status-adequate maintenance" of the person so obligated. It is at least debatable whether in certain cases assistance is not morally obligatory, even when it adds up to the amounts mentioned above. But the collectivity, nonetheless, renounces such demands in all cases, because the downward mobility of an individual from his "status-adequate" position would result in harm to the status structure of society which would appear to transcend in social importance the material advantages derived from forcing him to that contribution. Consequently, the obligation of assistance does not include a right of the poor person *vis-à-vis* his well-to-do relatives. The obligation of assistance is no more than the general obligation of the State, but transferred to the relatives and without any correspondence to any action or claim whatsoever of the poor person.

The image of a channeled stream which we used previously was, however, inaccurate. For the poor are not only poor, they are also citizens. *As such,* they participate in the rights which the law grants to the totality of citizens, in accordance with the obligation of the State to assist the poor. To use the same image, let us say that the poor are at the same time the stream and the adjacent landowner, in the same sense as the wealthiest citizens could be. Undoubtedly, the functions of the State, which formally stand at the same ideal distance from all citizens, have, insofar as content is concerned, very different connotations, in accordance with the different positions of citizens; and though the poor participate in assistance, not as subjects with their own ends but merely as members of the teleological organization of the State which transcends them, their role in that function of the State, however, is distinct from that of well-to-do citizens.

What matters sociologically is to understand that the special position which the assisted poor occupy does not impede their incorporation into the State as members of the total political unit. This is so despite the fact that their overall situation makes their individual condition the external endpoint of a helping act and, on the other hand, an inert object without rights in the total goals of the State. In spite of, or better yet, because of these two characteristics which appear to place the poor outside the State, the poor are ordered organically within the whole, belong as poor to the historical reality of society which lives in them and above them, and constitute a formal sociological element, like the civil servant or the taxpayer, the teacher or the intermediary in any interaction. The poor are approximately in the situation of the stranger to the group who finds himself, so to speak, materially outside the group in which he resides. But precisely in this case a large total structure emerges which comprises the autochthonous parts of the group as well as the stranger; and the peculiar interactions between them create the group in a wider sense and characterize the true historical circle. Thus the poor are located in a way outside the group; but this is no more than a peculiar mode of interaction which binds them into a unity with the whole in its widest sense.

It is only with this conception that we resolve the sociological antinomy of the poor, which reflects the ethical-social difficulties of assistance. The solipsist tendency of the medieval type of almsgiving of which I spoke by-passed internally, so to say, the poor to whom the action was directed externally; in so doing, it neglected the principle according to which man must never be treated exclusively as a means but always as an end. In principle, the one who receives alms also gives something; there is a diffusion of effects from him to the giver and this is precisely what converts the donation into an interaction, into a sociological event. But if — as in the case previously cited — the recipient of alms remains completely excluded from the teleological process of the giver, if the poor fulfill no role other than being an almsbox into which alms for Masses are tossed, the interaction is cut short and the donation ceases to be a social fact in order to become a purely individual fact.

As we were saying, neither does the modern conception of assistance to the poor consider the poor as ends-in-themselves; but nevertheless, according to it, the poor, although they are located in a teleological series which bypasses them, are an element which belongs organically to the whole and are — on the basis given — closely related to the goals of the collectivity. Certainly neither now nor in the medieval form does their reaction to the donation fall to any specific individual; but by rehabilitating their economic activity, by preserving their bodily energy, by preventing their impulses from leading them to the use of violent means to enrich themselves, the social collectivity gets from the poor a reaction to what it has done to them.

A purely individual relationship is sufficient from the ethical point of view and perfect from the sociological point of view only when each individual is an end for the other — although naturally not merely an end. But this cannot be applied to the actions of a transpersonal collective entity. The teleology of the collectivity may quietly pass by the individual and return to itself without resting on him. From the moment the individual belongs to this whole he is placed thereby, from the beginning, at the final point of action and not, as in the other case, outside of it. Although he is denied as individual the character of an end-in-itself, he participates as member of the whole in the character of an end-in-itself which the whole always possesses.

A long time before this centralist conception of the essence of assistance to the poor became clear, its organic role in the life of the collectivity was revealed through visible symbols. In old England, assistance to the poor was exercised by monasteries and ecclesiastical corporations, and the reason for this, as has been duly noted, is that only the property of mortmain possesses the indispensable permanence on which assistance to the poor necessarily depends. The numerous secular donations derived from booties and penances did not suffice to attain this end, because they were not yet sufficiently integrated into the administrative system of the State and they were consumed without lasting results. Assistance to the poor then became based on the only substantial and fixed point in the midst of social chaos and turmoil; and this connection is shown negatively by the indignation aroused by the clergy sent from Rome to England, because it neglected assistance. The foreign priest does not feel intimately related to the life of the community; and the fact that he does not care for the poor appears as the clearest sign of this lack of connection.

This same link of assistance with the firm substratum of social existence appears clear in the later tie established in England between the poor tax and landed property; and this was cause as much as effect of the fact that the poor counted as an organic element of the land, belonging to the land. The same tendency is manifested in 1861, when part of the welfare charges were legally transferred from the parish to the welfare association. The costs of assistance to the poor were no longer to be carried in isolation by parishes, but rather by a fund to which the parishes contributed in relation to the value of their landed property. The proposition that in order to make a distribution the number of inhabitants should also be taken into consideration was repeatedly and expressly rejected; with it, the individualistic element was completely excluded. A suprapersonal entity, with its substratum in the objectivity of landed property, and not a sum of persons, appeared as the carrier of the obligation to assist the poor. Assistance in this case is so basic to the social group that the local administration only gradually added to this main activity, first the administration of schools and roads, and then public health and the system of registration. Elsewhere, also, the welfare administration has become a basis of political unity because of its success. The North German Confederation decided that in all of the territory of the Confederation no needy person should remain without assistance and that none of the poor in the Confederation should receive a different treatment in one region than in another. If in England external and technical reasons contributed to establish a link between assistance to the poor and landed property, this connection does not lose its profound sociological meaning when the addition of other branches of administration to public assistance institutions led to the crossing of county boundaries by the welfare associations despite the technical disadvantages involved. It is precisely this contradiction in the technical conditions which makes the unity of sociological meaning even more conspicuous.

Consequently, the conception that defines assistance to the poor as an "organization of the propertied classes in order to fulfill the sentiment of moral duty which is associated with property" is completely one-sided. Assistance is rather a part of the organization of the *whole*, to which the poor belong as well as the propertied classes. It is certain that the technical and material characteristics of their social position make them a mere object or crossing point of a superior collective life. But, in the final analysis, this is the role that each concrete individual member of society performs; about which one can say, in accordance with the viewpoint temporarily accepted here, what Spinoza says of God and the individual: that we may love God, but that it would be contradictory that He, the whole which contains us, should love us, and that the love which we dedicate to Him is a part of the infinite love with which God loves Himself. The singular exclusion to which the poor are subjected on the part of the community which assists them is characteristic of the role which they fulfill *within* society, as members of it in a special situation. If technically they are mere objects, in turn in a wider sociological sense they are subjects who, on the one hand, like all the others, constitute social reality and, on the other hand, like all the others, are located beyond the abstract and suprapersonal unity of society.

Owing to this also it is the general structure of the group that decides the question: Where do the poor belong? If they still exercise any economic activity at all, they belong to the segment of the general economy that includes them. If they are members of a church, they belong to it, insofar as it does not coincide with another group. If they are members of a family, they belong to the personally and spatially defined circle of their relatives. But if they are no more than poor, where do they belong? A society maintained or organized on the basis of tribal consciousness includes the poor within the circle of their tribe. Other societies, whose ethical connections are fulfilled essentially through the Church, will turn the poor over to one or another type of pious associations, which are the answer of the society to the fact of poverty. The explanatory reasons of the German law of 1871 on place of residence for assistance answer this question in the following manner: the poor belong to that community — that is, that community is obligated to assist them — which utilized their economic strength before their impoverishment. The principle just mentioned is a manifestation of the social structure which existed prior to the complete triumph of the idea of the modern State, since the municipality is the place which enjoyed the economic fruits of those who are now impoverished. But the modern mobility, the interlocal exchange of all forces, have eliminated this limitation; so that the whole State must be considered the *terminus a quo* and *ad quem* of all prestations. If the laws actually permit everybody to establish his residence in whatever community he wishes, then the community no longer has an integrated relationship with its inhabitants. If there is no right to oppose establishment of residence on the part of undesirable elements, one can no longer demand of the community a solidary give-and-take relationship with the individual. Only for practical reasons, and then only as organs of the State — thus read the explanatory reasons of the legislation — do the municipalities have the obligation to take over the care of the poor.

This is, then, the extreme condition which the formal position of the poor has attained, a condition in which their dependence on the general level of social evolution is revealed. The poor belong to the largest effective circle. No part of the totality but the totality itself, to the extent that it constitutes a unit, is the place or power to which the poor as poor are linked. It is only for this circle, which, being the largest, has no other outside it to which to transfer an obligation, that a problem pointed out by the practitioners of welfare in the small corporative entities ceases to exist; the fact that they frequently avoid giving assistance to the poor, for fear that once they have taken care of them they will always have them on their hands. We see manifested here a very important characteristic for human sociation, a trait which might be called moral induction: when an act of assistance has been performed, of whatever type, although it be spontaneous and individual and not demanded by any obligation, there is a duty to continue it, a duty which is not only a claim on the part of the one who receives the assistance but also a sentiment on the part of the one who gives. It is a very common experience that the beggars to whom alms are given with regularity consider these very rapidly as their right and as the duty of the giver, and if the latter fails in this supposed obligation they interpret it as a denial of their due contribution and feel a bitterness which they would not feel against someone who always denied them alms. There is also the person in better circumstances who has supported for some time a needy person, fixing in advance the period for which he will do so, and who, however, when he stops his gifts, is left with a painful feeling, as if he were guilty. With full consciousness, this fact is recognized by a Talmudic law of the ritual code "Jore Deah": he who has assisted three times a poor person with the same amount, although he had in no way the intention of continuing the assistance, tacitly acquires the obligation of continuing it; his act assumes the character of a vow, from which only weighty reasons can dispense him, such as, for example, his own impoverishment.

The case just mentioned is much more complicated than the related principle, homologous to *odisse quem laeseris,* which says that one loves the one to whom he has done good. It is understandable that one projects the satisfaction of his own good action on the one who has given him the opportunity for it: in the love for the one for whom he has made sacrifices he loves in essence himself, just as in the hate against the one to whom he has done an injustice he hates himself. The sense of obligation that the good action leaves in the doer of good, that particular form of *noblesse oblige,* cannot be explained with so simple a psychology. I believe that, in effect, an *a priori* condition is involved here: that each action of this type — despite its apparent free will, despite its apparent character of *opus supererogationis* — derives from an obligation; that in such behaviour a profound obligation is implicit which, in a certain way, is manifested and made visible through action. What happens here is the same as in scientific induction: if the similarity is accepted between a past process and a future one, it is not simply because the first one has this or that structure, but because a *law* can be derived from the first process that determines in the same way as it determines any other future process. There must be, therefore, a moral instinct which tells us that the first act of charity already corresponded to an obligation which also demands the second no less than the first action. This is clearly related to the motives which we touched on at the beginning of this study. If, in the final analysis, any altruism, any good action, any self-sacrifice, is nothing but a duty and an obligation, this principle may, in the individual case, be manifested in such a form that any act of assistance is, in its profound sense — if one wishes, from the viewpoint of a metaphysics of ethics — the mere fulfillment of a duty which, naturally, is not exhausted with the first action but rather continues to exist as long as the determining occasion obtains. According to this, assistance given to someone would be the *ratio cognoscendi,* the sign which makes us see that one of the ideal lines of obligation between man and man runs here and reveals its timeless aspect in the continuing effects of the bond established.

We have seen so far two forms of the relation between right and obligation: the poor have a *right* to assistance; and there exists an *obligation* to assist them, an obligation which is not oriented toward the poor as having a right, but toward society to whose preservation this obligation contributes and which the society demands from its organs or from certain groups. But along with these two forms there exists a third, which probably dominates the moral consciousness: the collectivity and well-to-do persons have the obligation to assist the poor, and this obligation has its sufficient goal in the alleviation of the situation of the poor; to this there corresponds a right of the poor, as the correlative end of the purely moral relation between the needy and the well-to-do. If I am not mistaken, the emphasis has shifted within this relation since the 18th century. The ideal of humanitarianism and of the rights of man, mostly in England, displaced the centralist spirit of the Elizabethan Poor Law, according to which work had to be provided for the poor for the benefit of the community. The ideal of humanitarianism substituted for this principle another one: every poor person has a right to minimal subsistence, whether he wants and is able to work or not. On the other hand, modern assistance, in the correlation between moral duty (of the giver) and moral right (of the recipient) prefers to emphasize the former. Evidently, this form is realized above all by private assistance, in contrast to public assistance. We are attempting now to determine its sociological significance in this sense.

First, we should point out here the already noted tendency to consider assistance to the poor as a matter pertaining to the widest political circle (the State), while initially it was based everywhere in the local community. This ascription of assistance to the smallest circle was, first of all, a consequence of the corporative ties that bound the community. As long as the supraindividual organism around and above the individual had not changed from the municipality to the State and freedom of mobility had not completed this process factually and psychologically, it was the most natural thing in the world for neighbors to assist needy persons. To this may be added an extremely important circumstance for the sociology of the poor: that of all the social claims of a non-individualistic character based on a general quality, it is that of the poor which most impresses us. Laying aside acute stimuli, such as accidents or sexual provocations, there is nothing such as misery that acts with such impersonality, such indifference, with regard to the other qualities of the object and, at the same time, with such an immediate and effective force. This has given at all times to the obligation of assisting the poor a specific *local* character. Rather, to centralize it in the largest circle and thereby to bring it about not by immediate visibility but only through the general concept of poverty — this is one of the longest roads which sociological forms have had to travel to pass from the immediate sensate form to the abstract.

When this change occurred, whereby assistance to the poor became an abstract obligation of the State — in England in 1834, in Germany since the middle of the 19th century — its character was modified with respect to this centralizing form. Above all, the State maintains in the municipality the obligation to participate in assistance, but considers the municipality as its delegate; local organization has been made into a mere technique in order to attain the best result possible; the municipality is no longer the point of departure, but rather a point of transmission in the process of assistance. For this reason welfare associations are organized everywhere according to principles of utility — for example, in England, they are organized in such a fashion that each of them may support a workhouse — and they have the deliberate tendency to avoid the partiality of local influences. The growing employment of salaried welfare officials works in the same way. These officials stand *vis-à-vis* the poor much more clearly as representatives of the collectivity from which they receive a salary than do the unpaid officials who work, so to speak, more as human beings and attend not so much to the merely objective point of view as to the human, man-to-man point of view. Finally, a sociologically very important division of functions takes place. The fact that assistance to the poor is still essentially delegated to the municipalities is especially useful for two reasons; first, because every case must be handled individually, something that can only be done by someone close at hand and with intimate knowledge of the milieu, and second because if the municipality has to grant assistance it also has to provide the money, since it might otherwise hand out the funds of the State too freely. On the other hand, there are cases of need in which bureaucratic handling is not a threat, since action can be determined on the basis of objective criteria: sickness, blindness, deaf-mutism, insanity, chronic illness. In these cases, assistance has a more technical character and consequently the State, or the larger institution, is much more efficient. Its greater abundance of means and its centralized administration show their advantages in those cases where personal and local circumstances have little importance. And aside from the qualitative determination of the direct prestations of the State, there is the quantitative determination that particularly differentiates public from private assistance: the State and, in general, public organizations attend only to the most urgent and immediate needs. Everywhere and particularly in England, assistance is guided by the firm principle that only the minimum necessary for the life of the poor should leave the purse of taxpayers.

All this is intimately related to the character of collective actions in general. A collectivity which comprises the energies or interests of many individuals can only take into account their peculiarities, when there is a structure with a division of labor whose members are assigned different functions. But when it is necessary to perform a united action, whether through a direct organ or a representative organ, the content of this action can only include that minimum of the personal sphere that coincides with everybody else's. It follows, in the first place, that when expenses are incurred in the name of the collectivity, no more may be spent than what the most thrifty of its members would spend. A community which is acting closely together may allow itself to be moved by an impetus of overpowering generosity; but when the will of each individual is not directly known, but has to be inferred by means of representatives, it must be assumed that no one wants to spend more than the strictly necessary. This is not, of course, an unshakable logical necessity — for the contrary thesis would not constitute a logical contradiction — but it corresponds to a psychological dogma which, by the enormous number of its empirical confirmations, has acquired the practical value of the logically demonstrable.

Mass action has the character of a minimum, owing to its need to reach the lowest level of the intellectual, economic ,cultural, aesthetic, etc. scale. The law which is valid for all has been designated as the ethical minimum; the logic which is valid for all is the intellectual minimum; the "right to work," postulated for all, can only be extended to those whose quality represents a minimum; affiliation to a party in principle demands that one accept the minimum of beliefs without which it would not exist. This type of social minimum is perfectly expressed in the negative character of collective processes and interests.[1]

Consequently, the fact that the prestation of the total community in favor of the poor is limited to a minimum is entirely in accordance with the typical character of collective actions. The motive for this — that such an action has as its basis only that which can be assumed with certitude in each individual — is also the second reason for this behaviour: the fact that assistance to the poor, limited to a minimum, has an *objective* character. It is possible to determine objectively with fair accuracy

[1] There is a digression here on the negative character of collective behavior which makes no specific reference to poverty. It has been translated by Kurt H. Wolff in *The Sociology of Georg Simmel* (New York: The Free Press, 1964 [paperback edition; 1st edition, 1950], pp. 396-401. [Translator's note.]

what is necessary to save a man from physical breakdown. All that exceeds this minimum, all assistance aimed at a positive rise in level, requires less clear criteria and depends on subjective judgments of quantity and quality. I said before that cases of subjectively not-very-differentiated need, and, therefore, not requiring subjective evaluation, are the ones best adapted to State assistance – particularly cases of illness and physical infirmity – while those which have a more individual character are better assigned to the narrower local community. This objective determinability of the need, which favors the intervention of the widest group, is present when assistance is limited to the minimum. We see here again the old epistemological correlation between universality and objectivity. In the field of knowledge, real universality, the acknowledgment of a proposition by the totality of minds – not historical-real, but ideal – is an aspect or expression of the objectivity of this proposition; on the other hand, there may be another proposition which is, for one or many individuals, absolutely certain and possesses the full significance of truth, but lacks this special stamp which we call objectivity. Thus, in practice, one can only in principle request a prestation from the totality on an absolutely objective basis. When the basis is to be judged only subjectively and there is no possibility of a purely objective determination, the demand may be no less pressing and its fulfillment no less valuable, but it will be directed only toward individuals; the fact that it refers to purely individual circumstances requires correspondingly that it be fulfilled by mere individuals.

If the objective point of view goes hand in hand with the tendency to turn over all assistance to the State – a tendency which certainly until now has nowhere been fully realized – the normative measure, whose logical application implies objectivity, is derived not only from the poor but also from the interest of the State. We see manifested here an essential sociological form of the relationship between the individual and the totality. Wherever prestations or interventions are transferred from individuals to society, regulation by the latter tends to be concerned either with an excess or with a deficiency in individual action. In compulsory education the State requires that the individual should not learn too little, but leaves it up to him whether to learn more or even "too much." With the legal workday, the State provides that the employer should not require too much from his workers, but leaves it up to him whether to ask for less. Thus this regulation always refers only to one side of the action, while the other side is left to the freedom of the individual This is the scheme within which our socially controlled actions appear; they are limited only in one of their dimensions; society, on the one side, sets limits to their excess or deficiency, while on the other side their deficiency or excess is left to the indefiniteness of subjective choice. But this scheme sometimes deceives us; there are cases in which social regulation includes in fact *both* sides, although practical interest only focuses attention on one side and overlooks the other. Wherever, for example, the private punishment of a crime has been transferred to society and objective criminal law, one only takes into account, as a rule, that thereby one acquires greater certainty in retribution, that is, a sufficient degree and certitude in its application. But, in reality, the goal pursued is not only to punish enough, but also not to punish too much. Society not only protects the person who has suffered damage, but also the criminal against the excess of subjective reaction; that is to say, society establishes as an objective measure of punishment that which corresponds to its social interest and not to the desires or interests of the victim. And this occurs not only in relations which are legally established. Any social class which is not too low sees to it that its members spend a minimum on their clothing; establishes a standard of "decent" dress; and the one who does not attain this standard will no longer belong to that class. But it also establishes a limit at the other extreme, although not with the same determination nor in such a conscious manner; a certain measure of luxury and elegance and even at times modernity is not proper, indeed, for this or that group, and he who overreaches this upper limit is treated on occasion as not belonging fully to the group. Thus the group does not allow the freedom of the individual to expand completely in this second direction, but rather it sets an objective limit to his subjective choice, that is to say, a limit required by supraindividual life conditions. This fundamental form is repeated whenever the community takes over assistance to the poor. While apparently it seems to have an interest only in setting a lower limit to assistance, that is, in seeing to it that the poor should receive the part to which they are entitled — in other words, that they should not receive too little — there is also the other consideration: that the poor should not receive too much. This latter consideration is in practice less significant. The disadvantage of private assistance lies not only in the "too little," but also in the "too much," which leads to laziness, uses the available means in an economically unproductive way, and arbitrarily favors some at the expense of others. The subjective impulse to do good sins in both directions and, although the danger of excess is not as great as that of deficiency, an objective norm — which determines a standard that is not derived from the subject but from the interest of the collectivity — is directed against that danger of excess.

The transcendence of the subjective point of view is as valid for the recipient as for the giver. English public assistance, by intervening only when there is an objectively determined absolute lack of means, renounces the investigation as to whether a person deserves assistance. This is so because the workhouse is such an unpleasant experience that no one except in extreme need, would choose it, and consequently the lack of means is objectively determined. For this reason its complement is private assistance, which is directed to a specific worthy individual and which can select individually, since the State already cares for the most urgent needs. The task of private assistance consists in rehabilitating the poor, who are already protected from starvation, and in curing need, for which the State offers only a temporary alleviation. It is not need as such, the *terminus a quo,* that determines the task of private assistance, but rather the ideal of creating independent and economically productive individuals. The State operates in a casual sense, private assistance in a teleological sense. To put it in other words: the State assists poverty; private assistance assists the poor. A sociological difference of the greatest importance becomes manifest here. Abstract concepts, which crystallize certain elements of a complex individual reality, often acquire life and consequences for practice which would appear to fit only the concrete totality of the phenomenon. This may be seen in very intimate relationships. The meaning of certain erotic relationships cannot be understood in any other way than that one of the parties seeks not the beloved, but love, often with notable indifference toward the individuality of the lover. This is so because what is wished by this person is to receive the emotional value – love – in and by itself. In religious relationships it often seems that the only essential thing is that there should exist a certain kind and a certain quantity of generosity, while its carriers are indifferent; the behaviour of the priest or the relation of the faithful to the community is determined only by this general consideration, without taking into account the particular motives which produce and color this sentiment in the individual. In this case there is no particular interest in those individuals, since they only matter as carriers of that impersonal fact or rather they do not matter at all. In the social and ethical perspective there is a rationalism which demands that the interaction of people should be based on absolute subjective truthfulness. Everyone may require the truth as an objective quality of any statement made to him, without taking into consideration the particular circumstances or special qualifications of the statement; there can be no right to truth modified in an individual way by those qualifications or circumstances. The truth, and not the speaker or the listener in their individuality, is the assumption, content, and value of group interaction. The same problem is also the basis of divergences among criminologists. Is the punishment directed at the crime or at the criminal? An abstract objectivism demands punishment because a crime has occurred which requires a reinstatement of the violated real or ideal order. It demands punishment based on the logic of ethics, as a consequence of the impersonal fact of the crime. But, from another point of view, only the guilty subject should be punished; the reaction of punishment results not because the crime has occurred as something objective, but because a subject who expressed himself in the criminal act requires expiation, education, and control. For these reasons, in the degree of punishment, the individual circumstances of the case will have to be taken into account to the same extent as the general fact of the crime.

This twofold attitude may also be adopted with respect to poverty. It is necessary to start from poverty as an objectively determined phenomenon and to attempt to eliminate it as such. Whoever the poor may be and whatever the individual causes that produce it and the individual consequences it produces, poverty requires assistance, compensation for this social deficiency. But, on the other hand, interest may be directed to the poor person, who is assisted unquestionably because he is poor, not for the purpose of eliminating poverty in general *pro rata,* but rather to help this particular poor person. His poverty operates here as an individual and specific characteristic; it serves as the immediate occasion for being concerned with him; but the individual as a whole should be put into such a situation that poverty would disappear by itself. For this reason assistance derived from the first attitude is directed more to the fact of poverty; and assistance derived from the second attitude, on the other hand, to its cause. Incidentally, it is of sociological importance to observe that the natural distribution of the two types of assistance between the State and private individuals is modified as soon as one follows up the casual chain one step further. The State – in England more clearly than elsewhere – meets externally visible need; private assistance attends to its individual causes. But the fundamental economic and cultural circumstances which create those personal conditions can only be changed by the collectivity. The task of changing those circumstances in such a way that they should offer the least chance for impoverishment due to individual weaknesses, unfavorable propensities, misfortune, or mistakes belongs to the collectivity. Here, as in many other respects, the collectivity, its circumstances, interests, and actions, surrounds and affects the individual in his specificity. The collectivity represents a kind of immediate reality to which the elements contribute their own existence, the results of their own life. But, on the other hand, it is also the ground in which individual life grows, a ground in which it grows in such a way that the diversity of individual proclivities and situations contributes an endless variety of unique and colorful manifestations to that overall reality.[2]

The principle that governs assistance to the poor in England and which led us to these generalizations is the direct opposite of the French one. In France, assistance to the poor is incumbent upon private associations and persons, and the State only intervenes when these are insufficient. This inversion naturally does not mean that in France private persons would take care of the most pressing needs (like the State in England), while the State would handle what exceeds this minimum and is individually desirable (like private persons in England). What the French principle actually implies is that the two levels of assistance cannot, insofar as content is concerned, be separated as clearly and fundamentally as in England. For this reason, in practice, the condition of the poor will frequently be the same in both countries. But it is obvious that in terms of sociological principles there is a fundamental difference. We

[2] Simmel uses a footnote to expound his basic conception of the relationship between the individual and the social, without any specific reference to the topic at hand. Since this footnote states in metaphorical and highly abstract terms ideas much better presented at length in his basic theoretical writings, we decided to leave it out. [Translator's note.]

are dealing here with a particular case of the larger process, by virtue of which the direct interaction which obtains among the elements of the group becomes an action of the unitary and supraindividual community; once this has happened, constant compensations, substitutions, and changes in priority result between both types of social arrangements. Should this tension or social disharmony which is manifested as individual poverty be directly resolved among the elements of society or through the unity formed by all the elements? This is a question which has to be decided in a formally similar way for every aspect of society, even though it is only rarely posed with such clarity and purity as here. This is mentioned here only so that we should not forget to what extent "private" assistance is also a social phenomenon, a sociological form, which no less definitely attributes to the poor a position as organic members of group life — something that may escape superficial observation. This fact acquires particular clarity by virtue of the transitional forms between both levels: on the one hand, the poor tax, and, on the other, the legal obligation of assistance to poor relatives. As long as a special poor tax exists, the relationship between the collectivity and the poor does not have the abstract purity which places the poor in a direct relationship with the whole as an indivisible unity; the State is only the intermediary that channels the no longer voluntary individual contributions to their beneficiaries. As soon as the poor tax becomes part of the general tax obligation and the resources of assistance are drawn from the general income of the State or municipality, this relationship between the total community and the poor has reached its full development; assistance to the poor becomes a function of the totality as such, and not of the sum of individuals, as in the case of the poor tax. When the law requires the assistance of needy relatives, the interest of the totality is expressed in even more specialized terms. Private assistance, which in all other cases is also affected by the structure and teleology of the collectivity, here in a conscious overemphasis is dominated by it.

We said above that the relationship between the collectivity and its poor contributes to the formation of society in a formal sense as much as the relationship between the collectivity and the civil servant or the taxpayer. We are going to develop this assertion from the point of view which we have just reached in our discussion. We compared above the poor person with the stranger, who also finds himself *confronted* by the group. But this "being confronted" implies a specific *relationship* which draws the stranger into group life as an element of it. Thus the poor person stands undoubtedly *outside* the group, inasmuch as he is a mere object of the actions of the collectivity; but being outside, in this case, is only, to put it briefly, a particular form of being inside. All this occurs in society in the same way as, in the Kantian analysis, spatial separateness occurs in consciousness: even though in space everything is separate and the subject, too, as perceiver, is outside of the other things, the space itself is "in me" in the subject, in the wider sense. If we consider things more closely, this twofold position of the poor — as well as that of the stranger — can be found in all elements of the group with mere variations of degree. However much an individual may contribute positively to group life, however much his personal life may be tied with social life and submerged in it, he also stands *vis-à-vis* that totality: giving or receiving, treated well or poorly by it, feeling inwardly or only outwardly committed to it; in short, as part or as object in relation to the social group as subject, to which he nevertheless belongs as a member, as a part-subject, through the very relationships based on his actions and circumstances. This twofold position, which appears logically difficult to explain, is a completely elementary sociological fact.

We have already seen this in such simple structures as marriage. Each of the spouses, in certain situations, sees the marriage as an independent structure distinct from himself, confronting him with duties and expectations, good things and bad, which proceed not from the other spouse as a person, but from the whole that makes each of its parts an object, in spite of the fact that the whole consists only of these parts. This relationship, this fact of finding oneself simultaneously within and without, becomes more and more complicated and more and more visible as the number of members of the group increases. And this is true not only because the whole then acquires an independence that dominates the individual, but because the most marked differentiations among individuals lead to a whole scale of nuances in this twofold relationship. The group has a special and different relationship with respect to the prince and the banker, the society woman and the priest, the artist and the civil servant. On the one hand, it makes the person into an object, it "handles" him differently, it subjects him or recognizes him as a power standing against power. On the other hand, the group incorporates him as an element of its life, as a part of the whole, which in turn stands in contrast to the other elements. This is perhaps a completely unitary attitude of social reality, which manifests itself separately in these two directions or which appears different from these two distinct viewpoints: comparably, a particular representation stands with respect to the soul, so distinct from it that it can be influenced by the total mood — colored, heightened or toned down, formed or dissolved — while at the same time it is still an integral part of that whole, an element of the soul, of that soul which consists only of the co-existence and interlocking of such representations. In that scale of relationships with the collectivity the poor occupy a well-defined position. Assistance, to which the community is committed in its own interest, but which the poor person in the large majority of cases has no right to claim, makes the poor person into an object of the activity of the group and places him at a distance from the whole, which at times makes him live as a *corpus vile* by the mercy of the whole and at times, because of this, makes him into its bitter enemy. The State expresses this by depriving those who receive public alms of certain civic rights. This separation, however, is not absolute exclusion, but a very specific relationship with the whole, which would be different without this element. The collectivity, of which the poor person is a part, enters into a relationship with him, confronting him, treating him as an object.

These norms, however, do not appear to be applicable to the poor in general but only to some of them, those who receive assistance, while there are poor who do not receive assistance. This leads us to consider the relative character of the concept of poverty. He is poor whose means are not sufficient to attain his ends. This concept, which is purely individualistic, is narrowed down in its practical application in the sense that certain ends may be considered as independent of any arbitrary and purely personal decision. First, the ends which nature imposes: food, clothing, shelter. But one cannot determine with certainty the level of these needs, a level that would be valid in all circumstances and everywhere and below which, consequently, poverty exists in an absolute sense. Rather, each milieu, each social class has typical needs; the impossibility of satisfying them means poverty. From this derives the banal fact that in all advanced civilizations there are persons who are poor within their class and would not be poor within a lower class, because the means they have would be sufficient to satisfy the typical ends of that class. Undoubtedly, it may happen that a man who is really poor does not suffer from the discrepancy between his means and the needs of his class, so that poverty in the psychological sense does not exist for him; just as it may also happen that a wealthy man sets himself goals higher than the desires proper to his class and his means, so that he feels psychologically poor. It may be, therefore, that individual poverty — insufficiency of means for the ends of a person — does not exist for someone, while social poverty exists; and it may be, on the other hand, that a man is individually poor while socially wealthy. The relativity of poverty does not refer to the relation between individual means and actual individual ends, but to the status-related ends of the individual, to a social *a priori* which varies from status to status. The relationship between individual means and actual ends, on the other hand, is something absolute, independent in its basic meaning from anything outside of the individual. It has a very significant socio-historical difference *which* level of needs each group considers as a zero point above which or below which wealth or poverty begins. In a somewhat complex civilization there is always a margin, often a considerable one, to determine this level. In relation to this problem there are many important sociological differences; for example: the relationship of this zero point to the *real average;* whether it is necessary to belong to the favored minority in order not to be considered poor or whether a class, out of an instinctive utilitarian criterion to prevent the growth of feelings of poverty, sets the boundary below which poverty begins very low; or whether an individual case can modify the boundary, as for example the moving into a small town or into a closed social circle of a wealthy person; or whether the group holds on rigidly to the boundary set between rich and poor.

A result of poverty's being found within all social strata, which have created a typical level of needs for each individual, is that often poverty is not susceptible to assistance. However, the principle of assistance is more extensive than what its official manifestations would indicate. When, for example, within a large family the poorer and richer members give one another presents, the latter take advantage of a good opportunity to give the former a value which exceeds the value of what they have received; and not only that, but also the quality of presents reveals this character of assistance: *useful* objects are given to the poorer relatives, that is, objects which help them to maintain themselves within the level of their class. For this reason, presents from a sociological point of view turn out to be completely different in the various social classes. The sociology of the gift coincides in part with that of poverty. In the gift it is possible to discover a very extensive scale of reciprocal relationships between men, differences in the content, motivation, and manner of giving as well as in that of accepting the gift. Gift, theft, and exchange are the external forms of interaction which are directly linked with the question of ownership and from which an endless wealth of psychological phenomena that determine the sociological process are derived. They correspond to the three motives of action: altruism, egoism, and objective norms; the essence of exchange is in the substitution of some values by others which are objectively equal, while subjective motives of goodness or greed are eliminated since in the pure concept of exchange the value of the object is not measured by the desire of the individual but by the value of the other object. Of these three forms, gift is that which offers the greatest wealth of sociological situations, because here the intention and position of the giver and of the recipient are combined in the most varied ways with all their individual nuances.

Of the many categories which make possible, so to speak, a systematic ordering of these phenomena, the most important for the problem of poverty seem to be the following basic alternatives. On the one hand, does the meaning and purpose of the gift consist in the final condition achieved by it, in the fact that the recipient will have a valuable specific object, or, on the other hand, does it consist in the action itself, in the gift as the expression of the giver's intention, of a love desirous of sacrifice, or of a reaching out of the self which is manifested more or less arbitrarily by the gift? In the latter case, the process of giving is, so to say, its own ultimate end and the question of wealth or poverty evidently plays no role whatever, except in terms of the practical problem of what people can afford. But when the one to whom one gives is a *poor man,* the emphasis is not on the process but on its results: the main thing is that the poor person receives something. Between these two extremes of the concept of gift there are innumerable mixed forms. The more the latter type predominates in its purest form, the more impossible it often is to give the poor person what he lacks in the form of a gift, because the other sociological relationships between individuals are incongruent with that of giving. The gift is almost always possible when a great social distance intervenes or when a great personal intimacy prevails; but it becomes difficult to the extent that social distance decreases or personal distance increases. In the upper classes, the tragic situation frequently occurs in which the needy person would willingly accept assistance and he who is in a well-to-do position would also willingly grant it; but neither can the former ask for it nor the latter offer it. In the higher classes the economic *a priori,* below which poverty begins, is set in such a way that this poverty very rarely occurs and is even excluded in principle. The acceptance of assistance thus excludes the assisted person from the premises of his status and provides visible proof that the poor person is formally *déclassé*. Until this happens, class prejudice is strong enough to make poverty, so to say, invisible; and until then poverty is individual suffering, without social consequences. All the assumptions on which the life of the upper classes is based determine that a person may be poor in an individual sense, that is, that his resources may be insufficient for the needs of his class, without his having to recur to assistance. For this reason, no one is socially poor until he has been assisted. And this has a general validity: sociologically speaking, poverty does not come first and then assistance – this is rather fate in its personal form – but a person is called poor who receives assistance or should receive it given his sociological situation, although perchance he may not receive it.

The social-democratic assertion that the modern proletarian is definitely poor but not a *poor man* fits this interpretation. The poor, as a sociological category, are not those who suffer specific deficiencies and deprivations, but those who receive assistance or should receive it according to social norms. Consequently, in this sense, poverty cannot be defined in itself as a quantitative state, but only in terms of the social reaction resulting from a specific situation; it is analogous to the way crime, the substantive definition of which offers such difficulties, is defined as "an action punished by public sanctions." Thus today some do not determine the essence of morality on the basis of the inner state of the subject but from the result of his action; his subjective intention is considered valuable only insofar as it normally produces a certain socially useful effect. Thus too, frequently, the concept of personality is not defined by an inner characteristic that qualifies the individual for a specific social role, but on the contrary, those elements of society that perform a specific role are called personalities. The individual state, in itself, no longer determines the concept, but social teleology does so; the individual is determined by the way in which the totality that surrounds him acts toward him. Where this occurs, we find a certain continuation of modern idealism, which does not attempt to define things by an essence inherent to them, but by the reactions that occur in the subject with respect to them. The binding function which the poor person performs within an existing society is not generated by the sole fact of being poor; only when society – the totality or particular individuals

— reacts toward him with assistance, only then does he play his specific social role.

This social meaning of the "poor man," in contrast to the individual meaning, makes the poor into a kind of estate or unitary stratum within society. The fact that someone is poor does not mean that he belongs to the specific social category of the "poor." He may be a poor shopkeeper, artist or employee but he remains in this category, which is defined by a specific activity or position. In this category he may occupy, as a consequence of his poverty, a gradually modified position; but the individuals who, in different statuses and occupations, are in this state are not grouped in any way into a particular sociological whole different from the social stratum to which they belong. It is only from the moment they are assisted — perhaps already when their total situation would normally require assistance, even though it has not yet been given — that they become part of a group characterized by poverty. This group does not remain united by interaction among its members, but by the collective attitude which society as a whole adopts toward it. However, an explicit tendency toward sociation has not always been lacking. Thus in the 14th century, for example, there was in Norwich a *Poorman's Gild,* and in Germany the so-called "guilds of the miserables." Some time later we find in the Italian cities a party of the wealthy, of the *Optimates* as they called themselves, whose members were united only by the fact of their wealth. Similar unions of the poor soon became impossible because with the growing differentiation of society, the individual differences in education and ideas, in interests and background, among those who might have belonged to the unions were too great to lend to such groups the necessary strength for true sociation.

It is only when poverty implies a positive *content,* common to many poor, that an association of the poor, as such, arises .Thus, the result of the extreme phenomenon of poverty, the lack of shelter, is that those who find themselves in such a situation in the large cities congregate in specific places of refuge. When the first stacks of hay arise in the vicinity of Berlin, those who lack shelter, the *Penner,* go there to take advantage of the opportunity to spend a comfortable night. One finds among them a type of incipient organization, whereby the *Penner* of each district have a kind of headman who assigns to the members of the district their places in the night shelter and arbitrates their quarrels. The *Penner* scrupulously see to it that no criminal infiltrates them, and, when this happens, they denounce him to the police to whom they often render good services. The headmen of the *Penner* are well-known persons whom the authorities always know how to find when they need information about some obscure character. Such a specification of poverty, as the lack of shelter implies, is necessary today to contribute an element of association. Moreover, one may note that the increase of general prosperity, the greater police vigilance and, above all, social conscience which, with a strange mixture of good and bad motives, "cannot tolerate" the sight of poverty, all contribute to impose on poverty increasingly the tendency to hide. And this tendency to hide logically isolates the poor increasingly from one another and prevents them from developing any feeling of belonging to a stratum, as was possible in the Middle Ages.

The class of the poor, especially in modern society, is a unique sociological synthesis. It possesses a great homogeneity insofar as its meaning and location in the social body is concerned; but it lacks it completely insofar as the individual qualification of its elements is concerned. It is the common end of the most diverse destinies, an ocean into which lives derived from the most diverse social strata flow together. No change, development, polarization, or breakdown of social life occurs without leaving its residuum in the stratum of poverty. What is most terrible in poverty is the fact that there are human beings who, in their social position, are just poor and nothing but poor. This is different from the simple fact of being poor which each one has to face for himself and which is merely a shade of another individually qualified position. The fact of being just poor and nothing but poor is particularly apparent where expanding and indiscriminate almsgiving prevails, such as during the Christian Middle Ages and in Islamic lands. However, so long as one accepted it as an official and unchangeable fact, it did not have the bitter and contradictory character which the progressive and activistic tendency of modern times imposes on a whole class: a class which bases its unity on a purely passive characteristic, specifically the fact that the society acts toward it and deals with it in a particular way. To deprive those who receive alms of their political rights adequately expresses the fact that they are nothing but poor. As a result of this lack of positive qualification, as has already been noted, the stratum of the poor, notwithstanding their common situation, does not give rise to sociologically unifying forces. In this way, poverty is a unique sociological phenomenon: a number of individuals who, out of a purely individual fate, occupy a specific organic position within the whole; but this position is not determined by this fate and condition, but rather by the fact that others—individuals, associations, communities—attempt to correct this condition. Thus, what makes one poor is not the lack of means. The poor person, sociologically speaking, is the individual who receives assistance because of this lack of means.

3. Sociological Aspects of Poverty: A Conceptual Analysis*

Donald R. Whyte

The principle thesis of this article is that poverty is phenomenologically different in modern industrialized societies than in pre-industrial or non-industrial societies. To the extent that its empirical manifestations have changed with industrialization, its theoretical conceptualization has likewise undergone some modification. This analysis undertakes to examine the evolution of the concept of poverty, from one based on subsistence criteria to one affirming relative deprivation, and to extract from relevant theoretical and empirical studies a series of propositions which provide an explanation of the causes and consequences of poverty and reveal how sociological and psychological factors interact to perpetuate the conditions of the poor.

POVERTY AS SUBSISTENCE

The concept of poverty was prominent in a number of early theories of society and social change. One of the first and most explicit formulations of poverty as defined in terms of subsistence is found in Malthus' *First Essay on Population*. Malthus' fundamental postulate was that "the power of population is indefinitely greater than the power in the earth to produce subsistence for man."[1] The imbalance between population growth and food supply decreed that a portion of society would be undernourished and in poverty. Because man's needs for food and his sexual passions were not likely to diminish, Malthus foresaw an increasing incidence of poverty. The Malthusian postulate that nature decrees inequality received scientific stature with the publication of Darwin's *The Origin of Species* in 1859. Later Herbert Spencer applied the principles of natural

*Reprinted from *The Canadian Review of Sociology and Anthropology,* 2:4 (1965), by permission of the author and the publisher.

[1] Thomas R. Malthus, *First Essay on Population* (London, 1926), 13.

selection and survival of the fittest to society, thereby reinforcing Malthus' conclusions that interference in the social process served only to upset the natural laws and perpetuate those who were "naturally" less fit.[2]

The practical influence of Spencer's Social Darwinism was more profound in North America than in England, but in its application American sociologists introduced significant modifications in the Malthusian interpretation of the causes and consequences of poverty.[3] Ward and Giddings, though adhering to the basic tenets of Social Darwinism, incorporated a reformist orientation characteristic of American sociology until well into the twentieth century, into their interpretations of the causes of poverty. Thus Ward stated that whereas some were more advantaged than others due to basic biological differences, disadvantage could also derive from adverse social conditions. The same "psychic factors" which produced natural inequalities could be invoked to eliminate and reduce artificial inequalities.[4] Giddings however, pointed out that a system of decentralized communal administration would simply substitute competing communities for competing private organizations and the path of evolution would thereby lead to communal inequalities. A centralized socialism would, by definition, impose such a rigid social organization as to bring an end to progress and hence to the natural improvement of society. Though socialism could not eliminate poverty, it did reveal the fundamental truth that society, because it benefits from progress, ought to assume the costs of progress.[5]

The view that poverty is a consequence of social conditions and not of natural inequalities is most clearly expressed by Cooley, who affirmed that "poverty is unfitness, but in a social and not a biological sense."[6] The main cause of poverty, stated Cooley, is "without a doubt some sort of maladjustment between the individual, or the family or neighborhood group, and the wider community, by reason of which potential capacity does not yield its proper fruit in efficiency and comfort."[7] Poverty, he concluded, is an "unintended consequence" of economic development.

TOWARD A REDEFINITION OF POVERTY

Although Cooley's affirmation could have provided a fruitful point of departure for the development of a broader theory of social causation, its allegation of economic determinacy was sufficient to explain the social inequalities which accompanied the industrialization of American society. Concurrent with industrialization was an emergent affluence which released large aggregates of the population from subsistence levels of living. A growing confidence in science and technology tended to preclude the possibility that poverty could ever again be a serious social problem. This optimism was somewhat undermined by the impact of the Depression of the 1930's, but the poverty of that era merely served to reaffirm

Cooley's assertion that the causes of poverty are lodged in the structure and functioning of the economic sector of society.[8]

The theory of economic determinacy has recently been under serious reconsideration, both in the light of developments in sociological theory and research and in response to an increased awareness of marked disparities in social welfare prevailing under conditions of material wealth. Mills' assertion that "of the three broad strata composing modern society, only the new middle class has steadily grown in proportion to the whole" implied that greater equality of income and of living standards was being realized.[9] His conclusion was recently challenged by Kolko, who offers evidence that "the basic distribution of income and wealth in the United States is essentially the same now as it was in 1939, or even 1910." "Most low-income groups live substantially better today," he continues, "but even though their real wages have mounted, their percentage of the national income has not changed."[10]

The growing awareness among the middle class that a sizable proportion of the population shared a standard of living considerably below the average, and resurgence of equalitarian values,[11] gave support to the belief that the existence of a low-income class contradicted the North American creeds of equality and conformity.[12] Popular sympathy for the war on poverty was aroused by appealing to a sense of moral obligation. In addition, by emphasizing that such a war was an investment in human capital which would eventually pay dividends to all members

[2] Herbert Spencer, *The Principles of Sociology* (London, 1877-96), I, especially Part II. See also Herbert Spencer, *The Study of Sociology* (Ann Arbor, Michigan, 1961).

[3] See Richard Hofstadter, *Social Darwinism in American Thought* (Boston, 1955).

[4] Lester F. Ward, *The Psychic Factors of Civilization* (Boston, 1893).

[5] Franklin H. Giddings, *Studies in the Theory of Human Society* (New York, 1922), 231-2.

[6] Charles H. Cooley, *Social Organization* (New York, 1925), 296.

[7] *Ibid.,* 293-4.

[8] A number of well-known literary works have depicted the economic and social conditions which prevailed among the poor during the Depression. One which stands out both for its literary supremacy and its empirical astuteness is by James Agee and Walker Evans, *Let Us Now Praise Famous Men* (Boston, 1960).

[9] C. Wright Mills, *White Collar* (New York, 1956), 63.

[10] Gabriel Kolko, *Wealth and Power in America* (New York, 1962), 3.

[11] Seymour Martin Lipset, "A Changing American Character?" in *Culture and Social Character,* Seymour Martin Lipset and Leo Lowenthal, eds. (New York, 1961), 136-71.

[12] These creeds of equality and conformity are explained in Robin M. Williams, Jr., *American Society* (New York, 1960), 432. Evidence suggests that Canadian society reflects value patterns fundamentally similar to those of the United States, differing only in degree and primacy. Seymour Martin Lipset has outlined the patterns of similarity and divergence in "The Value Patterns of Democracy: A Case Study in Comparative Analysis," *American Sociological Review,* XXVIII, 4, August 1963, 515-31. A recent summary of this article focuses specifically on Canada and the United States. See Seymour Martin Lipset, "Canada and the United States: A Comparative View," *The Canadian Review of Sociology and Anthropology,* I, 4, November 1964, 173-85.

of the community and society, appeal was made to the values of achievement and progress. As the middle class came to be the point of reference in American society, and as the differences between it and the lower class became more apparent, it became increasingly harder for the lower class to accept the inevitability of their relatively low standard of living. With the resurgent equalitarian ethos, the legitimacy of the existing class structure came into question. Under these conditions, as Merton has shown, "members of some strata are more likely to contrast their own situation with that of others, and shape their self-appraisals accordingly."[13] He continues: "This variation in the structure of systems and in the degree of legitimacy imputed to the rules of the game may help account for the often-noticed fact that the degree of dissatisfaction with their lot is often less among the people in severely depressed social strata in a relatively rigid social system, than among those strata who are apparently 'better off' in a more mobile social system."[14] The conclusion generally accepted has been that in advanced industrial societies, such as Canada and the United States, "individuals and families whose resources over time, fall seriously short of the resources commanded by the average individual or family in the community in which they live . . . are in poverty."[15] Thus we see the evolution of the concept of poverty from one related to subsistence to one affirming relative deprivation, Riendeau gives a clear account:

This evolution has accompanied first the civilization of societies and the industrialization of countries. The definition of misery which was originally in relation to need-survival, changed to that of need-aspiration; from then on, it became accepted to define the needy as one unable to satisfy what were considered, without question, normal aspirations by the milieu; this development has brought us to the point where what had been considered legitimate aspirations, became rights.[16]

POVERTY AS RELATIVE DEPRIVATION: A THEORETICAL INTERPRETATION

The Operationalization of Poverty

The reconceptualization of poverty in terms of relative deprivation rather than in terms of subsistence provides a bridge between the empirical phenomenon and contemporary sociological theory. It necessitates examining poverty in the context of a system of action. *Relative* deprivation implies a social context and a set of normative standards which serve as a basis for comparative evaluation. The systems model, which has emerged as a central analytical element in contemporary structural-functional analysis,[17] makes it possible to examine those conditions of the system which produce relative deprivation and the consequences for other parts of the system and for the system as a whole.

Before examining the conditions and consequences of poverty it is necessary to clarify the conceptual and operational definition of relative deprivation. Poverty, as Riendeau stated, is relative deprivation, but not all relative deprivation is poverty. In addition to the absolute criterion of need which characterized earlier subsistence definitions of poverty, there is added the criterion of need aspiration when poverty is defined in terms of relative deprivation. Obviously, individuals who are unable to satisfy fundamental nutritional requirements aspire to a higher nutritional level; in such cases the criterion of need-aspiration is irrelevant. As pointed out previously, subsistence is a problem for only a small minority of individuals in an industrialized society; need satisfaction is thus a relative matter, and is judged in relation to the increasingly important criterion of need aspiration. Poverty is now directly correlated with the discrepancy between need satisfaction and need aspiration.

Distinguishing between objective and subjective needs, Tremblay and Gosselin differentiate two types of poverty: *la pauvreté objective et la pauvreté subjective.*[18] Individuals unable to satisfy minimal needs for food, clothing, or shelter and unable to fulfil a normal occupational role to provide for these needs are said to manifest *la pauvreté objective.* There are different intensities of objective poverty ranging from conditions where survival is threatened to conditions where a family is unable to satisfy the educational, spiritual, and psychological needs of its children to equip them for satisfying occupations. The intensity of objective poverty is related to an objectively defined criterion of need, that is, a criterion defined by the society or group in which the individual lives, not one defined by the individual himself. Although extreme objective poverty, wherein the survival of the individual is threatened, is an absolute condition, most conditions of objective poverty in industrialized societies are relative.

Subjective poverty, on the other hand, refers to the sensation of deprivation. It does not depend on the absolute level of survival but results from a comparison of what an individual has with what he would like to have. Subjective poverty is directly related therefore, to the discrepancy between need satisfaction and need aspiration: *"Cette marge de différence varie en fonction de l'intensité des aspirations de l'individu et*

[13] Robert K. Merton, *Social Theory and Social Structure* (Copyright © The Macmillan Company, Glencoe, Ill., 1957) , 267.

[14] *Ibid.,* 267-8.

[15] P. Townsend, "The Meaning of Poverty," *The British Journal of Sociology,* XIII, 3, September 1962, 225.

[16] Robert Riendeau, "Poverty in Canada in 1964," paper presented at the Canadian Conference on Social Welfare, Hamilton, Ontario, June 1964, 286.

[17] Talcott Parsons, "Recent Trends in Structural-Functional Theory," in *Fact and Theory in Social Science,* Earl W. Count and Gordon T. Bowles, eds. (Syracuse, 1964) .

[18] M. Adelard Tremblay and Emile Gosselin, "Le Continuum pauvreté-prosperité: son utilité en tant qu'indicateur de désintégration sociale," *Service Social,* IX, 3, nov-dec 1960, 3-28.

de ses opportunités réelles ou 'chances de vie,' pour utiliser l'expression de Weber."[19] Whereas objective poverty is relative deprivation defined by community standards, subjective poverty is experienced relative deprivation, defined in terms of individual values rather than shared norms.

"Il peut y avoir coincidence entre pauvreté objective et pauvreté subjective chez les individus ayant un statut économique très bas mais desirant, par ailleurs, un rehaussement appréciable de leurs niveaux de vie."[20] A low level of living is a condition of absolute poverty while the aspirations for a higher level is the principle condition of subjective poverty. Though both conditions may prevail, objective and subjective poverty being manifest simultaneously, objective poverty can exist without being experienced subjectively and subjective poverty can be experienced without being objectively defined. That is to say, if an individual desires but is unable to achieve a higher standard, he experiences psychological deprivation or subjective poverty even though the community does not define him as poor. It is quite probable that in a highly mobile, achievement-oriented society, as in Canada or the United States, a considerable degree of psychological deprivation is experienced which would not be objectively defined as poverty. On the other hand, as the foregoing suggests, much of what is socially defined as objective poverty will also be experienced psychologically as subjective poverty. Even where objective poverty prevails without being experienced subjectively, the probability is high, under conditions of mass communication and universal elementary education, that aspirations will exceed achievements and conditions of deprivation will be subjectively as well as objectively manifest. As Tremblay and Gosselin point out, the coincidence of objective and subjective poverty has important psychological consequences, consequences which, as the subsequent analysis will show, further reinforce the conditions which produced them.

The definition of poverty in terms of relative deprivation affords a clearer understanding of the operational character of the phenomenon. Rather than being measured solely in terms of subsistence criteria, the poor are defined as those considered by others to be poor and who either consider themselves to be poor or would do so if aware of the standards held by the larger community to which they belong. Poverty, therefore, is a normative concept. The difficulty in employing such an operational definition is in determining which set of normative standards will serve as the basis for evaluation. A family may not be considered poor in relation to others in the community, but in relation to the larger regional or societal norms, the entire community may be considered poor. Ultimately, the decision as to which standards are to be employed will be a matter of judgment conditioned by rational or non-rational motives.

The Sterling County studies offer evidence that such an operational approach is possible. The investigators asked selected key informants in a given locality to name the poor and, by also asking the informants to define what they meant by poor, they were able to ascertain local standards of evaluation and hence to discern degrees of poverty.[21] Their analysis of the social and psychological characteristics manifested by these "county pariahs" is sufficient evidence to support the conclusion that the technique is empirically as well as theoretically useful.[22] Acknowledging the empirical implications of this normative definition, the authors conclude that "poverty will be phenomenologically different, and hence it will have a different meaning in a community in which everyone is poor as contrasted to one in which there is a wide range of economic difference."[23] This is illustrated by Vallee in his study of the Kabloona [whites] and Eskimos in Central Keewatin: "The Eskimos evaluate themselves and one another, in terms of material well-being, education, etc., on a scale which is separate from the scale on which Kabloona are evaluated, as though it were tacitly recognized that a good position on the Eskimo scale would be a poor one on the Kabloona scale."[24] As the standards of the white become better known and more widely adopted among the Eskimos, they come more and more to compare their own well-being with that of the whites. As Vallee points out, this comparison will be made by the entire population within a generation. It is inevitable, therefore, that the Eskimos, who have been objectively poor by white standards for generations, will come more and more to experience their poverty subjectively.

The Cause of Poverty

An explanation of the cause of relative deprivation, or, specifically, of poverty, presupposes an assessment of "which social processes initiate, sustain, or curb" an orientation to one's own position or membership group *vis-à-vis* other groups. Merton suggests that the degree of relative deprivation experienced will be inversely associated with the degree to which the normative component of the existing social structure is institutionalized.[25]

> *If the structure of a rigid system of stratification, for example, is generally defined as legitimate, if the rights, perquisites and obligations of each stratum are generally held to be morally right, then the individuals within each stratum will be the less likely to take the situation of the other strata as a context for appraisal of their own lot ... If, however,*

[19] *Ibid.*, 9.

[20] *Ibid.*

[21] Charles C. Hughes, Marc Adelard-Tremblay, Robert N. Rapaport and Alexander H. Leighton, *People of Cove and Woodlot* (Basic Books, Inc; New York, 1960), 61.

[22] *Ibid.*, 248ff.

[23] *Ibid.*, 315.

[24] Frank G. Vallee, *Kabloona and Eskimo in the Central Keewatin*, Report to the Northern Co-ordination and Research Centre, Department of Northern Affairs and National Resources (Ottawa, May 1962), 181.

[25] "Imputations of legitimacy to social arrangements seem functionally related to reference group behaviour." Merton, *Social Theory and Social Structure*, 267.

the system of stratification is under wide dispute, then members of some strata are more likely to contrast their own situation with that of others, and shape their self-appraisals accordingly.[26]

Thus, for example, Marx foresaw the alienation of the proletariat becoming manifest in a class consciousness as the legitimacy of the prevailing economic system came under attack. In Hindu India, the outcasts and lower castes were not considered to be deprived in relation to the higher castes because the system was legitimized both by the religious norms and by the laws of the country. In the United States, awareness of the depressed state of the Negroes has increased as White Supremacist attitudes and laws have been eroded. Parallel conditions which have stimulated the present awareness of the poor are less apparent but, on the basis of our knowledge of the social and cultural changes which accompany industrialization and urbanization, it is possible to formulate some hypotheses.

It is an established sociological fact that, as technology advances and population increases, there is a concomitant increase in the differentiation of functions and hence of social structures.[27] Structural differentiation affects all segments of the society, but its impact on the occupational structure is especially apparent Some occupations assume greater importance while others become less important to society. Ideally, a system of stratification operates to allocate facilities and rewards according to the functional importance of the role to society.[28] Though it may thus serve a positive function, it does become dysfunctional to the extent that it allows unequal access to the recruitment of manpower, concentrates power in a social elite, and "functions to distribute unequally the sense of significant membership in the population."[29]

The process of structural differentiation, particularly in rapidly changing industrialized societies, has the effect of inducing role obsolescence, that is, certain roles previously of fundamental importance no longer command strategic significance. The effect of this is that either those who perform those roles are relegated, through the operation of the system of stratification, to lower status, or their roles become completely obsolete and they are no longer subject to the workings of the system of stratification. It is not surprising, therefore, to find that the majority of the people generally considered to be poor are unemployed or in occupations which have diminished in functional importance.[30] The latter condition is implied in such expressions as "the invisible poor" or "the forgotten man," and is characteristic of such groups as the marginal farmers who have failed to adapt to the rapid innovations taking place in the field of agriculture, the aged whose social significance has been diminished in a youth-oriented society, and the unemployed who, because they lack training and skills, do not qualify for admission to the labour force.[31] The familiar term "loss of function" may appropriately be applied to these and similar situations.[32]

Accompanying this loss of function is a corresponding loss of power.[33] There is a direct relationship between the position of an individual or group in the system of stratification and the amount of power thereby commanded.[34] Occupying a low position in the stratification system, the poor are unable to compete on an equal basis with other groups in the society.[35] Consequently their potential for adaptation to the changed circumstances is progressively reduced.[36] Contrary to the Marxist predictions, the progressive loss of power and perceived deprivation among the North American poor has not manifested itself in the emergence of a class consciousness or organized class conflict. The main reason is that the poor do not constitute a class as such. There is little similarity in styles of life between the unemployed factory worker, the marginal farmer, and the old-age pensioner.[37] The definition of poverty in *relativistic* terms precludes a common style of life or set of aspirations among the poor. In addition, remnants of the Social Darwinist view that poverty is primarily the fault of the individual still exist, primarily among the

[26] *Ibid.,* 267-8.

[27] This proposition was first put forth by Durkheim in *The Division of Labour in Society* and more recently elaborated by Parsons, who states that "with many individual exceptions, technological advance almost always leads to increasingly elaborate division of labour and the concomitant requirement of increasingly elaborate organization." Talcott Parsons, *The Social System* (Glencoe, Ill., 1951), 507.

[28] Kingsley Davis and Wilbert E. Moore, "Some Principles of Stratification," *American Sociological Review,* X, April 1945.

[29] Melvin T. Tumin, "Some Principles of Stratification: A Critical Analysis," *American Sociological Review,* XVIII, August 1953, 393.

[30] "The essential sin of which our society is capable is not that of allowing people to remain poor but in making them useless. In an age of overactivity, to be unemployed is to be guilty." D.P. Moynihan, "Poverty and Progress," *American Scholar,* XXXIII, Autumn 1964, 594-606. Clark makes the point that whereas earlier social problems in Canada were associated with frontier economic developments, today they arise primarily from the malintegration of existing structures. See S.D. Clark, *The Social Development of Canada* (Toronto, 1942).

[31] Rowntree found that unemployment as a primary cause of poverty increased from just over 2 per cent of the individuals studied in a specific town in 1899 to over 44 per cent in the same town in 1936. See S.B. Rowntree, *Poverty: A Study of Town Life* (London, 1902); and S.B. Rowntree, *Poverty and Progress* (New York, 1941).

[32] Talcott Parsons, "A Functional Theory of Change," in Amitai Etzioni and Eva Etzioni, eds., *Social Change* (New York, 1964), 96.

[33] Talcott Parsons, *The Social System* (Glencoe, Ill., 1951), 508-9.

[34] H.H. Gerth and C.W. Mills, eds., *From Max Weber: Essays in Sociology* (New York, 1958), 180-1.

[35] With reference to rural poverty, Harrington maintains that "farm poor are, for the most part, without a real voice in the United States. The dominant voices are those representatives of the wealthiest, most conservative stratum of the farmers." Michael Harrington, *The Other America* (Baltimore, Md., 1963).

[36] The "opportunity factor" is discussed by Parsons in *The Social System,* 508-9, and more extensively in "A Functional Theory of Change," 89-97.

[37] The British Labour Party is endeavouring to create a class consciousness among these diverse aggregates, but there is little evidence of such consolidation in Canada or the United States.

"intellectually conservative" lower classes. It is, therefore, not surprising to find that the poor, "having been cast by the surrounding sociocultural environment as 'different' . . . have come to accept themselves as different and have incorporated into their self-image many of the attributes given them by outsiders."[38] The belief that one's plight is primarily one's own fault precludes a strong negative identification with an oppressor.

A further consequence of structural differentiation, which explains in part the increased awareness of deprivation, is its effect on the normative system. With an increase in structural differentiation, norms become more universalistic, that is, there emerge "more general complexes of institutionalized norms which apply not to one collective structure but to many."[39] Thus social aggregates and subgroups previously evaluated according to particular standards will be evaluated on the basis of more generalized norms to which numerous other groups are likewise subject. As standards become more universalistic, the relative positions of individuals and groups can more readily be discerned. The change in the normative system serves to explain not so much the cause of poverty as the increasing awareness of relative deprivation. The major causes are the changes in society itself, but the change in the evaluation standards which accompanies structural differentiation provides a standard basis for comparison. Combined with the re-emphasis on equalitarian values which was noted earlier, there results an increased awareness of, and concern for, the less privileged on the part of the affluent majority. As Riendeau points out, what was once considered a legitimate aspiration is now seen as a basic right.[40]

Conseqences of Poverty

Relative deprivation has certain consequences for the individuals who experience it and for the society of which they are a part. An examination of these consequences illustrates the reciprocal relationship between individual and social conditions and helps to explain the persistence of poverty.

Relative deprivation is experienced when one evaluates oneself and one's membership group according to standards of another group. An important function of out-group identification is that it is a form of anticipatory socialization.[41] By accepting the standards of the reference group, the individuals experiencing relative deprivation will be better qualified eventually to assume the rights and obligations accompanying membership in that group. However, Merton points out that "anticipatory socialization is functional for the individual only within a relatively open social structure providing for mobility."[42] Failing to gain acceptance in the group with which he identifies and, because of his out-group orientation, having lost acceptance in the group to which be belongs, the individual becomes the classic example of the marginal man, "poised on the edge of several groups but fully accepted by none of them."[43]

The social conditions producing relative deprivation are such as to preclude ready movement from one group to another. The consequences of anticipatory socialization then, although potentially positive, are in fact dysfunctional. A typical response is some form of substitute action or compensatory behaviour. Caplovitz shows, for example, that the poor frequently indulge in conspicuous consumption, compensating for their low and insecure status with consumer goods.[44] Similar forms of compensatory behaviour are known to be characteristic of minority groups who perceive themselves to be in some ways inadequate in terms of the standards of the dominant group.[45] This response is innovative: the goals of the majority are upheld but, lacking the normatively prescribed avenues for achieving them, alternative methods become symbolic of achievement.[46] While the social structure precludes the movement of deprived individuals, their identification with the standards of the reference group progressively alienate them from their own group.[47] This alienation is accompanied either by withdrawal from social intercourse or by overt rebellion against the established structure. Withdrawal weakens the vitality and legitimacy of the group structure, and, as it becomes more widespread, the group takes on an anomic character. "There is," affirms Merton, "continued and cumulative interplay between deterioration of *social relations* within the membership group and positive *attitudes* toward the norms of a non-membership group."[48]

The depressed areas of Sterling County provide evidence to support this proposition. "The most outstanding feature of social relationship in the Depressed Areas," the authors assert, "is . . . the almost total lack of voluntary associational life."[49] Evidence of the deterioration of social relationships was found not only in the absence of voluntary associations, but also in the weakening of friendships and community spirit, the high proportion of broken homes, the low esteem for education and the school system, and low expectations and aspirations of stability and advancement in occupations.[50] Similar, if less pronounced, observations have

[38] Hughes *et al., People of Cove and Woodlot,* 250.
[39] Parsons, "A Functional Theory of Change," 95.
[40] Riendeau, "Poverty in Canada in 1964."
[41] Merton, *Social Theory and Social Structure,* 263.
[42] *Ibid.,* 265.
[43] *Ibid.*
[44] David Caplovitz, *The Poor Pay More* (New York, 1963).
[45] Tamotsu Shibutani and Kian M. Kwan, *Ethnic Stratification* (New York, 1965), 527-8.
[46] Merton, *Social Theory and Social Structure,* 140.
[47] The meaning of the concept of alienation and its place in social action theory is described by Parsons, *The Social System,* chapters 7 and 8. More recently, Seeman has examined the concept of alienation in terms of its component elements. See Melvin Seeman, "On the Meaning of Alienation," *American Sociological Review,* XXIV, 6 December 1959, 783-91.
[48] Merton, *Social Theory and Social Structure,* 270.
[49] Hughes *et al., People of Cove and Woodlot,* 267.
[50] *Ibid.,* 268-94.

been recorded in numerous other studies of lower-class social organizations.[51]

The inconsistency and unpredictability of behaviour and rewards associated with the breakdown of the social structure contribute to a greater emphasis on immediate goals. Deferred gratification generally holds no reward significance because no predictable pattern has existed to enable forecasts of future rewards. It is not that future rewards are not expected: they are simply not envisioned. The mode of life is oriented to short-range immediate goals. These conditions have well-documented psychological consequences. From the studies of the depressed areas of Sterling County, the authors conclude that: "The socio-cultural situation contains manifold events apt to produce inadequate learning of roles, chronic and severe disturbance of the essential psychical condition, and the fostering of symptoms. These can be conceived in terms of malformation of personality, disturbance to adult personalities whether malformed or not, and a lack of remedial resources for the symptom patterns once they have emerged. The setting is ripe, in short, for malfunctional spirals and cycles."[52]

Social institutions are adapted to the more universalistic standards of the majority and thus are not generally effective in administering either to the social conditions of the poor or to their psychological needs.[53] Institutional means of achieving adaptation to social changes are simply not available to the poor. They are thus further removed from the centres of power, their adaptive potential is weakened, their perceived deprivation becomes more of a reality, and their feeling that "people here are mentally and morally inferior" is reinforced.[54] In short, the psychological consequences of poverty stabilize the generic social conditions, weakening the individual and hindering organizational means of adapting to the rapid changes which initiated the condition. The low level of aspirations and the absence of organizational support combine with the lack of social homogeneity to preclude extreme patterns of innovation or rebellion such as have characterized class, ethnic, or racial responses in the past. Rather, the response is one of psychological alienation and social withdrawal, accompanied by what Rodman refers to as the "value-stretch," a cultural accommodation which enables the lower-class person to accept and condone widely disparate and relatively unpatterned forms of behaviour.[55] The value-stretch serves to minimize the psychological strains which normally accompany anomic conditions, thereby easing frustrations and making it easier for the poor to accept their lot in life.[56]

A Propositional Summary

From the foregoing analysis some propositions concerning the causal conditions of deprivation can be deduced.

(1) An increase in technological innovation and population density has resulted in more elaborate division of labour, or structural differentiation.

(2) Structural differentiation results in a reorganization of roles in the occupational system.

(3) This reorganization results in the obsolescence of certain previously important roles and a decrease in the functional importance of others.

(4) Associated with this loss of function is a corresponding loss of power.

(5) A loss of power reduces the capacity of the individual or aggregate to adapt to the continuing changes which are taking place in the society.

(6) This failure to adapt leads to a decline in the relative position of the individual or group *vis-à-vis* the standards of the larger sub-system or of society.

(7) In addition to resulting in a reorganization of roles in the occupational system, structural differentiation is generally accompanied by a transition to more universalistic standards of evaluation.

[51] Genevieve Knupfer, "Portrait of the Underdog," in Reinhard Bendix and Seymour M. Lipset, eds., *Class Status and Power* (Glencoe, Ill., 1953).

[52] Hughes *et al., People of Cove and Woodlot,* 140.

[53] Evidence in support of this proposition is found in the following: Howard S. Becker, "Education and the Lower Class Child," in Alvin W. Gouldner and Helen P. Gouldner, eds., *Modern Sociology* (New York, 1963); Robert Coles, "Psychiatrists and the Poor," *The Atlantic,* July 1964, 102-6; and Frank Reissman, *The Culturally Deprived Child* (New York, 1962).

[54] Hughes *et al., People of Cove and Woodlot,* 295.

[55] Hyman Rodman, "The Lower-Class Value Stretch," *Social Forces,* XLII, December 1963, 205-15. Rodman notes that a practical consequence of the value-stretch is that the poor are less likely to give a definite response to a survey question, being less committed to a particular point of view on any subject. Consequently there is a greater likelihood of eliciting more "don't knows" and "no responses" in interviews, or of eliciting answers which conform with the perceived expectations of the interviewer.

[56] Not all of the functional consequences of poverty noted in the literature have been discussed. Myrdal notes, for example, that "the poor represent a suppressed demand which needs to be released in order to support a steady and rapid growth of American production." Gunnar Myrdal, "Poverty and Plenty," *American Federalist,* April 1964, 6-8. Similarly, Harper sees the continuation of poverty as the loss of a potential market. Marion Harper, Jr., "Marketing the Poverty Program," *Saturday Review,* May 9, 1964, 65-6. Ultimately poverty is seen as morally intolerable, an offence to the integrity of a nation. The reasons for this attitude have been suggested earlier but because the question is an ethical one it is not susceptible to scientific proof or disproof. Needham observes, on the other hand, that the Newfoundlanders, the majority of whom are poor by current standards, reflect many "positive" features such as low rates of alcoholism, divorce and suicide, and manifest a high degree of personal contentment which is reflected in the maintenance of strong family, religious, and neighbourhood ties. Richard G. Needham, "The Happiest Canadians," *Macleans' Magazine,* November 2, 1964, 15-17, 35-9. Durkheim observed almost a century ago that poverty is an insurance against suicide because it produces fewer needs, and Madden concludes that "what we require is a public program, a vast advertising campaign to convince those with lower incomes that their way of life is best." John Madden, "Some Aspects of Poverty in Canada," paper presented at the Canadian Conference on Social Welfare, Hamilton, Ontario, June 1964, 326.

(8) As norms become more universalistic, they are, by definition, applicable to an increasingly broader spectrum of the population.

(9) The more general the applicability of the standards of evaluation, the more apparent is a relative decline in the position of an individual or group in the society.

(10) Hence the major conditions giving rise to relative deprivation, and its perception by the majority of the population, are inherent in the changing social conditions of the society or sub-system.

The following propositions concerning the social and psychological consequences of deprivation are also suggested.

(1) Perceived relative deprivation is potentially functional for both the individual and society in that it entails a degree of anticipatory socialization.

(2) For these functional consequences to be realized there must be available means whereby the individual can seek membership in the group with which he identifies.

(3) The conditions giving rise to relative deprivation preclude the availability of such means; hence withdrawal from social intercourse is employed as an alternative mode of adaptation.

(4) The combination of withdrawal and out-group orientation leads to the disintegration of predictable patterns of social interaction among the deprived and a breakdown in their social relationships.

(5) The resulting state of anomie produces psychological effects and cultural adaptations which serve to reinforce the prevailing social conditions.

These propositions embody the thesis that conditions of poverty in an affluent society are the consequence of the extensive social and cultural changes which have accompanied technological innovation and scientific advance. They further suggest that the consequences of poverty, and the inability of the existing institutional structures to minister to the needs of the poor, tend to reinforce the prevailing conditions, resulting in the familiar "vicious circle" of symmetrical cause and effect.

CONCLUSIONS

In tracing the evolution of the concept of poverty in sociological writing, it has become apparent that a definition of poverty solely in terms of subsistence criteria, while useful under pre-industrial social conditions, is of little value in explaining poverty in an affluent society. In modern industrial societies, such as Canada and the United States, poverty is a relative condition, that is, the poor are experiencing, or are said to be experiencing, relative deprivation. Although most poverty in North America is relative deprivation, not all relative deprivation, however, is poverty. Tremblay's and Gosselin's definition of objective and subjective needs aid in distinguishing relative deprivation which is poverty from that which is not.

Corresponding to the changing conceptual and operational definition of poverty is a changing conception of the causes and consequences of poverty. Earlier conceptions of poverty based on subsistence, particularly those emanating from the writings of the Social Darwinists, saw the cause of poverty inhering in the natural order of the universe. The principles of natural selection and survival of the fittest were fundamental laws of social development which invoked a seemingly indisputable biological premise to explain social inequalities. However, as subsistence poverty slowly decreased and social inequalities continued to prevail, early twentieth-century sociologists recognized that poverty was primarily a social and not a biological consequence. Cooley foreshadowed contemporary thinking when he asserted that "poverty is unfitness, but in a social and not a biological sense." However, neither he nor his contemporaries pursued the problem further to ascertain why some persons were socially less "fit" than others. Indeed, sociologists have so far given little attention to poverty as a sociological phenomenon and there has been virtually no attempt to examine it in the context of contemporary theory.

The reconceptualization of poverty in terms of relative deprivation provides a link between the phenomenon and current sociological theory, making possible the development and adaptation of theoretical propositions to aid in the explanation of the causes and consequences of poverty. In the previous section these propositions have been summarized. Although they have not been directly operationalized and tested, supporting evidence has been cited from a number of empirical studies. The list of propositions is not exhaustive. No hypotheses are offered, for example, about possible positive functions of poverty for either the individual or society. Is a background of poverty a valuable experiential resource for the individual? In our reaction against Social Darwinism we tend to dismiss such a possibility, but we have little factual evidence to justify its complete dismissal. Again, is it possible that a minimal amount of poverty is functional for a dynamically operating society?

These are only two of the questions which have not been approached in this analysis. However, their investigation requires first and foremost a useful definition of poverty and an understanding of the conditions which produce it in an affluent society. The foregoing propositions are intended to suggest some focal points for research into these preliminary questions. The need for research into the nature and conditions of poverty is generally acknowledged. That little has been done to satisfy that need indicates the lack of a general sociological orientation to the problem. To the extent that a conceptual analysis of poverty affords such an orientation, it will provide some guideposts to the researcher.

4. *Poverty**

S. M. Miller

The exceptional rather than the modal frequently dominates thought. The formation of the poverty program in the United States was spurred by the "discovery" of poverty among a minority of citizens in our most affluent society rather than by its chronicity and preponderance in most of the nations of the world. Similarly, it has been the policy-oriented social scientists of the first industrialized society who have in recent years awakened our interests in social mobility and in poverty and inequality. In their work and that of their colleagues, David Glass and Richard Titmuss of the London School of Economics have focused attention on the barriers to opportunity and to well-being and have forced us to reassess not only the roles of education and social welfare but also the meanings that we wish to assign to societal well-being.

As such, poverty has not been analyzed in the poor nations. The concern rather has been with issues of economic development. The assumption has been that the first task (at least in chronology) of economic development will adequately handle the second task, improving the well-being of people over time.

The disparities between the rich and poor societies make it rather embarrassing at times to discuss in the same breath the poverty of the affluent economy and the poverty of the low-income society. The poor are so much poorer in poor societies that some writers believed that poverty had been ended in the richer societies. Since our conceptualizations and policy orientations may be inadequate even for dealing with poverty in the rich nations, we shall have to exercise great caution in our discussions to insure that the ways of thinking about poverty and its eradication are not mechanically applied to situations where they may prove inappropriate. Also, the situations in societies with differing social systems may be significantly contrasting. We must search for the discontinuities of poverty analysis as well as for the continuities.

* Reprinted from *Transactions of the 6th World Congress of Sociology*, pp. 173-185, by permission of the author and the publisher.

In the richer societies poverty is essentially a minority phenomenon in that the majority of citizens are believed to be living above a poverty line. For most societies, however, the struggle is to move a dominant poverty into a minority poverty. How different is poverty when it is in the majority or in the minority position?[1]

We can categorize different patterns of poverty:

A. Dominant Poverty

1) Most people are poor except for a small but very rich section; the distribution is perhaps 90-10.

2) The poor are in the majority, but there is a sizable number of non-poor in the nation; the distribution of poor to non-poor may be 70-30 or 60-40. That is, a sizable middle-income group has developed.

B. Minority Poverty

3) Although the majority of the population is not poor, a sizable slice is; the distribution of poor to non-poor may be 30-70. The poor may be made up (to a substantial extent at least) of a low-income class group (a regional peasantry) or a caste group (e.g., Negroes in the United States).

4) Most of the population is not poor, except for special groups dependent on special sources (e.g., the aged) or suffering from economic decay (e.g., chronically depressed regional areas). The distribution of poor to non-poor is perhaps 15-85.

These may not be the best categories to denote different poverty situations, but some classification is needed. As with much of the analysis of this paper, the effort is to open doors to discussion rather than to provide a narrow structure to frame discussions.

The analysis of poverty is complicated by the varied meanings and shades attached to the term. To some it is the poverty of mind, of spirit, that is most important, and they are willing to declare, with varying degrees of specificity, what qualities of mind and spirit are the standards. By such standards an affluent society could be poor. Those enamored of the now fashionable term of alienation would characterize many who are materially well-situated as suffering from a poverty of spirit. For others, poverty is essentially a question of income, of the capacity to buy a particular basket of goods which is defined as essential to life in that

[1] ". . . poverty becomes visible and measurable as an increasing proportion of the population attains a higher standard of living, and the poverty of the minority then stands out as a glaring disgrace to a progressive society. Poverty becomes a policy problem when it has been reduced to a manageable proportion at a certain stage of socio-economic development." Koji Taira, *Country Reports: 6, Japan,* International Trade Union Seminar on Low Income Groups and Methods of Dealing with Their Problems, Manpower and Social Affairs Directorate, Organization for Economic Co-operation and Development, 1965, mimeographed, p. 1. While this striking statement has much merit, I do not think it is entirely accurate. It will probably become less so, as I argue later.

society. For still others, poverty is an insufficiency in the command over important economic, social or political ingredients of a level of living. Our concern is largely with "poverty" as indicated in the last two sentences, but we have to be aware of the shifting focuses and goals of poverty analysis.

I suggest below the broad value of looking at poverty in relative terms — the poor are those who are falling behind the advances of the rest of society. In that sense, the concept of poverty applies to rich and poor, socialist and capitalist, industrial and non-industrial societies.

THE ABSOLUTE APPROACH

It is deceptively easy to believe that when we deal with poverty in the low-income countries we are dealing with a basic subsistence problem. The implication is that we are identifying those who fall — and these should be easily identifiable — below the subsistence level. We tend to assume that when we refer to the poverty of the low-income nations we are referring to situations where all or most of the population is barely able to survive. In some countries and in some regions of even well-to-do nations, this is undoubtedly an accurate statement. But in all countries we find that cultural factors affect the definition of poverty. Peter Townsend has alerted us to the possibility that even the basic sustaining caloric intake is probably not determined by sheer biological necessity but by the particular cultural phenomena defining an adequate diet.

Further, in all societies, no matter how low the economic level, there is probably a considerable amount of internal differentiation. Even among the poor we find many who are much poorer than others. We always have to be concerned with the public policy question: to which poor do we wish to direct attention?

THE RELATIVE APPROACH

Richard Titmuss, Peter Townsend and Brian Abel-Smith have made an enormous contribution in forcing us to look at poverty in welfare societies in new ways. Much of their analysis probably applies to low-income societies; how much is one of the problematics of [this article].

Their argument is that poverty is always relative to time, place, and circumstance. Poverty, then, is defined by some standard which changes as society changes. In the higher-income societies, we are not dealing with a subsistence level today in most poverty situations. Rather, poverty refers to those who have *fallen behind the rest of society* in important respects. In Parodi's conceptualization, "lagging income" rather than low income is the issue. He argues:

Certain social groups are in fact particularly vulnerable to the combined effects of an increase in the cost of living, a stationary or inade-

quately increasing income in nominal terms and the specific factors which are normally responsible for poverty. The persistence and even the extension of geographical and vocational areas of poverty and frustration in a country with a rapidly expanding economy are a serious threat to a country's social cohesion.[2]

Poverty, then, has to be analyzed in terms of the over-all conditions of a changing society.

Another great conceptual contribution of the Titmuss group has been to emphasize the varied dimensions of well-being today. The Titmuss group has seen that in the contemporary complex society a conventional and limited interpretation of income is inadequate for assessing the well-being of a population. Titmuss has argued that income has to be considered broadly; in particular, wage-connected benefits (e.g., pensions) and fiscal benefits (e.g., tax deductions for children which benefit the better-off more than the low-income tax payer) as well as welfare (transfer) benefits have to be included in any discussion of the *command over resources.* Poverty, then, is an insufficiency in the command over resources.[3]

This theme has been developed recently by Miller, Gross and Rein. The concept of income has been widened beyond current monetary income to the accumulation of and access to assets (e.g., pensions and housing) and the availability and utilization of services (public and private, as in wage-related medical programs).[4] Poverty lines could be drawn in each of these areas.

In the high-industrial society it may become increasingly important to recognize "the new income" – the evolving forms of social and political inclusions and exclusions, of social and psychological participation, of social distance. T. H. Marshall's "citizenship rights" concept is being applied in the United States, with considerable public furor and varying degrees of achievement, to include the "maximum feasible participation" of the poor in making decisions in the poverty programs. Not only voting rights but political and personal autonomy become new forms of resources which place individuals in a society.[5]

[2] Maurice Parodi, *Country Reports: 1, France, Ibid.*, p. 1.

[3] Richard Titmuss, *Essays on "The Welfare State,"* New Haven: Yale University Press, 1958; *Income Distribution and Social Change,* London: Allen and Unwin, 1962; Brian Abel-Smith, "Whose Welfare State?" in Norman Mac-Kenzie, ed., *Conviction,* London: MacGibbon and Kee, 1959; Peter Townsend, "The Meaning of Poverty," *British Journal of Sociology, 13,* 3, September, 1962.

[4] Bertram Gross and S. M. Miller, "The War on Poverty: Programs Without Objectives." *ditto,* 1965. S. M. Miller and Martin Rein, "Poverty, Inequality and Policy," in Howard S. Becker, ed., *Social Problems,* New York: John Wiley and Sons; 1966.

[5] S. M. Miller, "The New Income," Syracuse University Youth Development Center, 1965, *ditto.* In this paper, a case is made for treating education as a consumers' good and not only, in the now-fashionable lexicon of economists, as an investment in human resources. Education "adds enjoyment values to individuals who possess it, apart from the economic gains that they may receive because of

As the average per capita income of a society increases, the various dimensions of income probably become less coincident. Marginal increments in income do not guarantee better housing, better medical services, better education, more neighborhood amenities or more political effectiveness. The fragmentation and segmentalization of activities in high-industrial societies – contrasting with the functionalist's emphasis on integration and interaction – means that efforts have to be expanded in each institutional area. Across-the-board expenditures cannot solve all the problems of the poor. If we extend the range of amenities that the poor should have (e.g., decent housing), we may have to operate in many of the institutional areas affecting amenities as well as in aggregative economic areas. Organizational resistance to change will become increasingly important. (The sociology of organization has failed to provide an adequate perspective for those attempting to engineer change in educational and welfare bureaucracies.)

The relative approach to poverty – emphasizing the changing components and standards of a level of living – forces recognition of cultural and *ideological* issues. Scientific rigor cannot be applied in most poverty analyses.[6] If poverty is defined by society's standards, exactly where should the poverty lines be placed? And which defining publics are credible?

A more disturbing aspect of poverty analysis is that it can become a lever to raise questions about the character and direction of society. The concern with inequality is frequently presented in the form of statements about poverty. At times, efforts to reduce poverty require reductions in inequalities; this is probably the case of educational differentials in societies with rising educational requirements. But not every statement about inequality is a statement about poverty. It may be a useful political device to link the two – and to some extent they are inextricably linked – but for some purposes of analysis, it has been argued, the differences should be separated. A central issue raised by the Titmuss group and requiring further analysis is the degree of convergence between reducing poverty and reducing inequalities.

SOCIAL STRUCTURE AND POVERTY

The relative and new income approaches require understanding poverty in terms of the changing stratifications and structure of society. We lack adequate accounts of social stratification and structure in low-income societies which are industrializing, in high income societies which are in a "welfare-state" phase, and in socialist societies. Attention to poverty analysis forces reexamination of the transformations in stratification and social structure.

At one level, the question is: are the poor "pockets of poverty," statistical groups, or forms of classes? At another level, what are the new forms of income, authority and personal relationships, and how do various groupings in society appear on these indications of social structure? Obviously, the new income approach is defining a poverty level in terms of the classic dimensions of class, status and power. How should these categories be filled in contemporary societies with different social systems and economic production levels?

The question "what are the causes of poverty?" leads to an analysis of the interaction of social and economic forces and, some would argue, of psychological and physiological circumstances. A statement about the factors producing the poor – the people who fall behind – is a statement about *leads and lags in the social structure.*

For this reason as well as others, I suspect that the relative approach will be important in all forms of societies. This approach delineates a society in motion; industries, occupations, regions, special groups cannot share equally in the changes. In all societies, there is uneven advance. (We call the situation of those worst-off "poverty." Of course, we can disagree about the appropriateness or usefulness of such a designation.)

Statements about policy are implicitly statements about social structure. Such statements etch out not only assumptions about the character of society but, more importantly, the ways in which the society is to be shaped.

Perhaps the greatest lack in discussions of poverty – of the uneven advance of individuals and groups – is the inadequate depiction of contemporary and evolving social structures.

POVERTY STRATEGIES

While economic development and growth are the basic factors in poverty reduction, one cannot offhandedly say that they will solve the problems of poverty. For the issue is *who benefits at what rate* from the development or growth. A poor society may be industrializing at a rapid rate with a sharply rising gross national product. But the number of poor persons may be very slowly (if at all) reduced if the increased product is going into augmenting productive capacity and not consumption. An economic answer to a social issue never resolves the question of choice.

We can look at efforts to reduce poverty in terms of programs of improving social conditions and programs of improving social mobility. ("Social" is used in the widest sense to include all the dimensions of the new income.) Although these two approaches overlap, the distinctions are important. The social conditions approach attempts to change the distribution of benefits; the social mobility approach attempts to change the distribution of individuals.

education." "In the affluent society, those . . . with limited education . . . are not fully included in the society. They are not able to enjoy a variety of benefits of the society. They are differentiated in terms of their treatment by various kinds of agencies and the like." (p. 12).

[6] The uncertain empirical procedures in counting the poor leads Parodi to speak of "detection" rather than "assessment" of the number of poor persons.

Social Conditions Approach

The aim here is to improve immediately, directly or indirectly, the *conditions* of those who are poor. It differs from the social mobility approach in that the concern is not with moving some of the now poor into other social niches in society. We can delineate five variants of the efforts to improve social conditions:

1) Bringing the poor, or a substantial category of the poor, directly above the poverty levels; for example, increasing the incomes of low-income employed categories (e.g. unskilled laborers) through a measure like a minimum wage. Alternatively, the effort is to increase benefit levels of transfer payments to a specific group like the aged or female-headed households on public-welfare assistance. The effort is *not* to change the group in some way but to enhance the conditions of the group as a category of social humanity.[7]

2) Insuring against economic stress and old age. A variety of social insurances (old-age pensions, unemployment insurance, medical benefits) attempt to maintain the income of individuals and families so that they do not fall into poverty or are not at the lowest levels of poverty. The eligibility for and the adequacy of benefits as society changes are recurring issues.

3) Aiding those who are left behind in the general advance of society. The concern is to pinpoint aid to particular groups who are sharply falling behind the general advances of society. Supplementary and assistance schemes, aimed at helping a fairly specific population, are characteristic of this approach.

4) Providing amenities to a larger number of people. Since certain kinds of amenities — decent health, housing, recreation, social services, etc. — are important elements in the new level of living, programs are aimed at directly improving the quantity and quality of these amenities available to and used by the poor. Non-market policies offset the impact of market forces.

5) Enhancing social conditions to promote social mobility. The effort here is to provide improved family social conditions in order to accentuate or encourage some of the people in a category (especially the young) to become socially mobile. Occasionally, improving income levels is seen as a way to stimulate mobility aspirations and efforts. More frequently, as in the United States, social services (cast in the chastizing setting of "rehabilitation") are regarded as the fulcrum to prepare and motivate youth for seizing opportunity to be mobile.[8] To some extent, then, there is a dual function in the effort to better social conditions: improving the conditions of some and encouraging their offspring to be mobile.

Social Mobility Approach

The aim here is to improve the chances of individuals and groups to move into occupational niches which provide higher levels of income and amenities. If there is a great increase in mobility opportunities for a particular category (e.g., if 35 per cent rather than 5 per cent, of the sons of unskilled, low-income men move into considerably higher-paid and higher-valued occupations) we are dealing with a structural change in the distribution of life-chances. The social mobility approach is highly valued because it emphasizes the normal operation of market forces and the desirability of participation in the labor market. Economic development means to a large extent social mobility, for it requires and results in changes in the occupational distribution. But those most poor in a society may have less opportunity than other groups to change their occupations despite the growth of industry and new forms of economic activity.

When social mobility is looked at from the viewpoint of policy, education becomes the focus. The improvement of social mobility chances for the poor (and for many other sectors) requires an expansion and democratization of education. In less industrialized societies, education may be at first of less importance. But as a society advances along the industrialization continuum, educational credentials assume increased importance, undoubtedly much beyond their reflection of real skill needs.

The distribution of educational opportunity, then, becomes a cardinal issue in the social mobility approach to poverty reduction. Expanding educational opportunities across the board may be less important than expanding opportunities for low-income youth.

The social mobility approach is oriented to *opening doors* into the larger society for the poor; the social conditions approach, to *providing floors* so that no one can fall below a particular level. The two approaches obviously overlap. But they are aimed at different visions and values of society and different concerns about the poor. To a large extent, the low-industrial society implicitly emphasizes improving the conditions of the poor by increasing social mobility through opening up new kinds of occupational statuses. In high-industrial societies, there is likely to be a more conscious debate about the two approaches.

[7] This effort is aimed at increasing stratum mobility, the position of one category relative to others. (See S. M. Miller, "Comparative Social Mobility," *Current Sociology,* IX, 1, 1960.) I have not included it under social mobility because it is of a different character than other social mobility measures.

[8] The descriptions of and attitudes towards the poor are important elements in the formation of policy. In the United States, the metaphor "the culture of poverty" has unfortunately affected much of policy thinking. See Miller and Rein, *op. cit.;* Miller and Rein, "Poverty, Policy and Purpose: The Dilemma of Choice," *Social Welfare Assembly,* 1966; S. M. Miller and Frank Riessman, "The Working-Class Subculture: A New View," *Social Problems,* 1961; S. M. Miller, Frank Riessman and Arthur Seagull, "Poverty and Indulgence: A Critique of the Deferred Gratification Pattern," in Louis Ferman, Joyce Kornbluh, and Alan Haber, eds., *Poverty in America,* Ann Arbor, University of Michigan Press, 1965; S. M. Miller, "The American Lower Classes: A Typological Approach," in Arthur Shostak and William Gomberg, eds., *Blue Collar World,* Englewood Cliffs, N.J., Prentice-Hall, 1964.

To what extent do these approaches necessarily conflict, to what extent do they converge, and which one has precedence in what kinds of situations, are questions of extraordinary importance that social science has not dealt with adequately at present.

Some measures can promote both the improvement of social conditions and social mobility. Other measures can do only one and would be harmful or irrelevant perhaps to the other. We need more and more delineation of measures and assessments of their effectiveness under varying conditions in low-income and high-income societies. Although much has been written on social policies, we still lack a theory which provides a basis for the allocation of resources and the improvement of the operations of welfare and educational bureaucracies.

Are there different kinds of strategies for poor and rich societies? To what extent has Western society been emphasizing the improvement of social mobility opportunities and neglecting the improvement of social conditions? How to divide expenditures in a society between improving social conditions and improving social mobility is an extraordinarily complicated point which will need much more analysis of the economic costs and benefits as well as the social costs and benefits of each kind of program. We are concerned, in dealing with the poor, with tracing out the kinds of responsibilities and burdens we wish our society to have. For example, to what extent do we wish to improve the conditions of the aged or the conditions of youth?

These are value issues to a large extent, not narrow technical issues. It is the hallmark of a beneficent society that it recognizes principles and does not submerge social values into technical issues. To some extent technicism has led to underestimating the significance of the moral choice involved in the way we wish to allocate production and to shape the kind of society in which we wish to live.

RICH AND POOR NATIONS

Increasingly, rich and poor nations are part of the same international system. With the spread of communication and information, the relevant comparisons of economic standing will not be within a nation but with an international standard of well-being. The richer nations will be yardsticks to provide measurements of well-being in poorer nations. "The revolution of rising expectations" is the development of new standards of well-being, based on images of what is possible. These images, even in poor societies, reflect conditions in the richer societies. The lines which will demarcate poverty will be increasingly determined by *inter*national rather than *intra*national situations. Poverty, then, could be considered a great problem in nations where it has not been "reduced to a manageable proportion."

Gunnar Myrdal has been one of the few who have consistently addressed themselves to the interaction of poor and rich economies. His conclusions are that the disparities between the rich and poor nations have deepened: the rich nations are richer today relative to the poor than in previous decades. Moreover, in many low-income economies the absolute level of living may actually be going down. Thus, many of the poor nations in the world are not only falling behind the rich nations relatively, but they are also suffering a real decline in their conditions of life.

Frequently, one hears attacks upon the new nations as being unwilling to assume the kinds of burdens necessary to promote industrialization. Here, it is important to remember that a number of pieces of evidence now show that the level of living in these countries may be below the level which was achieved in Western Europe at the time of its rapid industrialization. Productivity in agriculture in these areas—frequently after hundreds of years of Western influence and control—is at a lower productivity level than was the productivity of agricultural lands in Western Europe in its time of "takeoff."

The political difficulties in these nations also parallel the political difficulties of many high-industrial nations in their early stages. The revolutionary wars, the wars for national independence, the long battles among various countries, the internal constraints and conflicts which took place in the industrialized societies at an earlier point are very similar to the kinds of strains and difficulties of the now industrializing societies.

We have had, perhaps, a lack of humility, respect and understanding for the difficulties of industrializing societies. We have rather assumed that the benefits which have been attained in Western society are unique manifestations of the good will and dedication of Westerners, rather than related to specific historical experiences and luck, particularly in terms of raw materials and geography.

How can the rich nations help the poor nations? Here we have had inadequate analysis. We need many more basic ideas (and their implementation!) than have been developed. Myrdal has analyzed the important kinds of changes that must take place in relationships among rich and poor nations. He emphasizes the need for changes in the terms of trade so that the poorer agricultural nations can benefit more from international commerce. The rich nations should be more willing to accept the trade restrictions devised by the poor nations to promote development. Sizable investments of capital will probably be needed if internal strain is to be reduced in industrializing societies.

There has been an enormous amount of activity in the general area labelled technical aid and "investment in institution-building." To what extent have we learned how to borrow most effectively from the experiences and expertise of advanced societies in helping poor societies to move ahead economically?

There are grave difficulties involved here, apart from the level of systematizing what is known or might become known. The great problem is that of colonialism in the intellectual realm. Many people in industrializing societies are concerned that a colonial situation may continue despite the formation of a national state. They see the development of various forms of technical aid as intellectual bases for colonialism. Is it possible to provide expert help without encouraging intellectual dependence of and disrespect for the society?

A serious issue which obviously deserves much more attention is the analysis of the *resistance* to aiding the poor of other nations. In many societies, of course, there is even resistance to aiding the poor of one's own society. In the rich societies there is general reluctance to think seriously about aiding the poor of other societies. True, some nations have provided aid on a sizable level to other societies. But as a continuous, deep responsibility, this kind of consciousness does not seem to be pervasive. In the United States aid has been primarily related to the need to limit the attractiveness of Communism. In other societies, the counter-emphasis has provided the push towards aid. Is there a perspective which goes beyond the peculiar and limited national interest in attempting to provide aid to other nations? To what extent is it possible to develop new ways of viewing national output so that it is considered in terms of international as well as national benefit?

A new stage has probably been reached in international relations. While it is undoubtedly true that the rich societies are benefiting mightily from many of their activities in less rich societies, it seems that internal markets have developed to such an extent in the large industrial societies that the heavy rewards from colonial possessions and trade are no longer as significant as they once were. If this is true, then, it presages new possibilities on the international scene. Why have we not moved as rapidly in making these kinds of changes as is now possible? To what extent has there been reluctance of particular kinds of elites to image new possibilities? What have been the obstacles to popular support for measures of aid to other societies? These are important issues which deserve much more attention from social scientists than they have received.

The issues of poverty open up questions about the direction of a nation internally and externally. To ask what we wish to do about poverty is a question about the goals and character of a society.

5. *Problems and Perspectives in the Study of Poverty**

John R. Hofley

S. M. Miller in the *Transactions of the Sixth World Congress of Sociology* remarks:

Perhaps the greatest lack of discussions of poverty – of the uneven advance of individuals and groups – is the inadequate depiction of contemporary and evolving social structures.[1]

The relative and new income approaches require understanding poverty in terms of the changing stratifications and structure of society.[2]

As a result of this inadequate depiction of contemporary social structures we become blind to the complexity of poverty. We fail to ask certain questions. For example: What is the character of poverty in an industrial society? What is the relationship between poverty and capitalism? What is the relationship between the individual's definition of reality and the social reality in which he finds himself? Why do differences in attitudes, values and behaviour exist between persons of different socio-economic strata? Are the poor homogeneous? Should most ameliorative programs be similar in content? Are our research methods adequate for the task of answering such questions?

If we are to take these questions seriously, and begin the arduous task of finding the answers, an attempt to reconcile the various views expressed above is essential. We need to develop a framework which is both descriptive and explanatory – one which would enable practitioners to make useful distinctions between different types of poor, thereby creating different types of programs. "The amount of diversity among low

* An original article prepared for this volume. I would like to thank Charles Gordon, John Harp and Judi Stevenson for their critical comments on an earlier draft.

[1] S. M. Miller, "Poverty," in *Transactions of the Sixth World Congress of Sociology*, Vol. II, 1967, p. 179.

[2] *Ibid.*, p. 178.

income families is too frequently underrated and overlooked in both professional and popular thinking."[3]

The following discussion relies heavily on the classical, theoretical frameworks of Marx, Durkheim and Weber, together with that found in Peter Berger and Thomas Luckmann's *The Social Construction of Reality.*[4] The present paper has two goals: 1) to sensitize the reader to the sociological conditions presently extant in Canada as they concern the poor, as well as to the reasons for their invisibility; and 2) to build a conceptual framework that will enable us to pursue our ideas concerning the poor, not merely to comprehend or to delineate correlates, but to come to some understanding and interpretation of both poverty and the poor. "The physical world exists and can be known; the human world is meaningful and can be understood."[5]

Until the late 1950's, theories of stratification, with the exception of Weber's "Class, Status and Party" and Sorokin's *Social Mobility,* stressed *either* the Marxian emphasis on structural variables such as the relationship of persons to the means of production (thus having capitalists, petit bourgeois and proletariat) and the relation of persons to the means of production (thus having land owners, owners of capital and labourers),[6] *or* the importance of the individual's values, norms, family and peer groups in enabling him to move up and down in a fluid, classless society. The latter position has its classic expression in the works of such social Darwinists as Herbert Spencer and W. G. Sumner, and its contemporary expression in the work of K. Davis and W. Moore and Talcott Parsons.[7]

North American sociology, with a few exceptions (notably C. Wright Mills and Gabriel Kolko),[8] has been dominated by the latter approach. Most Canadian and American sociologists see the *individuals* as the root of the problem, seldom looking beyond the individual to the institutions of the larger society which shape him. The Hinkles describe this characteristic of North American sociology as "voluntaristic nominalism:"

This term describes the assumption that the structure of all social groups is the consequence of the aggregate of its separate, component individuals and that social phenomena ultimately derive from the motivations of these knowing, feeling and willing individuals.[9]

This approach is dominant in the major empirical works on stratification such as the Yankee City series in the United States,[10] or the Sterling County project in Canada.[11] It is a central feature of the culture of poverty approach and of the major conceptual framework in North American sociology – functionalism.[12] Oscar Lewis, the main exponent of the culture of poverty approach, stresses the importance of a lower class subculture with different values, norms, ideals, and behaviour. These values serve to inhibit upward mobility. Lewis writes:

The culture of poverty has its own modalities and distinctive social and psychological consequences for its members. It is a dynamic factor which effects participation in the larger national culture and becomes a subculture of its own.[13]

And later:

Other traits include a strong present time orientation with relatively little ability to defer gratification and plan for the future, a sense of resignation and fatalism based upon the realities of their difficult life situation, a belief in male superiority which reaches its crystallization in machismo *or a cult of masculinity.*[14]

Warren C. Haggstrom, a psychologist, notes that the poor have particularistic values that stress the intimate, the sensory, the personal. They are also present oriented and believe it is futile to think of the future.[15]

Others are highly critical of this approach[16] yet remain firmly within the voluntaristic tradition. Drake and Cayton's study of blacks in Chicago prior to World War II, suggests at least three "styles of life."[17] Hylan

[3] Hylan Lewis, "The Contemporary Urban Poverty Syndrome," paper presented to Howard University Medical School, April 28, 1964, p. 7.

[4] Peter Berger and Thomas Luckmann, *The Social Construction of Reality* (New York: Doubleday & Company Inc., 1967) .

[5] H. P. Rickman, *Understanding and the Human Studies* (London: Heinemann Educational Books, Ltd., 1967) , p. 135.

[6] S. Ossowski, *Class Structure in the Social Consciousness* (Copyright © New York: Free Press of Glencoe, 1963) , p. 81.

[7] K. Davis and W. Moore, "Some Principles of Stratification," *American Sociological Review,* 10 (April 1945) , p. 242-50; and Talcott Parsons, "A Revised Analytical Approach to the Theory of Social Stratification" in *Class Status and Power* (1st ed.) , R. Bendix and S. M. Lipset (eds.) , (New York: Free Press of Glencoe, 1953) , pp. 92-128 .

[8] C. W. Mills, *The Power Elite* (New York: Oxford University Press, 1959) ; and Gabriel Kolko, *Wealth and Power in the United States* (New York: Frederick A. Praeger, 1962) .

[9] R. and G. Hinkle, *The Development of Modern Sociology* (New York: Random House, 1954) , p. V.

[10] For example, see W. L. Warner, *et. al., Social Class in America* (Chicago: Science Research, 1949) ; W. L. Warner and P. Lunt, *The Social Life of a Modern Community* (New Haven: Yale University Press, 1941) .

[11] See Alexander Leighton, *My Name is Legion* (New York: Basic Books, Inc., 1959) ; and Charles C. Hughes, *et al., People of Cove and Woodlot* (New York: Basic Books, Inc., 1960) .

[12] See series of articles in R. Bendix and S. M. Lipset, *Class, Status and Power* (2nd ed.) , (New York: Free Press of Glencoe, 1966) , pp. 47-72.

[13] Oscar Lewis, *The Children of Sanchez,* (New York: Random House, 1961) , p. xxiv.

[14] *Ibid.,* pp. xxvi-xxvii.

[15] Warren C. Haggstrom in H. P. Miller, *op. cit.,* pp. 67-81.

[16] See Charles A. Valentine, *Culture and Poverty: Critique and Counter Proposals* (Chicago: University of Chicago Press, 1968) . For a lengthy debate on this book, see *Current Anthropology,* Vol. 10, nos. 2-3 (April-June 1969) , pp. 181-201. An excellent article on the concept of the culture of poverty is Jack L. Roach and Orville Gursslin, "An Evaluation of the Concept, 'Culture of Poverty'," *Social Forces,* 45 (March 1967) , pp. 383-92.

[17] St. Clair Drake and Horace H. Cayton, *Black Metropolis* (New York: Harcourt, Brace & World, 1945) , p. 600.

Lewis, after studying lower-class blacks and whites in Washington, D.C. in the early 1960's notes that "it is probably more fruitful to think of different types of lower class families reacting in various ways to the facts of their position and to relative isolation rather than to the imperatives of a lower class culture. It is important that we not confuse life chances and actual behavior with values and preferences."[18]

Functionalists, such as Talcott Parsons and Davis and Moore,[19] posit a single and integrated value system.[20] Parsons, of course, does recognize that variability in adherence to these values occurs, but in individuals, not in such entities as "classes." Roger Brown seems to agree with Parsons when he notes:

Norms in the United States do not seem to be organized in terms of classes, but rather in terms of roles. Some of the roles fall in a continuum of SES but behaviour is prescribed in terms of the roles. This is the last reason for concluding that classes are not functionally real.[21]

Rossi and Blum, in a recent summary of the literature on poverty and social stratification, conclude that in the United States "there is little firm evidence for the existence of a culture of poverty which marks off the very poor as distinctly different from socio-economic status levels immediately above them. The poor appear to be quantitatively rather than qualitatively different."[22] The consequences of the voluntaristic approach are not confined to the discipline. This voluntaristic orientation permeates our whole society.

Many Canadians believe that Canada is a classless society,[23] that most Canadians are middle class, that we have conquered hunger and poverty, and that anyone willing to work hard can be upwardly mobile. It is true that we recognize that some *persons* are in need, and as a result we spend millions of dollars on welfare measures or donate to charities, but we seldom realize that these persons' difficulties are the *result,* not the cause, of inadequate institutions — economic, political and social.

This conception of the reality of our social structure works against our perceiving poverty and the poor, and against our seeing the potential intense and violent conflict among various strata in Canadian society. We must constantly remind ourselves that our conception of reality, our social consciousness, is very much a product of our location in that structure. Also, that it is important to realize that persons in positions of power will stress that society is "classless" and that persons in the lower strata may achieve mobility through personal, rather than collective effort. These are factors that prevent the poor from becoming organized.[24]

Canadians see their society as "classless" because the vast majority of persons with whom they interact are, just as they themselves are, members of the middle class. It is precisely because we perceive our structure in this way, that we ignore *both* the extremes — that is, the poor and the rich. The larger the middle class, the less visible the extremes. Objectively, as Porter has ably demonstrated in *The Vertical Mosaic* and in *Canadian Social Structure,*[25] the extremes exist. Subjectively, they are "invisible."[26] There are several reasons, both physical and social, why the poor (and the rich) are invisible.

To begin with, we must not minimize the importance of Canada's geography and history. We have placed our Indians on reservations, effectively hiding them from the comfortable majority. Small rural farms, the majority of which are poor, look quaint on a Sunday afternoon drive. Regions of Canada such as the Atlantic provinces, Western and Northern Quebec, Northern Ontario, many parts of the West (particularly the northern fringes), and the Northwest Territories and Yukon are seldom seen by the affluent except through uncritical tourist eyes. In some Canadian cities suburban commuters may drive through the urban slums, but they certainly do not experience them in any meaningful way. (In most Canadian cities, one can drive around or over the slums and thus avoid even seeing them, except from on high.)

Even when the more affluent see the slums and impoverished reservations and farm communities, all of which are *collectivities*, the social conclusion most will draw will be based on the voluntaristic assumption discussed earlier — that *individuals* are to blame. Such a reaction is strongest during a period of prosperity such as we are now experiencing. They will see these physical slums and depressed regions as the result of the poor's own lack of initiative, not society's. Martin Rein notes:

[18] Hylan Lewis, *op. cit.*, p. 24.

[19] Davis and Moore, *op. cit.*, Parsons, *op. cit.*

[20] At this point it is important that we heed Hylan Lewis' comment (*op. cit.*, p. 6), "Middle class values, highly advertised as they are, indeed may be well known. But that does not make them realizable. For many, particularly the young poor, the distance between knowing and being able to achieve them is the rub."

[21] Roger Brown, *Social Psychology* (New York: Free Press of Glencoe, 1965), p. 135.

[22] Peter Rossi and Zahava D. Blum, *Social Stratification and Poverty*, a paper presented at the annual meeting of The Sociological Research Association, San Francisco, 1967.

[23] See John Porter, *The Vertical Mosaic* (Toronto: University of Toronto Press, 1965), p. 3.

[24] See Ossowski's brilliant yet relatively unknown work, *Class Structure in the Social Consciousness, op. cit.*, pp. 154 and 176. He remarks: "From the viewpoint of the interests of privileged and ruling groups the utility of presenting one's own society in terms of a non-egalitarian classless society is apparent. In the world of today, both in the bourgeois democracies and the people's democracies, such a presentation affords no bases for group solidarity amongst the underprivileged; it inclines them to endeavour to improve their fortunes, and to seek upward social mobility by means of personal effort and their own industry, and not by collective action."
"The choice of a scheme of class structure in a particular instance is symptomatic either of the problems which interest those who apply the scheme or of their views on the reality which they are describing."

[25] John Porter, *Canadian Social Structure: A Statistical Profile* (Toronto: McClelland & Stewart, 1967).

[26] Michael Harrington, *The Other America* (New York: Macmillan, 1962).

During a depression a 'failure' can blame his plight on the system; during prosperity it is much more difficult to avoid blaming himself, and becoming hopeless and apathetic. The ethic of the prosperous — that their welfare is due entirely to their own virtuous efforts — is infecting the poor, in reverse.[27]

In short, we are a society that historically has believed in a work ethic, the Horatio Alger myth. Because of this, we dislike public dependency and admire autonomy. Even persons on relief subscribe to this ethic; at least they give lip service to it. The more affluent forget that they are where they are because of "luck," that is, the genes they have (what Philip Hauser calls "high preconception I.Q.") and the socio-economic status of the family of orientation. Part of the luck is the fact that occupational choice is far more rational for the wealthier persons in our society. The person born poor is much more dependent on short-term local fluctuations of the labour market for his mobility chances. Similarly, members of the middle class forget that they are daily dependent on various public and private agencies such as municipal, provincial and federal governments. The affluent of Canada ignore the fact that various government departments and agencies such as ARDA, Manpower and Immigration, Health and Welfare, and more recently, the Economic Council of Canada have documented the extent of poverty and the need; yet the poor remain both ignored and invisible. This historical and emotional attachment to the work ethic is well described by Ossowski: "Facts are powerless against stereotypes supported by emotional motivations."[28]

Another important feature of contemporary Canadian society that serves to obscure the gap between the poor and the rich is the "rational-legal bureaucracy." Our lives are lived in and around these man-made institutions. A bureaucracy as a form of social organization stresses individual competition. Authority is vertical and yet diffuse. It is difficult to pinpoint who makes the decisions that affect the participants and the clients. As long as persons within the bureaucracy — be it political, economic, religious or educational — feel that they can rise within the system (through examinations for example), the common interests that lower-level participants share will remain dormant or latent. In short, the more affluent members of a bureaucracy will not recognize the poverty of the lower level participants. This difficulty is even greater when we consider the place of the welfare recipient in the welfare bureaucracy. As Simmel pointed out many, many years ago, "within the modern relatively democratic State public assistance is perhaps the only branch of the administration in which the interested parties (the clients) have no participation whatsoever."[29] Welfare bureaucracies tend to serve the interests of dispensers rather than recipients. The poor of Canada are powerless and, as Vallee and Whyte point out, "There is no evidence that [this] disestablished element is developing an organizational structure through which it can express its views and apply its meagre weight."[30]

All the above conditions help to account not only for the invisibility of the poor, but for a lack of "class consciousness" and of violent struggle between classes. As long as the more affluent members of a society can convince everyone less affluent that they can rise in the social hierarchy as individuals, there is a minimum of conflict within the society; and what conflict exists can be handled through institutional procedures such as unions and courts. However, our society is presently undergoing rapid social change. Conflict between various groups in our society (French-English; White-Indian; within Quebec, Federalists-Separatists; students-teachers; parents-children; welfare workers-clients; farmers-urban dwellers) is coming to the surface, is no longer polite and is not always manifested through institutionalized mechanisms. There is also in many cases a coalition of these various groups — for example, students and Indians, or students and labour, or Indians and blacks and students. This intense conflict (so far, much more serious and violent in the United States than in Canada) was not expected even by sociologists. Indeed, the functionalist, voluntaristic approach would predict that the higher the correlation between various measures of status (income, education, occupation, prestige), the greater the stability of the social system.

However, what has occurred and is still occurring in Canada is a higher correlation between characteristics deemed "undesirable;" that is, persons who are poor are more likely to be non-white, of Eastern European descent, and low in education, income and occupation. The first two characteristics mitigate against their being able to improve on the last three characteristics. In addressing himself to this type of situation Dahrendorf remarks:

If the social condition of industrial workers, who are as such excluded from authority, falls below a physiological subsistence minimum or "poverty line," the effects of such deprivations are likely to be different in kind from those of relative deprivation. I would suggest that in this case, and in this case only, the superimposition of scales of status and the distribution of authority is likely to increase *the violence of class conflicts.*[31]

In other words, the expectation by functionalists such as Talcott Parsons, that such a "superimposition of scales" would bring stability, in fact brings conflict. It does so because it heightens the group consciousness of the "disinherited." These various groups who are "low" in socio-economic status and prestige — that is, on objective criteria — become

[27] Martin Rein, "The Strange Case of Public Dependency," *Trans-Action,* 2 (March-April 1965), p. 21.

[28] Ossowski, *op. cit.,* p. 38.

[29] Georg Simmel, "The Poor," *Social Problems,* 2 (Fall 1965), p. 123.

[30] Vallee & Whyte, *op. cit.,* p. 845. Also see James Harding, "The Powerless Minority," this volume, pp. 239-252.

[31] Ralf Dahrendorf, *Class and Class Conflict in Industrial Society* (Stanford, California: Stanford University Press, 1959), p. 217 (italics mine).

aware of their common interests and begin to formulate goals for organized action; they form a "class."[32] The development of "class consciousness"[33] is facilitated by a political climate that permits organized dissent and by social conditions and technical conditions, especially radio and TV, that permit such groups to communicate their needs and goals to each other.[34]

I hope that so far I have sensitized the reader to the sociological conditions presently extant in Canada *vis-à-vis* the poor, and to the reasons for their invisibility and status. I have also tried to hint at the potential development of such persons (particularly in terms of "class consciousness"), which has serious and fascinating challenges for the social scientist, the practitioner and the politician. There follows an examination of the particular problem of poverty and a suggested conceptual framework that is firmly grounded in stratification theory.

In recent years, three sociologists — a German, Ralf Dahrendorf; an American, Gerhard Lenski;[35] and a Pole, Stanislaw Ossowski — have tried to synthesize the various strands of European and North American views on stratification. All three see the development of stratification theory in terms of a conflict between two opposing schools. Dahrendorf calls the two schools Utopian (its members, for example, Talcott Parsons, stress coherence through consensus) and Rationalist (its members, for example, Marx, stress cohesion by constraint and domination). Lenski uses the words Conservative and Radical to depict the same phenomena. Ossowski distinguishes between two approaches and breaks each down into two categories. Category A connotes schemes based on relations of dependency — that is, classes differ in their attributes. An attribute refers to a quality which has an all-or-none existence. Category B contains schemes based on ordering relationships — that is, classes differ in the degree of their variables. The diagram below illustrates the model, and I have included examples of each type in brackets.

Diagram 1
*Models of Stratification**

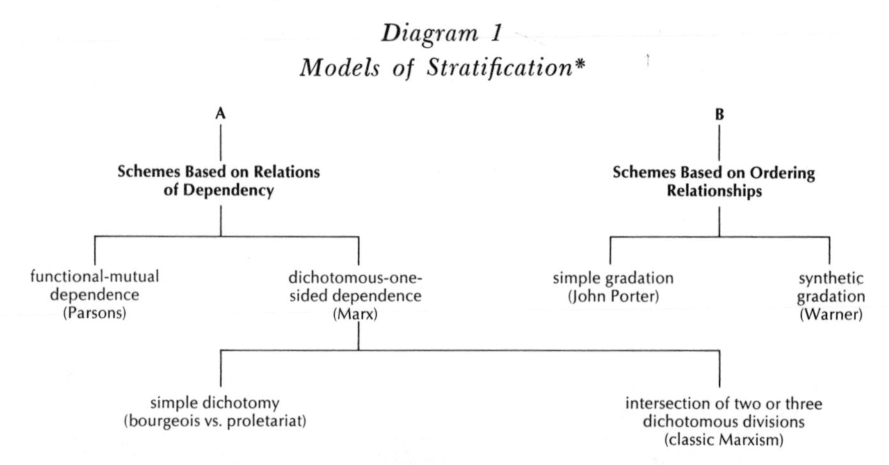

* Adapted from S. Ossowski, *Class Structure in the Social Consciousness* (New York: Free Press of Glencoe, 1963), p. 152.

The basic dichotomy all three authors allude to is that between consensus and conflict. We have already noted that North American sociology has generally fallen into the first camp — that is, it stresses consensus. As Max Weber noted at the turn of the century in his analysis of authority systems and legitimacy, the relationship between consensus and the emphasis on values is complementary to the emphasis on conflict and tension. The two are not diametrically opposed. Both consensus and conflict are omnipresent characteristics of any society. "Society is Janus-headed, and its two faces are equivalent aspects of the same reality."[36]

Any attempt to deal systematically with poverty must recognize the constant interaction between these two aspects of reality, between conflict and consensus. Another way of looking at this interaction and tension within society is to see it as the result of an encounter of two realities or conceptions of society, society as subjective reality and society as objective reality.[37] This is the result of a dialectic that involves three processes:

1) *Externalization.* "The production of institutions that serve to order man's existence, that possess a reality of their own, a reality that confronts the individual as an external and coercive act."[38]

2) *Objectivation.* "The process by which the externalized products of human activity attain the character of objectivity."[39] An example of objectivation is language.

3) *Internalization.* "The immediate apprehension or interpretation of an objective event as expressing meaning."[40] (Best expressed in the writings of the "symbolic interactionists", particularly George Herbert Mead.)

These three processes remind us that society is a human product and an objective reality, and that man is a social product.

Berger and Luckmann's basic framework will enable us to develop a typology, a conceptual framework within which poverty can be understood, that will be cognizant of the fundamental points raised by Dahrendorf, Lenski and Ossowski and of the tension between the two realities.[41]

[32] As Marx has pointed out, "... individuals form a class only insofar as they are engaged in a common struggle with another class." Quoted in Dahrendorf, *ibid.*, p. 14.

[33] "Class consciousness" is the articulation and transformation of interests, both latent and objective, so that the members of a class become subjectively conscious of their class position and begin to organize and develop goals that will change their class position. See Karl Marx, *The Communist Manifesto.*

[34] For an excellent discussion of these conditions, see Dahrendorf, *op. cit.*, pp. 179-89.

[35] Gerhard E. Lenski, *Power and Privilege* (New York: McGraw-Hill, 1966).

[36] Dahrendorf, *op. cit.*, p. 159.

[37] Berger and Luckman, *op. cit.*, p. 60.

[38] *Ibid.*, p. 58, cf. Emile Durkheim, *The Rules of Sociological Method* (New York: Free Press of Glencoe, 1964), p. 3.

[39] Berger and Luckmann, *op. cit.*, p. 60.

[40] *Ibid.*, p. 129.

[41] The purpose here is to *outline* the framework and point out its implications. There is no intention of following all the permutations and combinations to their logical conclusions.

THE FRAMEWORK

We know that knowledge (including language) is *socially distributed* and that this distribution is, in Canada, closely linked with the occupational structure, or more broadly, with the division of labour. We often distinguish empirically and analytically among the middle class, working class and lower class persons on the basis of this occupational structure. It is the occupational structure, *par excellence,* that represents the society as objective reality. The position of one's father in the occupational sphere, particularly his authority or lack of it, is an important determinant of the habits, norms and values one encounters and internalizes as a child.[42] As Karl Marx noted:

On the different forms of property and the social conditions of existence a whole superstructure of various and peculiarly formed sentiments, illusions, modes of thought, and conceptions of life is built. The whole class creates and forms these out of its material foundations and the corresponding social relations.[43]

These conceptions represent objective reality and are part of the process of objectivation. Roles, norms and values can be passed on as entities (*choses*).

Broadly speaking, those persons at or near the bottom of the occupational structure are considered to be lower class. We would suggest that such persons have a different subjective construction of reality than those persons in other occupational categories or in what we might call the stable working class and the middle class. Hence, the distinction in Diagram 2 between the two sides.[44]

It is within the family unit that the process of primary socialization occurs. This process is very emotionally charged and thus must be separated analytically from secondary specialization which occurs in the other institutions of the society and is relatively impersonal.[45] The crucial process during the primary socialization stage is the internalization of the society's values, norms, and so on – that is, the process of creating social beings. This process crystallizes our identity and reality. This reality is established, maintained, legitimized and reinforced through everyday contact, especially through conversation. Since knowledge is socially distributed, the construction of society as subjective reality will differ by social class, or more broadly, by the structural position of the family unit, usually determined by the occupation of the father.

The content of the subjective reality is an empirical question although we already have some evidence that the values learned in the two classes are quite different. Rossi and Blum, after inspecting much of the literature on child rearing, conclude:

1. *Lower SES (socio-economic status) children are socialized to a pattern of obedience to authority rather than to the understanding of rules.*
2. *Lower-lower children are much more likely to be reared in an unstimulating environment in which children are frequently rejected and often neglected.*[46]

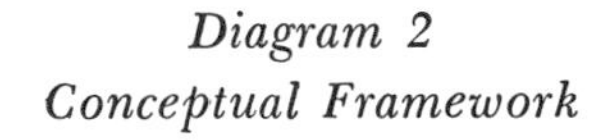
Diagram 2
Conceptual Framework

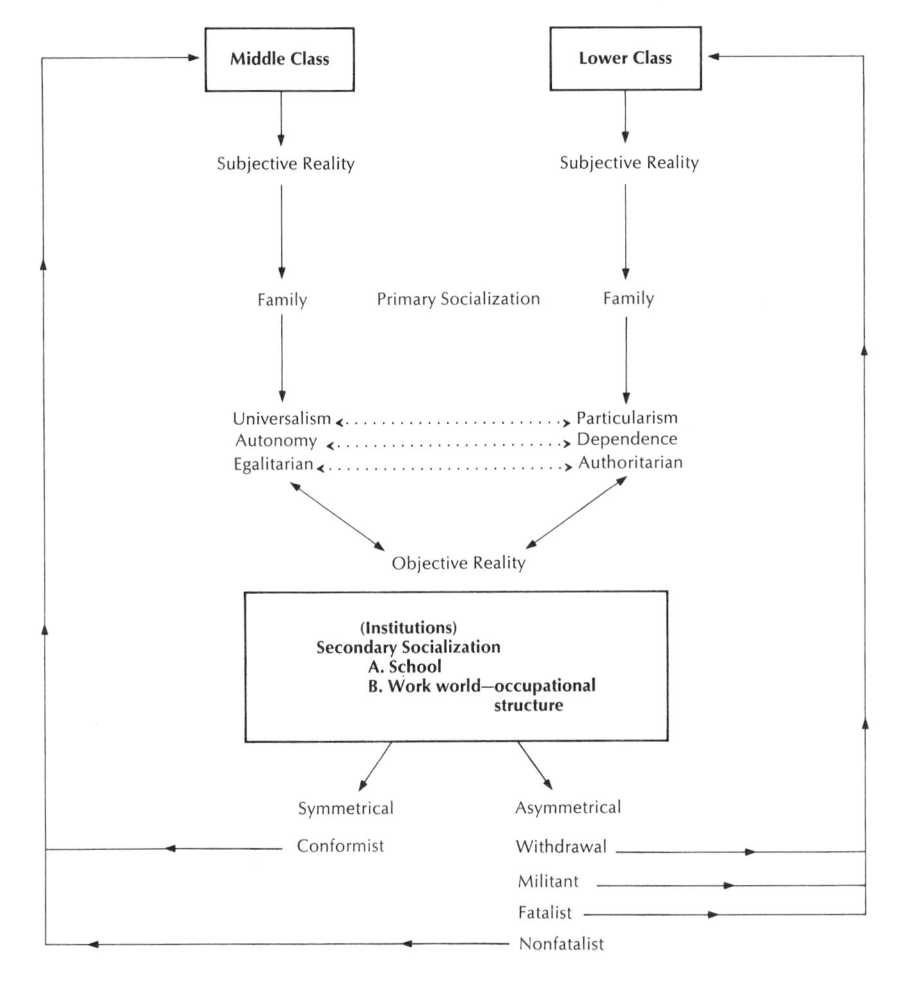

[42] This is, of course, one of the most crucial reasons why most French Canadians speak English but few Anglophones speak French. The occupational structure is controlled by the Anglophones, both Canadian and American.

[43] Karl Marx, *The Eighteenth Brumaire of Louis Bonaparte,* quoted in Dahrendorf, *op. cit.,* p. 14.

[44] I am well aware of the methodological difficulties inherent in this framework and of the debate in sociology as to the "reality" of social classes in the Marxian sense. I feel we must leave a discussion of these issues for another time. Tentatively, I would agree with Dahrendorf's analysis in *Class and Class Conflict in Industrial Society, op. cit.*

[45] I think we must never forget, however, that much of secondary socialization can be, and is, emotionally charged. Much of a relationship between teacher and student can even be brutal. See J. Kozol, *Death at an Early Age* (Boston: Houghton, Mifflin Co., 1967).

[46] Rossi and Blum, *op. cit.,* p. 37.

The lower class family socializes the child in such a manner so as to heighten dependence and thereby create a low "need achievement." The lower class family and milieu nurture the development of a particularistic value orientation — that is, a "disposition to receive and give specific gratifications in reciprocal relation with a particular object possessing special qualities."[47] Universal and collective values are learned and reinforced essentially through participation, first in the family and then in voluntary associations. The lower class individual is not permitted to participate in family decision-making and he is seldom a member of any organization other than the church.[48]

The framework stresses that the values internalized during primary socialization exist on a continuum and it is quite possible that empirically we may find middle class and working class parents who transmit to their children a lower class construction of reality. Recent work by Hylan Lewis in a study of lower-class families in Washington, D.C. underscores the immense variability in values among the poor and one should proceed with caution. Children of such parents may have "attitudinal exposure" to the values and attitudes of lower class persons through kin, peers, and neighborhood friends.[49] These would serve to legitimize, reinforce and maintain a reality different from that usually found in the middle class.

The process of reality maintenance also enables us to deal conceptually with the question of the influence of mass media, such as television, on the values of lower class children. It suggests that the middle class values transmitted by television do not become an integral part of the subjective reality since they would not, presumably, be legitimized and reinforced during the primary socialization process. Thus, in a real sense, among lower class children, myth (TV), and reality are separated. This is not to say that TV has no influence. Given certain conditions, its influence may be great. These are empirical questions which the framework suggests would be worthwhile exploring.[50]

The institutions of society outside the family represent the process of secondary socialization, in which the individual acquires role specific knowledge which is usually related to the occupational structure of our society. These institutions, by virtue of their existence as objective reality, are external and coercive. Diagram 2 suggests that society as objective reality is encountered by the individual primarily through the school system. The school system in Canada is essentially middle class in its orientation and the values it transmits. Both lower class and middle class persons encounter this objective reality; both must deal with the tension, however minimal, that results, yet I am suggesting that the tension will be greater (and the responses more asymmetrical) if individuals are from the lower class. "Success" in our society is to a large degree contingent upon schooling and this heightens the tension. In other words, both one's future and one's construction of reality will be affected by his experiences within the educational system.

When the lower class person attends school it is as an immigrant to a foreign land. Educators estimate (and the Head Start program has verified the estimation) that lower class children are two or four years behind at grade one and they tend to fall further behind as time goes on. The values learned during the primary socialization stage are not at all conducive to "success" in the institutions of the larger society.

The result of the encounter of subjective and objective reality may be either symmetrical or asymmetrical. If the socialization is "successful," the relationship will be symmetrical — that is, the amount of tension will be minimal. The values internalized will be reinforced and legitimized through this dialectical interaction (hence the double arrows in the diagram) of the processes of internalization and objectivation.

However, the relationship may also be asymmetrical. Society as subjective reality, learned through primary socialization, may not be consistent with society as objective reality. This creates considerable tension, which must be resolved. As Diagram 2 indicates, we are suggesting that the probability of the relationship between subjective and objective reality being asymmetrical is greater if the person comes from a lower class milieu, although the model permits such asymmetry to emanate from the middle class. It is important to emphasize here that it is more probable that institutions indigenous to the lower class — for example, the store front churches — will be symmetrical, but that those imposed from above, such as the school, will be asymmetrical. Symmetric lower institutions may facilitate withdrawal from non-symmetric schools, work, and so on. I am also suggesting that the poor are not a homogeneous group, that the constructions of society as subjective reality, learned and reinforced during primary socialization, may, in interaction with society as objective reality, create different solutions to the ensuing tensions. These tensions may be resolved in at least one of four ways:[51] withdrawal, militancy, fatalism and non-fatalism.[52]

[47] Talcott Parsons, *The Social System* (New York: Free Press of Glencoe, 1951), p. 109.

[48] I cannot stress enough the relativity of such statements. Many middle-class children do not participate either in decision-making or in organizations.

[49] Robert Merton's discussion on reference group theory is particularly appropriate here, especially his discussion on different types of reference groups — for example, normative and comparative — and the importance of reference groups for the development of different norms and values. See Robert Merton, *Social Theory and Social Structure* (Glencoe: Free Press of Glencoe, 1957), pp. 225-386, with particular attention to 284-307, 326-32 and 336-53.

[50] One could pursue at this juncture all the studies and theories which deal with aspirations and expectations among persons in different social classes and their effect on social mobility.

[51] I see these resolutions as chiefly dependent variables, the effect of structural variables impinging upon the individual.

[52] These are somewhat analagous to Merton's categories of retreatist, rebel, ritualist and innovator. I agree with Merton when he says: "It is a primary assumption of our typology that these responses occur with different frequency within the

Each of the responses involves different behavioral consequences. The conformist is more likely to be a stable working class or middle-class person.[53] There are two types of withdrawal: 1) those under 65 who are what Merton calls true "aliens" (the hobo, for example), and 2) those over 65, the old-age pensioners who are rejected by the "youth" culture and withdraw "voluntarily." The militant may exhibit his adaptation in at least one of two ways: 1) aimless rebellion such that he is defined as "deviant," or 2) purposeful rebellion (he may still be defined as a deviant) such as that found in the Indian and French-Canadian movements. The fatalist has given up, lives his life from day to day, and performs activity, including his job, ritualistically. The non-fatalist possesses values that are more consistent with the dominant value system and thus he is a potential "striver," one who is likely to be upwardly mobile.

The crucial question remains, however, "Why do some lower class people become non-fatalists?" We would hypothesize that the lower class non-fatalist internalizes the goals of the dominant value system during primary socialization, and during secondary socialization, unlike the fatalist, he assimilates the means to attain the goals. The non-fatalist does this because of strong reinforcement, which may be the result of a variety of factors – for example, the influence of a "significant other," attendance at a school that is predominantly middle class, and "attitudinal exposure" to middle class values.

I feel this framework, outlined above, has several advantages:

1) it stresses the dialectical and developmental aspects of reality and moves us away from a strictly "functional" approach;

2) it permits flexibility in that the concepts are treated as variables thus avoiding a "normative" position;

3) the "poor" are not treated as a homogeneous group but as a heterogeneous mixture, the product of a multiplicity of factors.

The major difficulty with this framework and others dealing with the poor revolves around methodological considerations. A weakness found in much of the literature on poverty by North American sociologists can be traced to an overreliance on survey data such as the Census. We see the *individual* as the root of the problem and consequently reason that information on the individual obtained through survey techniques is sufficient. We seldom look beyond the individual to the institutions of the larger society which shape him. The framework suggested here sensitizes us to this danger. "What we need are full accounts case histories, and descriptions of how people experience life in concrete situations."[54] We require qualitative information on how persons construct their reality, and this is obtainable only through sustained contact and observation and a heavy dose of "sociological imagination."

I have tried to suggest in this paper a conceptual framework that would integrate the literature on poverty with the general literature on theory and social stratification and that would see the poor as an aggregate of persons struggling and adapting in various ways to a number of institutions imposed upon them by the more powerful members of Canadian society; further, that these adaptations can serve to perpetuate poverty, can be an "opiate of the people." The framework is at best preliminary. I have also attempted to point out the various problems and how they tie in with existing perspectives. Much work needs to be done.

various sub-groups within our society, precisely because members of these groups or strata are differentially subject to culture stimulation and social restraints." The framework differs from Merton's in some minor respects and one major respect, e.g., Merton's innovator assimilates the goals but not the means. Our nonfatalist has assimilated the goals during primary socialization and the means through secondary socialization, in *response* to the tension, and because he has done so he is a prototype of the "upwardly mobile person." A major difference between the framework is, I feel, the ability of this framework to 'explain' rather than 'describe' a phenomenon. The framework sensitizes the researcher to explore certain critical areas which will enable him to establish causal sequences and give meaning to the particular adaptation. Merton echoes this himself when he says: "... but what has until lately been overlooked is that the family largely transmits that portion of the culture accessible to the social stratum and groups in which the parents find themselves."

[53] Theoretically it is possible, though in practice unlikely, that the school will be symmetrical with a lower-class value system and thus we would have a lower class "conformist."

[54] Rickman, *op. cit.*, p. 48.

Section III

Opportunity Structures and the Culture of Poverty

A. Sources of Variations

The articles included under this section illustrate the bases for differential access to our society's rewards. Equalitarianism, at least in the sense of equality of opportunity, is often defined as a value in Canadian society but the evidence suggests it is an ideal yet to be achieved. That differentials exist with respect to the distribution of income and education is hardly surprising, and the evidence for the Canadian case is well documented. But the continued influence of ascribed characteristics in determining access to society's rewards is cause for concern. The articles refer to regional disparities in income and education, rural-urban differences and variations resulting from minority group status.

Podoluk points out the need for dynamic criteria in defining the poor, since economic circumstances and quality of life can change over time. Her article also presents an excellent profile analysis of low-income families and documents the importance of sex and/or age as crucial variables. One is reminded of Arnold Rose's typology of the unemployables, i.e.: individuals who reside in an area where the major industry has declined or undergone automation; older persons whose occupations have become displaced; youth or high school dropouts who lack education; and certain minority groups discriminated against in employment.

Brewis' article centres on the first item, residence in a "depressed" area. He reports a "growing discontent with the magnitude of the differences between income and employment opportunity which exist not only between countries but also between various regions of the same country." It is not only regional variations in income and employment that are of interest to students of poverty, but the persistence of these differences over time. Other research on this topic documents the existence of pockets of exceptionally heavy structural unemployment.

Rural poverty, Harp points out, is even more difficult to measure and perhaps to detect than its urban counterpart. Given a choice between natural-state migration and development strategies as programs designed to alleviate the problem, a combination of programs built around the growth-centre concept is advocated.

Emile Gosselin's comments are part of a larger research report on urban poverty conducted in the city of Montreal. The study documents the incidence of poverty, including its geography, and concludes with a general discussion of the causes of poverty.

Regional differences in income and employment opportunities also apply to education, as shown by excerpts from the *Sixth Annual Review* of the Economic Council of Canada. The discussion focuses on the role of education in growth and development. It should be recognized that, because of the character of the data, interprovincial differences in the quality of education are not discussed.

The final article in this section reflects another class of unemployables, the minority groups. Borovoy presents the case of poverty among Canadian Indians. The prejudice and discrimination to which the Indian has been subjected is well documented by several Canadian studies.[1] Indeed the history of the Indian on this continent has for the past century been one of categorical exclusion from the mainstream of society.

[1] H. B. Hawthorne (ed.), "A Survey of the Contemporary Indians of Canada" in a *Report on Economic, Political, Educational Needs and Policies,* Vols. I and II, (Ottawa: Indian Affairs Branch, 1966).

1. *Low Income and Poverty**

Jenny R. Podoluk

DEFINITION OF POVERTY

The notion of a measurable boundary marking off the range on the lower part of the income scale that can be designated substandard has crept into our thinking about size distributions of income practically unchallenged. Theorists of all persuasions utilize such a concept implicitly while proponents of various types of social policy exploit the 'poverty line' determining this measure for a given time and place, the theorist will deny the possibility of a unique answer and the propagandist will settle for any one of many solutions if the result suits his purpose.[1]

Perhaps more attention has been focused on the lower end of the income distribution than on any other aspect of the income structure. In popular terms, the family units clustered at the bottom of the income scale have been termed the "poor" or the population living in "poverty." Dictionaries define poverty as "indigence, want, scarcity, deficiency, poorness or meanness," and point out that the dominant sense of present-day usage of the word is that of having little money or property. In turn, it is implicitly assumed that this also connotes deprivation in respect to various aspects of consumption – that low income is accompanied by malnutrition, inadequate health care, poor housing and so forth.

A concern with poverty, its characteristics and its implications for economic and social policy motivated much of the early research on the income and consumption patterns of families and households. A well-known study at the end of the nineteenth century collected data on incomes in York, England, and, using such statistics in conjunction with minimum budgets, developed estimates as to the proportion of the population with incomes inadequate to satisfy minimum needs.[2] The methodology developed in this study has influenced much of the research that

*Reprinted from the Dominion Bureau of Statistics' Monograph "Incomes of Canadians" (Ottawa: Queen's Printer, 1968), by Dr. J. Podoluk, with the permission of the author and the Queen's Printer for Canada.

[1] Dorothy S. Brady, "Research on the Size Distribution of Income," *Studies in Income and Wealth,* Vol. XIII, p. 30. National Bureau of Economic Research, New York, 1951.

[2] B. Seebohm Rowntree, *Poverty, A Study of Town Life.* Thomas Nelson & Sons, London, (No date).

has followed in the twentieth century. This study developed "a poverty line" and statistically estimated the proportion of the population living in poverty. It stated in conclusion:

That in this land of abounding wealth, during a time of perhaps unexpected prosperity, probably more than one fourth of the population are living in poverty, is a fact which may well cause great searchings of heart. There is surely need for a greater concentration of thought by the nation upon the well-being of its own people, for no civilization can be sound or stable which has as its base this mass of stunted human life. The suffering may be all but voiceless, and we may long remain ignorant of its extent and severity, but when once we realize it we see that social questions of profound importance await solution. What, for instance, are the primary causes of this poverty? How far is it the result of false social and economic conditions? If it be due in part to faults in the national character, what influences can be exerted to impart to that character greater strength and thoughtfulness?[3]

Examples may be readily found in many contemporary studies which, in effect, make the same statement about current conditions in North America that Rowntree made about the Britain of 1900. The characteristics of poverty may have changed but the problems of defining it, analyzing it and eliminating it have not.

Most studies concerned with the measurement of the extent of poverty are faced with the problem of defining poverty. Many studies have described eloquently the physical, social and economic manifestations of poverty – ill health, slum housing, unemployment and so forth.[4] A satisfactory determination of the extent of poverty requires, in effect, surveys designed to measure the levels of living of the population – food consumption and its adequacy, housing conditions, the adequacy of medical care and the state of health. Such statistical data are not available and, in their absence, statisticians and others have usually fallen back upon other approaches which invariably involve the use of income levels as the primary indicator of poverty.

Statistical Measurement of Poverty

Broadly, the various methods developed in studies can be categorized as of two varieties – the use of a fixed income point below which incomes are considered, in some sense, to be substandard or, alternatively, the construction and pricing of minimum budgets which are then compared with the existing income distribution to determine what proportion of the population has incomes inadequate to purchase the suggested budget. The use of a fixed point on the income scale such as the bottom quintile or on a family income figure of $3,000 as a poverty line is probably influenced by the fact that families below these points receive a share of aggregate income which is small in relation to their numbers and so they must be "poor." The rationale for the budget approach has been expressed this way: "Whether those at the bottom of the income distribution are or are not poor depends on whether their income level is or is not, by objective standards, sufficient to cover their needs."[5]

A budget approach to the examination of the adequacy of income is superior to the use of income criteria that ignore differences in family characteristics and, implicitly, in family needs. The use of a family income figure such as $3,000 does not take into account that family living requirements are affected by the size of family, its age composition, its place of residence such as farm or urban, and the price levels in the area. In the United States, although, initially, specific income figures were used to designate poverty, the deficiencies of this criterion resulted in the adoption of budget data as indicators of poverty or income inadequacy.[6] Other recent studies have also used a budget criteria for defining poverty.[7]

The budget-income approach has its own limitations as a statistical measure of poverty. In a recent U.S. Bureau of Labor Statistics publication it was noted: "There is not, and indeed in a rapidly changing pluralistic society there cannot be, one standard universally accepted and uniformly applicable by which it can be decided who is poor. Almost inevitably a single criterion across the board must either leave out of the count some who should be there or include some, who all things considered, ought not to be classed as indigent."[8]

An examination of the sixty-year history of using budgets to define poverty in the United States makes evident the existing problems. Budgets are devised for families with specific characteristics and in specific living circumstances. In earlier years these tended to be budgets for working families of four or five persons living in urban areas; such budgets would not be representative of families in rural areas, families who were retired, etc. In recent years, budgets have been constructed for many more family characteristics and these have been matched to the income distribution of families with the same characteristics. No account is taken of the fact that some families may have an imputed income from capital assets and thus have lower money income requirements than other families. There may also be differences in respect to access to free services such as medical care, education and so forth. Ideally, as well as

[3] *Ibid.*, p. 360.

[4] For example, Michael Harrington in *The Other America: Poverty in the United States*, The Macmillan Company, New York, 1963, a study that has influenced policies in the United States.

[5] Oscar Ornati, *Poverty Amid Affluence*, The Twentieth Century Fund. New York, 1966, p. 16.

[6] See Mollie Orshansky, "Counting the Poor: Another Look at the Poverty Profile," *Social Security Bulletin*, Vol. 28, No. 1, January 1965.

[7] As for example, in the analysis of poverty in *Income and Welfare in the United States*, Chapter 16, "Poverty in the United States," James N. Morgan, Martin H. David, Wilbur J. Cohen and Harvey E. Brazer. McGraw-Hill Book Company, New York, 1962.

[8] Mollie Orshansky, *Social Security Bulletin*, Vol. 28, No. 1, January 1965, p. 3.

income data, information is needed on other aspects of consumer finances such as asset holdings and the stocks of consumer durables owned. Obviously a family of three with an income of $3,500, a house owned free of debt and savings of $10,000, is better off than a family of three renting accommodation and having no accumulated assets. Recent budget studies have at least recognized that there are differences between the circumstances of farm families and those of non-farm families as the former are often able to produce food and other commodities and to own their own homes. Money requirements of farm families are assumed to be lower than those of other families.

Another major problem in the use of annual income data as an indicator of poverty is that annual data in themselves may not be representative of what might be termed the "permanent income" status of an individual or family. The shorter the time period used for the measurement of receipt of income, the more probable it is that the amount received is affected by transitory factors. Although some segments of the population such as the retired category live on fixed incomes, the majority of family income patterns pass through cycles and from year to year the income position undergoes change — some families are gradually improving their position while for others the long-run expectations are for a worsening. Although little data exist to verify the supposition, annual data may tend to overstate the degree of inequality existing in the income distribution and the proportion of families with permanent low-income status may be lower than annual data suggest.

For example, in the United States the Council of Economic Advisors, in examining the characteristics of families in poverty, used some data collected from a sample survey of families for the year 1962 and income data for the year 1963 were collected from the same sample of families a year later, It was found that 30 per cent of families with incomes below $3,000 in 1962 had incomes above $3,000 in 1963 although the over-all proportion of families with incomes below $3,000 showed little change. This indicates that the majority of low income families were largely an unchanging group of families but it also indicates that many families with low incomes in a one-year period might have a temporary low-income status. As might be expected, the families most likely to improve their positions are those with male heads under 35. Younger families contained the highest proportions of families whose incomes changed most between 1962 and 1963; the greatest change occurred among families with heads aged 35 to 44, in which group nearly half of those with incomes below $3,000 in 1962 had incomes above $3,000 in 1963.[9]

Definition of Needs

The long-run experience with developing standards of poverty is that standards are not static but the designation as to who is poor is greatly influenced by contemporary opinion as to what are the "minimum needs" of families. The poor are those who do not have sufficient income resources to satisfy these "needs". The standards set as needs usually rise as over-all real incomes rise. One study has concluded:

There is a strong factor of circularity in the standards upon which workers' budgets are based. Not only do they reflect what society thinks men "ought" to spend for "subsistence," "minimum adequacy," or "minimum comfort" but also what contemporary low-income people customarily do *spend when they buy what is budgeted for. Workers' family budgets, especially at the "subsistence" level, thus reflect the customary contemporary life style of the poor as society judges it ought to be and as the poor expect it to be. Society's judgment as to what workers' families "ought" to spend tends to reflect the extent of its concern about poverty at any time.*[10]

The decisions as to what the components of family budgets should be are, to a considerable extent, subjective decisions, not objective ones, and are very much influenced by the current over-all level of living of the remainder of the population. Thus, if the overwhelming majority of the population come to consume or use a certain commodity, it tends to be regarded as a need of the total population. The history of working-class budgets in the United States, for example, shows that in earlier days items included in the budget tended to be items that society felt working families should have rather than items they could acquire out of the existing distribution of incomes. As a result, when such budgets were priced, it was found that the majority of working families had incomes that were too low to purchase the complete budget.[11]

The conclusion as to how many people are poor will be greatly influenced by the decision as to what commodities and services people should be able to have in order not to be poor. There is general agreement that incomes should be sufficient to provide for subsistence, however that may be defined, and some of these budgets have been called "subsistence" budgets. However, in an affluent society the notion that incomes should provide subsistence and no more is often unacceptable and other budgets have been drawn up to provide what is sometimes called a "modest but adequate" level of living. It follows that the more generous the budget contents, the higher the proportion of families considered to be poor when incomes are compared with the cost of purchasing the budget. The numbers of poor families in the United States

[9] See pp. 161-166 of *Economic Report of the President,* January 1965. United States Government Printing Office, Washington, 1965.

[10] Oscar Ornati, *Poverty Amid Affluence,* The Twentieth Century Fund, New York, 1966, p. 131. For a discussion of the conceptual and statistical problems involved in the construction of budgets, see the articles by N. N. Franklin "The Concept and Measurement of 'Minimum Living Standards'," *International Labour Review,* Vol. 95, No. 4.

[11] See discussion by Dorothy S. Brady in "Scales of Living and Wage Earners' Budgets," *The Annals of the American Academy of Political and Social Science,* March 1951, Vol. 274.

in one set of estimates increase by 50 per cent if two budgets are drawn up with one budget containing more generous allowances for consumption as minimum budget requirements.[12]

It is because poverty is a relative concept that poverty or low income does not diminish as much as might be expected in view of the real income growth of a country. The extent of change can be evident only if contemporary standards are applied to the income structure of an earlier day. A study in the United States, using as a criterion of poverty the 1935 New York City Welfare Budget adjusted for price change, demonstrated that in 1935 some 28 per cent of United States families had below subsistence-level incomes while by 1960 this ratio had dropped to 10 per cent. If the 1960 subsistence-level budget were applied to the 1935 income distribution, then 47 per cent of families in 1935 were below the 1960 subsistence level.[13]

Thus, even though the level of living of the poor improves through time, poverty never seems to be eliminated because a wide gap persists between the level of living attained by some segments of the population and those enjoyed by the majority of the community. In Canada, the subjective element in discussing the needs of the poor is implicit in some contemporary views as to what are symptoms of poverty. For example, the lack of bathrooms, running water and central heating in rural housing have been cited as evidence of substandard housing. The 1941 Census showed that at that time half of Canadian households had no installed baths or showers (nearly 25 per cent in urban areas) and 45 per cent of households had no inside toilets. Amenities which in the mid-1960s are considered to be necessities as recently as 25 years ago were not available to nearly half of Canadian households. Other examples of items that might be considered necessities of the 1960s are consumer durables such as television sets or automobiles. When television sets first became available in the early 1950s only the middle and upper income classes could afford them; currently, families who do not own television sets appear to be those residing in parts of the country still not reached by television stations, or families who can afford television but consider it a status symbol not to own one. Budgets for welfare purposes now recognize that expenditures on television ownership should not disqualify recipients from receiving assistance. Similarly, in 1961 the majority of families with incomes above $2,000 owned automobiles and a surprising 40 per cent of those with incomes below $2,000 also owned automobiles. Statistics suggest that non-owners tend to consist of groups such as the aged who may no longer be able to operate a car. In the postwar years it is obvious that an automobile has joined the list of family "needs;" in pre-war years it would still have been considered a luxury item. It might be noted that the U.S. Bureau of Labor Statistics budget, designed to provide a modest but adequate level of living for a retired couple, includes provision for the ownership and operation of an automobile.[14]

It should also be noted that in the United States, experiments with a range of criteria to define very minimum income requirements either using minimum budgets or fixed income points have tended to produce very similar results as to the probable size of the population that may be experiencing poverty. However, the more sophisticated approaches show lower proportions of poor families than the more arbitrary approaches and show fewer adults and more children in this group than the simpler criteria. Further, although the estimated number of persons is much the same under the different criteria, each shows a different composition as to age, family size, place of residence and so forth.[15]

LOW-INCOME POPULATION IN CANADA

There is no existing official statistical concept of poverty in Canada, primarily because no minimum standard budgets have been constructed that would allow for a location of points in the income distribution below which income inadequacy might exist. For purposes of this study, low-income families are defined as those families whose incomes fall into those income groups in which, on average, most of the income received must be spent upon essentials such as food, clothing and shelter. An examination of family expenditures data collected from a sample of approximately 2,000 spending units living in urban centres of 15,000 or more in population showed that, on average, families of different sizes allocated about half of their income to expenditures on food, shelter and clothing.[16] It was assumed that where expenditures on these components were well above average, that is, where they accounted for 70 per cent or more of family income available, such families might be in straitened circumstances. They would have little "discretionary income" left after expenditures on basic essentials, or income to pay for medical care, education of children, recreation and so forth or for savings. The expenditures data suggested that a single person with an income below $1,500, a family of two with less than $2,500, and families of three, four, five or more with incomes of less than $3,000, $3,500 or $4,000, respectively, had such expenditure patterns. The same income limits were used for all families although possibly lower limits should have been used for rural families.

It should be stressed that the universe being considered probably includes the great majority of families who are in genuine need but it

[12] See Mollie Orshansky, "Recounting the Poor — A Five-Year Review," Table 7, p. 31, *Social Security Bulletin,* April 1966.

[13] See Herman P. Miller, *Measurements of Alternative Concepts of Poverty,* Institute of Government and Public Affairs, University of California, Los Angeles, November 1964.

[14] See "The Cost of a Retired Couple's Budget", *Monthly Labor Review,* November 1960, Vol. 83, No. 11, United States Department of Labor.

[15] See Mollie Orshansky, "Counting the Poor: Another Look at the Poverty Profile." *Social Security Bulletin,* Vol. 28, No. 1, January 1965, Washington, D.C.

[16] These data are for the year 1959 and are unpublished data from the DBS 1960 Survey of Family Expenditures. The results of this survey were published in DBS *Urban Family Expenditures, 1959,* (Cat. No. 62-521), Ottawa, March 1963.

must not be assumed that all of these were living in poverty. The U.S. Bureau of Labour Statistics budget estimates of incomes that may be indicative of poverty are 1960 urban incomes of $1,700 to $1,900 for a family of two, $2,000 to $2,600 for a family of three, $2,500 to $3,200 for four $3,100 to $3,800 for five and $3,600 to $4,200 for six or more, so that the income levels used in this report for families of two to four persons for Canada are higher than those developed for the United States as poverty lines.[17] The Bureau of Labor Statistics estimates developed for families of different age compositions and sizes assume that young families need less than families at later stages of the income cycle. The minimum figure represents the requirements of families with heads under age 35 and the maximum those with heads aged 55 to 64. Further, Canadian incomes are lower, the average non-farm family income being only 85 per cent of the American average. The over-all level of living is probably lower in Canada than in the United States.

Attributes of Low Income

Although poverty is a chronic social and economic problem, studies in industrial societies such as the United States and Britain indicate that the characteristics of the population in poverty have changed through time as real incomes have risen. To an increasing extent, poverty is becoming associated with specific groups rather than remaining a characteristic widely found through all segments of the population.[18] In North America during the depression years of the 1930s poverty was probably prevalent among all age groups and in all areas; in present times it has tended to become concentrated among the non-working population.

A number of studies have attempted to specify the population characteristics associated with above-average levels of low income; that is, the characteristics that carry with them high probabilities of poverty. One study concluded that, among families, the significant family characteristics in decreasing order of importance were: head a non-earner, head aged 65 or over, rural farm residence, female head of family, non-white, head aged 14-24, six or more children under 18 years of age. Among unattached individuals the significant factors were: non-earner, age 65 or over, rural farm residence, female, non-white, 14-24 years of age.[19] Another study of poverty gave the following ranking of factors which helped explain the existence of poverty among families: age, disablement, families with children and only one parent, unemployment, non-white, self-employed business man or farmer.[20] Families with only one parent present are primarily families headed by women. There is considerable similarity in the factors suggested, such as age and unemployment. A combination of these characteristics increased the probability of poverty.

[The Appendix to this article] shows in more detail the characteristics of the families and persons not in families who compose low-income groups in Canada. Data are not available in the Census on some of the characteristics associated with low income such as disability or the extent of unemployment but other characteristics affecting the level of income such as age, education and occupation are shown separately; most of the tables present data separately for families with male and female heads.

In a general way these tables describe how many family units in 1961 were in low-income circumstances, where they were located regionally and what sort of families they were. As to how many, 916,000 families or 25 per cent of all non-farm families had the combined income and family-size characteristics outlined above; 416,000 persons living alone or 44 per cent met this low-income criterion. In total, these family units contained approximately 4.2 million persons or nearly 27 per cent of the non-farm population.

Table 1 presents a summary of selected characteristics of low-income families. These show that the incidence of low income is very high when these characteristics are present: no member of the family worked during the year, family resides in a rural area and/or in the Atlantic Provinces, the head of the family is 65 years of age or over, the head of the family is a woman, the head of the family was outside the labour force, the head of the family had no education beyond the elementary level. These characteristics then are very similar to those isolated in the United States as primary characteristics of poverty.

. . . Table 1 [reveals] that in the Atlantic Provinces a much greater proportion of families had low incomes than in other regions of Canada, and that Ontario contained the lowest proportion of low-income families. The table also confirms again that low incomes were much more prevalent among the rural population, where nearly half of families had low incomes, and among the small urban centres; the frequency of low incomes in the largest cities was only a little over three fifths of the national average.

An examination of the absolute number of low-income families with different characteristics rather than the proportion with low incomes shows that the greatest number of these families were concentrated in Ontario and Quebec, as might be expected because, in total, 63 per cent of the population resided in these provinces. Although 45 per cent of families in the Atlantic Provinces had low incomes, 58 per cent of all

[17] United States data are from Herman Miller, *Measurement for Alternative Concepts of Poverty,* Institute of Government and Public Affairs, University of California, Los Angeles, November 1964.

[18] Rowntree, for example, in resurveying York in the 1920s found poverty was less likely to be an attribute associated with low levels of wages and unemployment than to be attributed to such characteristics as old age.

[19] See Oscar Ornati, *Poverty Amid Affluence,* pp. 43-44. Twentieth Century Fund, New York, 1966.

[20] See Morgan, David, Cohen and Brazer, *Income and Welfare in the United States,* Chapter 16. McGraw-Hill Book Company, New York, 1962.

Table 1

Selected Characteristics of All Families and of Low-Income Families, Year Ended May 31, 1961

SELECTED CHARACTERISTICS	NUMBER OF FAMILIES		PER CENT OF TOTAL		INCIDENCE OF LOW INCOME PER CENT
	ALL FAMILIES	LOW-INCOME FAMILIES	ALL FAMILIES	LOW-INCOME FAMILIES	
Totals	3,626,964a	916,050a	100.0	100.0	25.3
Region —					
Atlantic Provinces	348,887	157,938	9.7	17.3	45.3
Quebec	988,307	275,505	27.2	30.1	27.9
Ontario	1,362,618	253,760	37.6	27.7	18.6
Prairie Provinces	556,251	149,998	15.3	16.4	27.0
British Columbia	368,116	78,359	10.1	8.6	21.3
Place of residence —					
Metropolitan centres	1,901,221	314,540	52.4	34.3	16.5
Other urban municipalities	958,767	249,713	26.4	27.3	26.0
30,000 - 99,999	276,397	54,162	7.6	5.9	19.6
10,000 - 29,999	270,001	64,573	7.4	7.1	23.9
1,000 - 9,999	412,369	130,978	11.4	14.3	31.8
Rural	766,856	351,797	21.1	38.4	45.9
Size of family —					
Two	960,421	280,199	26.5	30.6	29.2
Three	734,111	147,991	20.2	16.2	20.2
Four	757,883	157,283	20.9	17.2	20.8
Five or more	1,174,549	330,577	32.4	36.1	28.1
Sex of head —					
Male	3,343,756	795,494	92.2	86.8	23.8
Female	283,208	120,556	7.8	13.2	42.6
Number of children under 16 —					
None	1,382,913	329,949	38.1	36.0	23.9
One	699,114	143,571	19.3	15.7	20.5
Two	678,546	155,849	18.7	17.0	23.0
Three or more	868,391	288,681	23.9	31.3	33.1

a Includes Yukon.

continued . . .

Table 1

Selected Characteristics of All Families and of Low-Income Families, Year Ended May 31, 1961 — concluded

SELECTED CHARACTERISTICS	NUMBER OF FAMILIES		PER CENT OF TOTAL		INCIDENCE OF LOW INCOME PER CENT
	ALL FAMILIES	LOW-INCOME FAMILIES	ALL FAMILIES	LOW-INCOME FAMILIES	
Age of head —					
Under 25	149,134	43,179	4.1	4.7	29.0
25 - 54	2,508,658	553,891	69.2	60.5	22.1
55 - 64	491,119	109,026	13.5	11.9	22.2
65 or over	478,053	209,954	13.2	22.9	43.9
Labour force status of head —					
In current labour force	2,995,847	572,843	82.6	62.5	19.1
In non-current labour force	99,605	48,814	2.7	5.3	49.0
Not in labour force	531,512	294,393	14.7	32.1	55.4
Education of head —					
No schooling or elementary only	1,680,323	625,040	46.3	68.2	37.2
Secondary 1 - 3 years	1,068,314	207,847	29.5	22.7	19.5
Secondary 4 - 5 years	551,095	62,160	15.2	6.8	11.3
Some university	137,234	12,727	3.8	1.4	9.3
University degree	189,998	8,276	5.2	0.9	4.4
Number of earners —					
No earners	267,734	217,415	7.4	23.7	81.2
One earner	1,870,344	529,361	51.6	57.8	28.3
Two earners	1,114,312	141,747	30.7	15.5	12.7
Three or more earners	374,574	27,527	10.3	3.0	7.3
Major source of family income —					
Wages and salaries	2,908,957	533,282	80.2	58.2	18.3
Self employment	306,478	76,435	8.4	8.3	24.9
Transfer payments	270,771	244,509	7.5	26.7	90.3
Investment income	75,010	26,397	2.1	2.9	35.2
Other income	54,980	24,659	1.5	2.7	44.9
No income	10,768	10,768	0.3	1.2	100.0

Source: Unpublished data from **1961 Census** of Canada. Tables are reproduced in the Appendix to [this article].

low-income families lived in Quebec and Ontario. Most low-income families resided in urban centres. Although 46 per cent of rural families had low incomes, only 38 per cent of low income families resided in rural areas; increasingly in urban societies, low income is becoming an urban rather than a rural problem.[21]

Low Income by Age and Sex

It has been suggested that: "Since the ranks of the poor have always been filled with widows and orphans, the halt, the lame, and the blind, a study of poverty must treat these groups separately if only to avoid confusing the effect of age, sex or disability with other factors."[22] The tables confirm that age and sex are important "handicapping" characteristics of low incomes especially among persons not in a family group. Among families, although only eight per cent of families had female heads, approximately 13 per cent of low-income families had female heads. Approximately 20 per cent of low-income families were headed by men aged 65 and over so that, in total, one third of low-income families appeared to be in this category because of the sex or age of the family head. If the assumption is made that age may affect incomes even earlier than 65, for example at age 55, then for 43 per cent of all families the sex or age of the family head is the probable explanation for low family income. The importance of age and sex as characteristics highly correlated with low incomes is even more pronounced if an income cut-off of $3,000, regardless of family size, is used to designate poverty; 53 per cent of all families below this limit were headed by women or by men aged 55 and over. Age and sex, in themselves, are only superficial explanations of low incomes. Other factors associated with these characteristics such as the inability to work or a low earning capability, especially among women, probably provide the real explanations . . .

The incidence of poverty follows a somewhat different pattern among families with male heads than among families with female heads. Among families with a husband or father present, the proportion of low incomes was above average when the head was young, especially under age 25, and declined steadily with the lowest incidence occurring when heads were aged 45 to 54, after which the incidence rose sharply. Among families headed by women, the proportion of families in low-income brackets was highest when women heads were under age 35 and lowest when they were age 55 and over. This confirms that, at certain stages of the family cycle, families were able to move out of low-income levels, at least for some years. Low income is more prevalent among young families because only the head might have been working. As children grow older, low earnings on the part of the head might compel wives to enter the labour force and, in turn, when children are old enough they also leave school to help supplement family income. This is especially the case with large families, when the combined incomes of all working family members, for a time, appear to provide an adequate income for the family as a whole. How-

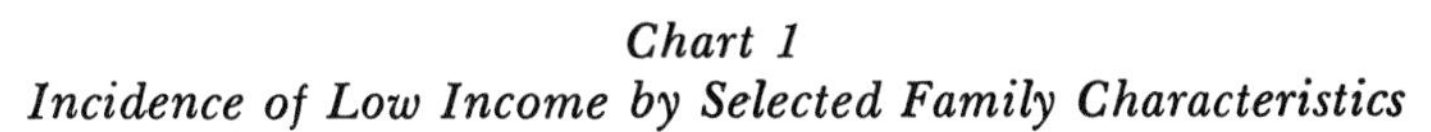

Chart 1
Incidence of Low Income by Selected Family Characteristics

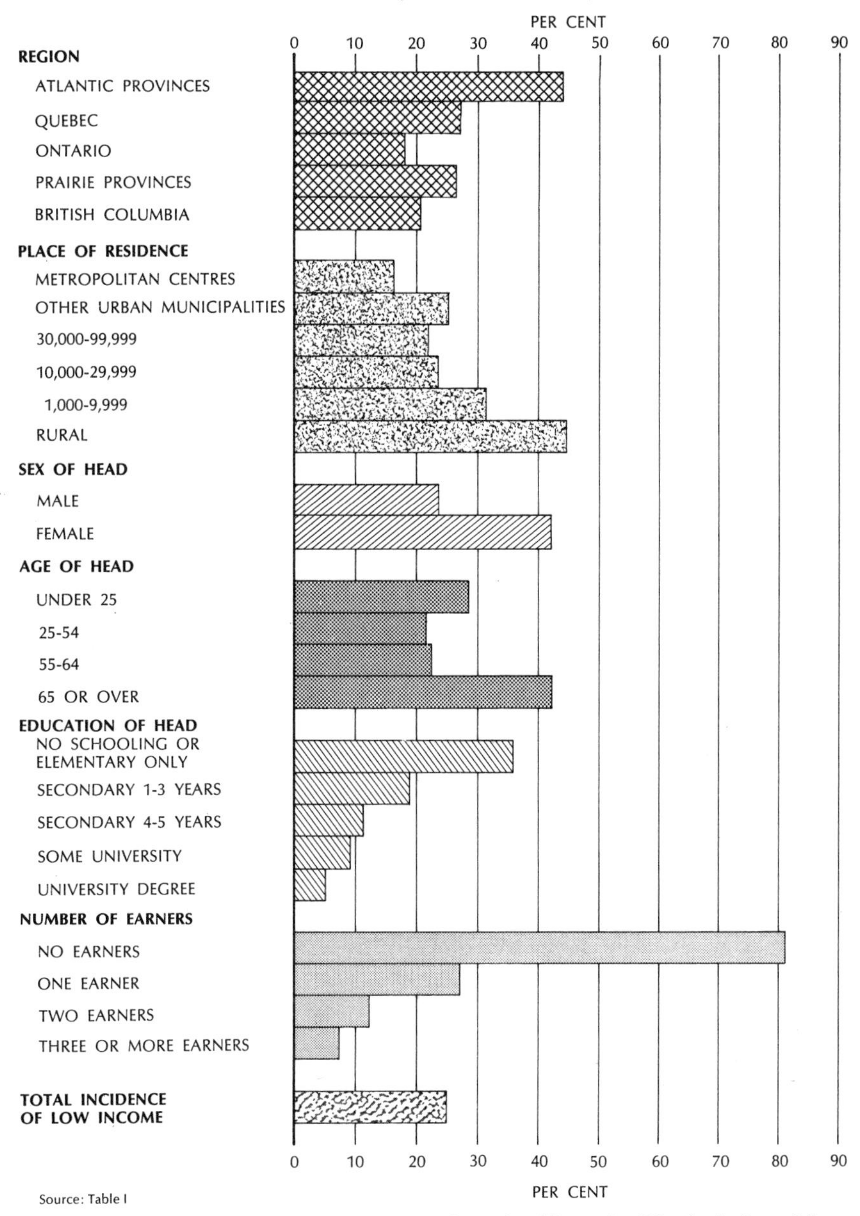

Source: Table I

[21] These statistics are, of course, for non-farm families only. The inclusion of low-income farm families would raise the proportion of low-income families resident in rural areas although the proportion would probably still not exceed 50 per cent.

[22] Dorothy S. Brady, "Research on the Size Distribution of Income," p. 34.

ever, where children enter the labour force at an early age with a limited education, and when they leave the parental home to marry and start their own families, the unskilled workers and the new families may in turn become part of the low-income population while the parents themselves may again lapse into poverty.

Young women heading families usually were widowed, divorced or separated and usually had small children dependent upon them. Such families tended to be supported by government social welfare assistance as most women heads of families were outside the labour force. Further, over half of women heads had only an elementary school education and since, even when fully employed, female earnings usually were substantially lower than male earnings, there might be little or no financial advantage for younger women to work. Expenditures on household help or on the cost of providing for the care of children may be such that there might be no real improvement in the income position of the family if women heads enter the labour force and attempt to support themselves from their own earnings rather than welfare assistance. When children grow up and begin working, the incidence of low incomes in such families declines; children, as long as they stay with the mother, take over the responsibility for the maintenance of family income. In families with women heads containing working family members, the workers are usually children or other relatives rather than the family head. If all the children leave home so that the mother is left alone, the probability is very high that her income will be insufficient for her needs. Years of labour force inactivity may also make it difficult for her to re-enter the labour force.

Labour Force Characteristics

Approximately 55 per cent of families whose heads did not work during the year had low incomes and approximately half of families whose heads had worked some of the time but withdrew from the labour force at census time were in a low-income category. In contrast, only 19 per cent of families with heads currently in the labour force reported low incomes. In total, some 40 per cent of these families had heads who had not worked during the year or who were currently not working; this ratio was higher for families headed by women where nearly three quarters of all family heads had this characteristic.

Among families whose heads worked, there was a correlation between occupation and low income. Over half of the families whose heads were farm workers, loggers, fishermen, trappers or hunters were in a low-income category and 40 per cent of the families of labourers had low incomes. However, although these families had the highest proportion of families with low incomes, they accounted for only one fifth of low-income families with male working heads. The largest number of families, approximately one third, were those whose heads were craftsmen and production workers.

Low income is also positively correlated with the education of the family head; the lower the level of education, the higher the probability of low income. Approximately 37 per cent of families whose heads had only an elementary school education had low incomes and such families constituted 68 per cent of all low-income families. In contrast, only 11 per cent of families whose heads had four to five years of secondary schooling had low incomes.

Family Composition

An examination of family size by age of head and number of children by family size shows that the characteristics of low-income families of different sizes were dissimilar. The two-person families who were nearly 40 per cent of all low-income families were largely the aged; three quarters of these had family heads who were aged 55 and over. One third of families of three persons had heads under age 35 so that three-person low-income families tended to be young families. Some 60 to 70 per cent of families of four or five or more had family heads aged 25 to 44. There were larger families where the children were still of school age and where the head was likely to be the only family member with an income. Families with three or more children under 16 had a higher incidence of low incomes than had families with fewer small children. Of all low-income families, approximately 400,000 or one half of families with male heads had heads who were under age 45. These are the families who have the greatest likelihood of improving their income position through time.

Sources of Family Income

As might be inferred from the characteristics already outlined, low-income families were, to a very substantial extent, dependent upon government transfer payments of various types for their income; this was especially so for families headed by women. In total, approximately 27 per cent of low-income families derived the greater part of their income from government sources. Low-income families, although they formed 25 per cent of families, received only 9.4 per cent of total family income. They earned only 7.5 per cent of all income from employment reported by families but 29 per cent of family allowances, 44 per cent of old-age assistance and pensions and 38 per cent of other government transfer payments, such as unemployment insurance and veterans' pensions, went to this group. An examination of the composition of the income receipts of low-income families shows that 70 per cent of the total income came from earnings, 24 per cent from government welfare payments and six per cent from miscellaneous sources, such as private retirement pensions and investment income.

In summary, at least one third of low-income families had characteristics suggesting that such families might have chronic low incomes and some 40 per cent were at a stage in the family life cycle in which they might, at least for some years improve their income position.

Persons Not in Families with Low Incomes

Age and sex are by far the most important explanations for low incomes among the population who are not members of a family group. Table 2 summarizes the age and sex characteristics of these persons. Although some 53 per cent of all unattached individuals were women, they formed 62 per cent of the low-income population. Approximately half of women living alone were aged 55 and older so that the majority would be widows with no children present. In total, 60 per cent of persons living alone and receiving low incomes were aged 55 and older; one third were over age 70. Another 16 per cent of low-income recipients were under age 25 so that three quarters of all persons in this category were in the youngest or oldest age groups. Most of those with low incomes who were under age 25 were young girls, many of whom might have only recently completed school and left their parental homes. The majority of these might eventually marry. Young males with low incomes might also improve their income position through time as they gained experience in the labour force.

Table 2

Incidence of Low Income Among Persons Not in Families, by Sex and Age, Year Ended May 31, 1961

SEX AND AGE	PERSONS NOT IN FAMILIES		INCIDENCE	DISTRIBUTION OF PERSONS	
	LOW INCOME	TOTAL	OF LOW INCOME	LOW INCOME	TOTAL
	No.	No.	p.c.		
Males	157,901	451,470	35.0	38.0	47.3
Females	257,647	503,572	51.2	62.0	52.7
Totals	415,548	955,042	43.5	100.0	100.0
Age —					
Under 25	65,566	168,954	38.8	15.8	17.7
25–34	31,084	147,049	21.1	7.5	15.4
35–44	27,563	108,052	25.5	6.6	11.3
45–54	40,288	121,979	33.0	9.7	12.8
55–59	28,716	70,009	41.0	6.9	7.3
60–64	38,889	76,690	50.7	9.4	8.0
65–69	51,289	79,991	64.1	12.3	8.4
70 and over	132,153	182,318	72.5	31.8	19.1

Source: Unpublished data from 1961 Census of Canada.

As with low-income families, the incidence of low income among individuals was much higher in rural areas than in urban centres. The majority of this group had only an elementary education although the women, on average, had more education than the men. As might be expected from the age structure, most individuals were not in the labour force during the year so that this group was more dependent upon income from sources other than earnings than were families in low-income circumstances. Only 38 per cent of males and 33 per cent of females received most of their income from employment. Thus the majority of individuals with low incomes who were not part of a family unit were likely to constitute a group with permanently depressed incomes. There was less likelihood that this group would be beneficiaries of rising national incomes; rather they were primarily reliant upon government welfare plans for income maintenance.

Table A.1

Estimated Number of Low-Income Units, by Size of Unit, Sex of Head and Size of Income,[a] *Year Ended May 31, 1961*

SEX AND INCOME SIZE	PERSONS NOT IN FAMILIES	FAMILY UNITS OF				TOTAL LOW-INCOME FAMILIES
		2 PERSONS	3 PERSONS	4 PERSONS	5 OR MORE PERSONS	
	No.	No.	No.	No.	No.	No.
Male heads —						
Under $1,000	112,393	48,670	17,652	12,640	21,092	100,054
$1,000–$1,499	45,508	63,347	15,554	10,401	19,257	108,559
1,500– 1,999		59,755	20,926	15,165	26,159	122,005
2,000– 2,499		53,418	30,385	22,201	37,423	143,427
2,500– 2,999			36,031	32,760	51,090	119,881
3,000– 3,499				47,036	70,288	117,324
3,500– 3,999					84,244	84,244
Low-income units	157,901	225,190	120,548	140,203	309,553	795,494
Total units	451,470	822,363	666,527	722,452	1,132,414	3,343,756
Per cent with low incomes	35.0	27.4	18.1	19.4	27.3	23.8
Female heads —						
Under $1,000	193,692	19,133	8,194	4,500	4,936	36,763
$1,000–$1,499	63,955	13,189	4,389	2,131	2,271	21,980
1,500– 1,999		11,191	5,749	3,090	2,750	22,780
2,000– 2,499		11,496	4,528	2,751	3,452	22,227
2,500– 2,999			4,583	2,224	3,067	9,874
3,000– 3,499				2,384	2,391	4,775
3,500– 3,999					2,157	2,157
Low-income units	257,647	55,009	27,443	17,080	21,024	120,556
Total units	503,572	138,058	67,584	35,431	42,135	283,208
Per cent with low incomes	51.2	39.9	40.6	48.2	49.9	42.6

[a] Non-farm population only.

Table A.2

All Families and Low-Income Families, by Provinces of Residence and Size of Place of Residence,[a] *Year Ended May 31, 1961*

SELECTED CHARACTERISTICS	LOW-INCOME FAMILIES (A)	ALL FAMILIES (B)	INCIDENCE OF LOW INCOME (A/B)	PERCENTAGE DISTRIBUTION OF FAMILIES	
				LOW INCOME	ALL
	No.	No.	p.c.		
Province of Residence –					
Newfoundland	45,638	81,957	55.7	5.0	2.3
Prince Edward Island	7,017	14,269	49.2	0.8	0.4
Nova Scotia	58,029	144,003	40.3	6.3	4.0
New Brunswick	47,254	108,658	43.5	5.2	3.0
Quebec	275,505	988,307	27.9	30.1	27.2
Ontario	253,760	1,362,618	18.6	27.7	37.6
Manitoba	45,719	175,054	26.1	5.0	4.8
Saskatchewan	49,569	142,550	34.8	5.4	3.9
Alberta	54,710	238,647	22.9	6.0	6.6
British Columbia	78,359	368,116	21.3	8.6	10.1
Totals[b]	916,050	3,626,964	25.3	100.0	100.0
Size of place of residence –					
Metropolitan centres	314,540	1,901,231	16.5	34.3	52.4
Other urban municipalities	249,713	958,767	26.0	27.3	26.4
30,000–99,999	54,162	276,397	19.6	5.9	7.6
10,000–29,999	64,573	270,001	23.9	7.1	7.4
1,000– 9,999	130,978	412,369	31.8	14.3	11.4
Rural	351,797	766,966	45.9	38.4	21.1

[a] Non-farm population only.

[b] Totals include Yukon Territory.

Source: Unpublished data from 1961 Census of Canada.

Table A.3

All Families and Low-Income Families, by Size of Family, Sex and Age of Head, Sex and Number of Children,[a] Year Ended May 31, 1961

SELECTED CHARACTERISTICS	LOW-INCOME FAMILIES							PERCENTAGE DISTRIBUTION OF FAMILIES	
	2 PERSONS	3 PERSONS	4 PERSONS	5 OR MORE PERSONS	TOTAL LOW-INCOME FAMILIES (A)	ALL FAMILIES (B)	INCIDENCE OF LOW INCOME (A/B)	LOW INCOME	ALL
	No.	No.	No.	No.	No.	No.	p.c.		
AGE OF HEAD									
Male head —									
Under 25	6,574	15,553	11,050	5,716	38,893	142,595	27.3	4.9	4.3
25–34	10,446	27,801	50,318	95,958	184,523	808,349	22.8	23.1	24.2
35–44	8,523	15,737	34,663	120,396	179,319	873,034	20.5	22.5	26.1
45–54	17,120	19,363	24,907	60,126	121,516	696,039	17.5	15.3	20.8
55–59	16,915	9,931	6,606	11,770	45,222	245,150	18.4	5.7	7.3
60–64	25,544	8,954	4,605	6,625	45,728	189,656	24.1	5.7	5.7
65–69	41,815	9,287	3,551	4,411	59,064	153,068	38.6	7.4	4.6
70 and over	98,253	13,922	4,503	4,551	121,229	235,865	51.4	15.2	7.1
Totals	225,190	120,548	140,203	309,553	795,494	3,343,756	23.8	100.0	100.0
Female head —									
Under 25	2,217	1,212	572	285	4,286	6,539	65.5	3.6	2.3
25–34	3,889	4,288	3,660	4,240	16,077	23,393	68.7	13.3	8.3
35–44	6,803	7,060	5,525	8,177	27,565	46,725	59.0	22.9	16.5
45–54	10,026	6,497	3,749	4,619	24,891	61,118	40.7	20.6	21.6
55–59	5,451	2,100	976	919	9,446	29,098	32.5	7.8	10.3
60–64	5,488	1,481	845	816	8,630	27,215	31.7	7.2	9.6
65–69	5,884	1,310	585	743	8,522	25,340	33.6	7.1	8.9
70 and over	15,251	3,495	1,168	1,225	21,139	63,780	33.1	17.5	22.5
Totals	55,009	27,443	17,080	21,024	120,556	283,208	42.6	100.0	100.0

[a] Non-farm population only.

continued . . .

Table A.3

All Families and Low-Income Families, by Size of Family, Sex and Age of Head, Sex and Number of Children,[a] *Year Ended May 31, 1961*—concluded

SELECTED CHARACTERISTICS	NUMBER OF LOW-INCOME FAMILIES BY SIZE OF FAMILY				TOTAL		INCIDENCE	DISTRIBUTION OF FAMILIES	
	2	3	4	5 OR MORE	(A) LOW-INCOME FAMILIES	(B) ALL FAMILIES	RATIO (A/B)	LOW INCOME	ALL
NUMBER OF CHILDREN[b]									
Male heads –									
No children	223,702	41,046	11,591	3,958	280,297	1,214,225	23.1	35.2	36.3
1 child	1,488	78,646	21,949	12,598	114,681	645,738	17.8	14.4	19.3
2 children		856	106,141	30,206	137,203	648,616	21.2	17.2	19.4
3 or more children			522	262,791	263,313	835,177	31.5	33.1	25.0
Totals	225,190	120,548	140,203	309,553	795,494	3,343,756	23.8	100.0	100.0
Female heads –									
No children	38,351	8,671	2,100	530	49,652	168,688	29.4	41.2	59.6
1 child	16,658	7,518	3,329	1,385	28,890	53,376	54.1	24.0	18.8
2 children		11,254	4,431	2,961	18,646	29,930	62.3	15.5	10.6
3 or more children			7,220	16,148	23,368	31,214	74.9	19.4	11.0
Totals	55,009	27,443	17,080	21,024	120,556	283,208	42.6	100.0	100.0

[a] Non-farm population only.

[b] Under age 16.

Source: Unpublished data from 1961 Census of Canada.

Table A.4

All Families and Low-Income Families, by Other Selected Characteristics,[a] *Year Ended May 31, 1961*

SELECTED CHARACTERISTICS	NUMBER OF FAMILIES		INCIDENCE OF LOW INCOME	PERCENTAGE DISTRIBUTION OF FAMILIES	
	LOW INCOME (A)	ALL (B)	(A/B)	LOW INCOME	ALL
NUMBER OF INCOME RECIPIENTS					
Male heads —					
No recipients	9,009	9,009	100.0	1.1	0.3
1 recipient	465,940	1,491,409	31.2	58.6	44.6
2 recipients	265,623	1,335,339	19.9	33.4	39.9
3 or more recipients	54,922	507,999	10.8	6.9	15.2
Totals	795,494	3,343,756	23.8	100.0	100.0
Female heads —					
No recipients	1,759	1,759	100.0	1.5	0.6
1 recipient	62,438	84,853	73.6	51.8	30.0
2 recipients	45,058	134,636	33.5	37.4	47.5
3 or more recipients	11,301	61,960	18.2	9.4	21.9
Totals	120,556	283,208	42.6	100.0	100.0
NUMBER OF INCOME EARNERS[b]					
Male heads —					
No earners	168,902	212,207	79.6	21.2	6.3
1 earner	475,782	1,747,785	27.2	59.8	52.3
2 earners	126,555	1,038,507	12.2	15.9	31.1
3 or more earners	24,255	345,257	7.0	3.0	10.3
Totals	795,494	3,343,756	23.8	100.0	100.0
Female heads —					
No earners	48,513	55,527	87.4	40.2	19.6
1 earner	53,579	122,559	43.7	44.4	43.3
2 earners	15,192	75,805	20.0	12.6	26.8
3 or more earners	3,272	29,317	11.2	2.7	10.4
University dgree	536	3,880	13.8	0.4	1.4
Totals	120,556	283,208	42.6	100.0	100.0
MAJOR SOURCE OF INCOME					
Male heads —					
Wages and salaries	484,979	2,722,469	17.8	61.0	81.4
Self employment	72,019	293,751	24.5	9.1	8.8
Transfer payments	188,393	210,670	89.4	23.7	6.3
Investment income	20,938	61,085	34.2	2.6	1.8
Other income	20,156	46,772	43.1	2.5	1.4
No income	9,009	9,009	100.0	1.1	0.3
Totals	795,494	3,343,756	23.8	100.0	100.0

[a] Non-farm population only.

[b] Number of persons in the family with income from employment.

continued . . .

Table A.4

All Families and Low-Income Families, by Other Selected Characteristics,[a] *Year Ended May 31, 1961*—continued

SELECTED CHARACTERISTICS	NUMBER OF FAMILIES: LOW INCOME (A)	NUMBER OF FAMILIES: ALL (B)	INCIDENCE OF LOW INCOME (A/B)	PERCENTAGE DISTRIBUTION OF FAMILIES: LOW INCOME	PERCENTAGE DISTRIBUTION OF FAMILIES: ALL
Female heads –					
Wages and salaries	48,303	186,488	25.9	40.1	65.8
Self employment	4,416	12,727	34.7	3.7	4.5
Transfer payments	56,116	60,101	93.4	46.5	21.2
Investment income	5,459	13,925	39.2	4.5	4.9
Other income	4,503	8,208	54.9	3.7	2.9
No income	1,759	1,759	100.0	1.5	0.6
Totals	120,556	283,208	42.6	100.0	100.0
EDUCATION OF HEAD					
Male heads –					
No schooling and elementary	551,434	1,528,359	36.1	69.3	45.7
Secondary 1-3 years	174,212	987,805	17.6	21.9	29.5
Secondary 4-5 years	50,889	510,912	10.0	6.4	15.3
Some university	11,219	130,562	8.6	1.4	3.9
University degree	7,740	186,118	4.2	1.0	5.6
Totals	795,494	3,343,756	23.8	100.0	100.0
Female heads –					
No schooling and elementary	73,606	151,964	48.4	61.1	53.7
Secondary 1-3 years	33,635	80,509	41.8	27.9	28.4
Secondary 4-5 years	11,271	40,183	28.0	9.3	14.2
Some university	1,508	6,672	22.6	1.3	2.4
University degree	536	3,880	13.8	0.4	1.4
Totals	120,556	283,208	42.6	100.0	100.0
LABOUR FORCE PARTICIPATION[c]					
Male heads –					
In current labour force	524,056[d]	2,871,478[e]	18.3	67.2	86.5
In non-current labour force	44,480	91,552	48.6	5.7	2.8
Not in labour force	211,056	355,690	59.3	27.1	10.7
Totals	779,592[d]	3,318,720[e]	23.5	100.0	100.0

[c] Heads in current labour force are heads in labour force on June 1, 1961. Those in non-current labour force were in labour force in year preceding the Census but not at census time. Heads not in labour force were those completely outside the labour force during the year.

[d] Excludes 15,902 families of farm operators residing off-farm for whom family income data were not complete.

[e] Excludes 25,036 families of farm operators residing off-farm for whom family income data were not complete.

continued . . .

Table A.4

All Families and Low-Income Families, by Other Selected Characteristics,[a] *Year Ended May 31, 1961*—concluded

SELECTED CHARACTERISTICS	NUMBER OF FAMILIES		INCIDENCE OF LOW INCOME (A/B)	PERCENTAGE DISTRIBUTION OF FAMILIES	
	LOW INCOME (A)	ALL (B)		LOW INCOME	ALL
In current labour force by occupation —					
Managerial	41,950	419,141	10.0	8.0	14.6
Professional and technical	11,822	255,447	4.6	2.3	8.9
Clerical	21,150	199,763	10.6	4.0	7.0
Sales	23,656	181,541	13.0	4.5	6.3
Service and recreation	49,937	246,281	20.3	9.5	8.6
Transport and communication	60,652	255,896	23.7	11.6	8.9
Farm workers	19,228	34,261	56.1	3.7	1.2
Loggers and related workers	20,048	35,351	56.7	3.8	1.2
Fishermen, trappers and hunters	13,696	20,384	67.2	2.6	00.7
Miners, quarrymen and related workers	7,850	44,252	17.7	1.5	1.5
Craftsmen, production process and related workers	182,939	991,291	18.5	34.9	34.5
Labourers	60,652	148,424	40.9	11.6	5.2
Not ascertained	10,476	39,446	26.6	2.0	1.4
Totals	524,056[d]	2,871,478[e]	18.3	100.0	100.0
Female heads —					
In current labour force	32,750[f]	99,105[g]	33.0	27.2	35.1
In non-current labour force	4,334	8,053	53.8	3.6	2.8
Not in labour force	83,337	175,822	47.4	69.2	62.1
Totals	120,421[f]	282,980[g]	42.6	100.0	100.0
In current labour force by occupation —					
Managerial	1,868	6,535	28.6	5.7	6.6
Professional and technical	1,418	11,865	12.0	4.3	12.0
Clerical	6,261	27,724	22.6	19.1	28.0
Sales	3,257	8,230	39.6	9.9	8.3
Service and recreation	14,314	27,298	52.4	43.7	27.5
Transport and communication	611	2,348	26.0	1.9	2.4
Craftsmen, production process and related workers	3,914	12,059	32.5	12.0	12.2
Labourers	483	1,161	41.6	1.5	1.2
Not ascertained	624	1,894	27.0	1.3	1.6
Totals	32,750[f]	99,105[g]	33.0	100.0	100.0

[f] Excludes 135 families of farm operators residing off-farm for whom family income data were not complete.

[g] Excludes 228 families of farm operators residing off-farm for whom family income data were not complete.

Source: Unpublished data from 1961 Census of Canada.

Table A.5

Income Composition of Incomes of Low-Income Families by Sex of Head,[a] *Year Ended May 31, 1961*

INCOME COMPONENT	MALE HEADS	FEMALE HEADS	ALL LOW-INCOME FAMILIES	PERCENTAGE $ OF AGGREGATE INCOME RECEIVED
	p.c.	p.c.	p.c.	
Income from employment	72.5	49.7	70.3	7.5
Family allowances	6.5	7.3	6.6	29.3
Old age pensions	8.4	11.9	8.7	44.3
Other transfer payments	7.3	20.9	8.6	38.0
Investment income	2.8	5.7	3.1	6.7
Other income	2.4	4.6	2.6	15.3
Totals	100.0	100.0	100.0	9.4

[a] Non-farm population only.
Source: Unpublished data from 1961 Census of Canada.

Table A.6

All Persons Not in Families and Low-Income Persons Not in Families, by Province of Residence and Size of Place of Residence,[a] *Year Ended May 31, 1961*

SELECTED CHARACTERISTICS	NUMBER OF PERSONS		INCIDENCE OF LOW INCOME (A/B)	PERCENTAGE DISTRIBUTION OF PERSONS	
	LOW INCOME (A)	ALL (B)		LOW INCOME	ALL
Province of residence —					
Newfoundland	7,755	11,940	64.9	1.9	1.3
Prince Edward Island	2,715	4,205	64.6	0.7	0.4
Nova Scotia	21,233	36,913	57.5	5.1	3.9
New Brunswick	13,682	24,120	56.7	3.3	2.5
Quebec	96,097	220,006	43.7	23.1	23.0
Ontario	144,067	366,534	39.3	34.7	38.4
Manitoba	23,481	51,810	45.3	5.7	5.5
Saskatchewan	24,672	49,105	50.2	5.9	5.1
Alberta	29,939	74,407	40.2	7.2	7.8
British Columbia	51,540	114,884	44.9	12.4	12.0
Totals[b]	415,548	955,042	43.5	100.0	100.0
Size of place of residence —					
Metropolitan centres	206,159	555,324	37.1	39.1	58.1
Other urban municipalities	110,391	239,262	46.1	27.1	25.1
30,000–99,999	30,399	74,193	41.0	6.4	7.8
10,000–29,999	29,133	64,808	45.0	7.0	6.8
1,000– 9,999	50,859	100,261	50.7	13.7	10.5
Rural	98,998	160,456	61.7	33.9	16.8

[a] Excludes persons resident on farms.
[b] Includes Yukon Territory.
Source: Unpublished data from the 1961 Census of Canada.

Table A.7
All Persons Not in Families and Low-Income Persons Not in Families, by Sex and Other Selected Characteristics,[a] Year Ended May 31, 1961

SELECTED CHARACTERISTICS	NUMBER OF PERSONS: LOW INCOME (A)	NUMBER OF PERSONS: ALL (B)	INCIDENCE OF LOW INCOME (A/B)	PERCENTAGE DISTRIBUTION OF PERSONS: LOW INCOME	PERCENTAGE DISTRIBUTION OF PERSONS: ALL
AGE OF PERSONS					
Males —					
Under 25	24,797	82,696	30.0	15.7	18.3
25–34	15,798	91,699	17.2	10.0	20.3
35–44	13,009	60,443	21.5	8.2	13.4
45–54	16,071	58,177	27.6	10.2	12.9
55–59	10,906	30,753	35.5	6.9	6.8
60–64	12,964	30,345	42.7	8.2	6.7
65–69	16,581	29,056	57.1	10.5	6.4
70 and over	47,775	68,301	69.9	30.3	15.1
Totals	157,901	451,470	35.0	100.0	100.0
Females —					
Under 25	40,769	86,258	47.3	15.8	17.1
25–34	15,286	55,350	27.6	5.9	11.0
35–44	14,554	47,609	30.6	5.6	9.5
45–54	24,217	63,802	38.0	9.4	12.7
55–59	17,810	39,256	45.4	6.9	7.8
60-64	25,925	46,345	55.9	10.1	9.2
65–69	34,708	50,935	68.1	13.5	10.1
70 and over	84,378	114,017	74.0	32.7	22.6
Totals	257,647	503,572	51.2	100.0	100.0
MAJOR SOURCE OF INCOME					
Males —					
Wages and salaries	55,064	309,017	17.8	34.9	68.4
Self employment	5,864	24,343	24.1	3.7	5.4
Transfer payments	65,421	70,977	92.1	41.4	15.7
Investment income	5,158	12,861	40.1	3.3	2.8
Other income	4,695	12,573	37.3	3.0	2.8
No income	21,699	21,699	100.0	13.7	4.8
Totals	157,901	451,470	35.0	100.0	100.0
Females —					
Wages and salaries	79,647	269,566	29.5	30.9	53.5
Self employment	6,129	15,815	38.8	2.4	3.1
Transfer payments	106,668	114,935	92.8	41.4	22.8
Investment income	19,823	45,726	43.4	7.7	9.1
Other income	8,772	20,922	41.9	3.4	4.2
No income	36,608	36,608	100.0	14.2	7.3
Totals	257,647	503,572	51.2	100.0	100.0

For footnotes, see end of table.

continued . . .

Table A.7
All Persons Not in Families and Low-Income Persons Not in Families, by Sex and Other Selected Characteristics,[a] *Year Ended May 31, 1961*—continued

SELECTED CHARACTERISTICS	NUMBER OF PERSONS		INCIDENCE OF LOW INCOME (A/B)	PERCENTAGE DISTRIBUTION OF PERSONS	
	LOW INCOME (A)	ALL (B)		LOW INCOME	ALL
EDUCATION					
Males —					
No schooling and elementary	106,319	228,310	46.6	67.3	50.6
Secondary 1–3 years	29,321	112,262	26.1	18.6	24.9
Secondary 4–5 years	12,021	65,024	18.5	7.6	14.4
Some university	5,585	22,528	24.8	3.5	5.0
University degree	4,655	23,346	19.9	2.9	5.2
Totals	157,901	451,470	35.0	100.0	100.0
Females —					
No schooling and elementary	147,935	206,919	71.5	57.4	41.1
Secondary 1–3 years	70,010	148,938	47.0	27.2	29.6
Secondary 4–5 years	31,866	108,087	29.5	12.4	21.5
Some university	5,538	24,039	23.0	2.1	4.8
University degree	2,298	15,589	14.7	0.9	3.1
Totals	257,647	503,572	51.2	100.0	100.0
LABOUR FORCE PARTICIPATION[b]					
Males —					
In current labour force	58,931[c]	319,188[d]	18.5	38.0	71.3
In non-current labour force	7,676	16,953	45.3	4.9	3.8
Not in labour force	88,487	111,510	79.4	57.1	24.9
Totals	155,094[c]	447,651[d]	34.6	100.0	100.0
In current labour force by occupation —					
Managerial	2,334	20,322	11.5	4.0	6.4
Professional and technical	5,759	35,965	16.0	9.8	11.3
Clerical	2,962	30,176	9.8	5.0	9.5
Sales	2,384	17,073	14.0	4.0	5.3
Service and recreation	8,694	35,191	24.7	14.8	11.0
Transport and communication	3,548	21,658	16.4	6.0	6.8
Farm workers	4,572	7,805	58.6	7.8	2.4
Loggers and related workers	1,919	4,815	39.9	3.3	1.5
Fishermen, trappers and hunters	1,196	1,904	62.8	2.0	0.6
Miners, quarrymen and related workers	453	44,833	9.4	0.8	1.5

For footnotes, see end of table.

continued . . .

Table A.7

All Persons Not in Families and Low-Income Persons Not in Families, by Sex and Other Selected Characteristics,[a] *Year Ended May 31, 1961*—concluded

SELECTED CHARACTERISTICS	NUMBER OF PERSONS		INCIDENCE OF LOW INCOME (A/B)	PERCENTAGE DISTRIBUTION OF PERSONS	
	LOW INCOME (A)	ALL (B)		LOW INCOME	ALL
Craftsmen, production process and related workers	13,649	95,163	14.3	23.2	29.8
Labourers	8,812	28,359	31.1	15.0	8.9
Not ascertained	2,649	15,924	16.6	4.5	5.0
Totals	58,931[c]	319,188[d]	18.5	100.0	100.0
Females —					
In current labour force	84,148[e]	278,979[f]	30.2	32.7	55.5
In non-current labour force	7,612	12,967	58.7	3.0	2.6
Not in labour force	165,150	210,772	78.4	64.3	41.9
Totals	256,910[e]	502,718[f]	51.1	100.0	100.0
In labour force by occupation —					
Managerial	2,002	8,375	23.9	2.4	3.0
Professional and technical	5,744	53,709	10.7	6.8	19.3
Clerical	8,617	76,080	11.3	10.2	27.3
Sales	4,390	14,307	30.7	5.2	5.1
Service and recreation	53,655	83,985	63.9	63.8	30.1
Transport and communication	1,037	6,247	16.6	1.2	2.2
Farm workers	313	376	83.2	0.4	0.1
Craftsmen, production process and related workers	6,687	24,820	26.9	7.9	8.9
Labourers	687	1,809	38.0	0.8	0.6
Not ascertained	1,006	9,246	10.9	1.2	3.3
Totals	84,148[e]	278,979[f]	30.2	100.0	100.0

[a] Excludes persons resident on farms.

[b] Persons in current labour are those in the labour force on June 1, 1961, those in non-current labour force were those not in the labour force on June 1st but in the labour force during the preceding year. Those not in the labour force were persons with no labour force attachment during the year.

[c] Excludes 1,506 farm operators residing off-farm for whom income data are not complete.

[d] Excludes 2,406 farm operators residing off-farm for whom income data are not complete.

[e] Excludes 82 farm operators residing off-farm for whom income data are not complete.

[f] Excludes 129 farm operators residing off-farm for whom income data are not complete.

Source: Unpublished data from 1961 Census of Canada.

2. *Spatial Characteristics of the Economy**

T. N. Brewis

There has been in recent years a notable growth in the study of regional economic problems. The subject indeed has become a field of academic specialization, albeit one with uncertain boundaries extending into the broad realms of regional science and attracting geographers, sociologists, and demographers, as well as economists.

Among the factors contributing to this expanded interest in regional problems has been a growing discontent with the magnitude of the differences in income and employment opportunity which exist not only between countries but also between various regions of the same country. In the less developed nations especially there is often a widening gap between the growth of a few industrialized urban centres and the stagnation of rural areas, and if not redressed the disparity that results can be a potent cause of political unrest. Though likely to be less extreme, regional differences in prosperity within advanced industrial countries are also a source of concern, and most countries have introduced policies to modify spatial economic patterns. Canada is no exception.

The inequality of income and employment opportunity within as well as between provinces of the country has long been one of the important issues in the Canadian scene. There is widespread agreement that this inequality is too great to be acceptable, and federal, provincial, and local governments have been devoting increasing efforts to the development of programs to reduce it. It is clear that market forces alone cannot be relied upon to redress the situation. Indeed poverty to some extent begets poverty. But as experience in other countries has shown, governments can do much to improve the fortunes of the less favoured communities by appropriate policies.

In his budget speech of 1963, the federal Minister of Finance drew

*Reprinted with permission of the author and publisher from *Regional Economic Policies in Canada,* by T.N. Brewis (Toronto: The Macmillan Company of Canada, Limited, 1969).

attention to the establishment of a special Area Development Agency (ADA), within the new Department of Industry, designed to assist in the economic development of slow growth areas of the country. In addition, the Atlantic provinces were to be given further assistance through the strengthening of the Atlantic Development Board (ADB). Two years earlier, in June 1961, a very important piece of legislation, known as "ARDA," had been introduced "to provide for the Rehabilitation of Agricultural Lands and the Development of Rural Areas in Canada," and this was followed in 1966 by further legislation to provide a fund for the implementation of comprehensive rural development programs in specially selected rural development areas (FRED). The poverty of many farm and rural workers was more extreme than was commonly realized, and one of the primary purposes of the legislation was to increase their income opportunities. More generally, the Economic Council has been directed in its terms of reference to study how national economic policies can best foster the balanced economic development of all areas of Canada, a task to which the Council has been devoting increasing attention. These various policies and measures are additional to the federal fiscal adjustments which are made in favour of the poorer provinces and which have a long tradition.

What may prove to be of particular importance is the establishment* . . . of a new department of government responsible for regional development. The functions of this new department have yet to be spelled out in detail, but its creation reflects the increasing concern of the federal government with regional problems and recognition of the need for closer integration of various policies relating thereto.

Provincial governments for their part have not been at all content to leave the initiative to Ottawa and are themselves developing programs of varying degrees of comprehensiveness and sophistication which are intended to modify the extent and location of economic growth. It is clear that these programs, which typically have as their prime objective the attracting of new industry, are prepared with scant, if any, regard for their implications at the national level. Thus the Committee on Manitoba's Economic Future, in a voluminous report published in 1963, urged among other things that more Manitobans be induced to travel in their own province and that efforts be made to reduce imports from other provinces as well as to increase exports to them. But it is not just at the *national* level that trade patterns are being modified by regional subventions and policies of one sort and another but at the *international* level too. Efforts to liberalize international trade could well be undermined by certain types of regional assistance which have the effect if not the intent, of subsidizing export industries or reducing imports.

Though for the most part federal assistance is welcomed by those provincial governments which expect to benefit by it, there is not much enthusiasm among the others, and some provincial governments view the

*EDITOR'S NOTE: In 1968.

regional policies of Ottawa with very mixed feelings, except when they take the form of money with no strings attached. Questions concerning the criteria for assistance, the designation of areas to receive it, and the amount and form such assistance should take are matters of concern to all levels of government, and there are often sharp differences of opinion on policy. Should aid be distributed widely, or concentrated on smaller areas of deep distress? And what criteria of distress should be used? Would it be preferable to assist areas with more potential growth even though their distress is less marked? Is it preferable to concentrate efforts on various measures designed to influence the relocation of industry, or on measures to encourage the migration of people? And which industry and which people do we have in mind? Some favour leaving the main initiative for change to the local communities themselves, even though the process of education and voluntary action may be slow. Others argue that the problems are too pressing and that there is little hope of achieving substantial results within an acceptable time period in this way. The chronic differences in educational achievement across the country, regarded as one of the causes of income inequality, are not likely to disappear if left solely to local initiative. The areas offering the poorest education are precisely those least able to help themselves.

At the township and municipal level prolonged distress may lead to apathy; but often rivalries are keen, and local development associations compete with each other to gain a greater share of the over-all economic expansion, bringing what pressure they can to bear on provincial governments to support them in their efforts.

Recognition of this rivalry, combined with experience in the implementation of specific measures, has led to a belief in the virtues of planning regional development in a more systematic way. Even when they have begun with a modest enough objective, those concerned with the formulation of policies have often found themselves faced with a situation where one step seems to lead inexorably to another. Assistance to the "marginal" farmer, to cite one example, has led to the question of his alternative employment, and from this to the limited opportunities available to rural workers in general. Proposals to expand those opportunities have given rise to recommendations and measures to improve education, encourage the mobility of workers, increase social capital, and provide incentives to induce industry to locate in certain areas. Each of these measures leads to still others. It soon becomes obvious that all of them are interrelated, and that their efficacy depends upon integrating them into a coherent program of development. Judging from the experience of certain other countries, moreover, effective planning for regional development may entail integration in a national plan. The issues involved raise fundamental questions of an ideological nature concerning Canada's social and political objectives, as well as the interrelationship of its various levels of government.

A great variety of policies bear on the subject of area development.

Some, designed to encourage the growth of specific sectors of the economy, may have very important regional implications, for sectoral growth has a spatial aspect. By way of illustration, the tariff on manufactured goods and assistance to particular primary industries benefits some areas of the country more than others. Federal defence and other expenditures may also have an uneven regional impact. These spatial effects may be as important as they are fortuitous. The present enquiry, however, is concerned with those policies which are framed specifically to influence regional patterns rather than with those whose regional impact is not deliberately intended.

The proliferating agencies and bodies at the national as well as the provincial level pursue their individual objectives, and overlapping functions as well as serious gaps and conflicts result. ARDA, for example, cannot fulfil the objectives of rural development without support in the form of industrial development, but little is forthcoming since ADA is concerned solely with designated areas and with the reduction of unemployment rather than with measures designed to sustain a viable industrial expansion. With the passage of time, certain bodies such as ARDA have changed and added to their objectives, but however desirable such changes may be, they have added to confusion in the public mind as to the direction in which we are going.

The rapidity with which changes in the structure of the economy are taking place and the magnitude of these changes add an urgency to policy decisions. An instance of this is the trend towards urbanization and the concentration of population in larger centres which necessitates major investment decisions that will affect the location of schools, hospitals, and other forms of social overhead capital. Projections of future population patterns will not only influence but be influenced by these decisions. Whether we intend it or not, capital expenditures on a large scale can be expected to have a significant and perhaps decisive bearing on future population distribution, hastening the decline of some areas and the expansion of others.

One of the basic difficulties in framing regional economic policies is the lack of reliable and adequate data on which to base such policies. The designation of areas for development by the Area Development Agency, to note one example, has turned upon statistical material which is both obsolete and suspect. There is an urgent need for more statistical information on a sub-provincial basis. This would not only make it easier to identify areas requiring assistance, it would also indicate the direction that remedial action might take.

A second and more fundamental difficulty in the designing of policies is the absence of an adequate theoretical framework for the study of regional questions. The works of Hirschman and Perroux, especially, offer revealing insights into the regional growth process, but the regional economist is obliged to rely heavily on his own intuition regarding the steps that should be taken to achieve whatever goals he regards as appropriate. He soon finds himself, moreover, immersed in the speculations of sociologists, in the niceties of inter-governmental administration, and in constitutional questions concerning responsibility for providing certain services such as education. He can, of course, take a detached Olympian view of the whole scene, but if he does this he is likely to find that his contributions to the discussion of policy are not taken very seriously by those on whom the burden of decision must fall...

* * *

Any government which seeks to influence the spatial patterns of economic activity and encourage development in the lower income areas of the country must reflect not only on the present situation but on those trends which can be expected to bear on the future. Information is necessary on the changing patterns of population distribution and industrial activity, the reasons underlying those changes, and the regional differences in income and employment opportunity with which they are associated. Developments in one region have repercussions on another, and a study of this interrelationship is desirable and perhaps indispensable. In undertaking such a study, decisions should be reached on the specific spatial boundaries to be considered, for variations in those boundaries may influence materially the picture which is presented as well as the action needed to effect such changes as appear desirable.

THE DISTRIBUTION OF POPULATION

The population of Canada is now four times as great as it was at the turn of the century and it is still growing rapidly; but except for the narrow strip north of the United States border extending unevenly across the country from the Atlantic Ocean to the Pacific the country remains sparsely populated and undeveloped, having a population density of nine per square mile, or five if the Yukon and Northwest Territories are included. Inhabitants of the Northwest Territories and the Yukon, which together take in an area of almost one and a half million square miles, total less than forty thousand. Most of this forty thousand, moreover, live in two or three centres, and vast areas of the North are completely uninhabited. Of the total population of the country over sixty per cent live in the two central provinces, Ontario and Quebec, the metropolitan areas of Toronto and Montreal alone accounting for about one fifth. Toronto and Montreal have a population as great as that of all four Atlantic provinces, and fifty times as great as that of the Yukon and the Northwest Territories combined.

The distribution of the population by province for the decennial census years and the factors involved in the growth of that population are shown in Tables 1 and 2.

It will be observed in these tables that the pace of development has been very uneven. There have been wide differences in the rate of population increase between the provinces and from decade to decade. The population of Saskatchewan increased over five times between 1901 and

Table 1

Distribution of Population and Percentage Change; Decennial Census Years 1901 to 1961

	1901	1911	1921	1931	1941	1951	1961
(numerical distribution in thousands)							
Newfoundland*	—	—	—	—	—	361	458
Prince Edward Island	103	94	89	88	95	98	105
Nova Scotia	460	492	524	513	578	643	737
New Brunswick	331	352	388	408	457	516	598
Quebec	1,649	2,006	2,361	2,875	3,332	4,056	5,259
Ontario	2,183	2,527	2,934	3,432	3,788	4,598	6,236
Manitoba	255	461	610	700	730	777	922
Saskatchewan	91	492	758	922	896	832	925
Alberta	73	374	588	732	796	940	1,332
British Columbia	179	392	525	694	818	1,165	1,629
Yukon Territory	27	9	4	4	5	9	15
Northwest Territories	20	7	8	9	12	16	23
CANADA	5,371	7,207	8,788	10,377	11,507	14,009	18,238
(% change from preceding census)							
Newfoundland	—	—	—	—	—	—	10.3
Prince Edward Island	− 5.3	− 9.2	− 5.5	− 0.7	8.0	3.6	5.4
Nova Scotia	2.0	7.1	6.4	− 2.1	12.7	11.2	6.1
New Brunswick	3.1	6.3	10.2	5.2	12.0	12.7	7.8
Quebec	10.8	21.6	17.7	21.8	15.9	21.7	13.6
Ontario	3.2	15.8	16.1	17.0	10.4	21.4	15.4
Manitoba	67.3	80.8	32.2	14.8	4.2	6.4	8.4
Saskatchewan	—	439.5	53.8	21.7	− 2.8	− 7.2	5.1
Alberta	—	412.6	57.2	24.3	8.8	18.0	18.6
British Columbia	82.0	119.7	33.7	32.3	17.8	42.5	16.5
Yukon Territory	—	−68.7	−51.2	1.8	16.2	85.1	20.0
Northwest Territories	−79.7	−67.7	25.1	14.4	29.1	33.1	19.1
CANADA	11.1	34.2	21.9	18.1	10.9	21.8	13.4

Note: Figures do not add to totals in all cases because of rounding.

*Populations of Newfoundland (not part of Canada until 1949) were: 1901, 220,984; 1911, 242,619; 1921, 263,033; 1931, 281,500 (estimated); 1941, 303,300 (estimated); and 1945, 321,819.

Source: D.B.S., *Canada Year Book, 1962,* p. 1196.

Table 2
Factors in the Growth of Population 1951-1961

	POPULATION (THOUSANDS)				
	1951 CENSUS	NATURAL INCREASE	ACTUAL INCREASE	NET MIGRATION	1961 CENSUS
Newfoundland	361	111	96	–15	458
Prince Edward Island	98	18	6	–11	105
Nova Scotia	643	128	94	–34	737
New Brunswick	516	119	82	–37	598
Quebec	4,056	998	1,204	205	5,259
Ontario	4,598	953	1,639	685	6,236
Manitoba	777	150	145	– 5	922
Saskatchewan	832	172	93	–79	925
Alberta	940	265	392	127	1,332
British Columbia	1,165	224	464	240	1,629
Yukon and Northwest Territories	25	9	13	3	38
CANADA	14,009	3,148	4,229	1,081	18,238

Note: Figures do not add to totals in all cases because of rounding.
Source: D.B.S., Canada Year Book, 1962, p. 1196.

1911 with the opening up of the wheat lands, but fell between 1931 and 1951. The population of Prince Edward Island was virtually the same in 1961 as it was at the turn of the century, whereas that of Alberta increased eighteen times. In the Yukon and Northwest Territories, in spite of a doubling of the population between 1941 and 1961, the total population was less in 1961 than in 1901, largely because of a sharp fall in the first decade of the century. Six provinces experienced a net out-migration between 1951 and 1961, while Ontario experienced a heavy inflow of migrants which was more than three times as great as that into Quebec.[1] The heavy migration into Ontario has offset the generally greater natural increase in Quebec, and has contributed to the dominance of Ontario in the economy of the country, a dominance not without political overtones.

Although net immigration from other countries has been very heavy at certain periods, internal migration from one province to another and from rural to urban areas has far exceeded it. Net immigration to Canada between 1921 and 1961 totalled almost a million and a half

[1] In his study "Regional Aspects of Canada's Economic Growth 1890-1929," *Canadian Journal of Economics and Political Science,* XXXIII, no. 2 (May 1967), 232-45, Alan G. Green estimates that by 1929 the Prairie provinces and British Columbia accounted for approximately 28 per cent of countrywide gross value added, whereas in 1890 they had accounted for only about 8 per cent, the bulk of this increase taking place by 1910. He notes too that the rapid countrywide economic growth between 1890 and 1910 was accompanied by a growing divergence in output per capita among the provinces.

Table 3

Distribution of Rural and Urban Population 1961

	RURAL			URBAN					RURAL AS % OF URBAN
				POPULATION OF CENTRE					
	FARM*	NON-FARM	TOTAL	1,000 TO 9,999	10,000 TO 29,999	30,000 TO 99,999	100,000 OR OVER	TOTAL	
					(thousands)				
Newfoundland	9	217	*226*	99	48	85	—	*232*	97
Prince Edward Island	35	36	*71*	16	18	—	—	*34*	296
Nova Scotia	57	280	*336*	75	49	—	276	*401*	84
New Brunswick	62	258	*320*	80	62	136	—	*278*	115
Quebec	565	788	*1,353*	606	278	385	2,638	*3,906*	35
Ontario	506	907	*1,413*	632	298	935	2,959	*4,824*	29
Manitoba	171	161	*333*	72	51	—	466	*589*	62
Saskatchewan	305	222	*527*	109	48	129	112	*398*	132
Alberta	286	203	*489*	158	44	35	605	*843*	58
British Columbia	78	370	*447*	161	153	—	868	*1,182*	38
Yukon Territory	—	10	*10*	5	—	—	—	*5*	191
Northwest Territories	—	14	*14*	9	—	—	—	*9*	157
CANADA	2,073	3,465	*5,538*	2,022	1,049	1,705	7,924	*12,700*	44

Note: Figures do not add to totals in all cases because of rounding.

Source: D.B.S., *Canada Year Book, 1965,* p. 165.

*Excludes 55,615 persons living on farms in localities classed as urban.

people, but that figure amounted to less than half the movement of people out of farming areas.[2]

The shift from rural to urban living has proceeded extremely rapidly in Canada. In fact the Economic Council has expressed the view that Canada may have had the fastest rate of urban growth among the countries of the Western world in the post-war period as a whole, and it foresees the possibility of a dramatically faster rate of urban growth than that of other industrial economies over the years ahead.[3] In 1901 the rural population accounted for some 60 per cent of the whole, by 1921 it had dropped to a little over 50 per cent, and by 1961 the urban population had risen to over 60 per cent, reversing the position at the turn of the century. The most notable drop was in agricultural labour, which constituted almost half the total work force in the final quarter of the last century and had dropped to less than 8 per cent by 1966.

The degree of urbanization, however, differs greatly among the provinces. As seen from Table 3, Prince Edward Island, New Brunswick, and Saskatchewan are predominantly rural, Newfoundland is about equally divided, and Ontario is the most urbanized.

The depressed conditions which prevail in many rural areas have constituted one of the spurs to migration and . . . have prompted a number of regionally oriented policies on the part of the government to encourage an improvement in economic conditions in those areas.

The urban population has not only increased, it has tended to concentrate in the larger centres. The two largest metropolitan areas may soon have a total population as great as that of all rural areas combined. Over one half of Canada's entire population now lives within 150 miles of the three largest cities. This concentration seems likely to continue unless measures are taken to reduce it.

THE DISTRIBUTION OF MANUFACTURING ACTIVITY

Manufacturing activity is also overwhelmingly concentrated in urban centres. In the decade between 1950 and 1960, the six metropolitan areas of Montreal, Toronto, Hamilton, Vancouver, Windsor, and Winnipeg gained 1,287 establishments; the rest of the country, by contrast, showed a *decline* of 547. In 1961, these same metropolitan areas, with approximately 32 per cent of the national population, accounted together for 48 per cent of the selling value of factory shipments in Canada.[4]

[2] See Isabel Anderson, *Internal Migration in Canada, 1921-61* (Economic Council of Canada, Staff Study No. 13 [Ottawa: Queen's Printer, 1966]). Miss Anderson also makes the point that the rates of internal migration in Canada have been even greater than those experienced over long periods in the United States. Foreign born people in Canada seem to be more mobile than native born, and this is true also of their children. Regional differences also manifest themselves, Westerners being readier to move than Easterners who are often native to several generations.

[3] Economic Council of Canada, *Fourth Annual Review: The Canadian Economy from the 1960's to the 1970's* (Ottawa: Queen's Printer, 1967), pp. 177-8.

[4] This is a much higher degree of concentration than in the United States where, in 1961, 37.5 per cent of the nation's value added by manufacture was accounted for by *ten* metropolises containing 27 per cent of the 1960 population.

Table 4
Distribution of Population, Labour Force, and Manufacturing Employment 1961

	%				
	ATLANTIC PROVINCES	QUEBEC	ONTARIO	PRAIRIES	BRITISH COLUMBIA
(a) Population	10.43	28.90	34.26	17.47	8.95
(b) Urban population	7.44	30.79	38.02	14.43	9.32
(c) Labour force	8.70	27.38	37.05	17.93	8.94
(d) Non-primary labour force*	8.40	28.19	38.91	15.13	9.37
(e) Employees in manufacturing	5.54	33.21	45.80	7.41	8.05
(f) Employees in manufacturing (excluding primary and local)†	2.79	37.21	50.39	6.24	3.37
DENSITY MEASURES (concentration of manufacturing jobs relative to other characteristics):					
(e) as % of (a)	53.1	114.9	133.7	42.4	89.9
(e) as % of (b)	74.5	107.9	120.5	51.4	86.4
(e) as % of (d)	66.0	117.8	117.7	49.0	85.9
(f) as % of (b)	37.5	120.9	132.5	43.2	36.2

Note: Figures do not add to 100% in all cases because of rounding.
*Excluding labour force in agriculture, fishing, forestry, and mining.
†Excluding foods and beverages, wood products, paper products, printing and allied industries, and primary metal.
Source: D.B.S., *1961 Census of Canada,* Vol. I (92-536) and Vol. III (94-518).

In 1962 the province of Ontario accounted for half the entire value of factory shipments in the country, Quebec for 30 per cent, the Prairies and British Columbia for 8 per cent each, and the combined Atlantic provinces for only 4 per cent. This high degree of concentration is still more marked when attention is paid to sub-provincial areas. For instance, within Ontario manufacturing is heavily concentrated in the Toronto metropolitan area and is very limited in the North.

Table 4 casts further light on the distribution of economic activity.[5] From this table, it will be noted that the concentration of manufacturing activity in Ontario and Quebec appears even greater if primary manufacturing and manufacturing for a local market are excluded. Manufacturing for markets outside the Atlantic provinces amounts to less than 3 per cent, in contrast to over 50 per cent for Ontario.

[5] The table is a modification of one prepared by D.W. Slater and presented in his paper "Trends in Industrial Locations in Canada" at the Resources for Tomorrow Conference held in Montreal in 1961. See *Resources for Tomorrow: Conference Background Papers* (Ottawa: Queen's Printer, 1961), I, 410. More recent data have been included here; Newfoundland has been added to the Maritime Provinces, and certain minor changes in classification have been made.

Table 5

Personal Income Expressed as a Per Cent of the Canadian Average 1926 to 1965 (various years)*

(as % of the national average)

	1926	*1929*	*1933*	*1939*	*1946*	*1950*	*1955*	*1959*	*1961*	*1963*	*1965*
Newfoundland						51	54	55	60	58	59
Prince Edward Island	57	59	51	53	58	56	55	62	62	63	69
Nova Scotia	67	71	77	76	86	74	73	75	77	74	75
New Brunswick	64	65	66	65	75	69	65	66	68	66	69
Quebec	85	92	94	88	82	85	85	85	88	87	88
Ontario	114	122	129	124	115	121	120	119	118	117	115
Manitoba	109	98	93	90	103	100	95	100	97	97	97
Saskatchewan	102	67	47	77	97	87	93	87	78	107	99
Alberta	113	92	74	87	108	103	103	104	102	100	99
British Columbia†	121	128	132	125	114	123	122	118	116	114	115

*Includes all transfer payments and imputed net income of farmers.
†Includes Yukon and Northwest Territories, 1926 to 1950.
Source: Calculated from D.B.S., *National Accounts, Income and Expenditure* (13-201), various years.

This high concentration of manufacturing activity in certain regions of the country is not peculiar to Canada. Throughout the world the output of manufactured goods is heavily concentrated in certain regions or belts of industrial production. Even in very industrialized countries such as the United States, or those of western Europe there are extensive areas which contribute little to manufacturing output. A variety of factors account for this, and any attempt to modify the situation must take cognizance of the various forces which have created the present patterns and which can be expected to give rise to further change.

DISPARITIES IN INCOME AND EMPLOYMENT

In a country as large and diversified as Canada, it is to be expected that there will be substantial differences in economic potential between one area and another. As seen from Table 5 and Figures 1, 2(a) and 2(b) average incomes are much lower and unemployment is higher in some provinces than in others. The degree of economic stability also varies, though unequivocal conclusions concerning the causes of this and other differences may be difficult — partly because of inadequate data and partly because, as noted below, different concepts of growth produce different results. Levels of income and of unemployment show a striking regional pattern. Marked fluctuations in income are characteristic of Saskatchewan. As might be expected, high unemployment rates tend to be associated with low labour force participation rates, and participation rates for both males and females in the Atlantic provinces are generally well below those in the rest of the country, though the gap is narrowing. Participation rates for Ontario are the highest.

On the issue of income differentials specifically, a distinction can be drawn between gross income and disposable income after taxes. Less income tax is paid by residents in the poorer provinces on the average, and as a result net disposable incomes show a smaller regional variation than do gross incomes. A wider regional variation in income is manifest if attention is confined to income derived from work, transfer payments contributing a somewhat larger proportion of income to the poorer areas of the country. Table 6 indicates the magnitudes involved for the year 1966.

It will be observed that while total personal disposable income in Prince Edward Island was 68 per cent of the national average, earned income was only 57 per cent. Nova Scotia and New Brunswick also showed a marked difference between the two measures, with earned income being 8 and 6 percentage points lower respectively.

As for the distinction between real and nominal incomes, the view is sometimes expressed that it is cheaper to live in some parts of the country than in others, and that comparisons of money incomes fail to reflect differences in purchasing power. There is some evidence that the distinction between real and nominal incomes could be an important one in certain cases. The very low incomes prevailing in

Figure 1
Percentage Unemployed, by Region, 1963 to 1967

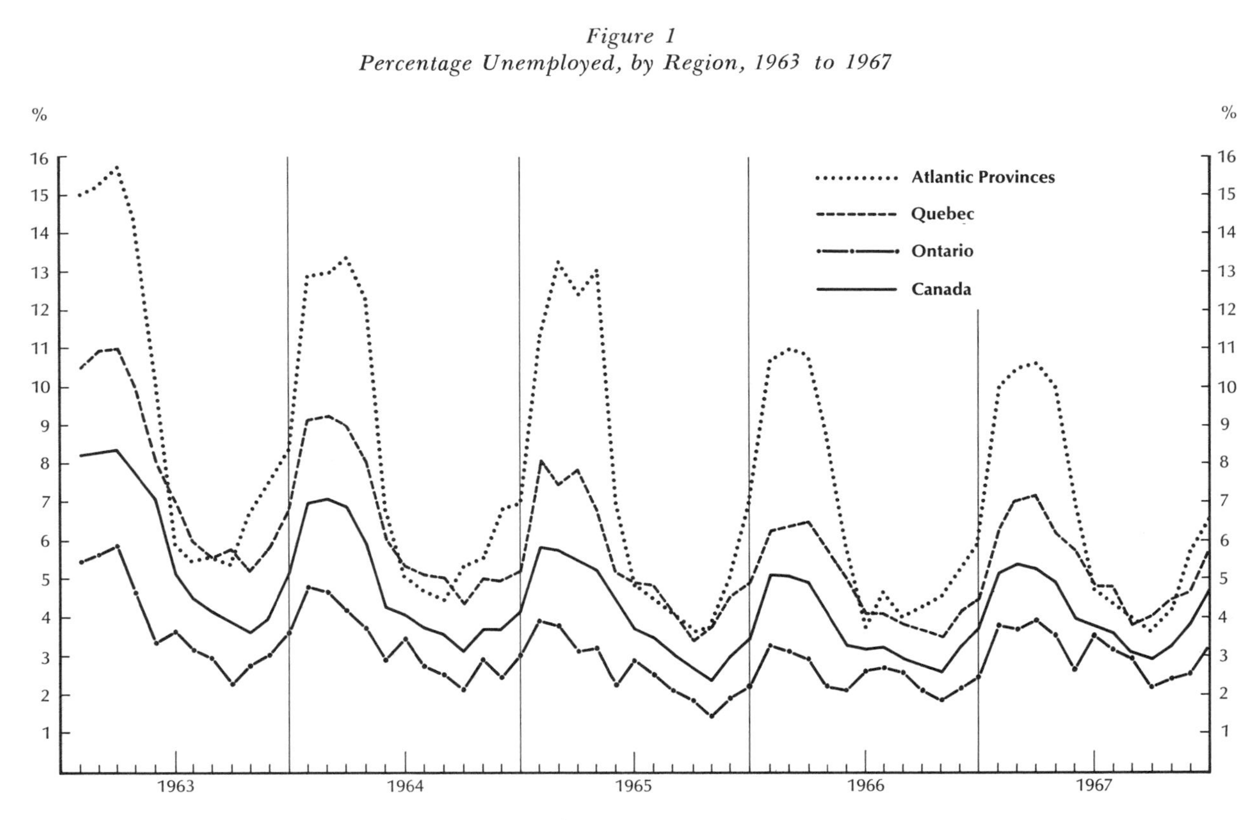

Note: Figures are unadjusted for seasonal variation.
Source: D.B.S., Canadian Statstical Review *(11-003), various months.*

Figure 2(a)
Participation Rates for Males, by Region, 1950 to 1967*

Figure 2(b)
Participation Rates for Females, by Region, 1950 to 1967*

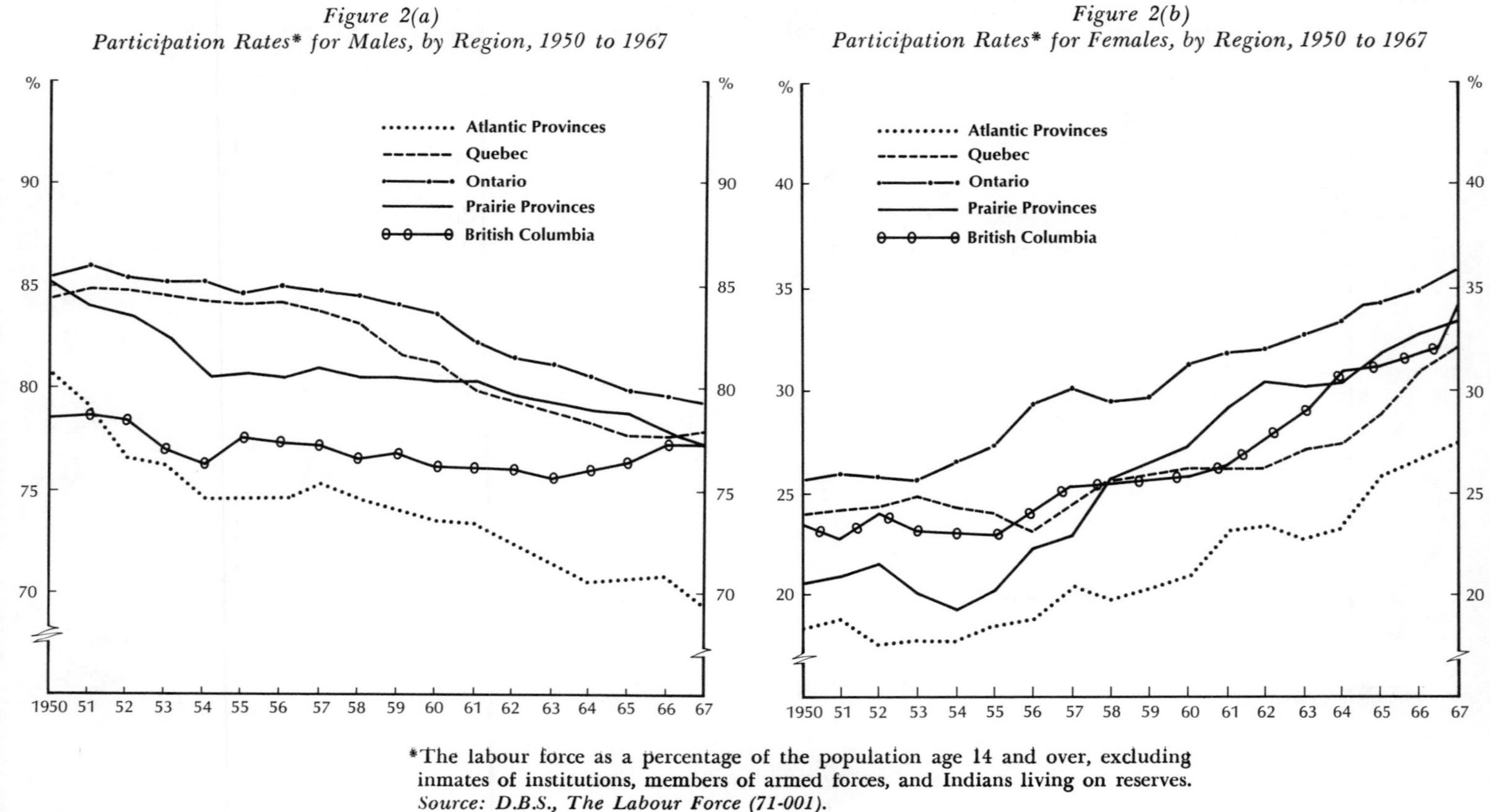

*The labour force as a percentage of the population age 14 and over, excluding inmates of institutions, members of armed forces, and Indians living on reserves.
Source: D.B.S., The Labour Force (71-001).

Table 6
Source of Income 1966

($ per capita, unless otherwise noted)

	NFLD.	P.E.I.	N.S.	N.B.	QUE.	ONT.	MAN.	SASK.	ALTA.	B.C.	CANADA
Wages and salaries (excluding military pay)	947	716	1,024	1,006	1,348	1,746	1,276	956	1,335	1,736	1,465
Net income from farm production	4	101	11	23	33	67	181	702	290	45	102
Net income from unincorporated businesses	108	156	147	125	117	155	172	169	171	188	147
Total earned income	1,059	972	1,181	1,154	1,499	1,969	1,629	1,826	1,796	1,970	1,715
% of national average	*62*	*57*	*69*	*67*	*87*	*115*	*95*	*106*	*105*	*115*	*100*
Interest dividends, net rental income	67	101	149	120	190	290	219	203	204	259	227
Government transfer payments	237	284	246	266	244	243	249	253	273	278	250
Balancing item*	–45	+19	+7	–41	–60	–71	–53	–46	–56	–85	–58
Total personal income	1,318	1,376	1,583	1,499	1,873	2,431	2,044	2,236	2,217	2,422	2,134
% of national average	*62*	*64*	*74*	*70*	*88*	*114*	*96*	*105*	*104*	*113*	*100*
Direct taxes	–77	–73	–112	–108	–203	–286	–188	–182	–177	–238	–222
Total personal disposable income	1,241	1,303	1,471	1,391	1,670	2,145	1,856	2,054	2,040	2,184	1,912
% of national average	*65*	*68*	*77*	*73*	*87*	*112*	*97*	*107*	*107*	*114*	*100*
Net transfer payments†	160	211	134	158	41	–43	61	71	96	40	28

Note: Figures do not add to totals in all cases because of rounding.

*Largely composed of military pay and allowances, less employer and employee contributions to social insurance and government pension funds.

†Government transfer payments less direct taxes as shown in the previous columns. Though data by province is not available, 50 per cent of the transfer payments at the national level were federal, 48 per cent provincial, and 2 per cent municipal.

Source: D.B.S., *National Accounts, Income and Expenditure* (13-201).

Prince Edward Island, for example, imply a lower standard of living than actually seems to be the case. Many recreational amenities which are free in some parts of the country are expensive in others; costs of travel to and from work and the time involved in such travel also vary greatly, as do capacities to supplement income from unrecorded agricultural and related pursuits. These differences in purchasing power, which are not reflected in statistical data, may explain in part the reluctance of many people to migrate to areas where incomes are nominally higher.

3. Trends and Regional Differences in Education*

Education is a process that has many facets and many values. It can enhance the quality of life and enrich the lives of individuals. It quickens appreciation of the wonders of knowledge and stimulates the yearnings of mankind for a better world. It stirs the imagination, sharpens the intellect and stimulates creativity. It can also help to generate economic growth; it increases the mobility, adaptability and productivity of people, and raises their level of living.

For these reasons, the Economic Council, in successive Annual Reviews, has given special attention to the need to increase and improve Canadian education. In our *Second Annual Review,* certain basic conclusions were reached about the economics of education. It was pointed out that the income of individuals is in general closely related to the extent of schooling, and that the rates of return from increased investment in education appear to compare favourably with the returns from other kinds of investment. Increased education was estimated to have accounted for a significant part of the increase in productivity and material well-being of Canadians over the past half century. But the differences in educational achievements between Canada and the United States were found to be at least one of the significant elements having a bearing on the persistent gap in living standards between the two countries. Our more recent work has revealed that through much of the postwar period Canada has been lagging behind not only the United States but also various European countries in the rate of improvement in the quality of the labour force attributable to education. In our *Fifth Annual Review,* attention was drawn to the close association between lack of educational opportunities and individual poverty.

Our study of the important role of education in Canadian growth and development is continuing. In this article, we review certain basic national and regional trends in education and attempt to illuminate, in a preliminary way, some of the interprovincial disparities.

*Reproduced with the permission of the Queen's Printer for Canada, from the Economic Council of Canada, *Sixth Annual Review,* (Ottawa: Queen's Printer, 1969), pp. 123-134, 137-8.

THE NATIONAL PERSPECTIVE

Historically, progress in Canadian education has been substantial but uneven over time and between educational levels. In the first two decades of this century, great strides were made at the primary level. Literacy and elementary education were strongly and widely promoted. Unfortunately, this momentum was not maintained during the 1920's into the secondary and postsecondary levels, nor was it restored under the stresses and strains of depression and war. As a result, the growth in the quality of the labour force, as affected by education, was relatively slow for a number of decades, extending into the 1950's.

Following the Second World War, Canadian education expanded with renewed vigour. Apart from the heavy, but temporary, demand on the higher educational facilities in the immediate postwar years as a result of government financial assistance to veterans, the new dynamism was largely concentrated at the primary and secondary levels of education through the 1950's. In the 1960's, although further substantial advances have occurred at the secondary school level, the most conspicuous advances have taken place at the postsecondary level. The expansion of enrolment has reflected, among other things, the high postwar birth rates. But at the secondary and postsecondary levels, the longer retention of students in the educational system (the reduction of drop-outs) has been a much more important factor in the growth of enrolment.

As we near the end of the 1960's, Canadian educators can look back with pride to a decade of accomplishment and progress under difficult conditions. It has been a decade of vigorous educational mobilization. Some of the benefits are just beginning to be reaped by society. The main pay-off is yet to come.

Canada's educational enrolment in the postwar period increased faster than that in any other industrialized country. From school year 1951-52 to school year 1967-68 combined elementary and secondary enrolment more than doubled (secondary enrolment alone more than tripled), reaching a level close to 5½ million in 1967-68 (Table 1). During the same period, university full-time enrolment quadrupled, reaching a level of over 280,000 in 1967-68. Other postsecondary enrolment, starting from a very small base, increased at an even faster rate and reached 90,000 in 1967-68.

This impressive expansion in enrolment was accompanied by various related changes—a substantial increase in the number of educational institutions and classrooms and more generally in the scale and quality of educational facilities, widespread consolidation of rural schools, a large increase in the number of teachers and improvement in their average level of qualifications, a very large increase in part-time students in higher education and adult education and training, and the emergence of new types of educational institutions.

The sharp increase in retention rates in the postwar period has moved Canada closer to the U.S. levels of enrolment ratios. The narrowing of the gaps has been most evident at the secondary level (Table 2).

Table 1
Full-time Educational Enrolment

	1951-52	1967-68	PROJECTED 1975-76	PROJECTED 1980-81
		(Thousands)		
Elementary and Secondary				
Elementary	*2,230*	*4,128*	*3,886*	*3,777*
Secondary	*395*	*1,325*	*1,776*	*1,667*
Total	2,625	5,452	5,662	5,444
Postsecondary*				
University	*71*	*284*	*560*	*750*
Other postsecondary	*3*	*89*	*290*	*380*
Total	74	372	850	1,130
Total enrolment	2,699	5,824	6,512	6,574

*Postsecondary enrolment, in this Table (and in the rest of the [article]), includes full-time enrolment of students with at least junior matriculation standing in universities and other educational institutions variously described as community colleges, junior colleges, institutes of technology, colleges of applied arts and technology and *collèges d'enseignement général et professionel.* Enrolment in teachers' colleges has been included with that of universities. Enrolment in nurses' diploma programs has been included from 1967-68 in the "other postsecondary" category. There are, of course, many part-time students in addition to the full-time students indicated here.

Source: Based on data from Dominion Bureau of Statistics and projections in forthcoming Staff Study No. 25, *Enrolment in Educational Institutions by Province, 1951-52 to 1980-81,* by Z. Zsigmond and C. Wenaas .

Table 2
Secondary and University Enrolment Ratios, Canada and United States

	1951-52	1965-66	PROJECTED 1975-76
	(As percentage of 14-17 age group)		
Secondary enrolment			
Canada	46	80	94
United States	77	92	98
	(As percentage of 18-24 age group)		
Full-time university enrolment			
Canada	5	11	18
United States*	12	19	24

*Full-time degree credit enrolment in institutions of higher education.

Source: Based on data from U.S. Department of Health, Education and Welfare; Dominion Bureau of Statistics; and projections in forthcoming Staff Study No. 25.

However, at both the secondary and post secondary levels substantial differences remain.

The projections suggest that future growth in Canadian educational enrolment is likely to be less rapid than in the past two decades. Combined elementary and secondary enrolment is expected to decline absolutely after the mid-1970's, reflecting the sharp decline in total births since the early 1960's and the fact that the increase in secondary school enrolment ratios will moderate as they approach very high levels. On the other hand, both the enrolment ratios and the numbers of young people attending postsecondary educational institutions should continue to rise (but at a decreasing rate). The increase at the non-university level will be particularly rapid. Some further narrowing in the gaps in enrolment ratios between Canada and the United States can be anticipated.

Total full-time educational enrolment for 1980-81 is projected at 6.6 million, compared with 5.8 million in 1967-68 (Table 1). Elementary school enrolment is projected to decline from 4.1 million in 1967-68 to 3.9 million in 1975-76 and to 3.8 million in 1980-81. Secondary school enrolment is projected to increase from 1.3 million in 1967-68 to 1.8 million in 1975-76 and then decline to 1.7 million in 1980-81. In contrast, postsecondary enrolment is projected to more than double between 1967-68 and 1975-76 and then increase by almost one-third over the following five years, reaching about 1.1 million in 1980-81. The projected growth rate in postsecondary education between 1975-76 and 1980-81 applies to both universities and other postsecondary institutions. The growth rate of the latter up to 1975-76 is expected to exceed that of universities.

Given the slowing in the rate of expansion in enrolment at the primary and secondary levels, opportunities for making improvements in the quality of Canadian education should be substantial during the coming decade. Within a national perspective of many competing needs, the challenge will be to improve educational performance — the effectiveness of educational systems in Canada — in meeting the complex demands of a rapidly changing social and economic environment, such as those arising from the growing concentration of Canadians in large cities and in service industries. The challenges posed specifically for the educational system will largely need to be met at the level of the individual provinces. But the benefits to education spill over provincial boundaries, so that there is a need for greater interprovincial co-operation on many matters affecting education, as well as continued intergovernmental sharing of some of the financial costs of education.

REGIONAL TRENDS

Many important factors in addition to formal education are involved in the wide and persistent regional disparities in incomes across Canada. We have drawn attention to some of these factors in our earlier Reviews. Nevertheless, educational disparities appear to be one of the significant elements involved.

Significant progress has been made in recent years in improving the educational performance in all provinces and, more particularly, in

Table 3
Retention Rates, by Province

	1960-61	1967-68	PERCENTAGE CHANGE
Newfoundland	38	49	29
Prince Edward Island	36	66	84
Nova Scotia	47	65	37
New Brunswick	44	60	35
Quebec	33	70	113
Ontario	56	73	32
Manitoba	61	80	32
Saskatchewan	56	70	26
Alberta	64	79	23
British Columbia	68	82	22
Canada	50	71	42

Note: The retention rate refers to enrolment in Grade 11 as a percentage of Grade 2 enrolment nine years earlier. The data underlying the estimates have been adjusted to remove the effects of student migration.
Source: Based on data from Dominion Bureau of Statistics.

Table 4
Full-time Postsecondary Enrolment as Percentage of 18-24 Age Group, by Province

	1951-52	1960-61	1967-68
Newfoundland	1	3	10
Prince Edward Island	3	7	13
Nova Scotia	6	9	15
New Brunswick	4	8	15
Quebec	6	10	19
Ontario	5	8	15
Manitoba	5	8	15
Saskatchewan	3	8	14
Alberta	3	7	16
British Columbia	6	10	16
Canada	5	9	16

Source: Based on data from Dominion Bureau of Statistics.

reducing some of the interregional educational disparities. Interprovincial differences in school retention rates, for example, have been reduced (Table 3). Quebec and Prince Edward Island, which in 1960-61 had the lowest retention rates to Grade 11, have moved up sharply to close to the national average. Yet, substantial regional differences in retention rates remain, especially between the Atlantic Provinces and British Columbia, Manitoba and Alberta. Newfoundland, which still had a particularly low retention rate in 1967-68, faces a formidable challenge in spite of major gains in recent years.

All provinces have also shared in the expansion of education at the postsecondary level (Table 4). This is evident despite the fact that differences in educational organization among the provinces make valid comparisons difficult. In Quebec and Newfoundland, for example, the equivalent of Grade 12 is included in postsecondary enrolment while in Ontario, Grades 12 and 13 are in the secondary level. Moreover, because there are numerous out-of-province students enrolled in postsecondary education, especially in universities, the figures in Table 4 do not exactly reflect the rates of participation of provincial residents in post-secondary education.

The higher school-retention rates and enrolment ratios achieved by all provinces have had considerable effect on labour force quality. In only five years, from 1961 to 1966, there was almost as much increase in the average years of schooling in the labour force as in the preceding 10 years (Table 5). There has also been a reduction of interprovincial differences.[1] Throughout the period from 1951 to 1966, the average years of schooling of the labour force in the Atlantic Provinces has been increasing faster than for Canada as a whole. Although the average years of schooling of the Quebec labour force increased only slightly between 1951 and 1961, there was a sharp improvement there between 1961 and 1966.

It is also important to note that due to interprovincial migration, some provinces are gaining highly educated people from other provinces. Immigration from other countries also affects average levels. It is highly significant, however, that the Atlantic Region has achieved its above-average rate of improvement in the average educational attainments of its labour force, in spite of substantial net out-migration. Yet in 1966 a disparity of 1.8 years of schooling still existed between the highest and lowest regions of the country. This is a substantial gap. For example, it is twice as large as the *increase* in the average number of years of schooling in the whole Canadian labour force in the 15 years from 1951 to 1966; and it is larger than the 1961 *gap* of 1.1 years in the average number of years of schooling between Canada and the United States.

The impact of the developments in education will continue to be felt in all regions for many years to come. Even without any further increase in enrolment ratios, the average educational levels of the labour force would continue to increase for several decades. This means that it will be a long time before the impact of the present large expenditures on education may be fully evaluated.

Labour force quality will also improve in all provinces with the expected further increases in the proportion of young people attending educational institutions, the expansion of adult education, and manpower upgrading programs of many kinds. The enrolment projections to 1975 and 1980 suggest that there will be a further reduction in, although

Table 5
Average Years of Schooling of Labour Force, by Province and Region

	1951	1961	1966
Newfoundland	*6.9*	*8.2*	
Prince Edward Island	*8.3*	*8.8*	
Nova Scotia	*8.5*	*9.2*	
New Brunswick	*7.7*	*8.5*	
Atlantic Region	7.9	8.8	9.3
Quebec	8.1	8.2	8.7
Ontario	9.1	9.5	9.9
Manitoba	*8.5*	*9.3*	
Saskatchewan	*8.2*	*8.8*	
Alberta	*8.8*	*9.6*	
Prairie Region	8.5	9.3	9.7
British Columbia	9.3	10.1	10.5
Canada	8.6	9.1	9.6

Source: Based on data from Dominion Bureau of Statistics and estimates by Economic Council of Canada.

perhaps not a complete elimination of, remaining provincial differences in the proportion of young people attending elementary and secondary schools. All provinces should also share in the upward thrust of post-secondary enrolment although substantial disparities may still remain in this sector.

... Chart 1 illustrates the expected regional pattern of the changes in enrolment. Two features stand out. The first is that elementary and secondary enrolment is expected to decline generally in 1975-80, and in some regions before 1975. The second is the relatively high, but gradually declining, rate of increase in postsecondary enrolment — from an average annual rate of about 15 per cent in 1959-67 to about 10 per cent in 1967-75, and to about 5 per cent in 1975-80.

DIFFERENCES IN PROVINCIAL EDUCATIONAL PATTERNS

Provincial differences in education are reflected in various ways: in enrolment ratios, both in total and at different levels of education; in types of educational institutions, systems, programs, and curricula; in student-teacher ratios; in teacher qualifications; in other types of resources provided for education; and in the magnitude of expenditures

[1] It will be recognized that the data do not allow for any interprovincial differences in the *quality* of education. They are of an entirely quantitative nature.

Chart 1
Full-Time Educational Enrolment, by Region

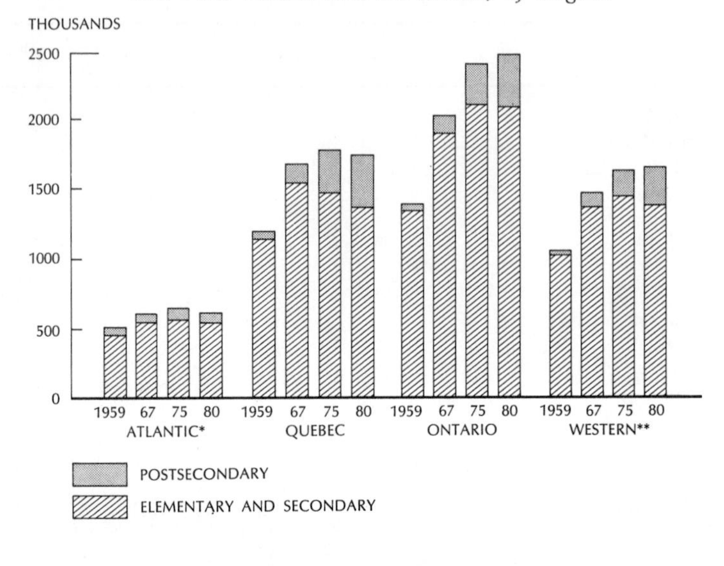

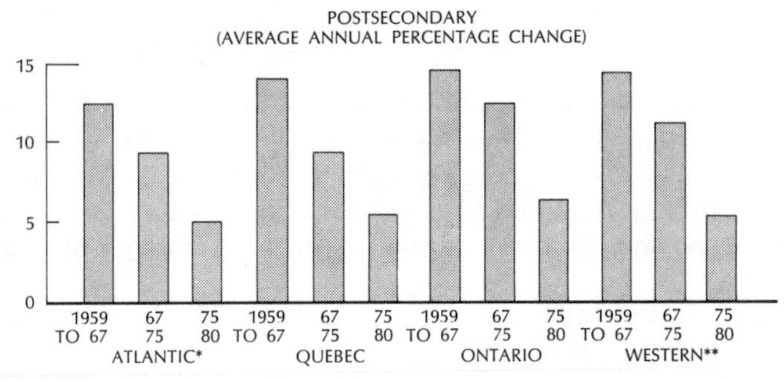

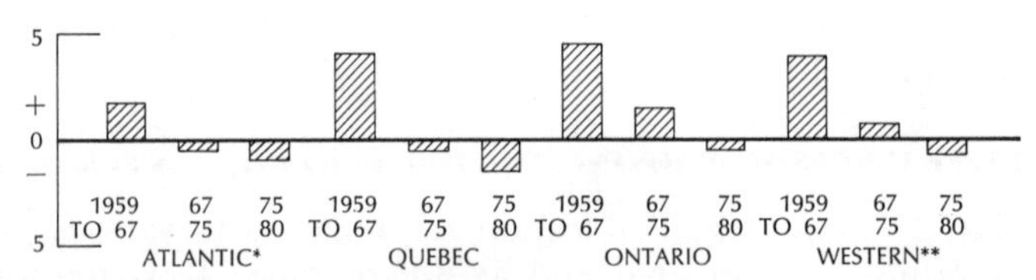

NOTE: These regional enrolment projections are affected by regional differences in fertility and migration rates. It has been assumed that fertility rates will undergo a further slight decline, and that interregional migration patterns will be similar to those of the recent past.

*Newfoundland, Prince Edward Island, Nova Scotia and New Brunswick.

**Manitoba, Saskatchewan, Alberta and British Columbia.

Source: Based on data from Dominion Bureau of Statistics and projections in forthcoming Staff Study No. 25.

per student and in total.[2] The differences are sometimes substantial and persistent, resulting from diverse combinations of cultural backgrounds and social attitudes, size of population and degree of urbanization, and, probably most of all, income levels and fiscal ability. Some of these provincial differences were discussed in the preceding section, and others are outlined below.

Structural Differences

An example of structural differences in education among the provinces is the difference in what is regarded as "elementary" and "secondary." In most provinces, Grades 1 to 8 are classified as elementary, but, in Quebec and British Columbia, Grade 7 is the final elementary grade and it will be changed from Grade 7 to Grade 6 in Quebec in the future. Moreover, the number of grades in the total elementary and secondary school system ranges from 11 to 13 with varying provisions for completing a senior matriculation year at university or other postsecondary institutions. The equivalent of Grade 12 is offered at university in Newfoundland rather than in the public school system, as in all other provinces except Quebec. The twelfth and thirteenth years in Quebec are offered at the *collèges d'enseignement général et professionnel (CEGEP),* which are neither universities nor secondary schools. There are wide differences both within and between provinces in postsecondary education. Further changes in the structure of education within various provinces can be expected in the future.

Student-Teacher Ratios

For Canada as a whole, in the school year 1966-67, there were approximately 29 students per teacher in elementary schools, 16 students per teacher in secondary schools and about 13 students per teacher at universities and colleges.[3] In part, these differences are accounted for by the greater number of subject options — and correspondingly greater staff — available at progressively higher levels of the system. At the university level, class sizes for first-year students are typically large — often much larger than at either the elementary or secondary level — but tend to fall rapidly in succeeding years of instruction. In part, too, the differences reflect the attempt to allow for more class preparation and research at the higher levels of education.

In spite of substantial variations among provinces in resources and

[2] The data on elementary and secondary education in this section are for public schools only, as defined by the Dominion Bureau of Statistics. This definition covers all schools "operated by local school boards or boards of education and supported by local taxation, including Roman Catholic and Protestant separate schools where such exist, and the denominational schools of Newfoundland." Over 90 per cent of total student enrolment in all provinces is covered by this definition.

[3] These data relate full-time student enrolment to full-time teaching staff. At elementary and secondary schools, principals and vice-principals are included with teaching staff even if they may not actually teach any classes. Specialist teachers are included whether or not they have a home classroom.

social and economic environment, most of the provinces had quite similar student-teacher ratios in elementary and secondary schools in 1966-67 (Table 6). In elementary schools, Prince Edward Island and Saskatchewan, reflecting their relatively larger rural component, had student-teacher ratios that were more than 10 per cent below the national average. British Columbia was substantially above the average. In secondary schools, Newfoundland was more than 20 per cent above the average while Prince Edward Island was about 10 per cent above. Although some provinces exhibited declining student-teacher ratios in elementary schools after 1960, the average for Canada had increased slightly by 1966. In contrast, the student-teacher ratios in secondary schools declined for Canada as a whole. For most provinces regional differences in student-teacher ratios at the postsecondary level are wider than at the elementary and secondary levels – reflecting, among other things, substantial differences among the universities in faculty orientation and course content. The range in 1965-66 was from about 15 full-time students per full-time teacher in the western Canadian universities to about 11 in Ontario.[4]

A lower student-teacher ratio may enhance the quality of education by providing the opportunity for greater individual attention by teachers and perhaps a greater variety of course offerings, although there may be significant exceptions. In a small school with only a few rooms, for instance, a low student-teacher ratio may exist with one teacher teaching all courses in several grades to a few pupils and accordingly unable to give as much individual attention as in a larger metropolitan school with higher student-teacher ratios. Student-teacher ratios in metropolitan areas have been declining for a number of reasons associated with rising quality, such as additional course offerings, new methods of teaching including team teaching, more effective language instruction requiring smaller classes, and greater individualization of instruction calling for more preparation and less time actually spent teaching.

Concluding Observations

This article has outlined trends and regional differences in formal full-time education. We caution, however, that it has left out some very important aspects of education. These include educational differences within provinces, which may be greater than differences among provinces, as well as part-time and nonformal education (e.g. adult education, in-plant training and retraining) which are increasingly important in a world of accelerating obsolescence of knowledge and skills.

The discussion has not drawn any specific policy implications . . . What [it] does do, however, is to raise certain questions about the performance of the educational system and to suggest additional areas that might well be investigated.

Questions are now arising about the possible relevance for educational performance of various changes in educational systems and patterns. What, for instance, would be the benefits from a more extensive

Table 6
Student-Teacher Ratios, Elementary and Secondary Schools, by Province
(Average number of students per teacher)

	1966-67	
	ELEMENTARY	SECONDARY
Newfoundland	28	20
Prince Edward Island	23	18
Nova Scotia	29	16
New Brunswick	28	17
Quebec	30	15
Ontario	28	17
Manitoba	27	17
Saskatchewan	25	17
Alberta	29	14
British Columbia	34	16
Canada	29	16

Source: Based on data from provincial Departments of Education and Dominion Bureau of Statistics.

kindergarten system as an alternative to one year of secondary schooling, or the substitution of one year of college for a secondary school year, or increasing use of new educational technology in place of a further reduction in student-teacher ratios, or the introduction of more flexible curricula as an alternative to the establishment of new institutions? Very little research has yet been done on many fundamental questions of this nature.

We are not suggesting that past decisions based on experience and sometimes even intuition have not produced beneficial results. But it does seem clear that in the future a more intensive assessment of the effects of alternative developments and of alternative allocations of resources in this field will be required. Also needed is a better understanding of the learning process itself. Obviously all of these matters will require much greater expenditures on educational research and analysis than are presently being made . . .

[4] In 1965-66, full-time enrolment and full-time teaching staff at Canadian universities were 200,000 and 16,000, respectively; there were also nearly 75,000 part-time students and about 9,000 part-time teachers.

4. *Canada's Rural Poor**

John Harp

In 1961 Canada ranked among the most urban countries in the world. Indeed the levels of urbanization reported for Canada and the United States are quite similar.[1]

Since the country is becoming increasingly urban, one can anticipate a tendency to overlook the rural poor. Harrington's notion of hidden poverty can well be applied directly to this sector of our society. The Canadian Association for Adult Education (C.A.A.E.) brochure gives an insightful description of the spatial distribution of the poor in Canada.

We find them [rural poor] *in a hundred minor locales where really bad lands merge with land which at one economic upswing or other might just possibly have been able to sustain a homestead for a time at least, and trap a homesteader and his family for a generation or two. Rural poor are found even in areas of good land and generally successful farms, but they are not numerous in such areas, and perhaps their problem is generically different from the problems of those who live in areas where low income is the norm.*[2]

Apart from their geographical isolation, other reasons for the invisible character of the rural poor derive from the special problems of measuring rural poverty. Buckley and Tihanyi's comprehensive analysis of rural adjustment policies documents certain limitations of the 1961 Census in its coverage of the farm population.[3] There are both conceptual and operational difficulties in measuring net farm income. The following summary results are provided by Buckley and Tihanyi and specify some dimensions of the problem.

1) At the beginning of this decade the average urban family income was $5,796; *in contrast, farm families averaged only* $3,645, *that is,* 37 *per cent less.*

* An original article prepared for this volume.

2) Out of 1.1 million families who resided in rural areas one half million or 44 per cent were poor — two fifths of the rural poor were families, three fifths were nonfarmers.

3) Roughly one third of the poorest farmers in Canada resided in counties which would rightly qualify as 'pockets of rural poverty' but two thirds of the hard core poor were dispersed in the more prosperous agricultural regions.[4]

Assuming that income data on farms were equal to the task of measuring rural poverty, we would still have ignored the non-economic aspects of the problem. Poverty is much more than income, for it also includes aspirations, wants and needs of rural people. Furthermore there are surely differences in standards of living which would lead us to examine the nature of housing, schools and social services in rural areas. Bonnen's statement about rural communities in the United States also applies to the Canadian rural scene: "One is forced to conclude that as an environment for the development of human capacities many rural communities are failures and have been for generations."[5]

We must begin by attempting to identify the various rural subpopulations that are affected by poverty. The General Census definition of farmer is obviously too inclusive for analytical purposes, for the population is extremely heterogeneous. There is a definite need for a more adequate methodology including criteria to measure efficiencies in the farming economy. More specifically we need a clear distinction between what is a viable economic unit and one destined to poverty. Given the present data we can begin by examining Canadian farms by economic class and value of agricultural sales. Buckley and Tihanyi suggest that "near the lower end of the $5,000–$7,499 gross sales/farm range there could be cases of destitution where the farm operation requires unusually high cost expenditures." We also have a situation where all farmers with gross sales of less than *$5,000* and representing 55 per cent of the total contribute only 14 per cent of the agricultural sales in Canada. This class of small farms represented 238,000 farms in 1966. The pressures for increased scale of operation in agriculture have been widely discussed and are dramatically shown by the 50 per cent decline in farms with less than $5,000 sales during the interval 1951-61.

The solution implied in increasing farm size is open to few farmers and this for a variety of reasons: for example, the lack of managerial

[1] Leroy O. Stone, *Urban Development in Canada,* D.B.S. Monograph, 1967.

[2] Canadian Association for Adult Education, *The Sixties: Rural Poverty: What Can A.R.D.A. Do?* (Toronto: C.A.A.E., 1966).

[3] Helen Buckley and Eva Tihanyi, *Canadian Policies for Rural Adjustment, A Study of the Economic Impact of ARDA, PFRA, and MMRA.* Prepared for the Economic Council of Canada, (Ottawa: Queen's Printer, 1967).

[4] *Ibid.,* Chapter 2.

[5] James T. Bonnen, "Rural Poverty: Programs and Problems," *Journal of Farm Economics,* May 1966, Vol. 48, No. 2.

Table 1
Canadian Farms by Economic Class in 1966

GROSS VALUE OF AGRICULTURAL SALES PER FARM	FARMS		GROSS VALUE OF AGRICULTURAL SALES, TOTAL		VALUE OF FARM CAPITAL, TOTAL	
$	NO.	PER CENT	$ MILLIONS	PER CENT	$ MILLIONS	PER CENT
35,000 & over	10,282	2.4	778	23.3	1,823	9.5
24,000 – 34,999	9,384	2.2	273	8.2	1,104	5.7
15,000 – 24,999	31,149	7.2	586	17.5	2,885	15.0
10,000 – 14,999	44,217	10.3	536	16.0	3,056	15.9
7,500 – 9,999	38,753	9.0	335	10.0	2,105	10.9
5,000 – 7,499	58,103	13.5	357	10.7	2,510	13.1
3,750 – 4,999	37,923	8.8	164	4.9	1,302	6.8
2,500 – 3,749	47,024	10.9	145	4.3	1,333	6.9
1,200 – 2,499	60,947	14.1	110	3.3	1,376	7.2
250 – 1,199	55,271	12.8	37	1.1	857	4.5
50 – 249	36,692	8.5	3	.1	547	2.8
Total	430,522	100.0	3,338	100.0	19,075	100.0

Source: The 1966 Census of Canada.

Table 2
The Geography of Small-scale Farming in Canada, 1966

	SMALL FARMS (SALES UNDER $5,000)		
PROVINCE OR REGION	NUMBER	PER CENT OF ALL FARMS IN REGION	PER CENT OF ALL SMALL FARMS IN CANADA
Atlantic provinces, Total	20,634	78.2	8.7
Quebec, Total	57,798	72.0	24.3
Northern fringe, Ontario	5,152	79.2	2.2
Northern fringe, Prairies	11,664	78.6	4.9
8 Counties, eastern Ontario	9,899	73.6	4.2
9 Counties, central and eastern Ontario	12,713	60.4	5.3
Parkbelt, Prairies	36,620	55.7	15.4
British Columbia, Total	13,054	68.5	5.5
All other, Ontario	30,326	44.1	12.7
All other, Prairies	39,997	35.3	16.8
Canada	237,857	55.2	100.0

Source: The 1966 Census of Canada.

Table 3
Comparison of Work Off-farm by Economic Class, 1961 and 1966

GROSS SALES PER FARM	PER CENT OF FARM OPERATORS REPORTING WORK OFF-FARM				AVER. NUMBER OF DAYS PER OPERATOR REPORTING 1–365 DAYS WORK OFF-FARM	
	1–365 DAYS		229–365 DAYS			
	1961	1966	1961	1966	1961	1966
$35,000 and over / 25,000 – 34,999	12	20	3	4	128	100
15,000 – 24,999	14	21	3	3	110	79
10,000 – 14,999	15	22	2	3	100	86
5,000 – 9,999	17	29	3	4	102	101
3,750 – 4,999	21	36	4	7	112	116
2,500 – 3,749	26	43	6	10	125	127
1,200 – 2,499	36	50	9	15	140	148
250 – 1,199	52	59	15	23	165	176
50 – 249	60	55	25	27	195	199
Total	32	38	9	11	148	139

Source: The 1961 and 1966 Census of Canada.

ability, the rising costs of land and restrictions in the availability of credit. A strategy practised by an increasing number of farmers is to obtain off-farm employment. Indeed, this has been suggested by some social planners as an alternative to the up or out hypothesis as applied to agriculture. There is insufficient evidence at present to know whether part-time farming is a transitory or a permanent phase for the structure of agricultural occupations. There is no doubt that it has become a pervasive pattern throughout agriculture as shown by the fact that 4 out of 10 Canadian farmers are employed to some degree in a non-farm job. Fragmentary evidence from several studies done in the United States suggests that many farmers regard their off-farm employment as a temporary phenomenon facilitating their return to full-time farming.

As to the Canadian scene, important regional differences in both amount and kind of off-farm employment undoubtedly exist. The pattern so well established in certain parts of the Maritimes where farming is combined with logging, fishing and trapping stands in sharp contrast to off-farm employment in urban occupations by farmers in Ontario. Buckley, reporting on unpublished Census data, claims that off-farm employment of the farm operator put more families above the poverty line in 1966 than in 1961. Nevertheless, if one is to view part-time farming as a transition to urban employment, opportunities for such employment must exist in the locale. There are, of course, innumerable barriers to mobility of the kind suggested by movement out of farming into urban occupations. Individuals must first be motivated to seek out and accept urban occupations.

Any programs designed to facilitate this overall mobility process must begin with some criteria for determining who is to be encouraged to stay and who will be assisted in obtaining employment other than farming. We are still without data that can provide us with a "clear distinction between what is a viable economic unit and one destined to poverty."[6] Buckley offers what is probably an accurate approximation of the nature of the macro-problem:

There are 430,000 farms in Canada. Perhaps only a third or so are — by today's standard — large enough for long-term viability. But the rest is not a homogenous group of problem people. Roughly they fall into two groups of about equal size — [a strata of poor and] a middle strata of moderately well off whose future may be uncertain but whose present needs are met at least at a minimum level. The middle group could greatly benefit from well designed long-term policies, helping some to viability, others to off-farm occupations. What distinguishes the really poor third of the farming population from the middle strata is the urgency of their needs.[7]

STRATEGIES OF PLANNED CHANGE: IMPLICATIONS FOR RURAL POVERTY

The purpose of the following discussion is not to review federal programs aimed at the elimination of poverty but to outline strategies of planned change that often form the basis of government policy. A majority of the relevant research on the strategies under review is based on data from the United States. Any extrapolation of these results to the Canadian scene must be done with full recognition of both similarities and differences in the nature of the rural poverty problems within the two societies.

The major types of strategies advanced to date, do have a striking similarity in both countries. One finds, for example, a continuing process of urbanization including the migration of rural residents to urban areas. The current debate centres on whether the natural state process of migration will solve the rural poverty problems, in other words, whether people will move on their own initiative from depressed to more developed population centres. Again, in the United States serious questions have been raised as to the effectiveness of this process in alleviating the poverty of migrants. The 1967 Manpower Report of the President suggests, "the rate of economic development in or accessible to rural areas needed to absorb all of the rural labour force seems at the moment far beyond the realm of achievement." Nor do we find much empirical support for economic growth by itself as a promising path for the quick reduction of poverty.

Anderson, in a much-quoted article, reports:

To the extent that low wages and near poverty incomes depend upon the absorption of the rural poor into the urban poor, a great deal of growth in income can take place without reducing the population in poverty. This is true to the extent the urban poor contribute more to measured GNP than the rural poor. Because of the chronic surplus of labour from the rural sectors, the U.S. in part may be an enclave economy similar to many underdeveloped countries. In an enclave economy as long as the reservoir of rural poor is full, a great deal of process without any substantial improvement in the lot of the poor can take place.[8]

The presence of these so-called "enclave economies" in Canada is part of the analyses of regional economic disparities by economists such as Brewis and others.[9]

Hathaway offers additional research evidence to dispel a common belief that occupational mobility will tend to reduce disparities in income between individuals and areas. Conventional wisdom again looks to migration to solve the low income farm problem. The first qualification to keep in mind is that gross data often show migration and not occupational mobility. Furthermore, they are not adjusted for age distribution and other social characteristics. A few salient results of this research warrant repeating, for they have broad implications for agricultural policy. Using a population of individuals classified as farm wage workers or farm operatives under Social Security, Hathaway reports:

1) Most farm workers do not migrate far, nor does long distance migration pay economic dividends.

2) More than 40% of those changing from farm to non-farm employment had lower earnings in their non-farm job than the last year in their farm job. A majority of those with this experience return to farm employment.

3) Much of the low income problem in agriculture may be transferred to rural non-farm and urban poverty by the mobility process.

[6] Alex McCalla, "A Review and Appraisal of Agricultural Policies in Canada," plenary paper presented to the Canadian Agricultural Economics Society, Thirteenth Annual Workshop, Guelph, University of Guelph, Ontario, 1968.

[7] Helen Buckley, "A Report to the Federal Task Force on Agriculture," Canadian Agricultural Congress, Ottawa, 1969 (Reproduced with the permission of Information Canada).

[8] W. Locke Anderson, "Trickling Down: The Relation Between Economic Growth and the Extent of Poverty Among American Families," *Quarterly Journal of Economics,* 78:4 (November 1964), pp. 511-24.

[9] It should be noted that not all observers of the Canadian scene are equally optimistic about the efficacy of a growth centre strategy. Professor Brewis comments that: "It is one thing, however, to reach agreement on such general observations as ... [the structural complexity of urban centres] and quite another to proceed to a selection of centres which are to serve as the focal points of growth, or to decide on the form that their development should take. Moreover the efficacy of such centres in promoting the development of the areas in which they are located is far from clear." See T. N. Brewis, *Regional Economic Policies in Canada,* (Toronto: Macmillan Company of Canada, 1968).

4) There is no evidence to suggest that the low-income area problem will be solved by the process of mobility. Indeed, off-farm mobility rates are not higher in low-income rural areas.[10]

These results have particular implications for the Canadian scene when the reader recalls that over one-third of the poor farms in Canada are located in areas where their proportion is so high that the areas themselves could be classified as poor.[11]

In addition to Hathaway's insightful analysis, which could profitably be repeated in terms of Canada, Duncan and Cowhig, working with data from the Current Population Survey of the Bureau of the Census and using a population of males in the 20–64 age group, answer some important questions about farm workers. For example, data on inter-generational occupational mobility may come as a surprise to those emphasizing the ascribed character of agricultural occupations. The authors find that only one respondent in nine had a father who was a farm labourer at the time the respondent was sixteen. It would appear that a majority of the present incumbents are recruited via downward mobility and not the inheritance of poverty.[12] Duncan and Cowhig emphasize the direct implications of their work for public policy:

If this nation does not do some forward thinking, it may soon be spending prodigious sums of public and private money to reverse its passively assumed solution that the rural poverty problem was to be solved by moving it to the city.[13]

Once again caution must be expressed in applying these results to the Canadian scene. We lack research of this scope at the present time. The salient results of a highly relevant but limited research project on the migration of farm operators in Canada deserve consideration.[14]

Although the sample for this study is quite restrictive, the analysis provides insights for future study of the adjustment problems encountered by rural migrants. The sample consists of one hundred farm operators living in Saskatoon but excluding sons of farmers who migrated, farm labourers or retired farmers. The author, Jane Abramson, reports that a self awareness of the respondents' inability to farm according to progressive standards was a factor influencing migration. The decision is further described as a "forced choice" for many farmers. Salient characteristics of the sample are as follows: median age 45, median formal schooling 7.6 years, and 45 per cent with less than $5,000 in assets.

Abramson speaks of a "clustering of disadvantages" for this group. For example, their unemployment rate at the time of the interview was nearly three times that of the Saskatoon labour force and more than half were employed in unskilled or primary occupations. These objective social facts are also reflected in the respondents' evaluations of their position: "rather than regarding city employment as a step toward upward mobility, many respondents considered it to be a come-down from the status of independent farm operator."[15]

Examining these studies and other related research, the question remains: How can we effectively intervene in the migration process in order to ensure that the end result will reduce the adjustment problems of migrants and alleviate poverty? The recently established (1965) Department of Manpower and Immigration coordinates a number of services which now receive a new emphasis. Occupational training, a knowledge about job opportunities, and assistance to movers are included among mobility programs. The participant's age is a crucial factor in programs of this type and for two basic reasons. First, the older age groups have fewer productive years remaining in the labour force and receptivity to new training plus attitudes towards changing job locations are often negatively associated with age. This would seem to suggest that an important subpopulation is represented by rural youth who also comprise a high proportion of the migrants. In this regard I refer specifically to the social determinants of levels of aspirations and expectations for this segment of the rural population. It is with this particular subpopulation that one can be most optimistic of achieving desired results.

On the macro or societal level, research on the relationship between educational attainment and income level shows a positive relationship.[16] Education appears to be a profitable investment both for the individual and for society. Negative correlations between educational level and economic poverty are widely reported for Canada.[17] Indeed, education comprises the most important single class of variables in accounting for variations in occupational achievement. This area of research is important in understanding further limitations of rural to urban migration as a panacea. One must remember that a significant change has occurred in the composition of the rural population – namely, the majority of those

[10] Dale E. Hathaway, "Occupational Mobility and Migration from Agriculture," in *Rural Poverty in the United States.* A report to the President's National Advisory Commission on Rural Poverty, Washington, D.C., May 1968, pp. 185-213.

[11] H. Buckley and E. Tihanyi, *Canadian Policies for Rural Adjustment,* Canadian Centre for Community Studies, Saskatoon, Saskatchewan, December 1966 (Reproduced with the permission of Information Canada).

[12] Otis D. Duncan and James D. Cowhig, *Social Backgrounds and Occupational Commitment of Male Wage Workers in Agriculture,* U.S. Census, Washington, D.C.

[13] *Ibid.*

[14] Jane A. Abramson, *Rural to Urban Adjustment,* ARDA Research Report No. RE-4, May 1968.

[15] *Ibid.,* p. 67.

[16] Podoluk reports that, "A ranking of male occupations by size of average annual earnings shows that occupations in the lowest deciles are characterized by limited education and substantial inequality resulting from insecurity of employment in these occupations and erratic employment problems." See J. R. Podoluk, *Earnings and Education,* Dominion Bureau of Statistics, Central Research and Development Staff, December 1965.

[17] For a review of research on this topic see, G. Albert Kristjanson and Rachel Alterman, "Vocational and Educational Aspirations and Achievements of Rural Youth," a position paper for the Task Force on Agriculture, September 1968, p. 4.

classified as rural are no longer engaged in farming. Added to this fact is the high migration rate for farm youth and the well documented inadequacies of their educational experience for survival in an urban environment. These data reaffirm my earlier statement that migration will not solve the problem of poverty, "for those who leave are marginal men in the new urban or semi-urban milieu."[18] On the subject of educational outcomes Kristjanson concludes that:

1) Rural youth tend to drop out earlier and are found in unskilled occupations.

2) The minority populations (Indians, Metis, Eskimo), have significantly lower levels of education than other rural populations.[19]

The general quality of education on the rural scene leaves much to be desired, with one-room schools and variability of teachers' salaries heading the list of inequities.[20] One concludes from the voluminous research on this topic in both the United States and Canada that school and home environments are less conducive to higher educational achievements in rural compared with urban areas. This results in many capable youth not attending university and consequently failing to receive a formal education commensurate with their ability.

Related to these situational and social determinants of educational opportunity is that complex of factors referred to as achievement values and levels of aspiration, both educational and vocational. There appears to be some limited evidence to support an increase in achievement values for the rural population, but measures of occupational or vocational aspiration are not always consistent with this pattern. Connor and Magill, for example, have commented on the unrealistic nature of professional aspirations of many rural youth.[21] These results are not necessarily a contradiction of Abramson's conclusions regarding more positive attitudes towards education among primary workers in underdeveloped areas.[22] It is important to separate unrealistic vocational aspirations by rural youth from an overall change in a generalized achievement value.

The implications of this research for educational programs is to emphasize the need for more information in the rural areas as to the kinds of occupations available. A partial answer to this problem rests with improvements in guidance counselling and more comprehensive public information about occupations and employment opportunities. All of the research on this topic to date serves to confirm our predictions that the educationally deprived are none other than the poor. What else can be done in this area, apart from costly improvements in the quality of education available to rural residents? Although the natural migration process has certain definite limitations for the reasons cited earlier, planned migration offers a constructive alternative.

Obviously, much more is required than simply "informing farm people of non-farm employment opportunities and personal adjustments required for new employment and new living environments," but these are surely necessary beginnings. Heady speaks to the point in the following statement:

Information and service should not be restricted to the sending end of transfers, but should be extended to the receiving end as well. Migrating farm families also need help in making friends, finding housing, becoming integrated into a community and so forth.[23]

In summary, then, if rural to urban migration continues — and many people have suggested that it will — and if rural areas cannot provide jobs for all who need jobs, then the debate as to whether rural poverty should be ameliorated in rural or in urban areas is pointless. No real choice exists. The problem of rural poverty must obviously be addressed in both rural and urban areas.[24] As always, a crucial question concerns the problem of who should be encouraged to migrate or remain.

An ideal complement of strategies designed to aid mobility and insure occupational training for that segment of the farm population for whom farming is not a viable alternative probably does not exist at the present time. Furthermore, there are those who are too old to make drastic changes in life styles. Migration of these individuals to urban areas, assuming this were possible, would not solve the rural poverty problem but only add numbers to the urban relief rolls. One is led to conclude, therefore, that a comprehensive poverty program must consider not only individuals but the communities in which they live. We must be concerned with evaluations of the differential needs of various subgroups of the rural poor. All of these questions can best be treated in a comprehensive regional planning approach to the problems of rural poverty. We are invariably caught up by the interdependent character of problems in an industrial society.

DEVELOPMENT STRATEGIES

Local Industry for Rural Areas

An important strategy in Canadian poverty programs is to create new jobs in unemployed and underemployed areas. The Area Development Agency, established in 1963 under the Department of Industry and now part of the Department of Regional and Economic Expansion, has used tax exemptions and capital grants to induce plants to locate in cer-

[18] *Ibid.*

[19] *Ibid.*

[20] See D. R. Whyte, "Rural Canada in Transition," Chapter 1 in W. Anderson and M. Tremblay (eds.), *Rural Canada in Transition,* Agricultural Economic Council, 1966.

[21] Desmond Connor and D. W. Magil, *The Role of Education in Rural Development,* ARDA Research Report, Ottawa: Department of Regional and Economic Expansion (formerly Department of Forestry and Rural Development), 1965.

[22] Jane A. Abramson, *Adjustments Associated with Migration from Farm Operator to Urban Earner,* Canadian Centre for Community Studies, Saskatoon, Saskatchewan, 1966.

[23] Earl Heady, *A Primer on Food, Agriculture and Public Policy* (New York: Random House Publications, 1967), pp. 110-11.

[24] Lee Rainwater, "Social and Cultural Problems of Migrants to Cities," in *Rural Poverty in the United States,* a report by the President's National Advisory Commission on Rural Poverty, May 1968.

tain areas. It should also be noted that provincial, local or private agencies are often engaged in similar activities.

One of the major problems with the overall strategy is that it tends to endorse a narrow economic approach to development.[25] Furthermore, some economists have suggested that the location of industry in rural areas will not occur given freedom of decision by industry. Apart from considerations of transportation and communication, the low quality of rural labour continues to be the major deterrent to employment. Suggestions of a wage subsidy program limited to the re-employment of rural labour have been put forth as a useful device in attracting industry to rural communities. Apart from the risk of further regional disparities, the subsidy would not solve rural unemployment nor would it eliminate rural poverty. Abramson's study of population mobility in the Atlantic provinces and Quebec shows the relationship between kind of industry and standard of living.

Talk about bringing in new industry, or the introduction of small-scale low-paying industries which will have little impact on the level of income or standard of living, may do worse than simply continue a subsistence level of living for the majority of working class people in the area. It may diminish out-migration and attach a backflow of earlier out-migrants with the result that the employment situation may be worsened rather than improved.[26]

It would appear much more efficacious to begin with a conception of development that includes a realistic appraisal of the labour potential in the region. One is led to concur with Abramson in advocating investments in health, housing, vocational education, and cultural and political development as a "surer route to human development than subsidies to small industries."[27]

Growth Centre Concept

Many of these ideas form part of a comprehensive approach to regional development which makes use of the growth centre concept. The latter is usually defined as "a point to which the population is brought together from a number of diverse places to provide a minimum viable urban size."[28] Understandably, consensus is lacking as to the *ideal* size of a growth centre, but current work on community growth and decline can offer valuable insights.

The advantages of this approach over the single industry idea are manifold and derive from the greater diversity of functional activities in the growth centre. A more highly differentiated social organization has a greater potential for further growth and development. Drawing extensively on Borts' discussion of the advantages in such a system, we conclude that:

1) A centralizing residence pattern can contribute to the continued urbanization of the population in addition to providing a necessary diversified labour pool.

2) In addition, the centre can serve as a "staging area" for migrants who will move to a larger city. Recognizing the adjustment problems alluded to by research in this topic, the advantages are self-evident.

3) The more direct advantages that derive from division of labour in a more complex social unit will also include a broader range of services available to the population in the hinterland.[29]

It can be seen that this particular strategy requires a highly sophisticated degree of social planning. Ideally, it suggests the creation of centres with a mixed population composition, including residents from congested urban areas and unemployed or underemployed rural. This is not to be confused with a natural migration strategy that simply involves moving people to the cities. Moreover, there is some research evidence to justify more serious consideration of comprehensive social and economic development programs that recognize the importance of growth centres. Hathaway, for example, has shown that "the probability of off-farm employment is highest for young multiple-job wage workers located in countries within 50 miles of an S.M.S.A. [Standard Metropolitan Statistical Area]."[30] We have also pointed out that off-farm mobility rates are not higher in low-income rural areas. Reliance on small local labour markets will result only in a low probability of a farmer successfully moving out of farm employment.

In conclusion, the growth centre strategy, when incorporated as part of comprehensive regional planning, would also seem to offer the best hope for minimizing the myriad social maladjustments that often accompany rural to urban migration. Sociologists and social scientists in related disciplines can assist by providing planners with certain kinds of intelligence. At present, for example, there is a dearth of research on comparative community or regional social systems analysis in Canada. More attention must be given to the simple task of completing an inventory of community capital. I refer in part to such items as facilities and organizations used to produce public services for communities.[31] Maki succinctly identifies certain key variables we must understand and explore if social planners are to function with maximum efficiency.

[25] Buckley and Tihanyi refer to development as ". . . the promotion of growth in the locale where the citizens of ARDA concern presently reside." Buckley and Tihanyi, *op. cit.*, p. 117.

[26] Jane A. Abramson, *Barriers to Population Mobility: From Economically Lagging Areas in the Atlantic Provinces and Quebec*, ARDA, Ottawa, June 1968.

[27] *Ibid.*

[28] George H. Borts, "Patterns of Regional Economic Development in the United States and Their Relation to Rural Poverty," in *Rural Poverty in the United States, op. cit.*, pp. 130-46.

[29] These ideas are treated in a more comprehensive manner by Borts. *Ibid.*, pp. 130-40.

[30] Hathaway, *op. cit.*, p. 202.

[31] Maki speaks of this as infrastructure. Wilber R. Maki, "Infrastructure in Rural Areas," in *Rural Poverty in the United States, op. cit.*, p. 86.

Lack of rural economic growth and development is fundamentally a function of low resource productivity, which in turn is influenced by a variety of considerations including the community and social capital that is a prerequisite for acquiring the individual skills and social attitudes that make possible high rates of resource productivity.[32]

The decision to give preferential treatment to certain depressed regions or areas in the country can be made only with due regard to the full range of strategies to alleviate poverty. These would include guaranteed incomes, negative income tax or assistance to migrate.

[32] *Ibid.*, p. 86.

5. *The Third Solitude**

Emile Gosselin

Poverty and its companion, misery, have ceased to be felt by a portion of the population of the Montreal area. Our life as it is presently organized does not expose us to poverty, so that the poor have become invisible, along with their problems and their destitution. Our individual and collective conscience is no longer shocked. We have become insensitive to poverty.

The city in which we believe we are living, with which we are familiar, is the city of skyscrapers and huge housing developments. The city we pretend to see is the city of the large building projects and wide boulevards which we are developing. Our conscience is put at peace by the rhythm of the city. We are impressed with the affluence of the scene but our octopus-like metropolis hides deep mires of misery.

The citizen who takes a comfortable drive to his office or his shop is more worried about getting a sufficient wage increase than about becoming unemployed. Memories of the 1929 and subsequent depressions are becoming fainter and fainter and are pushed back into oblivion like so many nightmares. The citizen is trying to convince himself that he is now living in an economy of affluence in which all may share without exception. Everything tends to suggest that it will always be so.

The present and immediate future cause less and less worry to the individual who earns a decent living. He is repeatedly told that, should it become necessary, the whole organized society, supported (as it claims to be) by plans for economic expansion, a flexible financial system, and adequate fiscal and monetary measures, will rush to his assistance. There is an attempt made to assure the citizenry that economic and social assistance will be at their disposal should there be a crisis. And will not various retirement programs reward such a satisfactory existence? As is

*Reprinted, with amendments to the translation, with permission of the author, from The Third Solitude, Montreal Labour Council, 1966.

repeated in some quarters, there is no cause for anyone to be poor unless he so desires, because we have solutions to all our social and economic problems. Yet . . .

NUMBERS OF POOR

Over twenty per cent of the families in Montreal live in poverty.* The poor who make up these families can hardly raise themselves out of this poverty, despite the economic and technical progress of the metropolitan area (Table 1).

Table 1
Family Incomes in the Montreal Metropolitan District

METROPOLITAN DISTRICT			MONTREAL		SUBURBS		
	NO.	%	NO.	%	NO.	%	% MTL.
Total	483,496	100	277,740	100	205,756	100	57.4
- 1,000	15,375	3.2	10,041	3.6	5,334	2.6	65.3
1,000– 1,999	25,359	5.2	17,258	6.2	8,101	4.0	68.1
2,000– 2,999	42,235	8.7	28,567	10.3	13,668	6.7	67.6
3,000– 3,999	79,222	16.4	50,035	18.0	29,187	14.2	63.1
4,000– 4,999	82,536	17.1	48,708	17.5	33,828	16.4	59.0
5,000– 6,999	112,328	23.3	61,308	23.2	51,020	24.8	54.5
7,000– 9,999	73,566	15.2	37,955	13.7	35,611	17.3	51.6
10,000–14,999	34,168	7.1	16,517	6.0	17,651	8.5	45.4
15,000 and over	18,707	3.9	7,351	2.6	11,356	5.5	39.3
Average	6,046				6,771		

Source: D.B.S. Census of Canada, 1961, Vol. IV, 4-13.

Should not recent large investments and tremendous technological advance guarantee the welfare of all? Yet a large percentage of impoverished immigrants from rural or other areas and a large proportion of low wage-earners blame their destitution on these very developments. These are the poor who are feeling the consequences of technological advance and economic changes which pushed them down to the bottom of the occupational ladder or simply wrote them out of the ranks of the labour force.

Every year the population, and particularly those elements of it who are better off, is astonished and more than slightly annoyed, when it is reminded of the existence of a little-known segment living in poverty—

* EDITOR'S NOTE: A brief submitted to the Senate Committee on Poverty by "Quebec's Corporation of Professional Social Workers" October 20, 1968 shows an increase in the number of welfare recipients in the City of Montreal from 9,349 in 1960-61 to 37,823 in 1968-69. It is recognized, of course, that part of this increase is due to changes in eligibility criteria for welfare recipients.

if not in a state of destitution – productive of countless miseries. Unfortunately, we are but momentarily shaken by tales which conform so little to what we pretend to be seeing in our cities. As a matter of fact, we feel that those who endeavor to remind us of our poor are talking rather about their own poor – like someone returned from a far-away mission land that we have just barely heard about.

Appeals and cries of alarm seem foreign, and deal with segments of the population which have very little in common with our own. We do not want to admit that there are poor among us, because it seems paradoxical; it appears to contradict the period of expansion and progress that our community life is going through. It is certainly annoying to be reminded that in the city of Montreal, over 55,800 families out of 217,000, or more than 20 per cent, are living below the normal vital minimum according to present standards. Therefore, we are tempted to overlook the problem, to define poverty in terms of individual cases, of a number of victims largely responsible for their own economic and social troubles. And after all, what else could we do?

Even our thriving suburban towns cannot completely escape the drama of poverty. Over 27,000 families, or 14 per cent of the total suburban families, are no better off than the poor families of Montreal.

Families

In addition to the families living below the normal minimum required to lead a tolerable social and human existence, there are also in the City of Montreal, 50,000 families, or an additional 18 per cent, who can be thrown into a state of poverty by a simple recession or prolonged unemployment, as was their fate in the 1929 depression. This economic inferiority, which allows little more than a precarious marginal existence, is the lot of over 29,000 suburban families, despite their apparent affluence.

The average Montreal family is made up of 3.7 persons living under the same roof. Therefore, in the City of Montreal proper (and our figures are conservative) there are over 207,000 individuals living in poor families. Regardless of the combined income of all their breadwinners and their other public and private sources of income, these families are unable to offer a quarter of a million people in the city of Montreal the minimum well-being considered necessary to lead a normal personal and social life.

In the suburbs, 100,300 persons live in poor families and in much the same situation as the poor of Montreal. In other words, in the Metropolitan area, over 307,000 persons are unable to obtain a decent minimum of well-being from their families, and these figures do not cover the poor who are living alone (Tables 1 and 1a).

If we add to the numbers who live in poor families those who live alone and have an income inferior to the accepted necessary minimum,

Table 1a
Distribution of Persons Not Living in Families According to Income, 1961

INCOME GROUPS	AVERAGE METROPOLITAN AREA		MONTREAL		SUBURBS	
	NO.	%	NO.	%	NO.	%
Total:	208,372	100	149,746	100	58,626	100
1,000	49,024	23.5	33,952	24.9	15,072	28.9
1,000 – 1,999	38,214	18.3	27,636	20.3	10,578	20.2
2,000 – 2,999	38,051	18.3	29,685	21.7	8,366	16.3
3,000 – 3,999	33,575	11.3	24,372	17.8	9,203	17.5
4,000 – 4,999	14,396	7.1	10,346	7.5	7,050	7.7
5,000 and over	15,628	7.5	10,745	7.7	4,883	9.4

we estimate the total of the impoverished population of Montreal at more than 395,000.

Thus, the poverty record of Montreal is far from satisfactory. Over 17 per cent of the families and 19 per cent of the whole population live in poverty. This is a scandal in any society claiming to be affluent.

The poor are not alone; a considerable number of families, while they cannot be actually considered poor, are on the brink of poverty and can fall back into poverty as a consequence of the slightest accident in their economic, social or personal life. More than a third of the families in the Metropolitan area (162,191) earn less than $4,000 per year and live either in poverty or in a condition close to it. In Montreal proper, 105,901 families, or 38 per cent of the total, are therefore kept at an inferior level of existence because of their low income.

If we add to these people living in families those who live alone, out of any familial context, we realize with astonishment that 33 per cent of the population of the Metropolitan area, or 706,830 live either in poverty or in an economic situation so inferior and precarious that any accident in life, such as a short recession, would soon reduce them to a state of poverty. In the city of Montreal itself, close to half a million (453,418) people, or 38 per cent of the total population of the metropolis, are in such a predicament.

PUBLIC REACTION TO POVERTY

Our bourgeois conscience, but slightly shaken by appeals to charity, usually remains indifferent to the economically weak. The charity drives have trouble reaching their objectives, despite the wealth being accumulated by some privileged few. Should we therefore draw the conclusion that in some circles, donations to charity are merely traditional ways of purchasing peace from one's conscience, and of shirking one's responsibility to relieve the miseries of the poor that one acknowledges after all? In many instances, according to experienced observers, charity drives are successful only because of the large proportion of donations coming from segments of the population which are less privileged or are on the brink of poverty. This spectacle of the economically weak, having his own serious problems yet sharing whatever little means he has with those who are even poorer, can inspire admirable speeches on the charity and great generosity of our people, but the heroic charitable gestures of some only emphasize and stigmatize the egotism of the others.

In 1965, to single out a case, the Red Feather campaign fell short of its objective by $125,000. Thus, because of accumulated deficits and the failure of their drive, this organization had to reduce their budget of assistance by $180,000 in 1965. This reluctance to contribute has the effect of reducing the original objectives even before the charity drives are launched. In other words, those who already receive so little will have to be content with a relatively reduced assistance. This indifference, not to say callousness, is unacceptable for a society in the full swing of progress. It is not understandable in a set-up of economic expansion which allows the well-off, or close to half the metropolitan population, to improve their own well-being, to increase their own material comfort and to partake of the various forms of cultural activity.

Our indifference to the state of poverty or deprivation of almost three quarters of a million people in the Metropolitan area is all the more scandalous since it tolerates the institutionalisation of poverty in our midst. The economically weak are coming to a point where they live outside organized life. This creates a community of the poor which tends to take root, to perpetuate itself, to sink into an increasingly isolated status as the margin widens between the level of existence of the poor and the level of well-being of the other elements of the population.

What is shocking and scandalous is not so much the gap between the various standards of living. Despite all our encouragements to contribute more to charitable organizations, those highly useful institutions will always get involved too late and too little, as long as we remain inactive. The actual root of injustice is our refusal to take the genuine economic and political decisions required to resolve the various levels of poverty. And those decisions should not only assist the poor as such, but above all give a new start to our whole economy and a more solid foundation to our society.

CRITERIA OF POVERTY: TOWARD A DEFINITION

It is no easier to find an accepted definition of poverty and to agree on the ways and means of evaluating it than it is to agree on what constitutes a good government, what is nice, ugly, warm or cold. Poverty is relative and is clearly determined by the culture and possibilities of a society. This relative quality of the level of well-being does not imply any arbitrary definition. Simple statistical calculations cannot create poverty where it does not exist or eliminate it where it governs the existence of many. Facts do not lie, provided they are correctly reported by reliable persons, and not purposely hidden or partially suppressed.

It was rightly said that there is no objective definition of the poor and of poverty. The reason is that there is no objective definition of need, want or deprivation.

Need is a movement toward an objective recognized as necessary by the individual or the family. If the objective is not reached, in other words, if the movement towards it persists, there will be frustrations and deprivation. Such deprivation will in turn generate some defence mechanisms such as regression or aggression. However, we feel that this reaction to deprivation is not so much due to the individual's character as such, as to his total social situation. Depending as to whether he belongs to this or that group, the individual will react differently to an identical case of deprivation. Furthermore, the objective is not defined as necessary by the individual but according to the standards of his group or the various groups to which he belongs.[1]

The co-authors, Messrs. Tremblay and Fortin, of Laval University, noted that age, income, occupation, education, residence and schooling are factors that influence each other and guide family structures in a given direction.[2]

Our country currently enjoys an unprecedented economic progress and standard of living. Just recently, the Canadian Minister of Finance had to revise his figures about the expected Gross National Product for 1965. He raised his estimations from $48,312,000,000 to almost $52,000,-000,000.

A quick examination of the most recent data and a comparison of the current situation and the situation as it was ten or twenty years ago, bring us to the following conclusions:

1) The Gross National Product and the individual annual income increased faster than the population in general and the labour force in particular.

2) The increase in the national income divided by the employed labour force, whether calculated in current or constant dollars, benefited the top two-thirds of the wage-earning families rather than the bottom third.

3) Almost one quarter of the Canadian population and an even greater proportion of the population of Quebec, had little or no share in the increase in well-being. This part of the population lives in poverty or in a situation close to it.

4) 16.5 per cent of the salaried heads of families in Canada and 17.5 per cent in Quebec do not have a sufficient level of income to satisfy even some of their essential needs and are condemned with their families to a life of poverty.

5) In the Metropolitan area, 11.3 per cent of the salaried heads of families earn under the threshold of poverty. If we add to this those whose annual earnings barely exceed the threshold of poverty, which prevents them from satisfying all the necessary needs of their families, we find that 21 per cent of the salaried heads of families in the Metro-

politan area barely make both ends meet. These families have to face the anxiety of daily existence and are unable to make any plans for the future.

INCOME AND RESIDENCE PATTERNS FOR FAMILIES AND INDIVIDUALS

Poverty appears as a situation in which many, due to insufficient means, cannot reasonably satisfy those needs considered essential, according to the standards and values determined by the group in which they live. The needs and services, according to those standards considered essential for a minimum of decent living, are not available to the poor, are beyond their material means and therefore cannot be obtained by the poor with the resources at their command.

The purpose of this analysis is to define the context of poverty in the District of Montreal. We have underlined the fact that social and economic interdependence made it difficult to segregate the Metropolitan area from the rest of the province and the country. Conditions which create poverty and its consequences are found everywhere, even though it is possible to notice local and regional variations of a non-essential nature. The interdependence of Montreal, the province and the rest of the country is such that we felt justified to start with a comparison of the various regions before attempting to analyse the nature of poverty and its most important aspects in the Montreal area.

Based on similar studies in Canada and the United States, we have established the following classifications:

I. *Families and individuals living in misery:* As a rule, any family of four with a total income of less than $2,000 per year and any individual living outside of family circles with an income of less than $1,000.

II. *Families and individuals who are poor or living in poverty:* Any family with a total annual income of less than $3,000 and any individual living outside family circles with an income of less than $1,500.

III. *Families and individuals living in deprivation:* Families with annual earnings of less than $4,000 and individuals with an income of less than $2,000 per year.

According to Table 2, 12.73 per cent of Canadian families and 12.44 per cent of families in Quebec, in 1961, were living in misery, in the most abject poverty. In the Metropolitan area, 8.41 per cent of the families live in misery, and in Montreal proper, this percentage rises to 9.8 per cent. In the suburban municipalities, 6.6 per cent of the families live in a state of abject poverty.

[1]Marc Adelard Tremblay and Gerald Fortin, *Les comportements économiques de la famille salariée du Québec,* (Les Presses de l'Université Laval, Quebec, 1964), p. 10.
[2]*Ibid.,* p. 11.

Table 2
Distribution of Non-agricultural Families
by Regions and Groups of Income (Absolute Figures and Percentage), 1961

INCOME GROUPS	REGION					
	CANADA		PROVINCE OF QUEBEC		METROPOLITAN MONTREAL	
	NUMBER	%	NUMBER	%	NUMBER	%
Under 1,000	163,590	4.47	41,158	4.14	15,375	3.17
1,000– 1,999	302,115	8.26	82,500	8.30	25,359	5.24
2,000– 2,999	382,235	10.45	117,894	11.86	42,235	8.73
3,000– 3,999	557,366	15.24	175,407	17.65	79,222	16.38
4,000– 4,999	603,192	17.49	165,674	16.67	82,536	17.07
5,000– 5,999	502,464	13.73	125,015	12.58	66,572	13.76
6,000– 6,999	353,405	9.66	80,994	8.15	45,756	9.46
7,000– 7,999	242,729	6.63	55,697	5.60	33,238	6.87
8,000– 9,999	262,787	7.18	65,367	6.57	40,328	8.34
10,000–14,999	194,303	5.31	55,390	5.57	34,168	7.06
15,000 and over	92,782	2.53	28,642	2.88	18,707	3.86
Total	3,656,968	100	993,738	100	483,496	100

Source: D.B.S. Census of Canada, 1961, Vol. IV, bulletin 4.1-3.

Poverty strikes 23.18 per cent of all non-agricultural families in Canada. This percentage is even higher in Quebec – 24.3 per cent. In Montreal, 20.1 per cent of families live in poverty and in the suburbs this percentage is 13.3 per cent. For the whole Metropolitan area, 82,969 families, or 17.14 per cent of the 483,496 families living in the area, live in poverty. We also notice that the percentage of poverty for persons living alone is higher. As a matter of fact, in Canada, 48.87 per cent of all persons living alone earn less than $1,500 per year, while 23.18 per cent of families are considered poor. In Quebec, 49.65 per cent of the persons living alone live in poverty compared to 24.3 per cent of families. Persons living alone represent a higher percentage of the poor than their percentage in the overall population. They represent 7.5 per cent of the population and 17.5 per cent of the poor. In Quebec, persons living alone represent 6.8 per cent of the population and 15 per cent of the poor in the province.

Income Distributions for Urban and Suburban Areas

When we organized our data to determine the number of persons living in poverty in each area, we obtained the following results.

1) Our analysis revealed that over one third of the population suffers deprivation or lives in poverty and that close to one half of the population (48.6%) in the Metropolitan area can be classified as eco-

Table 3
Distribution of Persons Living Outside of Family Circles by Regions and Groups of Income (Absolute Figures and Percentage), 1961

INCOME GROUP	REGION					
	CANADA		PROVINCE OF QUEBEC		METROPOLITAN MONTREAL	
	NUMBER	%	NUMBER	%	NUMBER	%
Without income	101,212	7.19	33,278	9.25	19,484	9.35
Under 1,000	429,123	30.49	108,438	30.14	49,024	23.52
1,000 – 1,499	157,522	11.19	36,911	10.26	20,135	9.66
1,500 – 1,999	116,183	8.25	31,782	8.83	18,079	8.67
2,000 – 2,499	119,358	8.48	32,960	9.16	20,709	9.93
2,500 – 2,999	97,318	6.91	26,466	7.35	17,342	8.32
3,000 – 3,499	119,962	8.52	30,621	8.51	33,575	16.11
3,500 – 3,999	75,111	5.33	17,699	4.92		
4,000 – 4,999	92,774	6.59	20,105	5.58	14,396	6.90
5,000 – 5,999	43,761	3.10	9,208	2.55	6,641	3.18
6,000 – 6,999	20,884	1.48	4,390	1.22	5,046	2.42
7,000 – 9,999	20,907	1.48	4,454	1.23	1,494	0.71
10,000 and over	13,161[1]	0.93	3,393[2]	0.94	2,447[3]	1.17
Total	1,407,276	100	359,705	100	208,372	100

[1] 1961 Census, Vol. IV, bull. 4.1-4, table D1, page D1-1.
[2] 1961 Census, Vol. IV, bull. 4.1-4, table D1, page D1-2.
[3] 1961 Census, Vol. IV, bull. 4.1-3, table C5, page C5-2 (N.B. for Montreal, the 3,000–3,999 income group is not divided as for Canada and Quebec).

nomically weak. It is almost unbelievable that a metropolitan area, where the average annual family income is $6,046, would have such a large number of poor, such a high percentage of people struggling in a marginal or precarious existence.

2) A simple glance at DBS figures would seem to indicate that the Montrealer's family has higher average incomes than the rest of the country.

3) The average income of the families in the Metropolitan area is above the Canadian average by about $600 per year. The average Metropolitan family earns $660 more per year than the average family in the rest of the province. Within the boundaries of the Metropolitan area, however, we noted that the Montreal family earned an average of $1,262 less per year than a suburban family and barely $122 more than the average family in the province.

4) We found that 50.6 per cent of families in the Metropolitan area earn less than $5,000 per year. We estimate that 63 per cent earn less than $6,000. In Montreal itself, 55.6 per cent of families earn less than $5,000 and, according to our estimates, 67 per cent of the families in the

City of Montreal earn less than $6,000. It therefore appears that if the average income of the families in the Metro area is so high, it is due to two interacting situations:

a) The higher incomes earned by suburban families;
b) the very considerable gap between the average income of a small number of families and the income of the other families in the area.

Montreal families represent 57.4 per cent of all the families in the Metropolitan area. Now, if we compare the proportion of Montreal families in each income group in the Metropolitan area, we would see that, compared to suburban families, Montreal families represent a disproportionate percentage of the marginal or poor families. But on the other hand, compared to the suburbs, Montreal has a relatively smaller percentage of well-off or wealthy families.

We can, without any risk of error, state that 4 per cent of the families in the Metropolitan area who earn $15,000 per year and over, earn over 10 per cent of the total income of all families in the Montreal area.

Poor families and those whose existence is marginal or precarious are not equally distributed in the various sections of the Metropolitan area. We already know that the City of Montreal has an excessive proportion of poor compared to its population. It was interesting to see how poverty was distributed over the territory, in what districts it had a tendency to concentrate, in what other districts it was submerged in the surrounding affluence. We therefore used the relative wealth of the various districts of the Metropolitan census to determine the distribution of the poor and the economically weak over the Metropolitan area territory.

Average Family Incomes: A Characteristic of Districts

Based on the average income of the families in each district, we have set a continuum of poverty and wealth. We distributed the population of the area in five sections or quintiles, according to the level of income of each district, each quintile representing about 20 per cent of the population. We were then able to spot on a map the relative concentrations of wealth and poverty (Table 4).

It must be pointed out at this time that wealth tends to concentrate in certain points of the territory and more particularly in some suburban municipalities. On the other hand, poverty and marginal existence tend to concentrate mainly in Montreal, although in a few suburban districts as well. Such a situation can result only in a local and regional dislocation of assistance, welfare, municipal and school-board finances.

We found that the better-off families were concentrated in some districts in the area and particularly in the suburbs. The data show that the families in the fifth quintile, or about 20 per cent of the total families,

Table 4

Percentage Distribution of Families, by Levels of Income and by Quintile

STATUS OF FAMILIES	INCOME GROUPS	METRO DISTRICT	QUINTILES 5TH	4TH	3RD	2ND	1ST
	1,000	3.2	0.2	2.1	2.8	3.1	5.6
Poverty	1,000 – 1,999	5.2	2.1	3.4	5.	6.	9.9
Precarious	2,000 – 2,999	8.7	3.7	6.3	8.8	10.1	14.8
Marginal	3,000 – 3,999	16.4	6.7	13.1	17.4	21.	21.9
Normal	4,000 – 4,999	17.1	9.7	18.	19.3	20.5	18.7
Well-off	5,000 – 6,999	23.3	21.2	28.5	26.	23.2	18.6
and wealthy	7,000 – 9,999	15.2	23.3	18.8	14.6	11.5	7.8
	10,000 – 14,999	7.1	17.1	7.3	4.7	3.8	2.3
	15,000 and over	3.9	15.8	2.5	1.4	0.8	0.4
			99.8	100	100	100	100
Low district average			6,700	5,500	5,100	4,600	2,300
High district average			39,000	6,600	5,400	5,000	4,500
Estimated average family income			10,400	6,000	5,350	4,900	4,150
Percentage of the total family incomes			34.3	19.5	17.5	15.2	13.5

Table 5

Percentage Distribution of the Income of Families in the Metropolitan Area, by Quintile, 1961

QUINTILE	%	NORMAL	INCOME VARIATION	PROPORTION OF POOR FAMILIES IN AREA (%)	DIFFERENCE FROM NORMAL
5th	34.3	20	plus 14.3	7.1	minus 12.9
4th	19.5	20	minus 0.5	14.4	" 5.6
3rd	17.5	20	" 2.5	19.7	" 0.3
2nd	15.2	20	" 4.8	22.8	plus 2.8
1st	13.5	20	" 6.5	36.	plus 16.
Total	100	100	0.0	100	0.0

earn over 34 per cent of the total incomes of the whole area. Families in the fifth quintile earn almost as much as all the families in the second and third quintiles for the Montreal area (Table 5).

Wealth Quintiles

We conclude that when the average income of a district rises, this district is more likely to have a proportion of well-off or wealthy families relatively higher than its population. Thus, the districts in the fifth quintile have only 6 per cent of families living in poverty, while 56.2 per cent are well-off or wealthy (Table 4). The percentage of poor families increases slightly to 11.8 per cent in the fourth quintile, or a lower percentage than the metro district. But, the percentage of well-off or wealthy families drops to 28.6 per cent, or slightly more than the metro district. This fourth quintile has the highest percentage of families which, while they are not exactly well-off, make both ends meet and are able to plan for the future. This fourth quintile would therefore be comprised of the most representative districts in the Metropolitan area. In fact, the distribution of family incomes closely matches the distribution for the area.

The families living in the districts grouped under the third, second and first quintiles are in a clearly unfavorable situation compared to the families in the other quintiles, particularly those in the fifth quintile. Indeed, quintiles one, two and three have proportionately more poor families, a higher percentage of marginal families and a markedly lower percentage of well-off families than the percentage of the population of the Metropolitan area. For instance, only 10.5 per cent of the families in the first quintile are well-off compared to 26.2 per cent of the families in the metro district. In the first quintile, 30.3 per cent of the families live in poverty, compared to 19.1 per cent of the families in the Metropolitan area (Table 4).

It would seem that the distribution of income in the various districts abnormally favors the fifth and fourth quintiles. Furthermore, there is a marked disproportion between the income of the families in the fifth quintile and that quintile's percentage of poor. Finally, the percentage of income of this quintile is disproportionate compared to its percentage of families in the Metropolitan area. This conclusion is the more evident since we estimate quite conservatively that less than 4 per cent of the families in the Metropolitan area earn 10 to 12 per cent of the total income earned by all the families in the Montreal area. These families have total incomes equal to over 30 per cent of the families in the fifth or wealthiest quintile, and almost equal to 80 per cent of the families in the first quintile.

SOCIAL CHARACTERISTICS OF LOW-INCOME GROUPS: REMARKS ON THE SOCIAL ORIGINS OF POVERTY IN SOCIETY

The state of poverty carries in itself its own accelerating factor, its own multiplier. The more one is poor, the more likely that other characteristics will tend to keep one in an economic and social status of inferiority. Poverty strikes not only the head of the family but all those he supports. Not only do the poor districts require more assistance, but they have the least educated, most poorly housed population. The poor have the largest number of families headed by widows, sick persons and senior citizens. A high percentage of large families live in poverty. The poor are found among the citizens who are the least prepared to face the demands of an urban and industrial civilization.

Due to the lack of income, the territories where the poor are concentrated lag behind in the number of public services available, and welfare plans tend to be highly inadequate. The greater the needs of these low-income-earning sectors of the population, the less they are able to satisfy those needs. Such a situation is caused by the deep inequality of the distribution of incomes over the territory. This engenders a bad geographic distribution of the poor families in municipalities likely to support a relatively higher level of tax and welfare.

A better knowledge of the various social and economic characteristics of the poor and the economically weak in general will permit us to explore the reasons for their poverty. We may thus prevent some proposed remedies from falling short of their actual objectives and from eliminating mere effects rather than tackling the profound causes of poverty.

For instance, we have already found that a large number of families in Montreal and the district are poor or live in the most marginal status, despite the fact that the head of the family belongs to the labour force and is a wage-earner. Unfortunately, we lack some important information about certain characteristics of the poor in Montreal. On the other hand, we feel that indications we have found for Canada and Quebec are not too far from the real poverty situation in the Montreal area.

The aspects of poverty remaining to be considered cover only the situation in 1961. The data we could obtain for any period prior to 1961 is less comparable. However, based on serious authors who examined the situation since the depression of the thirties, we must note that the largest decrease in the number of the poor since the war was due to the gradual elimination of the economic cycles and a better control over the effects of inflation. But North America has a high percentage of population which is very little affected by economic and social progress. The rate of growth of income among the lowest fifth of families has not met the demands implied by the purely egalitarian measures. However, the share of the lowest quintile in income has not increased in the twentieth century. What are the socio-economic characteristics of the poor in our contemporary society?

The poor could be classified in three main categories:

1) Those whose poverty results from social, political or purely individual factors and could not be defeated through measures of a strictly economic nature.

2) Those whose poverty results from the faults of the economy and the labour market.

3) Those whose poverty is linked both to economic and social factors.

Social and Personal Correlates

Those who are poor because of illness, old age, inadequate training for life, broken homes, etc., owe their poverty to the inadequacy of social and political measures meant to combat the causes or remedy the effects of an abnormal personal or social situation. This type of poverty cannot be fought by purely economic means. For instance, our society would not accept giving employment to senior citizens as a means of offsetting their poverty. Social and political measures would most likely be to assist those classes of the poor, while recognizing that a high level of employment and appropriate economic measures would greatly increase the efficiency of adequate social and political measures.

Economic Correlates

In an expanding economy, it would be normal for the poor to come exclusively from the ranks of those who do not participate in production. In other words, the fruits of an increase in the national income and productivity should be equitably distributed to all the economic agents. All those who produce should at least have access to the standard of living that is considered necessary, and even progress beyond the vital minimum, even if each sector's share of the total income were not identical.

The number of poor in our population who belong to the labour force demonstrate our economy's inability to insure a reasonable distribution of economic advantages to the whole labour force. Measures to maintain a high level of employment, to facilitate worker reclassification and mobility at both the industrial and regional level, to combat inflation, to insure economic stability between and within the various regions, and to remedy unemployment, particularly structural unemployment, are more likely to counteract poverty in groups consisting of people able to work. Indeed, an inadequate economic context is the only thing that prevents those people from obtaining a just share of the national wealth and to insure themselves and members of their families of a decent standard of living.

Social-Economic Correlates

People whose poverty is due to social-economic factors must also be the object of appropriate consideration and measures. This would be the case with wage-earners' families relegated to a state of poverty or of marginal existence by too many children and inadequate earnings. In such cases, the government must offer some kind of compensation.

Government economic measures will be necessary to prevent, for instance, a deterioration of pensioners' incomes through inflation. Such measures will also be essential to protect women workers who often have wages inferior to those paid to males for the same work. A widow, even if engaged in gainful employment, may be poor for two main reasons: 1) disappearance of the main family breadwinner; 2) the discrimination she is faced with on the labour market.

REMEDIAL MEASURES AND TYPES OF POVERTY

It is obvious that since there are many causes of poverty, remedies should vary according to an adequate definition of the poor and his surroundings. While recognizing the importance of a policy of economic progress, full employment and price stability, and the necessity of counter-inflationary measures, we feel that none of those measures can by itself defeat the various forms of poverty. Not any more, for that matter, than a single reform of education of apprenticeship may remedy all the faults of a market economy if there is no employment available to a better-educated and better-trained labour force. Total war against poverty, with a total conscription of society, must accompany very precise individual measures.

The legions of poverty are numerous. A detailed knowledge of their devastated social context is imperative before launching an attack. In this fight there is no universal remedy or weapon. It is also important to make a distinction between the real causes of poverty and attendant conditions. It is above all important not to confuse causes, accompanying phenomena and the effects of poverty itself.

Poverty and Family Size

According to all research made to date we conclude that in Montreal, a family earning less than $3,000 per year is condemned to poverty. In order to facilitate our analysis and comparisons we set the following thresholds:

1) *Poor families and individuals:* families of 4 whose annual income is inferior to $3,000 and individuals living alone whose income is less than $1,500 per year. These persons have resources which allow them to satisfy only some of their needs, but not their total needs.

2) *Deprived families and individuals:* families with an income below $4,000 per year and persons living alone with an annual income of less than $2,000. These families and persons can at the most make both ends meet, without any possibility of looking ahead to the future.

3) *Families or individuals whose existence is precarious or marginal:* families with an income of less than $5,000 per year and single persons with an income of less than $2,500 per year.

If we consider the other types of families (with one, two, three, four or more dependents), we find for the whole of Canada and the province, that the percentage represented by this type of family for the total number of poor families tends to decrease with the number of dependents, then to increase sharply with the sixth dependent.

This decrease of the percentage of poor families with a greater number of dependents seems to be linked with many factors:

Table 6
Percentage of Poor Families According to Size

NUMBER OF DEPENDENTS	2	3	4	5	6 and over
CANADA	38.0	14.1	13.8	12.1	21.9
QUEBEC	39.8	14.3	14.2	13.2	27.2

1) The percentage of couples over 65 with dependents decreases with the number of dependents and the number of heads under 65 increases with the number of children. Therefore, 19.24 per cent of Canadian families whose head is from 55 to 64 earn less than $2,500 compared to 37.95 per cent for heads of families aged 65 to 69, and 50.21 per cent for heads of families over 69.

2) Heads of families with one, two or three dependents tend to be older, therefore earning more on the labour market than the younger ones (under 25). In Canada, 11.17 per cent of heads of families between 35 and 44 earn under $2,500, compared to 24.07 per cent for those under 25. In Quebec, this percentage is 12.54 per cent compared to 23.77 per cent for those under 25.

3) Families increase the number of their breadwinners when they increase the number of their dependents.

The abrupt rise in the percentage of poverty among families with four or more dependents seems to result from two main causes:

1) The number of breadwinners per family tends to decrease when the children grow older and leave the family.

2) The income of the head of family decreases for a high percentage of workers over 50. Thus, 25.11 per cent of families headed by persons over 54 are poor, compared to 17.74 per cent of those aged from 45 to 54, in the province of Quebec. For Canada, percentages are 24.75 per cent compared to 16.70.

While earnings tend to stabilize or even decrease with age, the number of dependents tends to increase with the age of the head of family and the expenses to insure a vital minimum also tend to increase proportionately.

Now, if we established a percentage of poverty within a category of families of any given size we would find that families without dependents have, as such, the highest percentage of poor families of six (four dependents) or more.

In Canada, the income median is the lowest for households without dependents. It increases with the first and second dependent, levels off with the third and decreases with four or more dependents. In fact, if we consider the percentage of families, according to the number of dependents within each income group, we find that for incomes under $4,000 the percentage decreases with the increase in the number of dependents up to the third dependent and increases with the fourth and other dependents. For instance, of the families earning between $2,000 and $2,499 per year, 32.82 per cent have no dependent, 23.89 per cent have only one, and 10.06 per cent have three, but the percentage rises to 16.91 per cent for families with four or more dependents.

Poverty and Age of Family Head

The age of the head of family greatly affects family income. Youth or old age for a head of family, increases the risk of poverty. A comparison of data for Canada and Quebec shows uniform trends.

1) The percentage of poor families increases in families whose head is over 45 and this rise becomes sharper after 55.

2) Over one-third of all young couples live in poverty. Even though they represent less than 1 per cent of the population, they account for 4 per cent of the poor.

3) The median income of households increases with the age of the head of family, but at a slower rate in Quebec. In any case, whether it be a Canadian or a Quebec family, the median income of the head of family decreases at 55 and this drop gets sharper at 65 and after.

4) Families whose heads are under 25 or over 64 represent a disproportionate percentage of the poor families compared to the place in the total number of families. But families whose heads are 25 to 54 have a lower percentage of poor than their percentage of the total number of families.

The close relation between the age of the head of family (and indirectly, between the size of the family) and the income level is clearly apparent. For each income group under $5,500 per year, the percentage of families with a given income reduces with the aging of the head. In Canada, for instance, 6.29 per cent of the heads of families aged 65 to 69 earn between $2,500 and $2,900, compared to 24.99 per cent of those aged 25 to 34. On the other hand, this percentage goes up to 10.12 per cent for heads of families over 70. The heads of families under 25 have the lowest percentage in each income group. This stems from the fact that the average income of these heads of families is at a clearly inferior level compared to older heads of families and that these heads of very young households are more equally distributed within the various income groups below $4,500.

We examined heads of families under 25 years of age in Canada and Quebec. Throughout the country, over 54 per cent of these heads of families earn under $4,000 per year and 23.4 per cent under $2,500. In Quebec, 61.89 per cent of heads of families under 25 earn less than $4,000 per year, and 23.77 per cent of them live in poverty with their families and earn under $2,500 per year.

Age and Unemployment

The relation between poverty and age is not direct, but is clearly apparent in any examination of the unemployment index according to age, for both male and female. As we found, poverty for the wage-earners is such that 40 per cent of the poor in Canada belong to wage-earning families. In Quebec, this percentage is 42.5 per cent for the whole province and 39.1 per cent for the Metropolitan area. Bad distribution of incomes and unemployment are mainly responsible for the fact that 50 per cent of the poor families in Quebec and Canada are families with a wage-earning head. We found that unemployment is much more severe for young people from 14 to 25 years of age than for any other group.

Families Headed by a Woman

There are in Canada 247,026 families headed by women. In Quebec, 16,914 families are in the same situation. The situation of these households is the more severe since the woman must sometimes neglect her care for her family to earn a decent income. One observes that despite all forms of social assistance offered families of this type and despite the earnings of their members, over 53 per cent of them are indigent in Canada (53.28) and about 50 per cent (49.62) in Quebec. We also estimate that an income of $3,000 per year is clearly inadequate to satisfy the needs of this type of family. Many of these families whose heads are deceased must incur additional costs to enable the women to work or to compensate the extra-familial work caused by the absence of the head of the family. Raising the level of poverty to $3,500 for these families, we find that 60 per cent or more families headed by women live in poverty across Canada.

Education of Head of Family

Poor schooling, as was confirmed by all studies to date, is a characteristic of people living in poverty. Having little geographic and social mobility, the poor are mainly the little educated.

Due to a low level of education, their training for life is not only made more difficult, but technical changes make rehabilitation extremely difficult. Sixty-nine per cent of the heads of poor families have an education level below high school. This percentage for Quebec is 75.43 per cent. However, a higher degree of education did not help 31 per cent of the heads of poor families to find a good job. The same goes for 24 per cent of the heads of families earning less than $3,000 per year in Quebec.

There is undoubtedly a very close relation between the level of education of the heads of families and their annual earnings. But in itself, as indicated in the table, a higher degree of education is not a foolproof guarantee against poverty. We should explain in more detail why 25 per cent of the poor in Quebec and 31 per cent of those in Canada are relatively uneducated. Age and illness must be taken into account. But how many of them had an education or some apprenticeship that did not prepare them to face life? The vast studies now being conducted are likely to give us satisfactory answers to these questions.

Single Residents, Age and Income

We already pointed out the high proportion of persons living alone in the ranks of the poor. In Canada, 48.87 per cent of persons living alone live in poverty, earning less than $1,500 per year and 57.12 per cent of them live in precarious or poor conditions with an income under $2,000. In addition, 65.60 per cent of all persons living alone earn less than $2,500 per year (see Table 3).

Persons living alone represent 16.9 per cent of the poor in Canada. In Quebec, the percentage is 15 per cent. In Montreal, 22 per cent of the poor do not live with families.

If we compare the income of heads of families and of persons living alone, we find that poverty is slightly higher among persons living alone than among married persons.

1) Persons living alone have in each age group a much higher percentage of poor than heads of families in the same age groups. Furthermore, this percentage is considerably higher in Quebec compared to the rest of the country.

2) Persons living alone and under 25 years of age are proportionately poorer than persons living alone between 25 and 54. On the other hand, there are more poor among persons living alone of the 55-to-65 age bracket than the under-25 bracket, or heads of families in the same age groups.

3) While among poor heads of families the percentage of poverty decreases in the 25-to-45-years-of-age bracket, it decreases only between 25-34 for persons living alone. It increases rapidly from that point so that the persons living alone in the 55-to-64 age bracket represent proportionately twice as many poor as persons living alone in the 25-to-34 age bracket.

4) The income median for each age group is much lower among persons living alone than among heads of families of the same age. In addition, the income median decreases earlier and much faster as age increases among persons living alone. In Canada, as in Quebec, the income median for persons living alone increases up to age 34 to decrease past that age while it keeps increasing among heads of families until age 54.

It will also be noticed, when comparing people living alone in Quebec, according to their age groups with their counterparts across the country, that the income median for this group in Quebec is much lower than for the rest of the country. The same phenomenon was noticed when we compared the income median for the heads of families in Quebec, according to age groups, with those of Canada.

The fate of the poor living alone and aged over 45 deserves our full attention. As long as the poor person living alone is able to fit in to the labour market, his situation, if not comfortable, seems bearable, especially if he is younger. After 35, the percentage of poverty increases — more rapidly so in later years. But at age 65 the situation turns to catastrophe.

Table 6a

Characteristics of the Poor, Canada, Quebec, Metropolitan Area, 1961

	CANADA	QUEBEC	METROPOLITAN AREA
Population	18,696,000	5,259,211	2,109,509
1) Poor persons	4,079,617	1,193,146	395,629
% of the population	21.8	23.7	18.8
2) Living in families	3,391,760	1,014,519	306,986
% of poor	83	85	87
3) Living alone	687,857	178,627	88,643
% of poor	17	15	13
4) Persons, in salaried families	1,720,700	506,404 (est.)	154,660 (est.)
a) % of poor persons	40	42.5	39.1
b) % of persons in poor families	51	58.5	50.5
5) Persons, families without dependents	1,302,526	173,945	
% of poor	31.9	30.7	
6) Persons, families with 4 dependents and more	748,542	153,997	
% of poor	18.3	27.2	
7) Persons, families whose head is under 25	162,963 (est.)	43,140 (est.)	
% of poor	4	4	
8) Persons in families headed by a woman	526,640	133,644	
	12.9	11.4	
9) Persons in poor families according to education of head	2,345,600	728,892	
(Elementary)	57.5	61.2	
10) Persons living alone			
a) -25	91,327	27,947	
% of poor	2.2	2.4	
b) over 65	256,881	71,912	
% of poor	6.3	6.	

In Canada, 82.1 per cent of senior citizens living alone earn under $2,000. In the province of Quebec, this percentage is 83.65 per cent. These persons require medical care and often need costly personal care. At the least, setting the poverty threshold for these people at $2,500-$3,000 per year, close to 90 per cent of our senior citizens living alone live in pitiable conditions.

Table 7
Distribution of Families in Canada and Quebec, According to Certain Characteristics and Percentage of Poor Families Having These Characteristics

	CANADA		QUEBEC	
	% OF FAMILIES	% OF POVERTY FAMILIES	% OF FAMILIES	% OF POVERTY FAMILIES
Total families	100	23.3	100	25.5
Without dependents	29.34	36.9	18.03	31
With 4 and more dependents	15.32	21.9	20.8	27.2
Head under 25	4.6	6.4	4.05	5.6
Head over 65	12.3	25.2	10.6	20.8
Headed by woman	6.7	15.4	6.7	13.2
Wage-earners	74.9	49.4	74.5	50.2

In Table 6a, we offer a general picture of some characteristics of the population of the poor. We also compare the poor in Canada with those in the Province of Quebec and the Metropolitan area, according to those characteristics.

After an examination of the percentages, we find that the poor seem to have more than one characteristic. For instance, the members of a poor family may belong to a family whose head is a wage-earner. The same family may on the other hand be headed by a widow under 25 years of age with elementary education, etc.

Through an examination of the factors related to poverty in Table 6, we find that half the population of the poor (40 per cent in Canada and 42.5 per cent in Quebec) is represented by wage-earners' families, which indicates the relative impossibility of our economic system upgrading out of poverty a large portion of our labour force. In addition, we find that a large proportion of poor live in families without dependents or with more than four dependents or come from families whose head is very young or over 65 years of age. The table also underlines the very close relation between poverty and an inadequate degree of education.

Table 7 is a distribution of families in Canada and Quebec and of persons living alone according to certain characteristics, and compares the degree of poverty of these families or individuals according to their representation in the population of the total number of families. How is the enormous proportion of poor families and individuals in Canada and Quebec distributed? Unfortunately, we do not have sufficient data in connection with this for the Metropolitan area, but since the area accounts for close to 40 per cent of the total population of Quebec, the same trends will most probably be apparent.

We find that families without dependents or with four or more dependents have a superior percentage of poor families compared to their own percentage in the total number of families. The same goes for families whose heads are under 25 or over 65 and for families headed by a woman. We also notice under a different form a partial failure of the economic system. Indeed, the wage-earners' families which represent ¾ of the total also represent half the poor families.

The risk of joining the ranks of the poor is greater for one who is a wage-earner or a member of a wage-earners' family. The risk becomes enormous for one who has only elementary education. It becomes very high for members of a family whose head is either very young or very old. It is high for families without dependents or with four or more dependents. There is one chance out of six of being poor, if one is among persons living alone or those living in a household headed by a woman.

CONCLUSION

A shocking proportion of the Montreal area population lives in poverty or has an existence on the brink of an economic and social abyss.

We tolerate the existence, continuation and aggravation of the scandal of poverty among us at the same time that skyscrapers are rising all over the metropolis. We are agreeably surprised by the meteoric increase of private and public investments, and by the rapid growth of the various sectors of our metropolitan economy; it has repeatedly been said that our province, and more particularly our area, currently enjoys the highest rate of economic growth in the country. Yet the poor seldom find a place at the banquet table, and are eternally overlooked by economic and social plans.

Poverty as a Relative Concept

The notion of poverty changes with the times, because the standard of living considered necessary changes with economic and social progress. The poverty threshold therefore tends to rise because of accelerated progress. We cannot evaluate poverty today by yesterday's standards. It is the society where the poor live that determines the required minimum necessary to live in decency and dignity. This minimum is determined according to society's own criteria, values and environment. It is normal that it be so.

A constant economic progression and a more abundant social legislation do not by themselves constitute an indication that poverty is vanquished or disappearing. What is important is that the population with the lowest income really benefit from progress, to such an extent that it may eventually be freed from an excessively low standard of living.

Society constantly modifies the need it considers essential. The threshold of poverty can therefore never be arbitrarily determined. The phenomenon of poverty, of deprivation, is within human experience itself, but it is society which decides the threshold of poverty. Because of technological advance, of increased investments, of the discovery of new products or services, society constantly modifies both needs and aspirations and thus raises the poverty threshold. "There are new definitions of what man can achieve, of what a human standard of life should be . . . Technology has consistently broadened man's potential: it has made a longer, healthier, better life possible. Thus, in terms of what is technically possible, we have higher aspirations."[3]

While economic progress and technological changes increase man's potential and modify his aspirations we find that much too high a proportion of the metropolitan population cannot follow the trend and does not share the advantages resulting from the general improvement of standards. According to Michael Harrington, poverty is the fate of all those who cannot attain a minimum degree of health, housing, food, and education as required by the present status of technical and scientific knowledge for existence, as it is in our country.[4]

However, the gap between the possible standards of living and the status of a great number is not enough to give a just idea of the level of poverty and to measure it with accuracy. What mainly characterizes poverty and gives it urgency and acuteness is that it exists in a society which could wage total war against poverty with the means it has at present, if it wanted to.

What defines poverty best is the gap between its own situation and the situation of the affluent society. "They [the poor] are dispossessed in terms of what the rest of the nation enjoys, in terms of what the society could provide if it had the will. They live on the fringe, on the margin."[5]

Institutional Poverty and the Culture of the Poor

There is no simple definition of poverty. Even though the poverty threshold must eventually be defined, as we have done, in terms of a vital minimum income to satisfy a minimum set of needs considered as essential at a given moment, even though this threshold may tend to rise in a progressive economy, poverty cannot be defined by strictly economic factors. Poverty reflects more than a simple lack of material resources. It constitutes an index of the isolation of a whole sector of the population; it conditions and explains that sector's absence from participation in organized life. It is evidence also of a relative impoverishment of the whole society. As long as the poor are kept away from economic life or until political decisions do cause them to integrate in a normal existence,

[3] Michael Harrington, *The Other America: Poverty in the U.S.A.*, (Baltimore: Penguin Books, 1963), p. 174.
[4] *Ibid.*, p. 175.
[5] Michael Harrington, *ibid.*, p. 174.

our society will tolerate and institutionalize an acceptable waste of material and human resources, which can only cause a weakening of our collective existence and make more difficult any attempt at eradicating and eliminating poverty.

Too many of our people have not benefited from the expansionary economy and the considerable progress since the last war. The poor, isolated and hidden in our metropolis, have for a long time been bypassed by a social and economic life elaborated without their participation and even sometimes against them. They are without leadership and are no longer seen. Everything in our society invites us to turn our back on the poor and their environment. The very structures of our towns, the development of suburbs, everything prevents us from seeing, hearing or understanding the poor. They are making themselves less and less visible. Since they have stopped participating in the various manifestations of our mass society, the poor remain on the fringe. Their dreams have for too long been broken. Without leaders, they have lost their political influence, or at least the influence they had during the depression.

Our poor wage-earners were born at the wrong moment in our political life and appeared at the wrong places in our economic organization. This seems to condemn them in our eyes. Badly educated, ill-trained, their fate is to have the wrong occupations at the wrong time and in the wrong place.

The poor seem to offer no interest to our elite. Forgotten, anonymous, without political strength, without leadership and adequate material and cultural resources, they are disorganized. They cannot be heard either by themselves or through the voice of convinced and active representatives. While the other sectors of our population join the existing organizations or create new ones when needed, the poor have become not only invisible but speechless.

The great tragedy of poverty today is that it renders one insensible to any progress. Kept outside, rejected, the poor man hears a world buzzing around him where he has no place. This world surrounds him without his participation in it, because he has convinced himself that he does not belong. Unable to adapt to the rhythm and the changes of his environment, because in many cases nothing prepared him for this existence, the poor man turns away from the society of "the others" to live his ghetto-like life. He gradually reaches districts where one does not have to participate but simply be tolerated. The poor man ends in slums, in poor accommodation, both inadequate and overcrowded. The moral and physical destitution initiated long ago, because of successive impoverishment periods, will continue to turn into various forms of physical, moral or social deterioration.

THE THIRD SOLITUDE

The reasons which create and perpetuate poverty in our midst constitute a new social dimension, a third solitude. This hardly visible solitude is populated by the poor who often are only the rejects of other sectors of society. Within this solitude, great tragedies are not likely to make headlines. But they occur all the time. "The suffering of the poor is not as well known as their crimes," said Fielding two centuries ago. Those who live in the solitude of the poor, often have nothing in common except the tragic experience they have accumulated.

This accumulated experience cannot be of any use, cannot be transformed into positive and constructive objectives by the poor left to look after themselves. A long succession of broken ideals, of failures, convinced them that it would be futile to take any new start or any new collective initiative, and often killed any desire in them to get out of their deplorable situation. A total and concerted effort by all sectors of our population supported and coordinated by governments with adequate policies and rapid means of action, can alone tear the poor away from their pitiable economic, social and cultural inferiority.

Our society will never have peace of mind until selective and adequate measures are taken to defeat poverty in all its forms. It is increasingly urgent that the poor be taken out of their isolation, or their material, social and cultural solitude. Such a victory would be that much more valuable since it would also eliminate the ignorance, the callousness, and the harshness which separate the poor from those who are already living in comfort in the other two solitudes.

In our study we tried to analyze the most important sides of poverty in our area. We hope more thorough analysis will one day show us the hideous face of a misery our society seems to be purposely ignoring. We hope that a greater sympathy for the poor will result from it, a greater desire to defeat this solitude, this isolation into which poverty is sinking. We hope that the various sectors of our economy and politics will from now on assume their responsibility for those who for too long have been ignored.

It is not enough to bring some little relief to the poor. While our collective passivity may increase the urgency of the charitable drives in the future, it profoundly devalues them. Private charity, which does not fit in to an enlightened scheme of social security supported by a dynamic economic policy, appears to us to be pointless. It only succeeds in disguising poverty all the more, and also serves to merely appease one's conscience.

The elimination of poverty may to some people seem like an unattainable objective. But why? Should we abandon all political prudence, all care for the present and the future, under pretence that ten years from now there will still be poor among us, even though they will be half as poor as our poor of today? To abandon our efforts or even to slow them, would endanger the existence of the next generation, which will probably seek a standard of welfare which will undoubtedly raise the threshold of poverty again.

Even if the task is a difficult one, it will be conducted with success provided we lose our indifference toward poverty. Education for harshness must be replaced by an education which will facilitate the understanding of poverty and provide a means of eradicating it. We must at all costs revise our attitudes.

We may base our attitudes on the best of principles and condemn certain antisocial activities, but we must then admit that the remedy comes too late. By themselves, the nice expressions of principles bring very little food to the plate of those who are hungry or are fighting permanently to get the required vital minimum. This is a time for concerted action, for a total effort supported by basic energetic positions.

Our conscience must be redressed and our judgment corrected if we want to stop the indifference toward the poor, toward close to half a million people living among us. More than any other sector of society, the poor have a right to reintegrate themselves, to have a normal life in the economic and social order. In many cases this calls for a total reeducation.

The poor will regain confidence and react to the positive standards of the environment, will really participate in the progress of our society, only if our society stops being a real enterprise of education for harshness. This is a responsibility for the well-off. Intermediate bodies and governments must support each other in this final war against poverty, which should not stop until poverty, the third solitude that cannot be tolerated in our midst, has been eliminated.

6. *Indian Poverty in Canada**

A. Alan Borovoy

The poverty of the Indian staggers the imagination of the white man. It simply drains our mental resources to conceive of how in the technological Canada of 1966 over 80% of Indian homes are devoid of such elementary facilities as sewers, septic tanks, flush toilets, running water, and telephones.

Before the current bout with inflation, most economists designated an annual income of $3,000 as the poverty line for Canadian families. How then can we believe that as of 1963, 75% of Indian families received an annual income of $2,000 or less and that during the same year, 47% of Indian families earned $1,000 per year or less?

Of course, these are only statistics. The greatest number of Canadians never come face to face with the wretched suffering which these statistics represent. While most Canadians live in highly industrialized urban centres, most Indians live in remote underdeveloped rural areas. Thus, we simply do not *see* their despair with our own eyes. Nor do the great majority of us ever experience the bitter cold which is so prevalent in many Indian communities. The suffering occasioned by their poverty is intensified by temperatures of 40 and 50 degrees below zero. Being so far removed, we cannot feel the horror which lies behind the fact that Indian preschool mortality is eight times the national average and school age mortality, three times the national average.

Even those of us who go to conferences and seminars with Indians, meet the Indians on *our* grounds, in our well-heated, well-lit hotels, colleges, and board rooms. Rarely do we see them in their habitat. Most of the Indians we meet are those who live closer to us, and have begun to develop more economically viable communities, e.g. Six Nations, Walpole Island, etc. Consequently, Indian poverty has a quality of unreality

*Reprinted with permission of the author and publisher from *Canadian Labour,* 12 (Ottawa: December, 1966), pp. 13-15.

for us. The most sympathetic and imaginative Canadian cannot fathom the depths of human suffering through the medium of bland statistics.

Since the beginning of the white man's reign on this continent, Indian life has undergone a steady deterioration. We virtually deported the natives of this country to small parcels of land (reserves) far away from the main streams of our civilization. Then we began from every side to assault their culture and way of life. Our tourist industries encroached on their hunting and fishing resources. Our fur companies invaded their trap lines. Our dams flooded their wild rice fields. Our churches undermined their religion.

When Indians withdrew from the reserves to seek their fortunes in the white society, they were beset by severe handicaps. Many Indian reserves are not culturally in tune with the demands of the industrial society. Punctuality, for example, is not always accorded the reverence in some Indian communities that it receives in our society. This plus racial prejudice created a wide-spread reluctance on the part of employers to hire Indian labour. When Indians did get jobs, their industrial naïveté often made them vulnerable to vicious exploitation. For example, I have known Indians in the 1960's to work a 15-hour day and 7-day week for as little as $250 per month.

Education, the white man's panacea for all problems has enjoyed relatively little success in Indian communities. In the first place, formal education is a white man's institution; it has no roots in Indian life. In the second place, even when there has been a favourable response to education, Indian children have found it virtually impossible to study in overcrowded hovels which lack adequate heating and lighting. In the third place, the efforts to integrate the education of Indian children with that of white children has often met rigid resistance by white bigots who resent having their offspring exposed to "uncivilized barbarians" and by reluctant Indians who feared having their children separated from their families.

Having been denuded of their own way of life and having been isolated from ours, the Indians found themselves increasingly with nowhere to turn and nowhere to go. The result has been a growing sense of despair. Despair in turn has fathered unemployment, alcohol and welfare cheques — the components of poverty. With each generation of our galloping technology, the gulf between them and us has grown wider and deeper.

Of course, not all white men have been hostile or indifferent to Indian suffering. Significant segments of white society have reponded with great concern and effort.

Unfortunately, however, white effort has been marked by over-participation on the part of the white man and under-participation on the part of the Indian. From the clothes collections of the do-gooders to the community planning of the Indian Affairs Branch, the white man has run the show. As a result, one well-intentioned project after another has fallen flat on its face.

The missing link has been Indian participation in the decision-making by which he is governed. The concerned white man has made the same mistake as the hostile and unconcerned white man. He has left the Indian out of the decision-making process; he has failed to consult the Indian about the policies which would determine his future.

To be sure, the federal government and many provincial governments have recently made significant efforts to correct this defect. The new community development programs stress consultation and participation with the Indian in policy formation. Government-appointed community development officers go into Indian communities with instructions to consult and plan with the Indian band councils.

As welcome as the new government approach is, there is still a missing link. The persisting gap is Indian bargaining power. What happens, for example, when a plan is conceived which requires government help to carry it through and the government help is not forthcoming? Government-appointed community development officers can exercise only limited pressure on their political superiors. Indians are inexperienced in the art of political and economic pressure. Thus, the Indians face the risk that many of their best laid plans might never see the light of day because they lack the bargaining power to enlist the cooperation of government or other community agencies. Recently, for example, an Indian community went to great expense to convert its reserve into a recreation park. But they are now being frustrated because the government has failed to improve a road linking the reserve with the main highway. As long as that road remains unbuilt, the Indians' ability to attract tourists to their park will be negligible.

It has been said that western democracy is essentially government by pressure groups. The rest of us are highly organized into pressure groups. Doctors, manufacturers, industrial workers, churches, ethnic groups band together in order to protect their various interests in the larger society. The policies and programs adopted by government reflect the balance of power among the many competing pressure groups.

But the Indian is left out. Being unfamiliar with the ways of the white man, Indians have found it difficult to impress their interests effectively upon our society. They have been forced to depend upon the good will of the white man's government.

The handicap is obvious. Only the naïve in our society are prepared to rely upon the good will of others to protect their interest. Imagine a trade union relying solely on the good will of management in the negotiation of their collective agreements.

Thus, in order for the Indian truly to participate in the decisions by which he is governed, he must acquire power. Power grows out of the ability to generate pressures, both political and economic.

KENORA — A TURNING POINT

In November 1965, for the first time in their history, the Indians in the area of Kenora, Ontario, exercised the art of mass political pressure. On the night of Monday, November 22, 400 Indians marched down the streets of Kenora and engaged the Town Council in a historic confrontation.

The Indians asked the town to:

1) Petition the Federal Government to install radio-telephone equipment on the reserves so that they could communicate with the larger communities around them,

2) Petition the Ontario Government to lengthen the trapping season in order to shorten the lay-over between the trapping season and the fishing season.

3) Petition the Ontario Government to make available to the Kenora area the services of the Alcoholism Research Foundation.

4) Establish a Mayor's Committee to process grievances between the Indians and the town

This demonstration created a national news sensation. Radio, television, and newspapers all over Canada headlined the story. Editorials demanded government action.

Very soon afterwards, the Kenora Town Council granted all of the requests in the Indian brief. It appointed a Mayor's Committee and enacted the resolutions for which the Indians had sought its support. Then the federal and provincial governments swung into action. The trapping season was immediately extended. By now, almost all the reserves have telephones. Following the dispatch of its research staff to the area, the Alcoholism Research Foundation has established a treatment centre in Kenora.

This response to their demonstration infused the Indians with a sense of self-respect, pride and hope. It has shown its effects even in other areas of Indian life. Some Indian leaders have reported, for example, that Indians in unprecedented numbers are signing up and completing government-sponsored employment retraining courses. So often, government attempts to help Indians have failed because the Indians in their despair lacked the sense of hope which would motivate the exertion of effort on their own behalf. The experience of moving government and the community through the use of their own power creates that sense of hope so necessary to the success of anti-poverty activity.

Of course, this is not to exaggerate the results of the Kenora experience. The gains were modest; the problem is immense. Its importance arises from the lesson that in the field of Indian problems there is no substitute for the use of Indian power exercised on the Indians' behalf.

The good will of others is no longer sufficient. We cannot content ourselves with knitting woollies or running to the government with pious briefs demanding help for the Indians. The emphasis must be on getting the Indians into the act.

ROLE OF THE LABOUR MOVEMENT

It should surprise no one that the labour movement through its Human Rights Committee in Ontario played a key organizing role in the Kenora demonstration. Of all the organizations in this country, the labour movement is uniquely qualified to help the Indian act on his own behalf.

No other organization in the community combines both the idealism and the practical know-how in social action. The reference to idealism needs no further elaboration. Our capacity for effective social action arises out of our identification with the relatively unvested interests in society. The more-vested-interest organization does not as willingly engage in social controversy. On the boards of virtually every major community group, we find business, industrial, and commercial entrepreneurs whose economic self-interest requires that they tread cautiously. They would not as readily man picket lines, conduct demonstrations, and openly fight some of the very enterprises which periodically threaten the Indian's position. We are the only functioning group with both the disposition for and experience in the kind of social action that this problem so often requires.

What the Indian can use is labour's priceless experience with mass pressures and collective bargaining. These are the two skills which can give the Indians the power to get effectively involved in the decisions which shape their lives. These were the skills which we put at the disposal of the Kenora Indians. First, we helped them to organize the demonstration and then we helped them to negotiate with the three levels of government.

Canadian labour should offer to share these skills with the Indian people throughout this country. We should publicly invite the Indians to come to us if they need help in their conflicts with government and the vested interests of this community. This has already begun to happen. Following the Kenora episode, one Indian organization approached the Human Rights Committee of the Ontario Federation of Labour for assistance in pressuring the federal government about recent encroachments on their treaty rights regarding hunting and fishing. Our Ontario Committee helped them to prepare a brief and is now assisting in the organization of a delegation to meet with the appropriate federal authorities. One band council has requested our assistance in mobilizing pressures for government service to maintain their roads; another has asked us to help them to bring about the correction of certain tax inequities sustained by lessees of reserve property.

General pleas for government help to the Indian are of little value. Every band council, every reserve has unique problems. To be helpful, we must assist specific Indian organizations with the specific problems that are bothering them. We should take the initiative. From the Canadian Labour Congress to the remotest labour council, labour leaders should seek out Indian leaders for consultations and discussions about Indian problems.

Our role is to help them develop the kind of social action which will generate the pressures they need. Then we should offer to assist in the ensuing negotiations with government or special interest groups.

Through Kenora, our Human Rights Committee in Ontario has taken the first step. It remains for the house of labour to follow through.

Section III

Opportunity Structures and the Culture of Poverty

B. Culture of Poverty

A culture is a whole way of life created, followed and passed on by human groups. The term has traditionally been used by anthropologists to depict the way of life of primitive peoples. In the last decade, Oscar Lewis and others have used the concept of culture and applied it to the poor in highly industrialized nations such as Canada and the U.S.A. Lewis estimates that about 20 per cent of the poor exhibit characteristics qualitatively different from those found in the majority of the middle class. This culture of poverty is characterized by a low level of organization, is not integrated with the major institutions of society, contains a deep-rooted hostility towards representatives of the larger society – for example, social workers, politicians and police – and persons within the culture possess feelings of hopelessness, dependence and inferiority.

This emphasis on the discrepancy between the values of a significant proportion of the poor and the values of the majority of persons within Canadian society is reflected in the articles included in this section. Moreover, all four writers see these discrepancies remaining, perhaps widening, unless we become aware of not only the content of the "culture of poverty" but also its causes.

Howard Becker illustrates the immense discontinuity between the values of a lower class child and the values of the educational system. Members of boards and professional educators are mostly members of the middle class and I.Q. tests usually reflect middle-class standards. The school, instead of providing an opportunity for a lower-class child to become upwardly mobile, serves to "label" the child as "inferior". Tremendous pressures, both cultural and economic, are placed on the lower-class child to conform to a set of values and modes of behaviour inappropriate to his milieu. Some do, but the majority do not. Education serves not the children in the lower-class, but the children of the affluent.

James Harding documents the consequences of this situation for the Indian in Canada. He delineates the poverty of the Indian as well as the Metis and points out the historical and structural reasons for their deprived position in Canadian society. Harding also stresses that the "culture" of poverty of the Indian is a *dependent* phenomenon. It is a means of adaptation to a position imposed upon the Indian and Metis by the rest of Canadians. This is a different emphasis than that found in the article by Lewis, and represents one of the difficulties with the "culture of poverty" approach.

There is often a lack of specification of "causes" — that is, culture is seen as both a dependent (Harding) and independent variable. In actuality it is both. The difficult question, both theoretically and methodologically, is how much weight do we assign to cultural factors and how much to structural factors in accounting for 1) the extent of poverty, 2) its perpetuation over time and 3) its alleviation?

A related difficulty is the extent to which the concept "culture of poverty" subsumes a *variety* (rather than a homogeneity) of distinctive traits and patterns. We need to know the variety of values, modes of life among the poor — the significance, the basis and the organization of these differences. It might be more fruitful, for example, to see how many different ways lower-class families react to the facts of their marginal existence rather than suggesting that they act in response to the imperatives of a lower-class culture. We should not confuse life chances and actual behaviour with values and preferences. As Miller and Riessman point out, "Having successfully overcome the dangers of a biological approach, we are now facing the dangers of a cultural approach that stresses the defects of the poor and does not focus on the possibilities of change."[1]

Finally an excerpt from the Economic Council of Canada's Sixth *Annual Review* provides us with data on consumer expenditures for poor families. The discussion serves to emphasize a view of the family as both a producing and a consuming unit, since recognition of this duality of functions is essential to developing programs that will alleviate poverty. A limited survey of anti-poverty programs conducted by the Economic Council suggests several problems, many of which derive from a failure to acknowledge the cultural dimension of poverty in society.

[1] S. M. Miller and Frank Riessman, *Social Class and Social Policy* (New York: Basic Books, Inc., 1968), p. 64.

1. *The Culture of Poverty*[*]

Oscar Lewis

Poverty and the so-called war against it provide a principal theme for the domestic program of the Johnson Administration. In the midst of a population that enjoys unexampled material well-being – with the average annual family income exceeding $7,000 – it is officially acknowledged that some 18 million families, numbering more than 50 million individuals, live below the $3,000 "poverty line." Toward the improvement of the lot of these people some $1,600 million of Federal funds are directly allocated through the Office of Economic Opportunity, and many hundreds of millions of additional dollars flow indirectly through expanded Federal expenditures in the fields of health, education, welfare and urban affairs.†

Along with the increase in activity on behalf of the poor indicated by these figures there has come a parallel expansion of publication in the social sciences on the subject of poverty. The new writings advance the same two opposed evaluations of the poor that are to be found in literature, in proverbs and in popular sayings throughout recorded history. Just as the poor have been pronounced blessed, virtuous, upright, serene, independent, honest, kind and happy, so contemporary students stress their great and neglected capacity for self-help, leadership and community organization. Conversely, as the poor have been characterized as shiftless, mean, sordid, violent, evil and criminal, so other students point to the irreversibly destructive effects of poverty on individual character and emphasize the corresponding need to keep guidance and control of poverty projects in the hands of duly constituted authorities. This clash of viewpoints reflects in part the infighting for political control

 An expanded version of this article appears in *La Vida,* by Oscar Lewis. Reprinted as it appeared in *Scientific American,* October, 1966, by permission of Random House, Inc.

†EDITOR'S NOTE: These figures apply to the U.S.A., 1965.

of the program between Federal and local officials. The confusion results also from the tendency to focus study and attention on the personality of the individual victim of poverty rather than on the slum community and family and from the consequent failure to distinguish between poverty and what I have called the culture of poverty.

The phrase is a catchy one and is used and misused with some frequency in the current literature. In my writings it is the label for a specific conceptual model that describes in positive terms a subculture of Western society with its own structure and rationale, a way of life handed on from generation to generation along family lines. The culture of poverty is not just a matter of deprivation or disorganization, a term signifying the absence of something. It is a culture in the traditional anthropological sense in that it provides human beings with a design for living, with a ready-made set of solutions for human problems, and so serves a significant adaptive function. This style of life transcends national boundaries and regional and rural-urban differences within nations. Wherever it occurs, its practitioners exhibit remarkable similarity in the structure of their families, in interpersonal relations, in spending habits, in their value systems and in their orientation in time.

Not nearly enough is known about this important complex of human behaviour. My own concept of it has evolved as my work has progressed and remains subject to amendment by my own further work and that of others. The scarcity of literature on the culture of poverty is a measure of the gap in communication that exists between the very poor and the middle-class personnel — social scientists, social workers, teachers, physicians, priests and others — who bear the major responsibility for carrying out the antipoverty programs. Much of the behaviour accepted in the culture of poverty goes counter to cherished ideals of the larger society. In writing about "multiproblem" families social scientists thus often stress their instability, their lack of order, direction and organization. Yet, as I have observed them, their behavior seems clearly patterned and reasonably predictable. I am more often struck by the inexorable repititiousness and the iron entrenchment of their lifeways.

The concept of the culture of poverty may help to correct misapprehensions that have ascribed some behavior patterns of ethnic, national or regional groups as distinctive characteristics. For example, a high incidence of common-law marriage and households headed by women has been thought to be distinctive of Negro family life in this country, and has been attributed to the Negro's historical experience of slavery. In actuality it turns out that such households express essential traits of the culture of poverty and are found among diverse peoples in many parts of the world and among peoples that have had no history of slavery. Although it is now possible to assert such generalizations, there is still much to be learned about this difficult and affecting subject. The absence of intensive anthropological studies of poor families in a wide variety of national contexts — particularly the lack of such studies in socialist countries – remains a serious handicap to the formulation of dependable cross-cultural constants of the culture of poverty.

My studies of poverty and family life have centered largely in Mexico. On occasion some of my Mexican friends have suggested delicately that I turn to a study of poverty in my own country. As a first step in this direction I am currently engaged in a study of Puerto Rican families. Over the past three years my staff and I have been assembling data on 100 representative families in four slums of Greater San Juan and some 50 families of their relatives in New York City.

Our methods combine the traditional techniques of sociology, anthropology and psychology. This includes a battery of 19 questionnaires, the administration of which requires 12 hours per informant. They cover the residence and employment history of each adult; family relations; income and expenditure; complete inventory of household and personal possessions; friendship patterns, particularly the *compadrazgo,* or godparent, relationship that serves as a kind of informal social security for the children of these families and establishes special obligations among the adults; recreational patterns; health and medical history; politics; religion; world view and "cosmopolitanism." Open-end interviews and psychological tests (such as the thematic apperception test, the Rorschach test and the sentence-completion test) are administered to a sampling of this population.

All this work serves to establish the context for close-range study of a selected few families. Because the family is a small social system, it lends itself to the holistic approach of anthropology. Whole-family studies bridge the gap between the conceptual extremes of the culture at one pole and of the individual at the other, making possible observation of both culture and personality as they are interrelated in real life. In a large metropolis such as San Juan or New York the family is a natural unit of study.

Ideally our objective is the naturalistic observation of the life of "our" families, with a minimum of intervention. Such intensive study, however, necessarily involves the establishment of deep personal ties. My assistants include two Mexicans whose families I have studied; their Mexican's-eye view" of the Peurto Rican slum has helped to point up the similarities and differences between the Mexican and Puerto Rican subcultures. We have spent many hours attending family parties, wakes and baptisms, responding to emergency calls, taking people to hospital, getting them out of jail, filling out applications for them, hunting apartments with them, helping them to get jobs or to get on relief. With each member of these families we conduct tape-recorded interviews, taking down their life stories and their answers to questions on a wide variety of topics. For the ordering of our material we undertake to reconstruct, by close interrogation, the history of a week or more of consecutive days in the lives of each family, and we observe and record complete days as they unfold. The first volume to issue from this study is to be published next month under the title of *La Vida, a Puerto Rican Family in the Culture of Poverty* — San Juan and New York (Random House).

There are many poor people in the world. Indeed, the poverty of the two-thirds of the world's population who live in the underdeveloped countries has been rightly called "the problem of problems." But not all of them by any means live in the culture of poverty. For this way of life to come into being and flourish it seems clear that certain preconditions must be met.

The setting is a cash economy, with wage labor and production for profit and with a persistently high rate of unemployment and underemployment at low wages, for unskilled labor. The society fails to provide social, political and economic organization, on either a voluntary basis or by government imposition, for the low-income population. There is a bilateral kinship system centered on the nuclear progenetive family, as distinguished from the unilateral extended kinship system of lineage and clan. The dominant class asserts a set of values that prizes thrift and the accumulation of wealth and property, stresses the possibility of upward mobility and explains low economic status as the result of individual personal inadequacy and inferiority.

Where these conditions prevail the way of life that develops among some of the poor is the culture of poverty. That is why I have described it as a subculture of the Western social order. It is both an adaptation and a reaction of the poor to their marginal position in a class-stratified, highly individuated, capitalistic society. It represents an effort to cope with feelings of hopelessness and despair that arise from the realization by the members of the marginal communities in these societies of the improbability of their achieving success in terms of the prevailing values and goals. Many of the traits of the culture of poverty can be viewed as local, spontaneous attempts to meet needs not served in the case of the poor by the institutions and agencies of the larger society because the poor are not eligible for such service, cannot afford it or are ignorant and suspicious.

Once the culture of poverty has come into existence it tends to perpetuate itself. By the time slum children are six or seven they have usually absorbed the basic attitudes and values of their subculture. Thereafter they are psychologically unready to take full advantage of changing conditions or improving opportunities that may develop in their lifetime.

My studies have identified some 70 traits that characterize the culture of poverty. The principal ones may be described in four dimensions of the system: the relationship between the subculture and the larger society; the nature of the slum community; the nature of the family, and the attitudes, values and character structure of the individual.

The disengagement, the nonintegration, of the poor with respect to the major institutions of society is a crucial element in the culture of poverty. It reflects the combined effect of a variety of factors including poverty, to begin with, but also segregation and discrimination, fear, suspicion and apathy and the development of alternative institutions and procedures in the slum community. The people do not belong to labor unions or political parties and make little use of banks, hospitals, department stores or museums. Such involvement as there is in the institutions of the larger society — in the jails, the army and the public welfare system — does little to suppress the traits of the culture of poverty. A relief system that barely keeps people alive perpetuates rather than eliminates poverty and the pervading sense of hopelessness.

People in a culture of poverty produce little wealth and receive little in return. Chronic unemployment and underemployment, low wages, lack of property, lack of savings, absence of food reserves in the home and chronic shortage of cash imprison the family and the individual in a vicious circle. Thus for lack of cash the slum householder makes frequent purchases of small quantities of food at higher prices. The slum economy turns inward; it shows a high incidence of pawning of personal goods, borrowing at usurious rates of interest, informal credit arrangements among neighbors, use of secondhand clothing and furniture.

There is awareness of middle-class values. People talk about them and even claim some of them as their own. On the whole, however, they do not live by them. They will declare that marriage by law, by the church or by both is the ideal form of marriage, but few will marry. For men who have no steady jobs, no property and no prospect of wealth to pass on to their children, who live in the present without expectations of the future, who want to avoid the expense and legal difficulties involved in marriage and divorce, a free union or consensual marriage makes good sense. The women, for their part, will turn down offers of marriage from men who are likely to be immature, punishing and generally unreliable. They feel that a consensual union gives them some of the freedom and flexibility men have. By not giving the fathers of their children legal status as husbands, the women have a stronger claim on the children. They also maintain exclusive rights to their own property.

Along with disengagement from the larger society, there is a hostility to the basic institutions of what are regarded as the dominant classes. There is hatred of the police, mistrust of government and of those in high positions and a cynicism that extends to the church. The culture of poverty thus holds a certain potential for protest and for entrainment in political movements aimed against the existing order.

With its poor housing and overcrowding, the community of the culture of poverty is high in gregariousness, but it has a minimum of organization beyond the nuclear and extended family. Occasionally slum dwellers come together in temporary informal groupings; neighborhood gangs that cut across slum settlements represent a considerable advance beyond the zero point of the continuum I have in mind. It is the low level of organization that gives the culture of poverty its marginal and anomalous quality in our highly organized society. Most primitive peoples have achieved a higher degree of sociocultural organization than contemporary urban slum dwellers. This is not to say that there may not be a sense of community and *esprit de corps* in a slum neighborhood. In fact, where slums are isolated from their surroundings by enclosing walls or other physical barriers, where rents are low and residence is stable and where the population constitutes a distinct ethnic, racial or language group, the sense of community may approach that of a village. In Mexico City and San Juan such territoriality is engendered by the scarcity of low-cost housing outside of established slum areas. In South Africa it is actively enforced by the *apartheid* that confines rural migrants to prescribed locations.

The family in the culture of poverty does not cherish childhood as a specially prolonged and protected stage in the life cycle. Initiation into sex comes early. With the instability of consensual marriage the family tends to be mother-centered and tied more closely to the mother's extended family. The female head of the house is given to authoritarian rule. In spite of much verbal emphasis on family solidarity, sibling rivalry for the limited supply of goods and maternal affection is intense. There is little privacy.

The individual who grows up in this culture has a strong feeling of fatalism, helplessness, dependence and inferiority. These traits, so often remarked in the current literature as characteristic of the American Negro, I found equally strong in the slum dwellers of Mexico City and San Juan, who are not segregated or discriminated against as a distinct ethnic or racial group. Other traits include a high incidence of weak ego structure, orality and confusion of sexual identification, all reflecting maternal deprivation; a strong present-time orientation with relatively little disposition to defer gratification and plan for the future, and a high tolerance for psychological pathology of all kinds. There is widespread belief in male superiority and among the men a strong preoccupation with *machismo,* their masculinity.

Provincial and local in outlook, with little sense of history, these people know only their own neighborhood and their own way of life. Usually they do not have the knowledge, the vision or the ideology to see the similarities between their troubles and those of their counterparts elsewhere in the world. They are not class-conscious, although they are sensitive indeed to symbols of status.

The distinction between poverty and the culture of poverty is basic to the model described here. There are numerous examples of poor people whose way of life I would not characterize as belonging to this subculture. Many primitive and preliterate peoples that have been studied by anthropologists suffer dire poverty attributable to low technology or thin resources or both. Yet even the simplest of these peoples have a high degree of social organization and a relatively integrated satisfying and self-sufficient culture.

In India the destitute lower-caste peoples — such as the Chamars, the leatherworkers, and the Bhangis, the sweepers — remain integrated in the larger society and have their own panchayat institutions of self-government. Their panchayats and their extended unilateral kinship systems, or clans, cut across village lines, giving them a strong sense of identity and continuity. In my studies of these people I found no culture of poverty to go with their poverty.

The Jews of eastern Europe were a poor urban people, often confined to ghettos. Yet they did not have many traits of the culture of poverty. They had a tradition of literacy that placed great value on learning; they formed many voluntary associations and adhered with devotion to the central community organization around the rabbi, and they had a religion that taught them they were the chosen people.

I would cite also a fourth, somewhat speculative example of poverty dissociated from the culture of poverty. On the basis of limited direct observation in one country — Cuba — and from indirect evidence, I am inclined to believe the culture of poverty does not exist in socialist countries. In 1947 I undertook a study of a slum in Havana. Recently I had an opportunity to revisit the same slum and some of the same families. The physical aspect of the place had changed little, except for a beautiful new nursery school. The people were as poor as before, but I was impressed to find much less of the feelings of despair and apathy, so symptomatic of the culture of poverty in the urban slums of the U.S. The slum was now highly organized, with block committees, educational committees, party committees. The people had found a new sense of power and importance in a doctrine that glorified the lower class as the hope of humanity, and they were armed. I was told by one Cuban official that the Castro government had practically eliminated delinquency by giving arms to the delinquents!

Evidently the Castro regime — revising Marx and Engels — did not write off the so-called *lumpenproletariat* as an inherently reactionary and antirevolutionary force but rather found in them a revolutionary potential and utilized it. Frantz Fanon, in his book *The Wretched of the Earth,* makes a similar evaluation of their role in the Algerian revolution: "It is within this mass of humanity, this people of the shantytowns, at the core of the *lumpenproletariat,* that the rebellion will find its urban spearhead. For the *lumpenproletariat,* that horde of starving men, uprooted from their tribe and from their clan, constitutes one of the most spontaneous and most radical revolutionary forces of a colonized people."[1]

It is true that I have found little revolutionary spirit or radical ideology among low-income Puerto Ricans. Most of the families I studied

[1] Frantz Fanon, *The Wretched of the Earth,* translated from the French by Constance Farrington, Copyright 1963 by Presence Africaine (New York: Grove Press, 1963), p. 129.

were politically conservative, about half of them favoring the Statehood Republican Party, which provides opposition on the right to the Popular Democratic Party that dominates the politics of the commonwealth. It seems to me, therefore, that disposition for protest among people living in the culture of poverty will vary considerably according to the national context and historical circumstances. In contrast to Algeria, the independent movement in Peurto Rico has found little popular support. In Mexico, where the cause of independence carried long ago, there is no longer any such movement to stir the dwellers in the new and old slums of the capital city.

Yet it would seem that any movement – be it religious, pacifist or revolutionary – that organizes and gives hope to the poor and effectively promotes a sense of solidarity with larger groups must effectively destroy the psychological and social core of the culture of poverty. In this connection, I suspect that the civil rights movement among American Negroes has of itself done more to improve their self-image and self-respect than such economic gains as it has won although, without doubt, the two kinds of progress are mutually reinforcing. In the culture of poverty of the American Negro the additional disadvantage of racial discrimination has generated a potential for revolutionary protest and organization that is absent in the slums of San Juan and Mexico City and, for that matter, among the poor whites in the South.

If it is true, as I suspect, that the culture of poverty flourishes and is endemic to the free-enterprise, pre-welfare-state stage of capitalism, then it is also endemic in colonial societies. The most likely candidates for the culture of poverty would be the people who come from the lower strata of a rapidly changing society and who are already partially alienated from it. Accordingly the subculture is likely to be found where imperial conquest has smashed the native social and economic structure and held the natives, perhaps for generations, in servile status, or where feudalism is yielding to capitalism in the later evolution of a colonial economy. Landless rural workers who migrate to the cities, as in Latin America, can be expected to fall into this way of life more readily than migrants from stable peasant villages with a well-organized traditional culture, as in India. It remains to be seen, however, whether the culture of poverty has not already begun to develop in the slums of Bombay and Calcutta. Compared with Latin America also, the strong corporate nature of many African tribal societies may tend to inhibit or delay the formation of a full-blown culture of poverty in the new towns and cities of that continent. In South Africa the institutionalization of repression and discrimination under *apartheid* may also have begun to promote an immunizing sense of identity and group consciousness among the African Negroes.

One must therefore keep the dynamic aspects of human institutions forward in observing and assessing the evidence for the presence, the waxing or the waning of this subculture. Measured on the dimension of relationship to the larger society, some slum dwellers may have a warmer identification with their national tradition even though they suffer deeper poverty than members of a similar community in another country. In Mexico City a high percentage of our respondents, including those with little or no formal schooling, knew of Cuauhtémoc, Hidalgo, Father Morelos, Juarez Diaz, Zapata, Carranza and Cardenas. In San Juan the names of Ramon Power, José de Diego Baldorioty de Castro, Ramon Betances, Nemesio Canales, Lloréns Torres rang no bell; a few could tell about the late Albizu Campos. For the lower-income Puerto Rican, however, history begins with Munoz Rivera and ends with his son Munoz Marin.

The national context can make a big difference in the play of the crucial traits of fatalism and hopelessness. Given the advanced technology, the high level of literacy, the all-pervasive reach of the media of mass communications and the relatively high aspirations of all sectors of the population, even the poorest and most marginal communities of the U.S. must aspire to a larger future than the slum dwellers of Ecuador and Peru, where the actual possibilities are more limited and where an authoritarian social order persists in city and country.

Among the 50 million U.S. citizens now more or less officially certified as poor, I would guess that about 20 per cent live in a culture of poverty. The largest numbers in this group are made up of Negroes, Puerto Ricans, Mexicans, American Indians and Southern poor whites. In these figures there is some reassurance for those concerned, because it is much more difficult to undo the culture of poverty than to cure poverty itself.

Middle-class people — this would certainly include most social scientists — tend to concentrate on the negative aspects of the culture of poverty. They attach a minus sign to such traits as present-time orientation and readiness to indulge impulses. I do not intend to idealize or romanticize the culture of poverty — "it is easier to praise poverty than to live in it." Yet the positive aspects of these traits must not be overlooked. Living in the present may develop a capacity for spontaneity, for the enjoyment of the sensual, which is often blunted in the middle-class, future-oriented man. Indeed, I am often struck by the analogies that can be drawn between the mores of the very rich — of the "jet set" and "café society" — and the culture of the very poor. Yet it is, on the whole, a comparatively superficial culture. There is in it much pathos, suffering and emptiness. It does not provide much support or satisfaction; its pervading mistrust magnifies individual helplessness and isolation. Indeed, poverty of culture is one of the crucial traits of the culture of poverty.

The concept of the culture of poverty provides a generalization that may help to unify and explain a number of phenomena hitherto viewed as peculiar to certain racial, national or regional groups. Problems we think of as being distinctively our own or distinctively Negro (or as typifying any other ethnic group) prove to be endemic in countries where there are no segregated ethnic minority groups. If it follows that the elimination of physical poverty may not by itself eliminate the culture of poverty, then an understanding of the sub-culture may contribute to the design of measures specific to that purpose.

What is the future of the culture of poverty? In considering this question one must distinguish between those countries in which it represents a relatively small segment of the population and those in which it constitutes a large one. In the U.S. the major solution proposed by social workers dealing with the "hard core" poor has been slowly to raise their level of living and incorporate them in the middle class. Wherever possible psychiatric treatment is prescribed.

In underdeveloped countries where great masses of people live in the culture of poverty, such a social-work solution does not seem feasible. The local psychiatrists have all they can do to care for their own growing middle class. In those countries the people with a culture of poverty may seek a more revolutionary solution. By creating basic structural changes in society, by redistributing wealth, by organizing the poor and giving them a sense of belonging, of power and of leadership, revolutions frequently succeed in abolishing some of the basic characteristics of the culture of poverty even when they do not succeed in curing poverty itself.

2. *Education and the Lower-Class Child**

Howard S. Becker

Schools, among their other functions, are avenues of social mobility in our society. They provide one of the means by which children of the well-to-do maintain their families' class position and children of the poor rise to new and higher slots in the social scale. Since our society is committed to the ideal of a relatively open class system, one in which everyone has a chance to rise, the degree to which our public schools give everyone a chance to acquire the knowledge, skills, and diplomas necessary for that mobility is a matter of public concern. To the degree that the schools discriminate against lower-class groups our class system is tightening up a little more. Social scientists have repeatedly addressed themselves to this problem, looking for the fact and consequences of discrimination.

The notion of "equality of educational opportunity" is extremely ambiguous and on its definition depends the diagnosis and treatment of the problem. Does it mean that every child, regardless of his class position, should be provided with equal facilities of a material sort, and then left to shift for himself? Or is simply providing an equal number of teachers, books, and school-rooms, without taking into account the differences in ability to learn what the school has to teach, only a more subtle form of discrimination against the lower-class child who has not been trained to take full advantage of these resources? Can we achieve equality only by providing better-than-average facilities for those of less-than-average ability, as we do for the physically handicapped? Or would this again fail to deal with discrimination, since an educational program built around middle-class ideals, no matter what the facilities offered, slights the skills of the lower-class child at the expense of those possessed by the middle-class child? Ought education to be adapted to the pupil, if necessary by radically altering the character of that education?

The dilemmas and paradoxes suggested by these questions constitute the basic themes of social science research in this area. An investigation of some of the major pieces of research reveals the complexity of the problem and suggests a number of directions in which change might be sought.

Early Research

George S. Counts was one of the pioneers in research in educational discrimination. In a series of publications in the 1920's he raised the question of who ran the nation's public schools and who reaped their educational benefits. He answered it in terms suggested by a theory that saw society as composed of conflicting economic-interest groups.

His studies "The Selective Character of American Secondary Education"[1] and "The Social Composition of Boards of Education"[2] used major occupational categories in analyzing the differential participation of the various economic classes in the educational system. The first showed clearly that lower-class children did not get to high school in the same proportion as middle-class children. Counts attributed this largely to economic circumstances that forced the lower-class child to go to work: "The free public high school . . . did not by any means equalize educational opportunity; for the cost of tuition is not the entire cost of education or even the larger part of it. Education means leisure, and leisure is an expensive luxury."[3] He suggested that if higher education were to be selective (as seemed economically inevitable) it should select on the grounds of the student's intellectual ability rather than of the parents' ability to support their child through more training.

His analysis of American boards of education tackled the same question from a different angle. Here he asked: Who runs our school systems, and what interests do they represent? The results demonstrated that control rested largely in the hands of the dominant economic classes of the community, and that manual laborers and the growing white-collar classes, who made up the bulk of urban population, were grossly underrepresented. His figures on more than five hundred city school boards make the point:

*Occupations of Male Members of School Boards**

OCCUPATION	PERCENTAGE
Proprietors	32
Professional Service	30
Managerial Service	14
Commercial Service	6
Clerical Service	6
Manual Labor	8
Agricultural Service	2
Unknown	2

*Adapted from George S. Counts, "The Social Composition of Boards of Education," *Supplementary Educational Monographs,* July 1927, p. 52.

Counts' fear was that school boards so composed would simply impose on the whole educational system the viewpoint dictated by the economic and social interests of their members or would become (a possibility his later study of the Chicago schools suggested) a mere reflection of the warring political interests of the community. In either case, important issues would be decided by a group in which one of the interested parties — the working class — had no representative.

Discrimination for Counts, is political and economic. Children are deprived of needed facilities or herded into segregated educational dead ends because it is to the interest of politically powerful groups to do so. The working-class child may be denied anything but an elementary or vocational training by such means. The remedy seems clear, if not sure. These depressed classes should be more adequately represented in policy-making bodies and should operate there to protect their class interest. The ends of democracy will be served if all children are provided with equal educational facilities and more adequately representative school boards will give the political process a chance to work so as to provide equality in that sense.

Today these seem to be dead issues. Many of the specific proposals and counterproposals are long forgotten. The new trend in accusations of inequality deals with quite different sorts of matters. There remain, however, in such matters as the allocation of funds for new school buildings, dangers of injustices such as Counts feared. These issues tend now to be ignored for what are considered more basic forms of discrimination.

The Middle-Class School

This new direction in reasearch is a direct outgrowth of the work of W. Lloyd Warner and his associates on American class structure. One of the by-products of the group's studies of communities in New England, the South, and the Midwest was *Who Shall Be Educated?* which introduced a different concept of educational discrimination.[4]

Noting that one of the school's functions in these communities was to sort children and select from among them persons destined for social mobility, they went on to point out that the people who actually operate the schools and who are of the greatest importance in this selective process — the teachers and principal — are themselves middle class. Each class grouping tends to meet different environmental problems and, consequently, to develop a somewhat unique culture. The lower-class child learns ways of behaving that are appropriate to the facts of lower-class life but are extremely inappropriate to a school that is an embodiment of middle-class values. His language, the things he strives for, the ways in which he strives for them — all these class-influenced styles of conduct form the basis of his teachers' judgments as to whether he has what

[1] *Supplementary Educational Monographs,* May 1922.

[2] *Ibid.,* July 1927.

[3] "The Selective Character of American Secondary Education," p. 148.

[4] W. Lloyd Warner and others, *Who Shall Be Educated? The Challenge of Unequal Opportunities* (New York: Harper, 1944).

it takes to get ahead. And these judgments determine how teachers will treat him and thus, in large part, influence his actual chances for mobility. If he adopts middle-class ways of behavior he will be encouraged and aided in getting the additional education necessary for further mobility. If he does not, school will be made so difficult for him that he will quit as soon as possible, thus condemning himself to a lower-class adulthood.

Intelligence Testing

This point of view was carried a good deal further, with more technical subtlety and a franker appreciation of all its implications, by Allison Davis and his colleagues at the University of Chicago.[5]

The bulk of the work deals with intelligence testing. IQ testing is viewed as one of the many items of middle-class culture giving the school its distinctive class tone and tending to favor the middle-class at the expense of the lower. This treatment of the IQ test as symptomatic is reasonable, in view of its widespread use as an indicator of natural ability.

Davis points out that these tests cover only a very small part of the total conceivable range of human mental abilities, concentrating almost entirely on verbal, bookish skills in which middle-class children tend to be systematically trained by their parents while lower-class children have far less contact with tasks involving their exercise. One would expect, therefore, that lower-class children would be less adept at solving these kinds of problems.

The Eells study, in which a number of conventional paper-and-pencil IQ tests were administered to over five thousand children in the Rockford, Illinois, schools, demonstrated that lower-class children did in fact get lower scores. But, as Eells carefully points out, the meaning of this is not entirely clear. It may mean that lower-class children are naturally less bright. Or it may mean that despite natural ability their environment has not stimulated them to learn so that they are developmentally unintelligent. Or it may mean that the tests are biased to produce these results — that is, that there are no real differences in actual ability, the differences in test scores being mere artifacts of the test construction. Although there is conflicting evidence and the results might be explained in terms of any one of these hypotheses, Eells favors the last of them, apparently convinced by his further analysis of those test items on which there is the greatest discrepancy between middle- and lower-class performance. For these items do tend to be primarily verbal, depending on skill with words and a large vocabulary.

Davis continues, in further support of the notion that there are no real differences in actual ability between the two groups with this argument:

> *If, however, it is granted that the genetic potential is equal between classes, it follows that there should be some major problem areas in which the more pertinent lower-class cultural experiences would render*

the lower-class superior. The middle-class may be expected to prove superior on the present tests, because this group has had more training on the specific test problems or on closely related problems. Their motivation is also more adaptive, as a result of their cultural training.[6]

He goes on to argue that although it may turn out that the middle-class children will do better on all kinds of test problems because of their cultural advantage in work habits and in motivation to do well in the testing situation, we do not know that this will be the case; in fact, it often happens that such training cannot be generalized in this way.

Unfortunately, the results of the Eells study do not support this, for lower-class children exhibit no such areas of superior ability, although there are some in which they appear equal. This may, of course, again be a function of the tests themselves, which may include no items which might tap these particular skills. It may also be due to the factor of motivation, of which Davis makes a great deal. If the lower-class child sees the intelligence test simply as another one of those incomprehensible things inflicted on him by the middle-class teacher – difficult because of his lack of training, and something for which he is not likely to be rewarded as the middle-class child is rewarded by his parents – he is not likely to try very hard and, consequently, not likely to do well. Eells' analysis of class differences in test mistakes gives reason to believe that many more lower-class children take tests in a hit-or-miss fashion, checking any answer and not caring much how it turns out, knowing they will do poorly and wanting only to get through the painful business as quickly as possible. Any test in which motivation is not controlled is thus likely to be unfair and discriminatory.

This critique of intelligence testing becomes the basis for a general indictment by Davis and Eells of contemporary educational practice, which presumably operates on much the same class-cultural premises. Discrimination in education is, in this view, a subtle and pervasive thing, built into the very tools of education, from intelligence tests to children's primers. The same cultural blinders prevent teachers from perceiving lower-class talent and ensure that they will perpetuate the social-class system by encouraging those who possess the same middle-class skills that have proved so useful to them. The principle of equality is thus violated by conducting education in a way that gives those students with middle-class training an unfair advantage. The lower-class child must run in a mobility race that is already rigged against him.

Quality or Equality?

A basic question here is clouded by the device of labeling all knowledge in social-class terms. Is everything the school has to teach – our whole heritage of literacy and culture – to be lumped together under

[5] See Kenneth Eells and others, *Intelligence and Cultural Differences* (Chicago: University of Chicago Press, 1951), and Allison Davis, *Social Class Influences Upon Learning* (Cambridge, Mass.: Harvard University Press, 1948).

[6] Eells and others, p. 28.

the term "middle-class skill?" Or is there something in this heritage that transcends class lines and cannot be dropped, even in the name of equality? Granted that there are obvious elements of middle-class bookishness in the way our schools do business, we need not on that account give up the ideal of a school that will transmit our cultural tradition; and how transmit it but by teaching those things so lightly passed off as "middle-class skills?" Granted that much "culture" is merely middle-class snobbery, a seeking after prestige rather than truth or beauty, we still cannot write off science, literature, art, music, philosophy — the truly great cultural achievements — in this simple way; they are something more than "middle-class" and must be among the major concerns of any good school.

If we want the schools to teach in such a way that the solid content of a humane education is not sacrificed, and yet do our best to see that opportunities for mobility are equitably distributed, we must realize that there are many kinds of discrimination against lower-class children that call for a different interpretation of the problem and different remedies. These are inequities produced, not by a class-slanting of subject matter and teaching style, but by matters of institutional functioning — administrative procedure, staff-recruiting arrangements, the nature of community organization — which, only on their face, appear to have no relation to the problem.

Another series of studies, done at the University of Chicago under the general direction of Everett C. Hughes, focused on precisely these matters.[7] Interviews with teachers, parents, and principals and statistical studies of school records, all in Chicago, concentrated on those elements of discrimination that were built into the operating structure of the school system. These tended to be things that might be altered so as to do away with some of the lower-class child's handicaps without forcing any drastic reduction of educational standards.

Although these studies have made much use of the Davis findings, they were concerned more with a set of problems that would probably persist even if the curriculum were tailored to the lower-class student. These are problems which, as things now stand, compound the difficulties of the lower-class child so that he has not only his own inadequacies of background to overcome, but an additional set of obstacles that does not confront the middle-class child. If these obstacles were done away with, the lower-class child might still be penalized by the difference in class cultures, but in all other respects he would have an equal opportunity to get an education.

What are these difficulties? In the first place, for the reasons that Davis has pointed out, the middle-class teacher finds it very difficult to teach lower-class children because of their poor background and motivation. Teaching them would require more time spent with each pupil for the "normal" amount of work to be accomplished. But two things interfere: the extreme overcrowding of many lower-class schools, so that there are more rather than fewer pupils in the average class, and the problem of discipline. Lower-class children are harder to control, and it becomes a matter of survival for the young teacher and a point of honor for the older one to "keep them in line." A large proportion of school time is spent in this enterprise so that precisely where more time should be spent on schoolwork actually less is available, the teachers devoting themselves to keeping order and in many cases hardly attempting any teaching at all.

Another obstacle is created by the administrative arrangements of a school system like Chicago's. Teachers are allowed to transfer from school to school at their own request, as soon as there are openings for which they are the first in line. A statistical analysis of their requests showed that many teachers want to teach in schools in middle-class areas and none want to leave, while teachers greatly dislike schools in the slums.[8] Because they find lower-class children difficult to work with, teachers flee the slums for the security and ease of the position in the more rewarding middle-class school; when they get one of these much-sought-after positions they keep it for life. The middle-class school acquires the immeasurable advantage of a stable and experienced teaching force, while the lower-class school is staffed year after year by new, inexperienced teachers (who accept the assignment only because they have not enough seniority to get anything better), and by those oldtimers who have made their peace with the situation and have given up trying. This kind of assignment system almost singlehandedly disables the slum school, whose pupils' chance at an education is greatly diminished by the inexperience and instability of the staff that teaches them.

Finally, the middle-class school must toe the educational line and do its job well, for it is watched over by parents who know what they want and have no qualms about complaining in effective ways when they do not get it. The lower-class parent tends to be resigned to his child's poor performance, to sullenly resent the school but to be afraid to combat it. He falls victim far more readily to the teachers' "conspiracy of silence," and is less likely to find out what is actually going on in school; even if he were ready to complain, he would find it more difficult to actually learn what there is to complain about. Unlike the middle-class school, the slum school is not prodded by its pupils' parents. But where

[7] This research is reported in Howard S. Becker, "Social-Class Variations in the Teacher-Pupil Relationship," *Journal of Educational Sociology,* April 1952, pp. 451-65; "The Teacher in the Authority System of the Public School," *ibid.,* November 1953, pp. 128-41; "The Career of the Chicago Public School Teacher," *American Journal of Sociology,* March 1952, pp. 470-77; and in Harold MacDowell, "The Principal's Role in a Metropolitan School System" (Ph.D. dissertation, University of Chicago, 1954), and John Winget, "Ecological and Socio-Cultural Factors in Teacher Interschool Mobility," (Ph.D. dissertation, University of Chicago, 1953).

[8] This analysis is reported in Winget.

there are no complaints, higher administration is less likely to check up; hence the school can carry on a lower grade of educational activity with little fear of being criticized for it.

The lower-class school, then, is staffed by inexperienced teachers who do not spend much time teaching and who are not watched over by anxious parents who know how to protect their children's interests. The slum child not only starts out with a cultural handicap, but administrative practice, the career aspirations of teachers, the power differentials between communities all combine to produce a situation in which he gets not even an equal chance to compete, much less the greater chance Davis and others desire to provide by remaking the curriculum.

The remedies suggested by this diagnosis do not require a complete recasting of our entire educational system, but rather concrete steps to remove each of these disabilities. For example, the system of assigning teachers might be arranged so that each school got its fair share of new and of experienced teachers; this one change alone would cut down lower-class school problems and would allow for a far higher standard of teaching. Again, class size might be reduced in those schools; discipline would become far less a problem and more school time could be devoted to teaching. It is even conceivable that the parents in a lower-class community might be organized to act as a watch-dog committee, performing a policy function similar to that of the middle-class PTA. (The PTA in lower-class communities is usually run by the teachers, and is used to coerce cooperation from the parents when the teachers find it useful.)

There would, of course, be difficulties in bringing about even such relatively small changes as these. Teachers would undoubtedly fight changes in the assignment procedure, and would be made unhappy by any effort to encourage further parental "interference" in the school. Any effort to cut class size in heavily populated slum areas would mean either an appreciable increase in the tax bill or a drastic cut in personnel and standards in middle-class areas, either of which would bring us face to face with the kinds of pressures Counts described twenty-five years ago. It is in this context, perhaps, that we see the larger import of his emphasis on the class composition of school boards.) The net effect of these changes, however, would be to ensure every child an equal share of an experienced teacher's effort. This would constitute a substantial equalization of the conditions of education for all groups, a long step toward the democratic sharing of the educational opportunity so necessary for the maintenance of an open-class system.

3. *Canada's Indians: A Powerless Minority*

Jim Harding

Because of the increased interest . . . in the so-called "Indian Problem" many observers look optimistically to the future when the pockets of racial discrimination in Canada will have disappeared.

Such optimism, in my view, is deceptive, and is based upon a superficial analysis of the problems facing people of Indian ancestry. Basic value questions regarding the self-determination of people and their right to participate in making decisions that shape their future, are not asked. Basic relationships between minority group problems and the society at large are ignored, and because of this, a crisis situation for democracy, which is directly related to the problems of people of Indian ancestry, is not foreseen.

THE STATUS OF PEOPLE OF INDIAN ANCESTRY

Since the publication, in 1962, of Michael Harrington's book, *The Other America,* poverty has become a topic of discussion in many North American circles. Partly as a result of the Negro movement in the U.S. bringing our attention to poverty among ethnic minorities, and partly because it is now acknowledged that poverty is still widespread in the so-called "affluent society," more political talk has centered around the issue of poverty in the past three years.

Harrington talks of our "emotional and existential ignorance of poverty" in North America. He describes *The Other America* as being the first minority poor in history and of being the "best dressed poverty the world has ever known." Because of this, he calls *The Other America* invisible. Many of the American poor are too old to be seen, and the

*Originally published by The Student Union for Peace Action, 1965. Reprinted with amendments by permission of the author.

poverty among the young does not disturb the dominant middle-class life in America. And, what we are especially concerned with in this paper, "the poor are politically invisible, too."

Harrington shows how interrelated are questions of socio-economic status and class with questions of power in society. For example, he reveals how the welfare state in fact benefits those who least require help; and how changes in technology and automation enhance, rather than alleviate, the problems of *The Other America*. For the poor, according to Harrington, "progress is misery."

The trouble is taken here to outline Harrington's book because it adequately shows the organic relationships among various aspects of a society. For instance, Harrington does *not* view the problems of ethnic minorities in isolation from *The Other America* in general; and to do so in Canada would be to fail to grasp the real nature of the problems facing people of Indian ancestry. The inherent relationship between the problems of ethnic minorities and the general problem of poverty and class in society will later be stressed, and the problem of power will be discussed in this regard. For now, Harrington has been mentioned to exemplify general socio-economic and political relationships in society.

With this organic concept in mind, let us discuss the status of people of Indian ancestry in Canada. There is increasing evidence that "Another Canada" exists, and that wherever one goes it is manifest. The growing population of people of Indian ancestry in Canada constitutes a large segment of that Other Canada.

The social scientist writing on social class often refers to the "life chances" of an individual or group. To describe the status of people of Indian ancestry, it is useful to think in terms of the "distribution of life chances" in Canadian society. By looking at the life chances of this minority in view of income and occupations, education, life expectancy and health, and the administration of justice and legal protection, one can obtain the overview of the general status of people of Indian ancestry that allows one to relate this minority to power in Canada.

Income

In discussing the income level of people of Indian ancestry one must remember that other sections of the population also exist at similar low-living standards. In this regard the Indian and Metis are but one part of The Other Canada. However, the striking fact is that poverty hits people of Indian ancestry far harder.

A Federation of Labour publication, *Poverty in Ontario,* defines "destitution" as living per year on $1,000 or less for an individual, or on $3,000 or less for an average Canadian family of four. The report notes that in Canada 13% of the population lives at this level of income.

It is shocking that over 40% of the Indian-Metis *families* in Canada obtain an income of $1,000 or less, the level set for abject poverty or destitution of an individual. Clearly, the Indian and Metis are solidly at the bottom of Canada's economic scale.

Seventy-five per cent of Indian and Metis families obtain $2,000 or less per year. In view of the larger family size, this suggests that this minority almost universally lives under conditions of abject poverty. In northern parts of Saskatchewan, it has been found that the average income of Indian and Metis families is around $500, putting these people at a level of underdevelopment comparable to many places in Africa, Asia or Latin America.

Employment

The 1961 Census reported that the Indian and Metis were the least employed segment of the employable labor force in Canada. Only 15.9% of the total employable Indians and Metis were in the labor force that year, compared to 35.7% for the rest of the population. But these statistics alone do not leave an accurate picture. Most of the employment of people of Indian ancestry is seasonal and short-term, and Census reports indicate that people of Indian ancestry are under-represented in every occupational classification except the most unskilled, low-status and menial.

Housing and Health

More than 16% of Indian and Metis families live in one-room shacks, and more than 50% of them live in three or less rooms. (Again, these figures have to be considered in view of the larger family size.) The Ontario Federation of Labour publication referred to, states that about 11% of Canadian homes lack running water. The fact that only 13% of Indian and Metis homes have running water blatantly reveals the housing conditions in which these native Canadians live.

The infant mortality rate for people of Indian ancestry is three times the national average – that is, for every 1,000 births among people of Indian ancestry there are 75 deaths. The pre-school age mortality rate is eight times the national average, and in teenage and adult groups it is between two and one-half and three times the national average. People of Indian ancestry require hospitalization twice as often as the rest of the Canadian population. When it is realized that few people of Indian ancestry are included in the so-called "universal" medical care programs now existing, the tragic health condition of this minority can be recognized.

Education

This same sub-standard trend is found in education. Only one-quarter of the Indian and Metis population attains a grade six level. Of the 7,000 Indian students in Canada in 1962-63, only 6% were in grades 9 to 12. The vast majority were in grades 1 to 4. In 1962-63, there were only 70 Indian students beyond high school in Canada. Six were registered in university, some were professional students, and the great bulk of them were in trade schools.

Administration of Justice

Unaware of their legal rights and privileges, or of the nature of charges made against them, it is typical for people of Indian ancestry to plead guilty without making any attempt to defend themselves. This is the case also for other segments of what is being called The Other Canada, but again the difference in degree exists. For example, in the Prince Albert Gaol for Women, it is standard for the Indian population to be greatly over-represented. More than 80% of the female population is Indian, and more than 10% is Metis. In a sample taken of the males in the Prince Albert Gaol in 1963, slightly more than 50% of the population between the ages of 16 and 30 was Indian or Metis. People of Indian ancestry in Saskatchewan constitute only about 5% of the total population.

The above evidence, plus the fact that the majority of sentences to people of Indian ancestry are for minor misdemeanors (chiefly intoxication and causing a disturbance) suggest that the administration of justice and legal protection is biased against people of Indian ancestry. For the same offenses, non-Indians often get no sentence, or only a fine. It is also common, especially in the north, for courts sentencing people of Indian ancestry to be held in the RCMP barracks and it has often been noted that the RCMP personnel suggest the sentence for people of Indian ancestry to the Justice of the Peace presiding.

THE SOURCE OF THE PROBLEMS

No one could argue that the above conditions . . . do not limit the participation of people of Indian ancestry in Canadian society. However, the argument begins when one starts to integrate the above descriptions into a theory of the sources of the problems facing these people. The statistics give a necessary, but not a sufficient, description of these problems. In addition, relationships, effects and sources of the problems have also to be discussed. (Far too often, social scientists stop after they describe a problem. It is my view that a social scientist also has the responsibility of explaining the basis of the problem so that prejudices, myths and superficial solutions are challenged.

One could say that the problems facing people of Indian ancestry occurred by accident, and are unfortunate results of the random growth of Canadian society. According to this view, it would be common to state that until the Indian and Metis completely assimilate into mainstream society and reject their cultural remnants, their underdevelopment will continue. Such a view would not point to any explicit factors underlying the problems.

I think, rather than this "random chance" view, that there is a systematic explanation for much of the development and maintenance of the problems facing people of Indian ancestry. I am not suggesting that the following view is a total one, only that it is basic to a full understanding. It is certainly a view which indicates that a systematic analysis can assist one to understand social problems or minority problems without resort to blaming the people involved.

A Colonial People

A strong argument exists for viewing Canadian people of Indian ancestry as a colonial people, who have been treated and in effect controlled by outside authorities over which they had no direct control. When one looks at the problems facing people of Indian ancestry with a historical perspective, such a view becomes highly tenable.

Erroneous explanations of the problems of people of Indian ancestry are common in Canada. While conventional wisdom in Canada regarding the situation of American Negroes is somewhat free of any superficiality, this is not the case regarding problems facing Indian and Metis. The fact that these problems are often referred to as the "Indian Problem" indicates the superficiality of thinking. Somehow the problems are viewed as arising from the Indian's or Metis' inherent inability to adjust to mainstream life. Such thinking lacks an appreciation of the interdependence of aspirations and motivations on the one hand, with socialization and opportunities on the other. Those who speak of the "Indian Problem" are explaining the problems in terms of the "Indian-ness" of some people.

Such erroneous thinking results from a confusion of correlation with causation. Because the historical and social treatment of a particular people correlates with particular physical characteristics (race) of that people, it does not mean that their characteristics – in this case, their "Indian-ness" – were the cause of the behavior arising from the treatment. The conventional view of this problem completely fails to recognize the cluster of social problems that people of Indian ancestry face, or the fact that these problems are not based on an Indian culture. Rather, as we shall see, they are problems resulting from a historical interdependence of the dominant society and this minority, which now lives within a "social problem milieu."

Indian reserves were established in the late 1800's as European settlements were being established in Canada with the aid of the railway. The decisions to have reserves were imposed on the native Indians. The reserve system is a product of non-Indian minds – a fact we often forget. Originally, the reserves were set up to concentrate the Indians, while allowing them to continue living in traditional ways. In addition to trapping, fishing and hunting, it was hoped that the reserves would enable Indians to develop an agricultural economy of their own.

As it turned out, the reserve system never did provide the expanding Indian population with a stable source of income, and thus, over the years, welfare payments have become a major source of their income. In fact, the reserve system as originally envisaged is now a complete anachronism. Few Indians have been able to earn a living from farming (especially in this day of farm "corporatization") and as the Indian population has doubled in the past 30 years, no chance of the reserve ever providing an independent source of income exists.

This fact of the failure of the reserve to provide a living for the Indian, and his consequent dependence on welfare from outside agencies, gives the first insight into the structural nature of the problems facing him. Because reserves separated Indians from communities where potential sources of income existed, and because this separation led them to view the reserve as security and the town and urban areas as threatening, much of the piling up of social problems for people of Indian ancestry has occurred over the years. Since these people have been cut off from mainstream life for 60 to 80 years, are unable to remain self-sufficient (because of imposed isolation on reserves), and are increasingly dependent on the growing welfare state in Canada, one should not be shocked at the apparent lack of morale, assertiveness or self-respect among many of them. (The fact that Indians were once legally restricted from leaving the reserve indicates the extent to which their isolation over the years has been imposed.) When this historical view is provided, comments like "they could get ahead if they wanted to" or "their values don't allow them to advance" are exposed as totally inadequate attitudes to the problem.

A historical view of the Metis provides the same kind of picture. The Metis, who were without reserve rights, waged a battle for the same political rights that easterners had fought for in the struggles for constitutional and responsible government in the first part of the 19th century. While history books distort much about the struggles of the Metis people (especially those under Louis Riel, which culminated in the North West Rebellion of 1885 at Batocho), factual accounts indicate that these struggles were on behalf of a people left without securities or guarantees of equality in the face of a conquering and more powerful social order.

The Metis never did receive the rights they fought for in the late 19th century. Because of their inability to maintain a subsistence living standard from the land and resources available for trapping, hunting and fishing, and because of their general isolation into northern communities, they became dependent upon provincial social aid in the same manner that the Indian became dependent on Federal welfare.

Indian Affairs

This historical picture must be supplemented with a discussion of Indian Affairs (which is a branch of the Department of Citizenship and Immigration in Ottawa), and of the role of churches in Indian Affairs. It is tragic and ironic that Canada's native population should be under the control of a branch of government in the Department of Immigration. Many people of Indian ancestry point to this irony as evidence of their colonial status. Canadians would perhaps be outraged if any other ethnic group in Canada existed under special control of one government branch, instead of having relations with all government branches as do other citizens. (However, cases have arisen in Canada where other minorities — the Japanese in World War II, and the Hutterites — have been under special control.)

The fact that all Canadian Indians, now totalling more than 200,000, are under the direct control of a centralized branch of government is another matter referred to by many as an indication of the colonial treatment of this minority. Under such a system, what amounts to a standard treatment of all people of Indian ancestry takes place, yet research is constantly showing how local and diverse are the conditions of these people throughout Canada. It is this centralized and standard treatment that most suggests a colonial form of treatment by the larger society and its agencies. In the past, no one could deny that the Indian was exploited economically in fur and fish dealings. This centralized and standard treatment is a continuation of older tendencies, both showing how structural are the conditions maintaining the low-life chances of this minority. With such treatment, and with distance between the decisions affecting people of Indian ancestry and their actual conditions, a bureaucratic relationship is almost inevitable. It is such bureaucracy that structurally impedes much progress among these people.

Obviously, if one does not allow a people to learn and develop responsibility, responsible behavior is unlikely. Often the failure to allow people of Indian ancestry to run their own affairs has created the conditions and attitudes whereby they are unable to run them. The self-fulfilling prophecy plays a major role in relationships between a dominant group and an ethnic minority, and there is no exception in the case of people of Indian ancestry. There are many examples of the treatment of Indian people that validate this statement. For example, Reserve Bands have their capital funds held in trust in Ottawa under Section 68 of the Indian Act, and have to ask permission to use it.* This paternalistic treatment is itself enough to maintain much of the bureaucratic psychology and dependent status of Indian people which underlies a great deal of the stagnancy of reserve life.

*EDITOR'S NOTE: The section of the act referred to by the author pertains to management of *revenue moneys* by the band and reads as follows:

68. (1) The Governor-in-Council may by order permit a band to control, manage, and expend in whole or in parts its revenue moneys and may amend or revoke any such order.

(2) The Governor-in-Council may make regulations to give effect to subsection (1) and may declare therein the extent to which its act and Federal Administration Act shall not apply to a band to which an order made under subsection (1) applies. 1951 c. 29, s. 68. Also see sections 61, 62, 63 re management of Indian Moneys Office.

Consolidation of the Indian Act. The Queen's Printer, Ottawa, Canada. Reprinted 1969.

Another example is the vote. The Indian right to vote federally was taken away in 1885, and until 1961 this minority was legally, not just socially, restrained from political participation. There are some who would argue that the Indian did not have the knowledge to vote, and that therefore the federal government had no alternative. However, such thinking fails to acknowledge the interdependence of expectations with behavior. At this time, voting rights are not yet universal for people of Indian ancestry† – legislation to give the provincial vote to Alberta Indians is just now on the books – and it will take a long time even after the vote is universal to counteract the effect of bureaucratic treatment over the years.

Until 1951, Band Councils did not have the right to make by-laws about the internal affairs of their reserve. This fact again points out how legislation has restricted the self-determination of this people. Perhaps, though, what I have called the colonial status of people on Indian ancestry is seen most clearly when one realizes the role of the churches in reserve life.

Religious education is the rule rather than the exception in Indian Affairs. Government money is provided to religious denominations to operate educational institutions for Indian students, both on and off reserves. The religious groups are empowered to hire the staff of their choice, which of course means of their denomination. What can only be labelled an indoctrination process of Indian students by the various churches, both Catholic and Protestant, is the result. At the expense of Indian self-determination, churches vie for potential "converts." It is a common story from the past, that where keen competition existed, church people would provide flour and grain in an attempt to persuade Indian parents to baptize their child into a certain denomination. Competition, at the expense of the freedom of Indian ancestry, has gone on to such extremes that in one southern Saskatchewan reserve there are eight denominations represented.

In provincial schools attended by Metis children, the power of the church is also common. It is not uncommon to find a nun as principal of public schools in northern areas, or for nuns to be the majority of the staff of such "public" schools. In some cases, whole Metis communities, such as *Ile à la Crosse* in northern Saskatchewan, are in effect operated by religious groups. Hospitals, schools, recreational facilities, etc., are to a large extent run by religious institutions, without the local people having any basic involvement in the major decisions.

This powerful association of church and state in Indian Affairs was clearly revealed some years back when government police (the RCMP) were used to remove Indian children to residential schools. These schools,

†EDITOR'S NOTE: Since this article was published, voting rights have been extended to people of Indian ancestry; however, Dr. Harding's comment regarding the time required to "counteract the effect of bureaucratic treatment" is probably still relevant.

operated by various churches, separated Indian children from their families for the bulk of the year, often by forcible means. Some could rationalize such treatment, but in all fairness these tactics are all too similar to the "colonial syndrome" to go unmentioned.

The word "colonial" may be too strong for some people. However, if the treatment of people of Indian ancestry has been of a colonial nature, the word should not be avoided simply because it bothers some people. Admittedly, it is difficult to actually document that a form of colonialism exists in the treatment of people of Indian ancestry. Colonialism is always something that some other country engages in — at least, we like to think so. However, a letter regarding tutorial services for Indian students in Regina, a letter written by an Indian Affairs official to Regina Indian students in high school, provides some insight into the interpersonal treatment of people of Indian ancestry. Part of this letter informs the students that the driver who picks them up is required to enter the house upon his arrival, introduce himself to the house mother and return with the student to the car. It is stressed that the driver is forbidden to merely stop and honk his horn for the student. The letter goes on to state that upon returning from the study group the driver is required to depart only after the student has entered the residence.

The letter shows the paternalism toward the Indian, and the psychology of Indian Affairs which, it is being argued here, largely underlies the maintenance of a dependent, low-life-chance status of this minority. Clearly, the official wouldn't see himself as a "colonial agent," or feel personally responsible for the historical treatment of people of Indian ancestry. However, such denial of responsibility is far too common in institutions through history that have in effect undermined the values of self-determination and freedom.

Impact of Dominant Values

The low life-chances of people of Indian ancestry, characterized by the cluster of problems that plague them and the fact that to a great extent these problems are based on, and enhanced by, a colonial status in society, are factors showing how necessary it is to analyze the total society to get a complete understanding of the nature of problems of a minority.

Not only is the interdependence of these problems with society at large shown by describing the structural and bureaucratic system that has affected people of Indian ancestry; but it is also shown by looking at the impact of dominant social values in this minority. In a centralized, industrial society, it is common for the dominant values to spread throughout all segments of the society, to permeate all socio-economic levels. This permeation of middle class aspirations and values into communities of people of Indian ancestry has been documented by an intensive motivational study, and it is one important factor creating their low life-chances and making them powerless over their own affairs.

As Paul Goodman states, this permeation of dominant norms throughout society is a standard phenomenon today. Speaking of the difference between the poor of today and the poor of the past, he writes: "Despite having minority traditions of their own, our present poor are absolute sheep and suckers for the popular culture which they cannot afford, the movies, sharp clothes, and up to Cadillacs."[1]

This permeation of the popular culture is the basis of a social contradiction that strikes minorities the greatest, and is one factor underlying their status. For instance, educational aspirations have been found to be important among the younger generation of Indian and Metis. A standard curricula exists for both this minority and the dominant groups in society, and thus the younger people of Indian ancestry have begun to adopt conventional aspirations. The contradiction exists because these aspirations are inconsistent with the life chances and opportunities of people of Indian ancestry. It is this contradiction that has led to the concept of "education for failure" which was coined after a study of education in northern Saskatchewan.

The fact that the Indian minority lives under structural conditions that greatly limit life chances and is confronted by the dominant aspirations of society, which are inconsistent with his life chances, suggests how powerless this minority is in its situation. On the one hand the individual has little or no self-determination, but is controlled by, and is dependent on outside agencies. On the other hand, he is constantly and increasingly subjected to pressures from the dominant culture which imply goals that are totally outside his reach.

The effects on the individual who lives within this predicament should not be overlooked. He may develop various psychological defenses to protect himself from the personality conflict arising from the dilemma he is in. He may displace his frustrated need to fulfill dominant aspirations onto some status system of some sub-culture. Such a reaction to his powerless and conflictful status may explain the extremely high delinquency rate among ethnic minorities confronted with a cluster of social problems.

When such alternatives are not available to a person living within this kind of social predicament, a frustration-aggression reaction may be the outcome of the conflict between low life-chances, and dominant aspirations. Violence and generalized hostility often become the means of expression, although in rare instances a person of Indian ancestry is able to articulate his dilemma into a meaningful political philosophy implying basic changes for Canadian society.

Minority Status and Power in Society

It is the thesis of this paper that the dilemma faced by many people of Indian ancestry is in fact related to a discussion of the power structure in Canadian society. Although no one has looked at the status of people of Indian ancestry from this point of view, the points made thus far in this paper suggest that the society at large (which means, along with other things, the power structure) cannot be ignored in achieving a full and valid understanding of minority problems. No one would dispute the statement that the stratification system of a society is related to the power structure. Modern sociology has recorded how the standard of living in a particular social class conditions the style of life of that class. Certain status roles are more closely related to power, and clearly the lower socio-economic style of life does not possess such roles.

This general principle of stratification and power of course applies to Canadian people of Indian ancestry. No one would suggest that they were a part of the power structure in Canada, no matter how one views it. While legally they have powers such as the vote, these are more of a nominal than a real nature. The possession of these nominal powers is not really the possession of power in any real sense of the word. In an organization and corporate era, to call such minor rights power is to make the concept of power useless.

In addition to the general limitations on people of Indian ancestry due to their socio-economic hierarchy, another factor, the factor of "race" or "ethnicity" further aggravates their condition. When racial or ethnic factors become a part of a stratification system, the term "caste," rather than solely "class" is applied. Rather than the life-chances being limited only because of a person's socio-economic environment, actual biological characteristics are related to opportunities. Regardless of one's personality, when ethnic factors play a part in stratification, the ethnic population is universally limited.

Such is the case when discussing people of Indian ancestry. Caste may be too strong a word for some who think immediately of the American south and of lynchings. However, caste relations can be subtle as well as overt. The fact is, a person of Indian heritage is limited not only because he comes from a deprived and isolated environment, but also because he is an Indian. While the degree to which this is the case varies throughout Canada, in all parts a stereotype of the "Indian" exists. In some northern areas, where caste relationships often are expressed overtly, local power structures remind one of the American south.

The significance of racial considerations in limiting the accessibility of positions of power in society is often underestimated, mainly because racial prejudice in Canada is expressed in a far more indirect manner than in places throughout the world where it has more dramatic overtones. For instance, that structural limits exist for all people of Indian ancestry is not generally admitted. (A Negro ghetto is evidence of discrimination, but an Indian Reserve is an unfortunate reality — this is the way Canadians think.) The common tendency is to view the problem as an Indian one arising from their own lack of initiative. The assumption, an erroneous one, is that we have left them alone, and that the problems they face have nothing to do with the policies of the larger society. When one points out that government social aid programs are a main factor in the great increase in population of people of Indian ancestry, and that government policies have untold repercussions on

[1] Paul Goodman, *Growing Up Absurd,* (New York: Random House, 1956), p. 65.

family life, migration, etc., people are often stunned. We have been ingrained with "racist thinking," and because we do not yet have racial conflict of major social consequence, we do not even know it. In large part, we have been able to deny the significance of caste because until lately people of Indian ancestry were completely isolated from most areas of Canadian life. Now, with the trend toward urbanization, as people of Indian ancestry cluster with lower-class, fringe groupings in the cities, it is more difficult to deny the importance of caste factors in Canada.

The position of people of Indian ancestry in the socio-economic hierarchy, with its direct limitations on life chances; the colonial, or quasi-colonial control of them over the years; and the added significance of racial factors, all challenge the common belief that a democratic social order exists in Canada. In terms of power (the ability to make and carry out decisions) or in terms of self-determination, people of Indian ancestry are in fact powerless.

But, is this a local, specific problem? Is the person correct who believes that this is a pocket of social problems that can be cleaned up with a little more time and effort? Or is the powerless character of people of Indian ancestry tied up with a general problem of the centralization of power? We have discussed the problems, and the source of the problems facing people of Indian ancestry to enable us to view this larger and more basic question.

Changing Class Structure

Harrington comments that the minority poor in the U.S. is not a part of mainstream society; that it is politically invisible, unlike the poverty of the depression. To understand this, one has to look at changes in the past few decades in the class structure of North America. Paul Goodman, in *Growing Up Absurd,* discusses these changes. He comments that the poor are now within an economy, unlike the pre-war economy, that no longer needs them.

Under these changed conditions, rather than, as in the past, a pyramid class structure where the different levels were economically interdependent, today a great bulge exists in the class structure. It is a bulge resulting from an economy of abundance for more, and it ". . . means those at the bottom tend to fall out of society altogether."[2] Whereas in the past, when a majority poor existed, the fight of socialists, labor leaders and radicals was to change the whole social order, today, with more people in affluent living, the minority poor has been nearly forgotten. This is not to say that there is more basic equality, but just that enough people now have economic security to stop the clamour for fundamental social changes. The result, as Goodman puts it, is that "our society is settling for the first time in its history into a rigid class system."[3]

While people of Indian ancestry have special problems because of their exceptionally deprived background of reserve and northern isolation, they will, as they urbanize, become but one aspect of this Other

Canada. While there is some validity in viewing their problems as particular because they are a native group with remnants of a traditional culture; with time and accelerating changes in the economy and power structure, their problems are best viewed in terms of their place within the larger class of displaced and dispossessed poor in the American "culture of poverty." People of Indian ancestry, unlike the American Negro, are certainly not closely related to the working class. But they are closely tied to the *lumpenproletariat* which is the new dispossessed, or de-classed part of the population that Harrington and Goodman are speaking of.

Once these changes in class structure are acknowledged, the idea that the problems facing people of Indian ancestry are simply pockets of problems to be mopped up with time appears superficial. And therefore, the powerless characteristic of people of Indian ancestry cannot be viewed as a special case.

IN CONCLUSION

Such an analysis as here provided indicates that organic relationships do in fact exist between the problems facing people of Indian ancestry and the society at large. The person seeing the problems as Indian problems . . . will fail to see these relationships. Both in terms of class structure and of power the problems of people of Indian ancestry cannot be isolated from a general description of the society at large. These factors, both analytically and in reality, are what link people of Indian ancestry and their problems to Canadian society and its overall social structure.

We might ask why some people fail to see these organic relationships in society. One major reason is that the values of a culture are usually so pervasive among all segments of society that they are rarely made explicit. People in Canada are so used to having power exist where it does, and major decisions made today within large, impersonal institutions, that they fail to ask basic and fundamental questions about power or social change. Most who are concerned with the problems facing people of Indian ancestry fail to ask one important question. They usually view the "solution" to the problems as the assimilation or integration of people of Indian ancestry into the "mass society," where they will have a slightly better opportunity of being socially mobile. It is, however, rarely asked whether they, along with other minorities and the "middle-class" stratum of society, should be involved in the decision-making and setting of priorities for the society at large. Most people fail to ask whether people of Indian ancestry and others in a powerless milieu should participate in asking what sort of society is desired, how

[2] Goodman *op. cit.*, p. 39.
[3] *Ibid.*, p. 40.

power and wealth should be distributed in it, and what kind of institutions would be necessary to achieve the social goals established (or, to participate in discussions about war and peace, since this is the area which most depicts the mass society and power elite dichotomy in our society).

It is my personal view that it is not enough to just talk of assimilating people of Indian ancestry into The Other Canada. While this may ultimately "free" people of Indian ancestry from the colonial form of treatment they now receive, it is hard to view a transfer of dependency from reserve living to urban welfare-state living as any great humanitarian victory. With the impact of technology and automation on our society, in all likelihood the class structure Goodman speaks of will become more rigid. So, while people of Indian ancestry may not in the future be isolated on reserves and in northern areas, they will still have a grossly unequal life-chance, and still live in a powerless milieu. And even if the much talked about "guaranteed annual income" is legislated for this section of society, as automation has its impact on society the fundamental question of the mass society and centralized power remains.

When one views the problems of people of Indian ancestry in an organic fashion, one is led to ask more fundamental questions than are usually asked by social scientists or groups interested in social problems. Questions about how wealth and power are distributed, how much participation actually exists in making major decisions, and whether groups have any fundamental control over their lives have to be asked.

When this approach is used one gets a different perspective on the problems facing people of Indian ancestry. One begins to see how minority problems relate to the way the economy is organized, to the way power is used, and to the social structure generally. One begins to see how necessary it is to understand a problem like that of the minority of Indian ancestry at its roots. Otherwise, a superficial solution will be advocated.

Will we simply bring people of Indian ancestry into a mass society, in all likelihood into the "culture of poverty" in Canada, where their involvement in making consequential decisions will be little more than nil? Or, from a study of their problems, will we find that to truly allow people of Indian ancestry to achieve equal status and rights in Canada, the social structure itself will have to be fundamentally altered? If we look deeply when we study this problem, we find a fundamental choice before us. Do we desire only a democracy of forms, where the welfare state keeps The Other Canada in dependency and consumer values dominate the rest of society? Or do we take the values of democracy, participation and self-determination seriously enough to create a society where these values are alive within the social structure? If more people were freed of superficial explanations of the problems facing the native Canadian, the chances of the latter choice being made would be greatly strengthened.

4. *The Effects of Poverty on the Poor*[*]

How does poverty affect the poor? The answer could fill volumes. Some of the effects are quite visible and obvious. Poverty breeds ill health. It engenders a sense of hopelessness and frustration. It frequently means interrupted employment, unrewarding jobs, poor housing and inadequate food. It prevents the poor from participating adequately in the life of the society.

Some indications about the ways in which the poor are deprived and about the degree of their deprivation can be gleaned from an analysis of the 1964 DBS Survey of Urban Family Expenditures. Chart 1 displays the relationship between the expenditures of the poor and the average expenditures of the nonpoor. In absolute dollar terms – the difference in the amounts spent – the poor are most deprived of sufficient food, clothing, shelter and transportation. However, viewing the expenditures of the poor as a percentage of the expenditures of the nonpoor, those living in poverty are most deprived, in a relative sense, of transportation, of recreation, of furnishings and equipment, of reading material, of medical care, of personal care, of clothing and of items to complement the formal education system.

One of the most important consequences of poverty is that it affects the ability of the poor to invest in themselves and thereby to lead more productive lives within the economy. This is illustrated by the lower relative expenditures of categories of goods and services which are particularly important as a basis for skilled and effective labour force participation, such as expenditures on education and reading.

A family's inability to invest in itself is likely to have particularly serious consequences on young children whose potential abilities are largely shaped in the years of early childhood. There is accumulating

*Reproduced with the permission of the Queen's Printer for Canada, from the Economic Council of Canada, *Sixth Annual Review* (Ottawa: Queen's Printer, 1969), pp. 115-121.

Chart 1
Average Expenditures of Poor Families as Percentage of Average Expenditures of Nonpoor Families

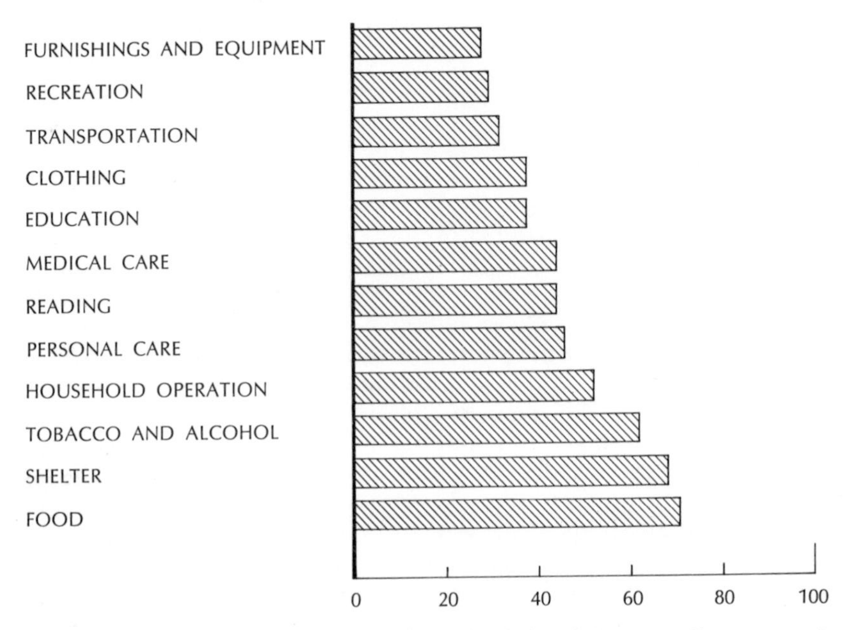

Note: Poor families are defined on the basis of the 1961 poverty lines set out in the *Fifth Annual Review,* updated to 1964.
Source: Based on data from Dominion Bureau of Statistics.

evidence to suggest that children of low-income families in Canada are most unlikely to have adequate access to needed resources in their early years. Even the possibility of significant child nutrition problems, seemingly so improbable in this country, must be taken seriously. A provincial minister of welfare recently stated publicly that some of the children in his province were too ill-clothed and ill-nourished to attend school. It is now well established that malnutrition in the early months of life will not only impair physical growth but may also damage mental development. From the infant born in 1969 to the school drop-out of 1985 is the short span of years that may comprise a poverty generation, and improved understanding of the experience of poor children in Canada is urgently needed if poverty is to be effectively eliminated in Canada in our time.

In the past there has been much concern about the deeply indebted poor. Yet, it is important to keep in mind that ready access to credit for the poor may also be a vitally important factor at certain times to facilitate improved income-earning capacity. For example, credit may be required for the purchase of a used car that may be needed to get to work

— or for something as ordinary as the purchase of stockings or clothing for a woman seeking to return to work — and may make all the difference in a family's progress out of poverty.

The fact that the family is the most common economic unit in our society is often forgotten, and the importance to society of the family's economic viability is frequently not fully realized. A family operates in many ways like a business firm selling a product on the market. The inadequate incomes of families in poverty put such families in a position similar to that of managers of firms whose costs exceed revenues. Unable to increase production and sales for various reasons, and unable in the long run to continue even a level of maintenance costs that would permit continued sales, a firm may ultimately be forced out of business. From the viewpoint of the economy as a whole, this may be a desirable result, especially if it frees resources that have been relatively inefficiently used to flow to other, more productive uses. In the case of the family, however, the social and economic consequences for society are quite different. While a firm may go out of business and disappear, the family remains. If the potential abilities of members of the family remain undeveloped and unused, the family members may not only become virtual nonparticipants in the nation's social and economic life, but also a continuing burden on the society. If society is to benefit from the potential abilities rather than merely support the costs of poverty, the adults in the family must be enabled to participate in the labour force currently *and to prepare their children to do so in the future.* Thus *the concept of a minimum standard of living must be based on a definition of the family not merely as a consuming unit, but also as a producing unit.* In our society, a substantial portion of the total investment in human capital is undertaken by family or individual initiatives. Public policies are needed to encourage this private investment process, and help to insulate it against the ravages of poverty.

We believe that one of the central tasks of antipoverty policies should be that of creating or restoring the economic viability of family units and of individuals not in families. This concern, if it is to be operationally effective, will require not only more carefully designed efforts to improve the income-generating capacities of the poor, but also substantially more cohesion and consistency than now exists in the provision of services and opportunities to the poor.

The overall structure of existing efforts in this field is currently one of extraordinary complexity, especially in operational terms, in our communities. Indeed, this structure essentially consists of largely unrelated efforts initiated by the three levels of government and by a great host of private organizations. The range of activities is so enormous that it is even difficult to collect information on their scope and nature. The federal government in 1967 issued an index to Human Resources Development Programs which listed over 200 different items. The New Brunswick Government's "Programs for People," listing close to 150 items, is an illustration of a similar effort to compile information about such programs at the provincial level. There are thus literally hundreds of items of legislation, thousands of regulations, and tens of thousands of administrative rules through which government efforts, by themselves, are carried out. To these must be added the vast array of private efforts of many different kinds.

In some communities, municipal or social planning agencies have attempted to compile directories about various forms of services and assistance available from public and private sources. And several cities, including Winnipeg and Ottawa, have attempted to go further, and to relate, at least in a preliminary way, the available services to local needs. But, in general, even reasonably comprehensive information is not readily available on the wide range of existing efforts in the social development field. In these circumstances, it is difficult to assess how well the present spectrum of antipoverty efforts is actually performing in bringing families out of poverty.

At the present time there are a great many undesirable and economically wasteful features associated with existing programs. Perhaps the most striking examples are to be found in the welfare programs. Welfare assistance is provided in a manner and amount that all too frequently undermines, rather than reinforces, the abilities and the aspirations of recipients to participate productively in the economic system. Taxed on incremental income at very high marginal rates, pervasively discriminated against by the economic system as discussed above, and singled out for public notice (a school principal in one Canadian city this year used the public address system to ask children of welfare recipients to stand up and come to his office for textbook vouchers), it is not surprising that recipients are alienated. The system often appears to provoke the very results it should be designed to avoid. In many cases, it discourages earnings, encourages school drop-outs, and creates the paradox of people who would prefer to work being unable to afford to get off welfare. Moreover, it generally does not come into operation in a timely way, so that families may be virtually driven into poverty before help is available. In some provinces it virtually forces the heads of large families with inadequate incomes to stop work in order to get welfare. The entire system urgently needs to be examined with particular reference to its overall economic effects, and to the need for strengthening its preventive and rehabilitative capabilities.

Those poor in receipt of public welfare assistance are, however, a minority of the poor, under the rather conservative definition of poverty in our *Fifth Annual Review*. The majority of the poor contribute more to general tax revenues than they receive in the form of government welfare expenditures. Thus the overall incidence of the fiscal system for the "non-welfare poor" is highly regressive. This system too should be examined for its overall economic effects on the poor.

In an attempt to obtain a better understanding, in a practical way, of the actual operation of antipoverty programs at the community level, the Economic Council undertook a limited survey of present activities in a number of Canadian cities early in 1969. From this survey, it is clear that the links between our welfare and manpower policies are greatly in need of review. There appears to be a widespread lack of co-ordination between welfare and manpower services; good co-ordination is needed here to help family units achieve economic viability. It is the poor who particularly need access to manpower programs, and this should be reflected both in the objectives and the operations of such programs in Canada.

Among some of the other results emerging from this survey are the following:

— A general concern that some of the poorest families, who may be the most backward in seeking needed assistance, are being missed by the existing programs, especially in the case of poor farm families.

— Encouraging progress in some communities towards bringing available services closer to those in need, especially through the establishment of neighbourhood centres in which a number of agencies, sometimes including government agencies, are co-operating.

— The inadequate information available to the poor, who often lack knowledge of the scope of welfare and other assistance, of what are their rights (under minimum wage legislation, for example), of eligibility criteria (for training programs, mobility grants, financial assistance through welfare offices), of rights of appeal from administrative decisions (with respect to welfare assistance, for example), of rights in law with respect to contracts (leases, door-to-door sales), of where to turn for advice and counsel (youth services, family planning, legal aid, nutritional consultants and consumer information).

— The unfortunate existence of significant barriers to employment of secondary earners in the family (especially of mothers who wish to work), as a result of the lack of day care nurseries and other ancillary services.

— The forward-looking separate and joint efforts of labour unions and co-operatives to develop self-help initiatives in the nonprofit housing field and to provide family budget counselling.

— The successful development of a number of community training workshops that are making special efforts to train disadvantaged poor persons in skills useful for gaining employment.

— Attempts to reduce the difficulties facing especially vulnerable groups — such as single parents, the ethnic minorities in some communities, and the handicapped — in seeking out productive employment opportunities.

— Constitutional difficulties that impair the effective operation of a number of important programs (such as manpower programs).

— Growing encouragement and opportunities for the poor to participate in defining their needs as a basis for more effective anti-poverty activities.

Canada's poverty problems are obviously different in a number of important respects from those of the United States. Nevertheless, as we observed last year, there is a great deal to be learned by Canadians from recent U.S. experience – both the successful experience and, even more perhaps, the unsuccessful. The explicit national commitment to eliminate poverty, the setting up of an agency to discover what specific antipoverty measures will work (and when they work, to spin them off to agencies with operating responsibilities), the major effort to co-ordinate all federal human development programs (and beyond this, to move towards better co-ordination among federal government programs, those of the state and municipal governments and those in the private sector), the focus in both the public and private sectors on the creation of job opportunities and increased training for the poor, and the special efforts directed towards enlarging opportunities for their children, are all very much in accord with the approaches recommended here. So too is the willingness to monitor and evaluate the effectiveness of specific programs.

Recent evaluations have in fact resulted in several changes in the structure of U.S. antipoverty efforts:

– Head Start (a preschool program for disadvantaged children) and the Job Corps (a job-training program for disadvantaged youth) have both been spun off from the Office of Economic Opportunity and put under the aegis of government departments which have been given administrative and operational responsibility for these programs.

– The Office of Economic Opportunity has become a program development agency where new programs will be tested and passed to operating departments when they show clear signs of being effective.

– Increasing numbers of on-the-job trainees are being financed under the Manpower Development and Training Act.

– Head Start evaluations which revealed that few if any tangible benefits from the program were discernible after a child had several months' experience in the regular school system have resulted in more extensive preschool programs, as well as adjustments within the educational system itself, and follow-up programs with the children.

– The business sector has been encouraged to co-operate in placing disadvantaged persons in jobs, and nearly 12,000 co-operating firms placed over 100,000 persons. In addition, certain labour unions in the model cities program have shortened required apprenticeship periods so that more of the disadvantaged workers in neighbourhoods affected by the program could participate.

The relevance of these and other similar programs for Canada should be explored and, if considered appropriate, should be effectively developed.

Section IV
Programs and Strategies

A wide and seemingly disparate array of programs and strategies have been advocated to alleviate poverty in Canada. We have chosen articles with the view to being representative of general programs and specific social action strategies. The regional planning perspective reflected in both the Richards and the Poetschke articles is currently favoured by federal agencies such as the relatively new Department of Regional and Economic Expansion.

Richards views social planning as planning for the public weal and offers a conceptual framework for analyzing regions. The process of development as described by Richards has an ecological character for "it embraces the worker and his job, the citizen and his living space". Poetschke, on the other hand, presents a concept of regional development that is adjustment-oriented. Furthermore, he picks up the problem after the area has been agreed upon. There are stages in the development process, Poetschke tells us, and these include a research phase, a program development and commitment phase, and an evaluation phase. The emphasis is understandably on program development, which includes mediating the objectives of federal and provincial programs in the light of objectives and needs of the designated areas. The latter objectives are presumably arrived at through the active participation of the local people in the region.

Continuing the local participation aspect of development, we have chosen an article on *Animation Sociale* by Marc Morency.[1]

[1] For another discussion of Social Animation, emphasizing strategies, the reader is referred to Michel Blodin, "Social Animation: Its Nature and Significance in *Le Conseil Des Oeuvres De Montréal*" in *Poverty and Social Policy in Canada*, W. E. Mann (ed.), (Toronto: The Copp Clark Publishing Co., 1970).

Prior to this discussion, a brief statement by the Economic Council of Canada provides the reader with some necessary background information about the innovative development project. It would seem that the closer one moves to program implementation the greater the likelihood that emphasis will be placed on the normative aspects of the locality or region. One finds a heightened interest in social structure and attitudes. However, participation can become a goal in itself rather than a means to an end.

Graham Parker's review of Ontario's legal aid scheme is quite germane to a discussion of poverty, for a number of reasons. First, the administration of justice should not be influenced by one's ability to pay. To quote from the Report of the Joint Committee on Legal Aid, "It [legal aid] is no longer a charity but a right . . . the stigma of charity should be removed from legal aid." It is of considerable interest to note the care taken by those responsible for planning this program to ensure that clients are not defined as welfare recipients. Finally, it has been documented by other research that certain poverty groups are often hapless victims of illegal business practices and have limited access to legal aid.

Brewis' paper presents an overview of government policy and programs in the area of regional economics. He reminds us of the range of policy objectives and variety of programs introduced over the past few years. The article serves to document the changing character of both agencies and programs in the recent past and this with little attention paid to evaluation. The issues and questions which Professor Brewis leaves with us are still part of the continuing debate on Canadian regional economic policy.

Although it is readily admitted that in some respects the American experience in the war on poverty is quite unique, the Economic Council expresses the point of view that certain general principles are applicable to the Canadian scene. Many of these ideas are the basis for contemporary discussion of programs designed to alleviate poverty. Specific recommendations are set forth in the report, which provides a guideline for measuring our current progress.

Cutt's article serves to emphasize the fact that the long run orientation of a welfare program must be part of an overall policy of redistribution of wealth. The author suggests that two programs, Negative Income Tax (NIT) and Children's Allowances (CA) require analysis relative to their effect on poverty. No simple decision criterion is possible, but Cutt offers a set of criteria consisting of economic efficiency, effect on work incentives, effect on expenditure patterns, stigma effects, administrative complexity, and social and political effects. He concludes that "we are left with the rather interesting fact that NIT and CA are really different programs altogether and may most effectively be seen as complements rather than as substitutes."

1. *Perspective on Regional Planning*[*]

J. Howard Richards

Few terms or concepts of such apparent respectability as "regional planning" are so susceptible to conflicting definition, approach and belief. To suggest that this is a field concerning which there is little definition, few basic and generally accepted concepts, but many brave and popular statements and generalizations, may cause pained surprise. Nevertheless, it is the intention here to discuss some of the theories and approaches to regional planning, stressing particularly the Canadian experience.

That Canada has a fairly long planning history may be demonstrated by the fact that Thomas Adams was brought from England to act as town planning adviser to the Conservation Commission created by Sir Wilfrid Laurier in 1909. Adams was essentially a regionalist in his approacch and his philosophy filtered through to the remote hinterlands of Canada, even to Saskatchewan. The 1917 Annual Report of the Saskatchewan Department of Municipal Affairs contained the following: ". . . An Act with respect to Town Planning and Rural Development was passed. This bill had been . . . carefully scanned by Mr. Thomas Adams, Town Planning Expert, Commission of Conservation, Ottawa . . . "

However, it is essentially since the Second World War that planning, as a concept and art, has become acceptable and even respectable, although in this country its greatest acceptability in the public sector has been in the field of urban planning. While planning may be applicable to the individual business or to a more diffuse entity of concern to the public rather than the entrepreneur, it still has the same basic intent – the substitution of order for disorder, the direction of resources, physical and other, toward a desired and designed goal; the

*Reprinted with the permission of the author and the publisher from *Community Planning Review,* Spring, 1967 (Ottawa) Community Planning Association of of Canada.

achievement of objective (s) through a process of planning. When we speak of planning separate from the art of entrepreneuring, we speak essentially of social planning, of planning for the public weal.

Such planning, with its welfare implications and its special societal values, may or may not be considerate of the individual business or the private sector at large. In some societies, certainly, the two last are inconsequential: in Canada the individual and his business, or residence, or privacy, or other attribute, may be sacrificed at specific times, so as to permit development of a system better adapted to the needs of the many. Examples of this are fairly common in: rural land use changes, as in the present attempt to convince recalcitrant dry-land farmers to convert to irrigation methods in the South Saskatchewan Dam irrigation project; urban changes, as in penalties induced via zoning, expropriation, taxation, or other social controls over property; transportation linkages, as exemplified by the creation of the Canadian National Railway, or in preferential freight rate structures and subventures.

Pragmatic Approach

Nonetheless, despite fairly frequent examples of the process, planning in Canada has been essentially pragmatic in character. As problems have arisen — or have become overwhelmingly obvious — concepts have been developed concerning the nature of the problem and its solution, and methods and administration devised to deal with them.

National planning relating to regional development is difficult under the Canadian system of confederation where control of natural resources, education and other sectors are the prerogative of the individual provinces. Except during periods of national emergency, national objectives involving these sectors may be achieved only through co-operation with the individual province; it is the province which assumes the planning function, and theoretically at least, deals with the problems and decides on the solutions and objectives.

Accepting this, we must also accept the fact there do exist federal programs, planned to meet regional problems and specific objectives relating to them, which have been relatively successful and have been characterized by considerable flexibility in that they have been susceptible to change as needs have changed. The latter type of program is exemplified in, for example, Prairie Farm Rehabilitation Administration (PFRA) projects in which a changed focus permitted the development of the Maritimes Marshland Rehabilitation Act — an application to a different type of region; and in the Canada Forestry Act, where changes in requirements and details led to its emergence as the Composite Forestry Agreements, dealing with specific resources located in a rather special region.

These and, to a certain extent, the Agricultural Rehabilitation and Development Act (ARDA) may be considered as programs designed to assist in regional planning and development. But they should be considered also, and properly, as programs concerned with problems of economic development in specific sectors of the economy, in these cases agriculture and forestry. It is coincidental (even if it happens to be axiomatic) that these sectors possess spatial or geographic arrangements and, therefore, that the program had to be applied not only to the structure of economic development but also to the geographic areas or regions involved.

Geographic Orientation

This last statement holds for all forms of sector development – single resource or grouped resources, transportation or other – so that while economic development deals essentially with the structure of development, it, perforce, must occur *somewhere,* i.e., it exhibits inherent spatial or geographical character. The geographical arrangement will differ according to the nature of economic development and will also change with time. In the cases cited, the areas affected are essentially rural: in the other cases, as under the National Housing Act, urban development or other aspect, the areas are highly localized in major cities.

This represents, roughly, the state of affairs in Canadian planning: the units of planning have as focus *either* the rural region *or* the urban centre. The statement may be modified to accommodate the emergence of "metropolitan" areas or regions as planning units in Toronto, Winnipeg and elsewhere, designed to accommodate a complex of closely associated urban, suburban and "rurban" or rural-urban activities.

Regional planning has a history in which problems in development of the physical resources have been the major interest. Incidentally to development, certain desirable socio-economic consequences were expected to occur, e.g., stabilizing of agriculture and the agricultural population in the case of some of the PFRA activities. Similar resource interests are inherent in the evolution of the Prairie Provinces Water Board and in the Saskatchewan Water Commission; and, in Ontario, in the watershed studies carried out under the Conservation Authorities Act in the Moira, Thames, Grand, and other areas where flood control, reclamation, reforestation or other natural resource may provide the reason for setting up a Conservation Authority. Note that under ARDA, rural development research, and presumably program development, permits the incorporation of full socio-economic studies, inclusive of small urban centres; as such, it differs from the usual resource-oriented program.

City planning, obviously, is different. It deals with a highly localized unit area in a specific and special institutional setting. In these last two, it differs from any regional planning attempted in this country. Some of the formal tools of planning, particularly zoning, are not uncommon in regional planning but, in the city, planning is directed essentially at problems in physical land use and design, attempting to preserve existing rental value and to facilitate movement of people, goods and services. In each case planning is specific to the individual city and, thus, to its internal structure. Occasionally "regional planning boards" have been set up to encourage reasoned development in urban-centred or supra-urban areas, a recognition of the impact of a large urban node on the surrounding area and of the implications of the latter to the city. More occasionally, metropolitan planning boards have been created in areas dominated by urban and suburban population dwelling in a number of closely linked centres and areas. . . .

Economic Analysis Systems

Despite this essential separation of the planning approach between natural resource-oriented region on the one hand and city-oriented on the other, numerous attempts have been made to develop systems of regions (or areas or zones) of different scale which would assist in the elucidation of problems and solutions in economic development. In most cases the systems were created in response to single objectives, as for example: the accumulation of consumer data for use in marketing; labour force/employment studies for cities and larger towns; labour/employment/input (public projects) relationships in a context of "commuting areas," etc.

In a White Paper of 1945 the federal government commited itself to a policy of high employment levels. At the same time it was recognized that planning for high total employment would not be good enough, that because of regional differences in activity, unemployment could be at high levels regionally while employment could be at a high level nationally. To provide basic data which could permit analysis of long-term issues and which would provide a more complete, if composite, picture of the economy, it was decided to devise a system of economic zones which could embrace city or cities but which were supra-urban in size.

The system evolved is known as the "D.D.P. Geographic Code,"[1] since adapted by several provinces to deal with various regional developments. Before examining the D.D.P. Geographic Code and its implications in the field of regional planning, it may be well to define "regional planning" and to place it in perspective.

Regional planning infers the formulation of policy, plan and programs necessary to the achievement of predetermined and acceptable socio-economic objectives: as such, it will encompass all aspects of social and physical planning. Concepts of regional planning have grown essentially out of two fields of study, geography and economics, and mainly from special theories of central place and location derived from these fields. The word "region" has changed greatly in connotation as it is applied to regional planning. Today, in planning, it tends to assume the commonplace sense of *space*.

"City Region" Theory

According to some theorists, this space (region) has a structure and organization provided by the system of nodes and linkages, (i.e., urban centres and transportation and communication lines) which occur within it. The argument of this school may be stated briefly. The city region must be the basic planning unit. This is necessary because the bulk of population is urban and further population growth will be in urban and metropolitan areas. With increasing concentration of population, the cities and their border areas also gain in economic power and in dominance in the fields of transportation and communication. Eventually (if it has not already happened) a pattern of urban settlement is established in which the city region possesses a dense urban core, a less densely populated margin where population growth has occurred along lines of access, and a system of satellites extending outward some distance and closely linked with the city.

It is suggested that theories of economic development support this concept of spatial structure, the focus having shifted from the *broad territorial base* with an emphasis on natural resources, to one of *city region* in which metropolitan resources – transportation, space and social organization – are the significant factors. Economic relationships between urban regions tend to develop specialized roles for each, while comparative advantages and disadvantages, in access to markets, in human resources and in resource endowment, lead to hierarchal systems of dominance and subordination among the regions.

Transportation is recognized as the most strategic advantage of the city region, influencing economic development, function and structure. All space resources, including non-populated sections, are significant and need be made susceptible to desirable controls. Further, the community itself, urban, neighbourhood, satellite, village etc., is a prime resource and only through full community efforts and life will the city region provide maximum advantages for living and working.

To conclude the advocacy of the city region as the regional planning unit, its protagonists claim that the old "regional" differences in the level of economic development are disappearing and that most of the densely settled parts of the country may eventually come within the influence of city regions, possibly 80 to 90 per cent of the total population becoming resident in such regions. They stress the special spatial structure as seen in the pattern formed by city regions and believe that functional planning must be related to this pattern. They believe the city regions are the nerve centres of national economic life and that within them all major decisions concerning areal development are made. As such, the city region can be the only form of areal structure capable of being properly used in a systematised program of planning and development.

What is a Region?

Acceptance of this form of regional planning unit points up an initial difficulty confronting regional planners (as distinct from natural

[1] *Economic Zoning of Canada and the D.D.P. Geographic Code* (Government of Canada, Department of Defence Production, Economics and Statistics Branch, Ottawa, 1953).

resource planners) and confounding or compromising concepts on regional planning. Obviously, the evaluation and creation of regions for planning are difficult tasks and the results are unlikely to be universally acceptable.

Even more fundamental is the decision whether the regional approach, however it is defined, is of consequence to planning and development. Some argue that regional planning has no place in national economic planning; that under a relatively free economic system, growth (economic development) does not occur everywhere at the same time; that once it has appeared it apparently concentrates around the starting points; that agglomeration tends to occur and to obviate costs of space (external economics) ; that growing centres tend to attract and accept new ideas and enterprises; and that the economy will develop one or more centres of economic strength – the growth nodes of the nation. These nodes tend to continue to attract (e.g., southern Ontario, with Toronto the primary node, constitutes c. 0.4% of the area of Canada, c. 20% population, and about 33% of Canadians engaged in industrial employment) and thus to develop regional growth complexes which will contrast markedly with peripheral areas characterized by small development. This argument, logical enough and substantiated by general concepts in location and central place theory, would suggest that planning at the national level, for both public and private sectors, would perpetuate the present hierarchy of growth complexes; further it would suggest that the latter could be identified and boundaries drawn, for example, around a significant urban complex and its market and influence zone – an academic exercise admitting of little meaningful application in itself.

D.D.P. GEOGRAPHIC CODE

This discussion has taken us a long way from the D.D.P. Geographic Code, and from concepts of planning units related to either rural region or individual urban centre. But it has provided a statement of background and does point up the lack of universally accepted principles as to what constitutes a planning region. Tiebout,[2] writing of the field of regional economics, succinctly places the dilemma in perspective:

In view of our inability to construct an "ideal" region, the selection of regional boundaries rests on other criteria. Usually the regional boundaries are suggested by the variables one chooses to study. Non-economic considerations, such as the availability of data and the location of political divisions, may, of course, be the basis for the demarcation of a region. The important point is not *which boundaries are chosen but the effect of this choice on the variables under study.*

Though its approach may be simple and pragmatic, the D.D.P. Geographic Code[3] does present a practical framework in which the economy may be studied and in which regional – including physical – planning could be organized and effected.

The spatial units of the D.D.P. Geographic Code are constructed as "aggregations related in a specific four-factor analysis," and the four factors in the "S.F.P.M." formula are used to set up a "matrix analysis of areas, a four-sector grid stratifying areas by the Structural and Functional factors on the one side and by Production and Marketing factors on the other." Thus:

S = Structural factors, defined here as referring to basic location of natural resources, as modified by the actual distribution of human and capital resources required for economic activity. (But since the latter resources are implicit, by definition, this may, in fact, become an identification of a "geographic zone").

F = Functional factors including a transportation and labour orientation and its agglomeration pattern. The agglomerative pattern is indicated by the description of the order of the centres in terms of population density and configuration.

P = Production Factors. In general the zones areb road production areas and the subzones even more uniform in terms of production.

M = Marketing Factors. In general the subzones are primary trading areas, but the zones are not necessarily wholesale trading areas, though they tend to perform some of this function.

Other relationships are treated – subjectively or otherwise – e.g., spheres of influence and hinterland relationships.

An example illustrating the use of the four factors of the SFPM formula could be the "Palliser Region" of southwestern Saskatchewan. *S* indicates "A dry southwest belt of short grass, brown-soil prairie;" *F*, the functional factors, refers to the fact that Moose Jaw is a third order centre and an *entrepôt;* Swift Current also is a third order centre; *P*, the production factors, stresses the agricultural nature and refers to minor manufacturing, etc.; *M*, the market factors, describes Moose Jaw and Swift Current as the marketing centres.

Code's Evaluation

That this system of geographic division possesses inherent difficulties is admitted by its inventors who raise their own questions concerning validity of units and permanency of the zonal pattern. Conceptually, because of its adherence to administrative boundaries, it runs counter to both the ideas of the region as neutral space, economically organized, and to traditional divisions of geographers and others who see natural units and geographic regions not conforming to administrative straitjackets. But workers in these fields have long recognized that neither "natural unit" nor "functioning zone" (except in the national sense) is

[2] Charles M. Tiebout, "Exports and Regional Economic Growth;" *Journal of Political Economy*, Vol. 64, April 1956 (Copyright © University of Chicago Press).

[3] This system, slightly modified, is described excellently and in shorter form in *Economic Georgraphy of Canada*, Camu, Weeks and Sametz (Macmillan, 1964).

coincident with areas of official statistics, that they do not coincide with land survey, municipal or census systems – and that these are unlikely to undergo changes which would prove satisfactory to both groups.

The Geographic Code has tried to accommodate: a) significant aspects of location and central place theory; b) concepts of natural regions; c) areas for which statistics may be derived. Without critically discussing the system as applied to Saskatchewan it may be stated, that while there may not be complete agreement with the absolute definition of units, the Code exhibits very reasonable appreciation of the functional organization of that province and, at the same, gives clear recognition of the major factors, physical and socio-economic, which create and characterize the organization. Thus, with some modification, these regions and zones would appear to provide valid bases for planning regions.

Intended to assist in the analyses of basic factors and to be used for the interpretation and forecasting of local conditions, these same divisions could be used – probably more satisfactorily than any existing system of areal units – for regional planning in the fullest sense, i.e., including all aspects of physical and socio-economic planning. Their definition and potential use approach closely to the needs and demands of those advocating regional planning based on the city region or other planning organization; further, they are likely to be more attainable as basic planning units, with new administrative structures, than any of the theoretical systems.

Planning is a function of government. At the highest level, it is a function of the federal government; at the next level, it rests with the individual provincial government; at lower levels, it is subject to planning agencies forming part of various municipal government systems existing within the provincial framework. The essential suggestion here is that, for most of Canada, regional planning per se does not exist; further, it is unlikely that effective regional planning could occur within the present framework of municipal and planning boundaries and with present agencies.

Therefore, a new system of municipal government, organization and planning area is necessary. The D.D.P. regions would seem to be eminently useable – indeed, compared with what now exist, pre-eminently so – as new administrative and planning units. They portray regions of reasonable uniformity, based on the S F P M weighting formula; they accommodate existing data-providing units; they make possible the use of computer methods; and they render feasible, because of recognition of city foci within the regions, the application of concepts inherent in the philosophy of city region.

Practical Application

The question still remains: is the concept of regional planning valid? The answer lies in the context of the individual and society. Sector planning has long been accepted and no one doubts that it has spatial, or regional, repercussions. Therefore, planning for the region must be a concomitant of sector planning; and, so, regional planning, involving complex multiple resources, human and other, must be acceptable.

The essential difference between sector development and regional development is that of complexity. Recognizing this difference we should not slough off its implications; further, we should not take refuge in the excuse that neither location nor central place theory provides us with an adequate practical framework for the purposes of regional planning. There is a need for the understanding of regional differences; there is a need to assess and, as necessary, encourage regions peripheral to the growth nodes; there is a need to feel, experience, and develop the total national economy. Such feeling and such experience may be gained through the analysis of meaningful and practical regional separates: it cannot be gained solely from national perspective.

Therefore, there is need for regional planning units. Their nature may be, relatively, ephemeral since all economic developments lead to shifts in the arrangement of economic space. But any system of planning areas which has some immediate application, shows possibilities of continuing interpretation and approaches closely to the acceptable, is likely to take precedence over theoretical systems and is worth trying out. One may hope to add to the system concepts of inter-provincial or even "sub-national" regions, as provinces admit of community of interests.

In this sense the system may be adaptable to the general concepts put forward by Professor D. F. Putnam in an unpublished paper of 1962:

> *. . . . the regional approach, a method which is applicable, indeed, . . . is fundamental to the planning of facilities for all human activities. A region is much more than the sum of its natural resources, and regional development comprises much more than the problems of resource use. Regional development must include the elements of broad social objectives such as housing, recreation and industrial relations. It embraces the worker and his job, the citizen and his living space. Man is part of his own environment, and population is the most important resource, whether it is viewed on a local, regional, or even on a national basis. To get the greatest benefit from the regional environment it is necessary for man to make the optimum use of all available resources; this is the ultimate objective . . .*

And in this context I would suggest that the system of economic regions, originally set out in *Economic Zoning of Canada and the D.D.P. Geographic Code* and further described in *Economic Geography of Canada* provides a structure of functional units well adapted to regional planning needs in Canada.

2. *Regional Planning for Depressed Rural Areas – The Canadian Experience**

L. E. Poetschke

Canada, by any international standard of comparison, is a wealthy country.[1] The gross national income, [in 1967] running at an annual rate of 60 billion dollars, generated by rich resources and by advanced technology, is distributed among a population of some 20 million people. Unfortunately, and for many reasons, almost 5 million Canadians fail to win a share which is adequate to meet basic requirements for food, shelter, health and education. All of these people are poor by Canadian standards. Almost two million are poor by any standards. It is this latter group, approximately one million of whom are located in six or seven large severely depressed rural areas across Canada, which is the present focus of attention of the Agricultural and Rural Development Administration's comprehensive planning efforts.

THE CHALLENGE

To provide meaningful assistance to the people of these regions, except on a welfare or simple transfer payment basis, is a singularly difficult task. Without exception, these areas are typified by their distance from viable and growing centres of major economic activity and by their dependence on a resource base which is in the process of being depleted or which, because of changing technology, can support only a much reduced work force. Taken together with the effects of a 19th century system of financing education, the result is large-scale unemployment

*Reprinted with permission of the author and publisher from the *Canadian Journal of Agricultural Economics,* 1, February 1968 (Ottawa: Agricultural Economic Research Council of Canada, 1968) , pp. 8-20.

AUTHOR'S NOTE: This paper is based on an address given to the regional Science Association Far East Conference, Tokyo, September 15, 1967. The author wishes to acknowledge the invaluable contribution of his colleague D. G. McClure in reviewing this paper but more particularly in developing the concepts and approach to our work as outlined in the text.

and under-employment, low levels of skills and, in many cases, potentials for development that can be realized only through a major redirection of the economic and social forces acting in the region.

In these circumstances, the conventional measures and approaches of government simply do not work. Over the last 45 years — embracing buoyant expansion, a severe depression, a prolonged war, and a period of revived national growth — the regional problem in Canada has remained substantially unchanged.[2] Large inter-regional disparities in per capita income have stubbornly persisted despite various forces working towards a better balance. These forces have included the significant reduction of population, far-reaching adjustments in the structure of economic activity at the national level, and certain public policies aimed at a greater equalization of regional incomes.

Fiscal and monetary policies and special sectoral development programs and policies of the federal government in the Canadian context are by necessity national in scope. They are designed for, and are most effective in, sectors and regions where the responses are the most sensitive. To do otherwise would seriously impair the nation's competitive position — a factor which a major trading nation such as Canada can ignore only at its peril. In addition, even in those sectors falling solely within provincial jurisdiction — and these comprise a substantial and important range of economic and social activities — the provinces encounter serious economic and political obstacles to other than province-wide programs.

This then is the dilemma. On the one hand, large areas in Canada are unresponsive or marginally responsive to national and province-wide policies and programs directed to various sectors but on the other hand, to gear such national policies and programs to the special needs of depressed areas would be tantamount to economic suicide. In addition to this economic problem, there are other well known barriers to regionally directed action. Providing special attention to selected areas of the country requires substantial political courage. Also there is the difficulty of working around the departmentalized, sector-oriented government structure — a feat which in our experience cannot be accomplished by legislative fiat or by building another bureaucratic structure.

THE AUTHORITY

A great deal might be said about how a federal government agency, which started business in 1962 under a brand new nine paragraph Act of Parliament entitled the Agricultural Rehabilitation and Development Act (ARDA), finds itself in the middle of this problem.

	1961	*1966*
[1] GNP million (current) dollars	37,500	56,000
Per capita personal income (current) dollars	1,564	2,100

Average annual rate of growth between 1961 and 1966 current dollars.

GNP	8.0%
Per Capita Personal Income	6.0%

[2] *Second Annual Report,* Economic Council of Canada, (Queen's Printer, Ottawa).

While a number of factors can be cited, the key to our present role can be found in the close relationships developed as a matter of basic policy with the (provincial) governments in the regions. As a result the whole ARDA program has developed in a manner which is more sensitive to individual regional needs than are most national programs. In addition, while the Federal government was understandably reluctant to undertake major regional *development* programs in the absence of a national framework for allocating resources, an adjustment oriented approach confined to regions of severe rural poverty did not present the same difficulties.

Accordingly in June 1966 the Fund for Rural Economic Development (FRED) Act was passed, legislatively incoprorating a planning process which had been worked out jointly between ARDA and the provinces two years earlier and providing a fund of $300 million to help the process along. This legislation provides the main basis for our comprehensive planning operations. It provides that areas, selected jointly by the provincial and federal governments, which are subject to widespread low income, possess major adjustment problems and have recognized development potentials, are eligible for special assistance, provided that the two governments can agree on a satisfactory comprehensive rural development program for the area. Such a program involves the following:

1) physical, economic and social studies and investigations to determine the development problems and potentials of the area;

2) the involvement of local people through the establishment of rural development committees or similar bodies.

3) the preparation of comprehensive rural development plans incorporating a broad range of projects to increase income and employment opportunities and to raise standards of living.

When a comprehensive rural development plan has been formulated and approved by both governments, a separate program agreement is drawn up. This agreement outlines the general strategy for development, makes provision for implementing projects within the plan and sets out the terms of financing. The projects may include:

1) Any of the resource development or adjustment programs provided for under the regular ARDA Agreement;

2) The application of other federal and provincial programs as they may be relevant to the area;

3) Major developmental projects in conformity with the comprehensive plan other than those provided in 1) and 2).

Contributions from the special Fund for Rural Economic Development provided under the legislation may be used to finance major new developmental projects under the plan, or to increase expenditures and supplement present programs as required by the plan.

In short, the legislation makes possible the incorporation into comprehensive plans of all relevant existing federal and provincial measures of assistance and, in addition, through the fund, makes it possible to either augment these programs or to undertake new programs which are indicated as being required to meet the special problems of the area.

Once an area has been agreed upon there are three more or less distinguishable phases in the life of a comprehensive rural development plan. These are the research phase, the program development and commitment phase and finally the implementation and evaluation phase.

To take them in order, the objective of [the] research phase is to identify the main problems and potentials of the area and to settle on broad strategy for adjustment and/or development. The most successful mechanism we have found for this is a task force which works under the close supervision of a steering committee composed of officials from several departments and agencies of both levels of government. The existence of the joint steering committee ensures that policy considerations are fully taken into account and that the various departments and agencies which are likely to have a role in the implementation of the final program, are given the opportunity to participate in and contribute to the preparation of the plan right from the beginning. An agreement by the committee on the strategy and broad programs provides the basis for the program development actvities of the second phase of the process.

Program development is essentially a process of assessing the wide range of available national and provincial programs in the light of the objectives and needs of the area, and of amending them, supplementing them or developing new programs to fill important gaps. The responsibility for overseeing this work is borne by a provincial program development and management group and by the federal ARDA staff. Most of the work is done by the departments and agencies who have a specific role to play.

When this material has been drawn together and incorporated into a draft plan, it is reviewed independently by senior staff at both the federal and the provincial levels. On the federal side, the mechanism for review is the Fund for Rural Economic Development Advisory Board — FRED Advisory Board. The members of this Board, appointed by the Governor-in-Council, include the deputy ministers and assistant deputy ministers of some ten departments and agencies of the federal government. The members of the Board review the strategy and programs as a complete package prepared largely by their own staffs. In each package, however, are invariably special measures of assistance to provincial programs or new programs which will be financed in part from the FRED Fund. Often these proposals break new policy ground and the Board provides a forum for review, comment and amendment to the proposals in the light of broader federal government policy considerations, prior to submission of the plan to the Cabinet.

The final phase of the process is rather misleadingly called the implementation stage. In fact the signed Agreement is mainly a commitment to action based on the best judgments that could be made about the relation between activities and desired results. Many operational details remain to be worked out and systems must be set up to ensure a thorough and continuing evaluation of the results of the action. This provides the only real information for testing the causal relationships both for continued effective planning in a dynamic situation and for building up experience for use in other areas.

While many of the programs are actually undertaken by government departments and agencies at the national or provincial level, our experience indicates that responsibility for management of the plan as a whole must be with a competent body working in the region. For this region we insist that the province establish an effective program development and management group before entering the second phase of the planning process and we carry a large part of the cost. At the same time a federal program administrative staff is appointed to work with the provincial group and together they form the core of the management team.

At all stages in this process the active participation of the local people of the region is encouraged and assisted. The form of this participation changes during the evolution of the program. The first step is the organization of the local people, through the community development or social animation process, into groups for discussing their problems and suggesting program activities. As their organization becomes more sophisticated and as they develop, with the help of experts, stronger views and a broader appreciation of their situation, they begin to take a more active part in the planning process. At the implementation stage, they perform an important advisory role in determining the manner in which the plan is executed and every effort is made to assist the development of close ties with the management team.*

RESEARCH APPROACH

Up to the present, our research process has been relatively unsophisticated. The objectives are to identify the major problems and constraints in the area together with the potentials for viable economic and social development. Because the areas studied are small relative to their economic impact on the Canadian economy as a whole, and because of the relatively limited amount of economic interdependence, the rather unsophisticated approach we have taken to research has not yet led to serious regional conflicts.

The first step in examining the area is to attempt an estimate of the demand for labour relative to the supply of different skills within the area. This analysis takes account of population growth, the expected

*EDITOR'S NOTE: Since the publication of this article a new department of regional and Economic Expansion has been created by the Federal Government. The reader is referred to the Information Service of the department for reports of current activities and programs. In the present volume, Professor T. N. Brewis' article, *Regional Economic Policy,* contains comments on more recent programs of the federal government.

labour that will be released from restructured resource sectors, and migration patterns, as well as the best range of forecasts that can be made sector by sector on the potential for growth and increased employment.

The second step is the construction of a simplified model of the area's economy in an effort to evaluate the pay-off to the regional economy as a whole of measures designed to promote growth or adjustment in the various sectors.

Simple as this analysis is, it has in every instance so far provided fairly clear guidelines for the evolution of the development strategy for each area. Moreover, as by-product, we are now convinced that, except in special circumstances, the traditional Canadian policy of assisting out-migration and making up income deficiencies by transfer payments cannot be expected to provide long-run solutions to the income disparity between most of these depressed regions and the rest of Canada.

To date, this analysis has been completed for six areas in Canada. For three of these, agreements have already been signed and, in the other three, we are at various stages in the pre-agreement period. For these areas, therefore, it is possible to give a brief indication of the strategy and broad programs shown to be most appropriate by the research work.[3]

1. Interlake Region of Manitoba

This area is heavily over-populated in relation to the resource base. For most of the area, its location militates against viable non-resource based economic activity, although in the southern portion of the region there is at least one urban centre where some industrial development appears feasible. In the light of this, the program for the area has three major aspects. First, structural adjustment will be made in fisheries and agriculture to establish viable economic operations. In agriculture this is provided by programs for acquiring lands of low agricultural capability and programs to consolidate and enlarge the improved acreage of farms on lands of good agricultural capability, combined with intensive management training for farmers. A second aspect of the program provides for extensive improvements in the levels of primary and secondary education in the area, and intensive adult education, technical and vocational training for individuals who are prepared to move from their present locations. A third aspect includes programs to exploit the industrial potential in the southern part of the area and the recreation potential along the eastern edge in an effort to reduce, to some extent, the required out-migration from the area. Because of its proximity to a major urban centre and the general ease of movement within the whole Prairie region, out-migration is both feasible and practical and in total, the effect of the program will be to increase the present rate.

[3] Negotiations and discussions between the Federal Government and the Government of the Province of Quebec are presently underway for the Lower St. Lawrence Gaspé area of the province and the description of the program and strategy has been omitted from this paper.

2. Newfoundland

The analysis of the Newfoundland economy indicates a substantial surplus of labour compared with the opportunities for viable economic employment. Unlike Manitoba, however, it is not reasonable to rely on out-migration, over the next decade at least, to bring about a labour force balance. While some urbanization is possible within the province, any extensive movement in this direction would only result in substituting urban poverty for rural subsistence living.

A basic weakness in Newfoundland is a highly fragmented and inadequate school system and the lack of an effective municipal structure. It is proposed, therefore, that within the broad area to be selected as the comprehensive planning area, the basic planning unit will be a small area defined as one that can be served by a consolidated secondary high school. Within these "mini-areas," part of the strategy will be to assist in concentrating communities around a consolidated school. This may be achieved either by the physical relocation of families from outlying communities or by the construction and improvement of roads and communication systems where these are feasible. For the first stages, it is also intended to provide assistance for marginal improvements in the fishing operations as well as in agriculture and forestry in regions where these are relevant.

There are, of course, a few communities within the broad region which have a potential for viable economic development, and this potential will be exploited to the optimum to absorb as many people as possible.

3. Prince Edward Island

The analysis of the economy of this province revealed a substantial unrealized potential for economic development in agriculture. The successful development of this potential is expected to make a major contribution to the reduction of the income gap between this province and the rest of Canada. Accordingly, in cooperation with the provincial government, we are in the process of developing programs which will assist in the realization of this potential. These will include programs of farm enlargement and consolidation, land development, intensive farm management training, and assistance in marketing, as well as exploitation of possibilities for processing agricultural commodities. Subsidiary to this activity, but important in their own right, will be programs to improve productivity in the fisheries and to exploit and control the recreation potential that exists in the province.

4. Nova Scotia — Northern Half of the Province

The basic problem in this area is an inefficient and declining industrial sector. Studies clearly indicate that, without some major effort to exploit the substantial potential that exists in this sector, efforts to restructure and improve the productivity in agriculture, fisheries and forestry may only aggravate the problem of low incomes and under-employment. While substantial out-migration will no doubt continue for a number of years, analysis indicates that the prolongation of the present situation, which gives rise to this movement, can only result in a further widening of the income gap between this region and the rest of Canada. In fact it may have a serious detrimental impact on the economy of the province as a whole.

The strategy of planning for this area has not yet been completed. It is our view, however, that the main emphasis must be on the development of manufacturing and service activities. Moreover, we expect that the program cannot be based on further support for the inefficient industries or an expansion of the existing small land regionally market-oriented manufacturing activities which are at present characteristic of the area. The objective must be accomplished through the promotion of developments which will take advantage of the area's locational and natural features, and which will entail a change in the total structure of the industrial sector, moving it towards large efficient operations oriented to export markets.

There is no doubt that the potential exists. If agreement can be reached on the strategy, the next step will be to work out the programs that will accomplish these objectives. In the Canadian context, the importance of this exercise cannot be over-stressed. It will be a major departure in policy, which in the past has concentrated on adjustments in the supply side of the labour market rather than on the demand side. The lessons learned in the techniques of promoting such development on a sound and viable economic basis will be extremely important for Canada. Obviously, this will require a close partnership between government and private industries, with industry supplying the capital and entrepreneurial expertise within a framework shaped by the planners.

5. Northeast New Brunswick

In September 1966, the federal government and the Province of New Brunswick signed a rural development agreement to implement a comprehensive plan for this area. Since this agreement, which resulted in a public expenditure commitment of about $100 million, is now in effect and the programs are underway, it might be worthwhile to outline in some detail the situation and the programs which are being undertaken.

There are, at present, approximately 106,000 people living in the area, largely scattered in ribbon developments along the coast and highways. The total labour force is estimated to be approximately 29,000, of which some 10,000 are seriously under-employed or permanently unemployed. In consequence, incomes are very low, averaging just over $600 per capita, or about one-half of the average for the Province of New Brunswick and one-third of the average for Canada.

Investments in social capital in the area, particularly in education, have lagged far behind those in most of Canada. Out of a total of 258 schools in the area, approximately 160 have only one or two classrooms, and in many of these, the teachers themselves have not studied beyond Grade Nine. It is not surprising, therefore, that 36 per cent of the labour force have an education level of Grade Four or less, compared with 13 per cent for Canada.

Unlike the situation in Nova Scotia, however, there are a number of major developments now underway in the private sector which will have a significant impact on the economy of the region. Large investments are being made, or are contemplated, in minerals in the central part of the regions and in pulp and paper in the west.

In statistical terms at least, it appears that a very rough balance can be achieved in the demand and supply of labour within the region, taking into account the scheduling of job openings and the time required to train and mobilize the surplus manpower in the region.

On the supply side, however, there are three distinct problems which have to be overcome. First, the bulk of the unemployed and under-employed population is located in the eastern portion of the region while most of the new employment will be generated in the western portion. Second, because of the generally low level of education, many of those requiring work are not at present in a position to benefit from occupational training programs. Finally, a large number of the under-employed are engaged in low income agricultural and fishing operations. Rationalization of these operations will free many of these people for more productive work elsewhere but, to be effective, the release and training of this labour force must keep in step with the expansion of job opportunities.

The key problem in the northeastern New Brunswick area is the extremely low level of education and skills possessed by the population. To meet part of this problem it is the intention to embark on a $32 million capital expenditure program for the expansion and modernization of school facilities over the next four years. The program will provide for extensive consolidation of school districts and for the assumption by the province, rather than municipalities, of the major responsibility for financing the construction and operation of new schools.

Success in achieving the objectives will also depend heavily on a substantial improvement in the skills and abilities of the labour force presently residing there. Accordingly, provision is made in the plan for a substantially expanded program of educational upgrading and occupational training for adults. The agreed objective is to provide technical and vocational training for 7,000 workers over a ten-year period. The cost of facilities and operation together with the generous training allowances paid to those undergoing instruction will amount to about $22 million over the ten-year period.

Another major problem in the area arises from the scattered location of the population. The present ribbon pattern of colonization along the coast and along the interior highways makes impossible the provision of adequate community facilities. Moreover, it is not likely that the attractions and advantages arising from education and training will in themselves overcome the difficult problems faced by people who might wish to move out of severely depressed rural areas. The plan, therefore, provides financial assistance to those families who choose to move out of these areas and into selected communities. Part of this assistance results from providing a market for the land of those rural families who would like to relocate near centres of employment and education. To make this effective, the plan provides about $8 million for the public acquisition of small marginal farms and for compensation to owners of commercial real property and to churches in small centres, where more than 80 per cent of the population using these centres have decided to take advantage of the measures available for moving from the area.

Because of the low productive value of land in the area, and the generally depressed conditions, it is not expected that the proceeds realized from the sale of the property to the Crown will provide a sufficient measure of security for families who choose to sell their land. In the light of this, and in the light of the urgent need to encourage the movement of families from isolated areas with an inadequate resource base, authority is also available under the plan to provide a grant of up to $2,400 for families in rural areas who choose to sell their land under the land acquisition programs and move to an approved centre. This will provide financial assistance for resettlement costs. Additional assistance is also provided to cover the costs of moving.

In addition to this financial assistance, the plan provides for the hiring of some 30 general counsellors to work in the area. These workers will provide general counselling services to inform rural residents of the range of government programs available to them and, for those who do move within the area, to help them make the adjustments from rural to urban or town environment. Services such as manpower counselling and placement, social welfare and others will be provided by the departments and agencies responsible.

To provide accommodation for families taking advantage of the assistance to move, the plan provides for the construction of some 3,000 to 4,000 housing units at the major centres within the area. It is recognized that, notwithstanding the funds available from property sales and re-establishment grants, the cost of adequate housing for some families may, for some time, remain above their earning capacity. It is therefore intended that, as a part of the housing program, consideration will be given to providing further assistance where required, for individuals unable to carry the full burden of their housing costs.

Another group of programs was devised to assist with structural adjustments in agriculture and fisheries, as well as assistance to recreational and tourism developments, industrial parks and some road construction.

It is estimated that the agricultural base of the area is capable of supporting no more than 100 large viable farming units. To achieve this, however, requires a major re-organization of the existing farm structure. The basic means of accomplishing this will be the allocation of land acquired under the public land acquisition program to ensure an adequate farm size. Assistance will also be provided for farm management training, soil and water conservation and land development.

The plan is intended to assist in the rationalization of the existing inshore fishery by training, regulation, assistance to mobility and some investments in the inshore fisheries. With the implementation of such projects, together with action to bring about fundamental structural changes, inshore fishing has the capacity to support up to 700 fishermen at reasonable levels of income. A re-organization of the fisheries along these lines, it is expected, will free some 900 workers, presently engaged in the inshore fishery to train for work in the deep sea fishery in this and other areas, or for other occupations as they become available.

The plan is designed also to facilitate and encourage the orderly development of investments in ancillary activities, which might be generated as a result of the growth in the mining-smelting-processing industries in the western part of the region. Financial assistance will be provided for the establishment of an industrial park.

Full exploitation of the development potential of northeastern New Brunswick will require substantial improvements in the transportation network. Under the plan, however, it was considered that a major road program was not essential to achieve the objectives of assisting the people of the area to obtain a satisfactory standard of living. In the light of this, road construction projects, considered to be within the framework of the plan, will be confined to those roads and road improvements required for the successful implementation of other approved sections of the plan. These will, above all, include improvements required in conjunction with the school-consolidation program.

Finally, funds are provided in the agreement to assist the province with the cost of continuing and comprehensive evaluation of the progress and with the costs of administering the program.

SUMMARY AND CONCLUSIONS

To date, the orientation of the comprehensive planning process of the ARDA administration has been largely toward the alleviation of extreme poverty in economically isolated areas of rural Canada. With the exception of the Nova Scotia region, most of the analysis and program planning has been done without the necessity of concerning ourselves too much with the position of the economy of each particular area in relation to broader economic regions or to the nation as a whole.

The most exciting aspect of the activities to date is the process which has evolved for developing a program and for co-ordinating all relevant activities in an area, in order to deal with the specific problems of that area. We have attempted, as a matter of basic policy, to obtain effective participation at all levels from the local people up to the senior national government to ensure that programs and plans developed through the research process are not left lying on the shelf, but are simply one aspect of an extensive undertaking to achieve desired objectives.

We have not been entirely successful, as yet, in developing the structure for the most effective participation of local people and of the industrial private sector. There is a great sense of urgency, however, not just to achieve the objectives of our present operation, but because if we fail to do this we will continue to be looking for solutions to the prbblems of "The Poor" instead of dealing with social and economic continuum in a developing economy. It will mean that whatever the capacity to successfully undertake regional development in earnest, the large pockets of poverty will remain, just as they do now in and around our most active growth centres such as Montreal and Toronto.

Hopefully, Canada over time will develop the administrative structures and the economic framework to be able to identify more clearly the barriers to sectoral and regional development and to be able to gauge the relative returns from intervention with sufficient confidence to take bold action in exploiting potential development situations. It is our hope that as the nation moves in this direction we will have developed the techniques and capabilities to ensure that plans turn into action and that the action does not continue to pass by the people who are in the most need of the benefits.

In the light of this we do not apologize for the fact that the ARDA comprehensive planning activities are adjustment oriented. We are prepared to seek authority and encourage public investment for development where this appears necessary and justified for adjustment purposes. In the absence, however, of any broad economic framework for allocating national or provincial resources either sectorally or regionally, and in the absence of real knowledge of cause and effect relationships of any specific activity, we tend to approach development very gingerly, only when we feel it essential to our objectives, and in a manner which we feel can be tested without large commitments of funds.

A second important aspect of the program, which is tied in with our long run objectives noted above is the contribution by gentle pressure, persuasion and by financial assistance, which we are making towards the establishment in several of the provinces of a planning, program development and co-ordinating group. These groups, which will gain experience and strength in the preparation and implementation of FRED plans will undoubtedly provide the core of the much stronger overall provincial government administration required to play a role in real development activity.

A third element which has contributed to our success so far is the existence of the Fund. Apart from limiting its application to a clearly defined area and to a package deal, there are few constraints on how it may be used. Accordingly it has permitted wide flexibility in programming. Perhaps, more important, however, it has expanded the financial capability of the provinces to undertake programs and has provided a means by which the provinces can be encouraged to take action on politically sensitive issues.

3. *Regional Economic Policy*

T. N. Brewis

Before proceeding to a discussion of future regional policies, it may be helpful to glance back for a moment at some of the lessons of past experience. Looking back is usually easier than looking forward, though this case would appear to be an exception. The past presents a picture of manifold changes in emphasis, administration, and policy, and the goals themselves present a picture of complexity. Reduction of unemployment, acceleration of economic growth and structural change, mitigation of poverty and the quest for social justice and national unity have all been woven into the fabric of policy. Over the last few years an observer who took his eye off what was happening for even a short while was apt to find that by the time he looked again the scene and the action had both changed.

Concern with rural poverty and unemployment led to the ARDA legislation of 1961 but an earlier emphasis on improving the physical qualities of land and increasing output to improve the lot of marginal farmers soon gave way to disenchantment and to new approaches. The Atlantic Development Board established in 1962 to provide special assistance to the Atlantic Provinces and which was originally given only advisory powers, was provided the following year with funds to finance projects likely to contribute to the growth of the economy of the region. But now, in a return to the original concept, the Board has been replaced by a Council with advisory powers only. The Area Development Agency which was created to encourage industrial development in areas of chronic unemployment began operations in 1963. Ambitious notions of planning development, however, were stillborn and the Agency limited its action to providing funds in an automatic way to firms engaged in secondary manufacturing that settled in those areas. Under the

*A paper presented to the Harrison Liberal Conference, Harrison Hot Springs, B.C., November 21-23, 1969 (Original title *Regional Economic Policies: The Issues Before Us*). Printed with permission of the author.

wing of the new Department of Regional Economic Expansion the Agency is now to be given a much more sophisticated role to play involving substantial discretion in the granting of aid. The emphasis henceforth is to be on the development of growth centres and growth potential in large regions whereas before it was on distress in small ones. In earlier statements of policy the objective of developing the more promising centres had been rejected categorically. As the Minister for Regional Economic Expansion has said, a fundamental change of policy is involved. FRED – the Fund for Rural Economic Development – appeared on the scene in 1966. Action thereunder began with tremendous verve. Several ambitious plans were introduced but within three years the legislation creating the Fund was superseded. During the few years that the government has been active in the regional field, policies have undergone a continual transformation and agencies have come and gone. As a result, and very understandably, the task of those entrusted with the implementation of action has been characterised by almost constant confusion and frustration.

Inevitably repeated changes of direction complicate the task of policy evaluation and evaluation is one aspect of policy to which inadequate attention has been paid.

The amounts spent by the government on the assessment of regional policies have been so trivial as to be derisory. This is one of the more serious deficiencies of policy. Substantial sums have been and continue to be spent on various programs but little analysis of the probable effects has been made public. In some cases little is known, and what is known is not always released. Some bodies and agencies are less ready to make information available than others.[1] It is strongly urged that a percentage of all expenditures be earmarked for evaluation and analysis, and that such evaluation not be left exclusively to those responsible for the implementation of the policies. Even crude estimates of a rate of return on federal expenditures may be better than none at all. It is difficult to escape the impression at times that government departments are less disposed to measure the value of their aid by what they accomplish than by what they spend. It may not be generally realized that the federal government alone has already expended and committed under its various regional aid programs in recent years a sum far in excess of a billion dollars, and this is additional to federal-provincial transfer payments.

Ideally in the appraisal of regional development policies, one would like to have more information on the determinants of growth. With regard to the latter, fashions have changed and confidence has waned.

[1] A number of the provincial agencies are especially secretive. Professor Rowat has pointed out that the United States has always had a much more open system of administration than our own. Donald C. Rowat "How Much Administrative Secrecy?" *The Canadian Journal of Economics and Political Science* XXXI, No. 4, November 1965, pp. 479-498.

There has been a disposition in some circles to look upon the determinants of economic growth much as one would regard a horse race. Thus a number of years ago stress was being laid on the crucial role of investment expenditures in machinery and equipment and physical assets generally. It is still seen by some as the crucial element in growth. But confidence is not as widespread as it was; that horse has dropped back. "Research" and "technological change" nosed ahead for a while along with "education" – and . . . a lot of money has been put on education. Outsiders such as "development corporations" and "management training" are attracting attention, especially the latter. Some psychologists appear to favour "achievement motivation." The sociologists talk about "participation," and financiers, as is their wont, talk about "risk capital" and "finance." It is a much more open race now and by the time the pack gets around the next bend I wouldn't be sure which horse the Economic Council or the Ministry of Regional Economic Expansion would be putting its shirt on.

The favourite now seems to be "growth centre." I like the look of it myself – it is worth a flutter – but I suspect that it may be a hard horse to ride and those who attempt it could well end up in the ditch. Banter aside, however, experience suggests that looking at economic growth in terms of possible winners is not a very fruitful approach. A large number of inter-related variables are involved in promoting growth and I suspect that concentrating on one or two of them may not get us very far.

The ADA program . . . is being completely revamped. Discretion in the granting of aid has much to recommend it in principle, but much harm may be done if those exercising that discretion lack the knowledge and competence which is required. It will call for a high degree of professional sophistication. In general ADA policies to assist depressed areas have achieved their greatest impact in those areas which are in the more prosperous parts of the country, those which are typically not far distant from major centres of activity. In contrast, peripheral areas of deep distress have shown little or no improvement. Some of the poorest of these have not attracted any firms at all. The same tendency is seen in the case of industrial estates – those that are relatively far removed from important centres of activity have been less successful than others.

It follows that if the most depressed parts of the country are to be assisted to develop they will have to receive preferential treatment, in some cases probably on a very substantial scale. Such help may appear warranted on grounds of social justice but not on economic, and if poverty is a prime concern it might be preferable to look at alternative policies such as guaranteed incomes, negative income tax or assistance to migrate. There is a limit to what the Department of Regional Economic Expansion can be expected to accomplish to reduce poverty.

It seems clear that there is a need for policies to facilitate the decline of economic activity in some industries and areas as well as the expansion [of it] in others. There is still considerable reluctance in a number of circles to recognize the desirability of encouraging the decline of some impoverished parts of the country and unless this attitude changes public money will be spent to little purpose in trying to restore them. Unless there are reasons for believing that an area can be revived and that it is worth reviving there is no point in bribing firms to move in. The fact that certain distributions of population and industry happen to exist at the moment is not a sufficient reason to maintain that distribution in the future.

The pursuit of policies whether for expansion or decline presupposes a view, however, on the prospects of individual areas. There is an urgent need in Canada for more information on which to base an assessment.[2] The nature and magnitude of technological changes involving new products, production and transport costs profoundly influence the locational patterns of industry. Without a knowledge of likely developments and their expected impact over the foreseeable future it is impossible to make sensible decisions on the courses of action that regional development should follow. The implications of these changes are far from being given the attention that they deserve. Admittedly, the future can never be foreseen with certainty, but to the extent that likely trends are discernible their neglect is almost certain to lead to a waste of effort. We have to have some notion of the forces at work which are influencing the location of industry and population.

Related to the above issue is the practice of closing the stable door after the horse is gone. Canadian policy has been characterised by concentration on the past rather than a view of the future. Only when unemployment was chronic, for example, was ADA authorized to step in and ARDA had no mandate to anticipate structural changes in rural areas which were not already depressed. What is needed are policies which will reduce the emergence of distress. This presupposes some understanding of the economic forces at work and the implications of these for the future development. If major transport changes, for example, are likely to change locational patterns, then steps to prepare for the consequences need to be taken before the dislocation results. Similarly, if economies of scale are likely to increase (and there are few who doubt it) there is no point in stimulating a multiplicity of small plants across the country by offering substantial incentives. Indeed the relatively small scale of many secondary manufacturing plants is regarded as one of the factors contributing to higher production costs in Canada than in the United States.

Reviewing the Canadian scene as it has unfolded over the past decade, it is apparent that there have been all sorts of programs but little overriding direction. In the case of the Atlantic Development

[2] In this connection some observers are very uneasy about the analysis which lies behind the FRED plans as well as the capacity and determination of respective governments to carry them out.

Board, project engineers and planners went their separate ways; and, especially in its early days, ARDA allocated funds to all sorts of miscellaneous projects recommended by the provinces without any regard for broader strategies of regional development.

The Department of Regional Economic Expansion should improve matters in time – its establishment was a most important advance, which I welcome – but it is still not certain how it will integrate its various functions or where it will place its emphasis. The Department offers the prospect of a more sophisticated approach to regional problems with [an] emphasis on developing growth potentiality and with a higher degree of administrative co-ordination than has existed hitherto. Legislative changes, however, are not enough and governments will be hard pressed to achieve their objectives unless they can achieve a high degree of expertise. As is well known to those faced with the task of recruitment, there is a severe shortage of people with the skills and judgment required.

When it comes to selecting ultimate objectives, the reduction of social injustice may be difficult to reconcile with steps to expand output in the more promising of the depressed regions and what seems like justice to one group of people may not seem like justice to another. With regard to national unity, another objective, it is questionable how far it can be furthered by actions which entail the transfer of funds from the richer to the poorer parts of the country. It may be worth recalling that in a number of federations, the effect has been the other way.

Decisions on the various steps considered necessary to create employment opportunities in some of the poorest areas will depend in large measure on agreement with the provinces, and there may well be conflicts of opinion. There are times when the provincial governments pursue ends which inhibit the development which some of us would like to see, and as has happened in Quebec, the actions of extremist parties can be a factor discouraging investment. In per capita terms, investment in the Atlantic Provinces now exceeds that in Quebec.

Provinces are competing with each other for industry and this can prove to be an expensive as well as [a] self-defeating practice. In a number of cases information on the inducements offered is not made public. These are serious matters. National interests will not be served if individual provinces act independently and offer whatever concessions they choose.

A number of provincial governments have been advocating the formation of regional governments, and specific proposals with regard thereto are currently under discussion. It is realized that many of the old administrative boundaries have little relevance in the world as it now exists. The redrafting of such boundaries, though not necessarily undertaken with economic development in mind, can be expected to improve the quality of services. Provincial boundaries are much more difficult to change, but some forms of closer economic integration between the provinces appear to be inevitable, for many of their regional economic problems cannot be solved in isolation. It is questionable indeed how far it will be possible to proceed with the ambitious policies which are now envisaged without becoming involved in a re-assessment of provincial powers and responsibilities. Certainly there will be a need for joint federal-provincial strategies.

One of the merits of the new approach to regional development in Canada is that small designated areas are to be replaced by larger regions. The designation of these larger regions should permit much more effective policies of structural adjustment.

A strong case can be argued for tailoring aid to the specific needs of individual regions and developing growth strategies on the basis of various assessments as is now intended, but it bears repeating that this is no mean task.[3] It is one thing, for example, to recognize the potential merits of growth centres and quite another to realize them. Quite apart from the political difficulties which are to be expected in their selection, it may be far from clear in individual cases whether growth will benefit or be at the expense of outlying localities where unemployment and poverty are likely to be more extreme. The centripetal effects may outweigh the spin-off.

Looking back over Canadian experience, a charitable observer might regard the frequent changes of course and administration as part of the learning process rather than one of inadequate thought being given to a highly complex problem at the outset. One would hope, however, that with the experience gained in recent years it would be possible to proceed with a clearer sense of direction in future.

With regard to future policy, there are a number of issues and questions which might profitably be the subject of discussion . . .

1. a) Whatever it may have been in the past, is our primary goal now that of increasing output in the more advantageous localities of larger depressed regions? (I gather that it is.)

b) If it is, who is going to select those localities, and what issues will determine the selection? In short, how are we to identify the growth centres?

c) If we are going to emphasize the development of the more promising localities, what (if anything) do we do about the *least* promising, which were the original subject of our concern?

2. Should we have differentiated regional and area incentives? Presumably the growth centres will be given preferential treatment. What about larger regions such as the Atlantic Provinces? . . .

3. If voluntary migration tends to be selective in terms of age groups and education (as it seems to be), should we follow the example

[3] As some sceptics have remarked, the government will be hard pressed to achieve as rapid a rate of growth in the depressed areas as in the number of officials concerned with it.

in Newfoundland and encourage, in particular cases, the migration of entire communities into localities with greater promise?

4. Growth appears to be "a system problem." It calls for a whole range of interacting conditions which cut right across conventional administrative boundaries. What are some of the implications of this?

5. The Minister has not been happy about various expenditures which have been made in the past, and with good reason. What arrangements should be made to ensure that the public is kept informed of the estimated costs and benefits of the programs that will be introduced in future? Nothing, in my mind, will kill public support for regional development expenditures in future more surely than doubts about the wisdom and efficacy of what is being attempted.

6. a) What steps should be taken to curb inter-provincial competition for industry?

b) Should federal aid be made conditional on full and frank disclosure of aid granted by provincial governments and their agencies?

7. Can we have an appropriate regional development policy without an indication of the major trends and forces which are likely to influence the location of industry and population in future? My own view is that we cannot, and one of the main functions of the Department of Regional Economic Expansion should be to supply that information.

4. *Anti-Poverty Planning in the Gaspé and Lower St. Lawrence Region**

Poverty in Canada is widely distributed geographically, with a considerable proportion of it taking the form of relatively small poverty pockets in otherwise well-off areas. There are, however, certain extensive areas or subregions where poverty is so widespread that its elimination can be treated in many ways as an area problem. In the United States, considerable attention has been focused on one such area, the Appalachian Region. In Canada, large parts of Eastern Quebec and the Atlantic Provinces could be looked at in the same way.

A comprehensive program now under way to deal with the poverty and developmental problems of the Gaspé and Lower St. Lawrence Region of Quebec, including the Magdalen Islands, has involved the use of some highly interesting and to some extent original techniques of socio-economic planning. With suitable modifications, some of these techniques may well prove of value in dealing with poverty problems in other parts of Canada, perhaps even in some urban areas. The program has been regarded from the first as a large-scale pilot project.

The region in question is mainly rural, with an average income per person only a little over half the average for the Province of Quebec as a whole. The economy is based largely on agriculture, fishing and forestry. In 1963, a regional planning agency, the "Bureau d'Aménagement de l'Est du Québec," was established as a nonprofit private corporation by two existing local economic councils. In the same year, the Bureau was provided with financing under the terms of the ARDA agreement between the Province of Quebec and the Federal Government, and given the task of preparing within three years a master development plan for the region. Two basic specifications for the work were an intensive program of research and full participation by the local population in the

*Reproduced with the permission of the Queen's Printer for Canada from the Economic Council of Canada, *Fifth Annual Review* (Ottawa: Queen's Printer, 1968), pp. 128-130.

preparation of the plan. Co-ordination and liaison with the provincial government were to be provided by way of relationships with a committee of ministers, a permanent committee of senior officials, and the Quebec Economic Council.

The research program undertaken by the Bureau was broad and interdisciplinary, involving the use of agronomists, ecologists, engineers, economists sociologists, geographers, cartographers and many other specialists. As the research work proceeded, it became evident that a solution to the problems of the region would require far-reaching structural changes in patterns of resource and land use and in political and social organization. This made it all the more important to ensure a continuing dialogue between the research workers and the people of the region, whose daily lives were in many cases likely to be profoundly affected by the changes in prospect. Such a dialogue was brought about by means of a network of local committees and through the efforts of a specialized team of 20 "social animators." Basically, social animation is a technique of stimulating and motivating people to define their existing environment and their wishes for a changed environment, and to organize and plan processes of social change. In this instance, use was made of all major means of communication, including group discussions, radio, television and special newspapers and films. A circular flow of ideas and suggestions from research workers to the population and back again to the research workers was thus assured.

The result of these endeavours was a development plan to 1982, submitted for public appraisal in 1966. The plan was subsequently modified somewhat and, on this basis, an agreement covering the five-year period to March 31, 1973, was signed by the provincial and federal governments in May 1968.[1] Total expenditure under the plan is projected as $258.9 million, of which $46.6 million will come from provincial revenues and $212.3 million from federal revenues. The principal objectives of the plan are as follows:

1) Modernization of the "traditional" economic sectors of agriculture, fishing and forestry.

2) Creation of new activities in manufacturing, mining and tourism — activities capable of absorbing at least part of the manpower flowing out of the "traditional" sectors.

3) Major improvements in the occupational and geographical mobility of the labour force.

4) Accelerated urbanization and regrouping of population in a few well-equipped urban centres.

5) Provision of infrastructure and other investment necessary for the success of the plan.

6) Establishment of a sound institutional structure, well adapted to the demands of a broad-based development policy for the region.

The agreement provides for the appointment of a provincial planning co-ordinator, a federal planning administrator, a management committee composed of these two officials, a federal-provincial liaison committee, and a provincial regional administrative conference made up of representatives of the various departments of the Quebec government involved in the plan. The previous emphasis on participation by the local population continues with the designation of the Eastern Quebec Regional Development Council, Inc., as the "privileged regional interlocutor."

[1] *An Agreement Covering the Implementation of a Comprehensive Rural Development for the Lower St. Lawrence, Gaspé and Iles-de-la Madeleine*, Ottawa, 1968.

5. *Animation Sociale: The Experience of the BAEQ*[*]

Marc A. Morency

INTRODUCTION

While any examination of the recent experience of the BAEQ [Bureau d'Aménagement de l'Est du Québec] in the sphere of *animation sociale* must reflect the short period of time to have elapsed since the end of the experience, it is also subject to two other limitations. First of all, such an undertaking must be limited by the unique nature of the experience itself and by the lack of specific terms of reference. Secondly, it is still too early to be able to examine adequately the results of a scientific evaluation of this process. Although such a sociological evaluation would produce a better description of the impact of *animation sociale*, it also would be restricted, of course, to a study of a limited number of events which took place during the life of the BAEQ mandate, neglecting those occurring after the BAEQ's work was finished.

Bearing these limitations in mind, in this report we will attempt tentatively to define, as empirically as possible, the *animation sociale* process as it was conducted from June 1963 until April 1966 by the BAEQ. However, before examining the *animation* activities, a few comments on the plan of this report would seem to be in order.

The first part of this report will try to make more explicit the conception of social change which led the BAEQ in this experiment in social action. At the very least, we will deal more extensively with the dominant concept in that respect. This concept involves the continual adherence, by the BAEQ, to the idea of integrated overall planning rather than piecemeal or project planning.

While this first part of the report may seem rather theoretical, it is very necessary to a complete understanding of *animation sociale* as practised by the BAEQ.

*Reprinted with permission of the author and Information Canada from *Rural Development Branch, ARDA, CR-No. 14,* Department of Forestry and Rural Development (Ottawa: Queen's Printer, 1968).

The second part of this study will look at the actual history of the BAEQ's *animation sociale* experience. This will involve an examination of the four distinct phases of the program: the launching (from May to the end of September 1963) ; the setting up of the first mechanism for intervention (from October 1963 to the end of October 1964) ; the setting up of a second intervening mechanism (from November 1964 to August 1965) ; and finally the consultative period. Each of these phases will be looked at from several standpoints: the dominant conception of committees; the formal and material goals sought; the group focus of *animation sociale*; the *animation* clientele; the clientele in training; the methods used; and the principal problems met.

PART ONE: SOME CONCEPTUAL CONSIDERATIONS

The BAEQ's Idea of Social Change

In order to begin to define *animation sociale* in any meaningful empirical way, we have chosen to examine the BAEQ's idea of social change from three directions: 1) the goals of intervention; 2) a description of the region's situation; 3) an attempt to interpret the intervention process. This descriptive work permits us to offer a first empirical definition of *animation sociale.*

Participation as a Means and a Goal of Development

Firstly, several scientific analyses have established that if culture (social structures and attitudes) is not changed along with changes in the other levels of society, be they economic or technological, then it is very difficult (if not impossible) to obtain a harmonious development through planning. Thus, the rejection of project or piecemeal planning in favour of overall planning clearly implies an intervention at the attitudinal level. Hence, in the eyes of the BAEQ, *popular participation* is seen as a *means* to such development.

In the second place, we should remember that our democratic society places great value on the participation of individuals or groups in the decision-making and change processes which affect them. Thus, *popular participation* also becomes a developmental *goal.*

In effect, since the plan represented a major decision affecting the region's population, two main tasks emerged. There was firstly the need to sustain and spread the BAEQ's conceptions of social participation in a social milieu which often blocks this form of participation, preferring instead to use the traditional structures of power which often do not favour development. There also was secondly the job of organizing an active way of particpating in the planning process, and hence in defining the goals and means of development.

Two further tasks could be distinguished in this second aspect. One of these called for the training of leaders to set up new participative structures. The other called for the use of *animation* in the consultative participation process itself.

These then are the dominant conceptions underlying the operations and very existence of the *animation sociale* agency.

We should say, too, that it is the second aspect, more philosophic than scientific, which most readily justifies the existence of *animation sociale*.[1] We also should acknowledge that the desired changes in attitude or organization do not necessarily justify the use of an *animation sociale* mechanism. This mechanism is introduced particularly by a philosophical belief in the participation of individuals and groups affected by the decision process. In a society where the neo-liberal philosophy is dominant it is conceded that means such as *animation* are used to promote this participation. However, the fact that this participation is not based on scientific criteria explains why this participaton and *animation sociale* are challenged by two different and opposed philosophies. These are the non-liberal and no longer dominant technocratic and conservative philosophies, each based on a paternalistic relationship between planners and planned.

In summary, we feel that the *animation sociale* efforts of the BAEQ have been useful in instilling the region's population with norms, values and attitudes that are suitable for and part of the developmental process. Moreover, we see this popular participation in decision-making as being both scientifically justifiable as a means of development, and philosophically desirable in a democratic political milieu.

These general conceptual considerations, then, lead us to look at the regional state of affairs in 1963.

The Region's Situation

The *animateurs* brought into the region found certain prevalent characteristics. There was a low population density, and this had promoted local solidarity and loyalty. On the other hand, they felt that the state of the region's culture had evolved suffciently to permit the employment of an *animation sociale* mechanism while the plan was being worked out. This consideration in turn led to the examination of several possible structural means of encouraging changes in attitudes and popular participation in the planning process.

Several known means of action were considered inappropriate to the goals of this venture in the Pilot Region. Thus, research in itself was not seen as a sufficient stimulant to action; nor were the mass media alone sufficient stimuli. These media were thought to be even less effective in a rural environment, where personal contact assumes a greater importance than in the urban environments where mass media are concentrated. Moreover, existing associations or voluntary groups were not felt to be sufficiently differentiated and adequately representative of all community interests; nor would the associations themselves permit actions aimed at bringing forth new leaders in their spheres. Finally the existing bodies would ask only to guide their specific projects, without having to consider the need to spread new norms and attitudes. Clearly, then, a new structural framework seemed necessary.

The Animation *Agency*

Perhaps it is appropriate at this stage to look at the BAEQ's *animation* agency. This was, basically, a specialized agency made up of multi-specialized *animateurs* who would be working at three levels: attitudes; understanding of planned development; and specific projects for development (silviculture, extension, etc.). These development agents, employing varying styles – oriented toward groups, and at the same time toward the goals of the agency – would also have their own public information unit (with radio-television and newspaper sections). The *animation* and information services were designed to work in complementary ways so that the information process could operate at two levels, in line with the notion of the "two-step flow" of information, and *animation* would proceed in parallel with the progress of the BAEQ's research teams.

The Processes and Phases of Social Change: An Attempt at Interpretation

Social change in the Pilot Region can be divided into three distinct periods.

a) Before 1963, change was not oriented in any overall systematic way. Social organization was unbalanced and deteriorating, and characterized by a dependence on governments. Structurally, there was little differentiation between elites and there was a general dependence of the population on the existing elites. Behaviour, too, generally was in accordance with established traditions.

b) The Intermediate Situation: (1964 to the beginning of 1966). The first intermediate phase involved the intervention of BAEQ's workers through an *animation* mechanism. Initially, this involved intervention at the role level through consultative study groups which helped local people to analyze rationally the local and regional situations.[2] At the same time these processes permitted developmental goals and means to be determined. This phase was characterized by occasionally rapid collapses of traditional patterns. We found that the setting up of the local committees, for example, was widely acclaimed by some segments of the population. This breaking down of patterns, however, in turn resulted in the dependence of rural elites on the imported leaders *(animateurs).*

The second step in this first phase centred mainly around mobilizing popular support for the idea of a plan, and preparing the leaders for permanent participation in the planned development of the region. This

[1] It should be understood that *animation sociale* is not always the only intervening mechanism available; moreover, it is not applicable in all types of societies nor in every stage of their development.

[2] The use of objective data provided by the research teams was a major asset and an important aspect of the *animation* strategy.

involved, essentially, a definition of specific roles for the associations in the region, and restructuring of economic councils.

The final intermediate phase presupposed the emergence of a new elite (*Le Comité de Liaison de l'Est du Québec*) some of whose members had already participated in local, zone, and/or regional committees. This new elite has been charged with restructuring councils in order to set up the Regional Development Council (CRD). It is this elite which has taken over the guiding role of the imported leaders of the BAEQ.

c) The Future Situation: (The 1982 Horizon). The dominant social condition of 1982 will be one of a balanced developing society. The region's social structures will centre around self-correcting social structures that provide a continuous rational process of change and development. During this phase the leadership will be differentiated in terms of socio-economic interests and the population, through an enlightened public opinion, will be able to identify new leaders. Finally, behaviour will be directed through carefully considered analyses of situations, goals and means.

PART TWO: THE HISTORY OF *ANIMATION SOCIALE* IN THE BAEQ

When looking at the history of *animation sociale* in the Pilot Region, we should remember that differences in conceptions, the novelty of the project, the problems of intervention in general, and the potential threat to the status quo of suggested social changes largely can explain the differences between the dominant conception of *animation sociale* and the actual application of the *animation* program. The present historical examination will be divided into four distinct phases.

Phase One (May to the end of September 1963): The Launching of the Program

This was a period of recruiting and training *animateurs* and of defining the strategy of change by means of a new structure.

The first recruitment of *animateurs* by the BAEQ took place in May 1963, following the March 1963 memorandum to Premier Jean Lesage of the *Conseil d'Orientation Economique du Bas St. Laurent* (COEB). This memorandum defined the BAEQ project as a participative survey and asserted that the participation of the local population was essential to the development of the region. During the period when the plan was being worked out, the memorandum recommended the creation of committees in each locality to meet with a social worker and agronomist or forestry or fisheries specialist. It is also interesting to note that the text proposed a multi-functional role for the development committee: a fact-gathering or research role and also an implementation role. The local organisms, at municipal, zone and regional levels, the COEB memorandum said, should make up the working groups to carry out the plan.

The *animateurs,* during the June-July self-training period, seized on this view of committee functions and, in early 1964, started to spread the idea to promote strong local participation, and strong critiques of established organizations such as municipal councils or school commissions. The first *animateurs* shared a conception of popular democracy which sometimes showed a tendency to differ from the *animation* goals and strategies finally adopted, and which constitute an alternative to community development.

Also in the summer of 1963, those in charge in the BAEQ sought to look into the possibility of having data gathered by the population concerned. However, as a result of a Quebec Department of Agriculture and Colonization general questionnaire, it was concluded that each person must be dealt with individually. This demolished the concept of participative survey promoted in the memorandum presented in May by the COEB. Through co-operation with the local committees, profiles on each locality were prepared. It was during this time that the *animateurs* began to study existing ARDA committees, their structures, operations and duties, to participate in a survey, and finally to set up descriptive files for each locality in the region. The *animateurs* at this time also restricted their activities to personal contacts. The information gathered was used to look at both the area and the occupational representativeness of the committees and to plan their re-organization.

In August, the *animateurs* had their first real chance to see the regional picture when they participated with their superiors in overall regional contact with the population. With the studying of existing scientific documents, including those made for the COEB, this total contact allowed the Planning Council to proceed to a first definition of the situation, to foresee some immediately realizable projects, to meet local elites and to diffuse the first information on the current experiment. The first information campaign was being delayed by difficulties in recruiting a specialist in this field. The information chief's job remained vacant until the spring of 1964.

Also in August an important discussion on the strategy of intervention was held. This discussion showed one group believing that existing leaders or associations could be re-oriented toward development, with a second group holding that the associations were not sufficiently different from one another, and not sufficiently regionally or developmentally oriented, to be influenced by a direct approach. It was this latter, dominant conception that showed these leaders and associations possibly seeking to use the *animateurs* to further local or particular interests. However, these local organizations, the *animateurs* felt, could be influenced and more easily redefined by the mobilization of their leaders into a thoroughly new structure. Thus the BAEQ limited its work among associations, sending only one *animateur* on information trips.

This strategy stressed the study aspect of the local committees, who would analyze the social, economic and physical environments, guided by local leaders or by the country *animateurs*. The next step would be improvement committees, which would utilize and develop general research in terms of action programs in each sector of socio-economic activity. This sectorial research was to be based on popular participation (through associations, for example, the *Union Catholique des Cultivateurs*, Chambers of Commerce, etc.) and on specialists.

Clearly, then, the functions of the committees had changed considerably from implementation to research since the COEB memorandum.

Phase Two (October 1963 to the end of October 1964): Setting Up The First Intervention Mechanism

The period between October 1963 and the end of October 1964 can be seen as the time when local development committees and the *animation-information* agency were being formed, and the participative survey and first training sessions were being held.

The visits to the associations were continued as the *animateurs* met with the existing committees and sought to focus on committee procedures and to inform the members on the roles of the BAEQ, the *animateurs* and the local committees. On October 23, 1963, the BAEQ professional teams took part in the meeting of the COEB at Cabano, and tried to impart development information. During the same month the first televised broadcast took place.

November brought the hiring of an official to take charge of the *animation* program. The five existing *animateurs* went into their territories to form local committees in each of the 200-odd localities in the region. In the case of ARDA committees to be restructured, the formation of sub-committees was the occasion for introducing new figures. In the local areas the *animateurs* made personal contacts before they held founding meetings. The *animateurs* were to serve their difficult apprenticeship at these meetings. They alone would have to face the local rural elites.

The first months of 1964 brought the regrouping of local elites and criticism of traditional solutions. During this time the *animateurs* concentrated on personal contacts, presiding at meetings, committee gatherings, forming sub-committees and sought to convince the leaders that research must precede action.

In doing this the *animateurs* wanted to discover the leaders who might benefit most from the first training sessions to be held in March, 1964. These weekend sessions, held at the county level, were conducted with the help of the specialists from the Research Service, as well as the now eight *animateurs*. The sessions dealt with regional development from economic, social, and biophysical viewpoints.

By the end of March a public information director was appointed and the second stage (the first had been the formation of committees) could be begun, and an occupational survey was launched. This study was to serve as an initiation for the local committees into collecting facts and making rational choices of the goals and means of development.

In March a training session for the *animateurs* was held in order to reach a consensus on *animation* techniques and on the orientation of the team. According to the reports sent by the *animateurs* to their superiors this objective seems to have been more or less attained. Some committees, too, were ready to do all the work expected of them and lent themselves to the pre-tests of procedures for the inquiry.

By May the approximately 160 French-speaking local (rural) committees received their copies of the labour-force questionnaire for approximately 220,000 respondents. Inventory and discussion guides for the committees were also circulated.

During this first year of the BAEQ's short life, an evolution had taken place. Past and present efforts had been assessed. The overall strategy had been planned and the Yellow Book outlining some of the ideas fundamental to the program had been released.

This Yellow Book, which became the foundation of popular participation in the BAEQ area, held that development of the region depended on the idea of each person participating as much as possible in his individual and collective growth. In order to redefine a situation, it advocated that the people should participate as fully as possible in decision-making. Popular participation was seen as a goal, and *animation sociale* as the means to achieve this participation.

Thus, by steps, the individual was to become his own master, leaving his traditional situation behind him. Through a truly participative structure, participation ought to be able to motivate itself.

These themes were to be carried in the BAEQ radio shows, *"Père Clophas,"* and the weekly newspaper *"l'Aménagement."*

It was during this period, too, that the various parts of the *animation* division began to assume quite distinct but related functions. Thus, we find an *animatrice* active among the women to mobilize them into local committees, a priest-sociologist among the clergy, and still another *animateur* working among the associations. In July the committees received the bulk of their inventory and discussion guides. The National Film Board, after its interesting experience with a film to help *animation* in St. Octave de l'Avenir (a remote settlement), was at work on films to be projected in the localities.

In August, as preparation for the zone committees to be formed in the autumn, the first urban committees were founded. In September *"l'Aménagement"* noted that six out of 12 urban committees had been formed and some 3,000 out of 4,000 possible committee members were enlisted. The *animation* team by then included 17 professionals, 14 of these working in the field. A new research section, too, had been added to the structure, an evaluation of the intervention began, and some of the more dynamic committees had evolved from investigating to public information. Others had begun to be interested in specific projects, for example a regional handicraft co-operative.

The officials in charge devoted some of their time during the summer to defining the functions and structure of the zone committees. By mid-October the principle outlined in the Yellow Book was accepted. This stated that the zone was to be formed from the group of communities situated in the zone of influence of a particular hub or centre. The zone committees were to represent the decision centres found inside such zones, and would comprise representatives of local committees. Certain association representatives also were to be attached to these bodies. These committees, with the representatives of all decision centres, were to increase communications in order to promote the identification of common goals.

At the regional level, too, the Yellow Book foresaw the setting up of sectorial improvement committees as subcommittees of the regional councils. These sub-committees would be formed from representatives of the zone committees and governmental agents, and would be charged with the exploitation and management of a single resource. The committees would evaluate specific projects suggested at the zone level.

After discussion among planners, the *animation* director and the political scientists and sociologists, the functions of a participative structure were redefined. These shifted the emphasis from working out a plan to the establishment of a continuous planning process with the preparatory and implementation processes going on simultaneously. In sum, the region's future society not only will have research and *animation* structures, but also local governments capable of making decisions and staffed by competent officials.

Phase Three (November 1964 to August 1965):
Transition and Setting Up a Second Intervention Mechanism

The late fall of 1964 was significant in the history of *animation sociale* in the region. At this time the annual meeting of the COEB studied the role of development committees, associations, governments, and other planning bodies in the preparation and implementation of a development plan. This meeting illustrated the consultative character of the development committees and economic councils, and pointed up the need to consider integrating them.

Another significant event at this time was the very successful adult education project sponsored by the BAEQ through local committees. This pilot *animation* project, designed to help remedy the lack of professional training found in the labour force, was without doubt greatly needed by the local population, especially since the analysis of the labour force aspects done by the local committees. The survey had spread the attitude that education was the right of all, and not merely of a select few.

Throughout this period the needs of *animateurs* to work through committees to ensure popular participation, and at the same time to use personal contacts to promote local leadership, sometimes conflicted. Such conflicting needs led to setting up a centre to train development leaders. By mid-December the Centre for Studies in Regional Development had held its first session, with some 20 persons from Gaspé south participating in the five-day session. Throughout 1965 and 1966 the Centre was to receive 1,000 such leaders. By mid-December, too, seven out of a possible eight zone committees were ready to operate, their first job being to consolidate local reports into zonal reports.

In order to reach a larger public, efforts were concentrated on persuading local committees to hold public information meetings. In these endeavours *Télé-Clubs,* using television broadcasts beamed to local information sub-committees who would discuss the subjects, were employed extensively with much success in this utilization of the "two-step flow" information process.

In January-February 1965, the team looked back over its successes. During 1964, 175 rural, 15 urban and 7 zone committees held some 7,000 meetings, and some 4,000 persons working in sub-committees produced 600 reports and 175 consolidations of local reports. In March alone some 7,000 persons were taking extension courses. In April 1965, the Télé-Club program came to a successful end with 324 clubs in existence instead of the forecast 200.

Meanwhile, the zone committees had finished their summary reports and were ready to compare their interpretations of the same data with BAEQ officials. Also, the local committees were busy analyzing the zone committee reports. During the summer the *animation* research staff met with 236 area leaders to assess the development of attitudes and opinions during the past year.

The end of this third phase brought a clarification of the constant evolution of *animation,* and showed it as definitely engaged in the process of consultation. This evolution is shown in three ways: the strategy planned; the addition of regional consultative committees at the top of the committee structure; and the alteration of the *information-animation* agency's structure.

Of these developments, perhaps the most relevant to our discussion was the restructuring of the agency to permit teams of *animateurs* to work together according to a certain specialization in tasks. The Planning Council's text, "Popular Participation in the First Plan for the Pilot Region" (September 1965), reiterated the importance of participation in the developmental process and explicitly linked *animation sociale* with developmental efforts. The report held that if development were to be seen as the coherent changing of socio-economic structures, then the people's participation would be necessary as both a means and an end. Moreover, such popular participation, the report suggested, could not be based on existing groups, since many groups had vested interests, very few were truly regional in outlook, and natural leaders were rare. This state of affairs required the creation of new structures.

The tasks of *animation* may be seen, then, as laying the bases for true long-term participative structures, and accelerating and making clearer the functions of popular consultation in order to prepare the First Plan more easily. It is this phase which will be outlined in the next section.

Phase Four (September 1965 to March 1966): Consultation

The shift in the prevailing idea of committees, so that they came to be regarded no longer as training grounds for leaders but as part of the consultative organization's sub-structure, was conspicuous throughout various aspects of the *animation* experience. However, the consultative approach, it was recognized, could involve the *animation* team not merely to the benefit of regional or zone committees but to the detriment of local committees, since the latter's tasks had been achieved. The *animateur's* clientele, then, would be local elites grouped into zone committees, representatives of associations, governmental bodies and a few specialized consultants.

The clientele of the Centre for Studies in Regional Development would be recruited among the local English-speaking leaders, the zone committee leaders, association representatives, mayors and presidents of school boards. The Centre also would utilize various training techniques. These techniques in turn would be tried out, and used by the committees in the field.

In September, when the zone committees were beginning their study of the Draft Plan, the first regional consultative committee, one for fisheries, was formed. The newly established committees' functions included study, *animation* and consultation, but not implementation or improvement as in the original conception. In addition, the regional committees were to study the zone reports.

At the end of September, the *Conseil Régional d'Expansion Economique de la Gaspésie et des Îles-de-la-Madeleine* (CREEGIM) proposed to integrate the participative structures with the regional councils, an idea which had been expressed in March 1964, and also in the Yellow Book. The *Conseil* also suggested that the councils be given an *animation* task after the presentation of the Plan.

As a whole, consultation on the Draft Plan was a difficult task to organize. The study of the plan called for the continuous presence of *animateurs* in zone sub-committees. However, the use of summary tables and lists of consultation points made real consultation possible despite the demands on time and attention resulting from intensive study of the draft. The draft in turn provoked the convening of the Estates-General of the cities of Rimouski and Rivière-du-Loup. Chambers of Commerce also sought to redefine themselves within the new institutional perspective and to redefine their conceptions of local and regional development.

In December the consultation was concerned with the structure of the regional development office to be set up following the end of the

BAEQ's work. Fundamentally the discussions centred around administrative deconcentration, with a parallel reorganization of governmental bodies, i.e, municipal regrouping and the creation of a new municipal or regional government.

The spring of 1966 was devoted to defining the institutional framework for consultation, *animation* and representation. It was then proposed to unify the regional councils into a regional development council. The establishment of the new council rested on the efforts of the regional elites and of the new body charged with continuing the structural change process in the region, the *Comité de Liaison de l'Est du Québec* (COLEQ).

In concluding the comments on this final phase, it is worthwhile to point out a few of the major problems of the BAEQ experience.

First of all, as regards goals, the training of professional *animateurs* revealed numerous difficulties resulting in different conclusions and actions. In some cases participation became the only goal of some *animateurs* and not just a means of development. Other *animateurs* had great difficulty in filling a multiple role. Still others differed over the type of *animation* required and in their conceptions of the role of group effort in *animation work*. Differences in rates of group change or in the effectiveness of intervention could not be too marked due to the constant necessity of obtaining consultation for the First Plan.

As for the internal structures of the agency, three positions – agency co-ordinator, *animation* chief and chief of information – were difficult to fill. Also information, with its reliance on some traditional techniques, did not play a thoroughly effective role among the general population. Instead, the information program concentrated on reaching leaders. Due to a general lack of information, the *animateurs* became the opinion leaders in the eyes of the local leaders, and this situation in turn helped to reinforce a traditional tendency to regard information as a privilege.

Due to the lack of precise scientific theories of social change, to the lack of a precise model of a modern society, and to the lack of a provincial plan and specific projects, the *animation* staff of the BAEQ had to place most of its emphasis on encouraging popular participation in working out the Plan, and in working out an experimental model of consultative participation.

CONCLUSION

In order to define an *animation* policy precisely, it seems to us, the BAEQ experience suggests that goals be looked at from two distinct viewpoints. The first of these is based on a scientific theory of economic and social development, and considers participation as a means of development. The second, for philosophical reasons, views participation as a goal in itself.

We also would like to offer a few recommendations for future *animation* efforts. We feel that an *animation* policy placed within a philosophical concept of development should take account of the usefulness of specialized agencies in achieving this end, that it should utilize multi-purpose specialists, and that *animateurs* in turn should employ a flexible approach. Moreover, emphasis should be placed on the need for information aimed at and written for the general public, and not just for a restricted elite. This should be planned and carried out in close co-operation with the *animation* team, making use of the "two-step flow" of information. After looking at the literature on the subject, it also seems to us that generally it is easier to set up new structures than to adapt existing ones to developmental thinking.

6.

Legal Aid - Canadian Style*

Graham Parker

The Ontario Legal Aid Act,[1] which was passed in 1966 and put into operation in April 1967, has received little attention[2] in the United States. This is surprising in the light of the great activity since *Gideon v. Wainwright*[3] and the outbreak of the War on Poverty. Perhaps, however, the very existence of these influences explains why the Ontario scheme has not had greater response in legal literature.[4] Although the national professional body, the Canadian Bar Association, has discussed the topic in a perfunctory manner for the last forty years,[5] there has been no centralized effort to provide legal aid. Similarly, the highest court in the land, the Supreme Court of Canada, has refused to emulate the United States Supreme Court by applying the so-called Canadian Bill of Rights to problems of the right to counsel so that the deprived accused would be acquitted automatically when due process was denied.[6] Therefore the administration and provision of legal aid has emerged as a provincial, *viz.* state, responsibility under the Canadian federal system.

*Reprinted from *Wayne Law Review,* Vol. 14, No. 2, 1968, by permission of the author and the publisher.

AUTHOR'S NOTE: My thanks to Mr. Andrew Lawson, Provincial Director of the Ontario Legal Aid Scheme, and his staff for their invaluable assistance. The views expressed are entirely my own.

[1] The Legal Aid Act, 1966, c. 80 (Ont.).

[2] The one known exception is Silverstein, The Ontario Legal Aid System and Its Significance for the United States, 25 Legal Aid Briefcase 83 (1967).

[3] 372 U.S. 335 (1963).

[4] The administrators of the scheme tell me that they have received many enquiries from organizations interested in legal aid, including many from the United States.

[5] Parker, Legal Aid — The Canadian Need, 6 Can. B.J. 179-82 (1963).

[6] O'Conner v. The Queen, 57 D.L.R.2d 123 (1966). This decision is typical of the lack of recognition given the Canadian Bill of Rights, 8 & 9 Eliz. II c. 44 (Can. 1960). The supposed constitutional guarantees were passed by the

Canadians have always tended to solve their problems other than by the direct approach to the courts in reliance on a constitutional document. Instead the country has looked to its civil service and the omnipresent Royal Commission or Departmental Committee.[7] This administrative device has been preferred first because it has enabled investigations, enquiries and studies to be carried out by, it is always hoped, independent, well-informed individuals or groups. Second, and no less important, the use of the Royal Commission has been an excellent pigeon-holing and delaying device providing a retreat from practical politics. One sometimes feels that a political party which is trying to justify its return to office expects the constituents to be as impressed by Royal Commission reports as by actual legislation. Furthermore, the Canadians have not been noted for their addiction to direct social action, official or otherwise, as a tool for reform. This can be explained partly by the fact that Canadian social problems have not been as great or as visible as those facing the United States.

Despite the inactivity of the Supreme Court of Canada and the morbidity of most Royal Commission enquiries, a committee appointed by the Attorney General of Ontario[8] made a careful study of legal aid and came forward with recommendations which now have been implemented in the Legal Aid Act of 1966.

I

THE IMPETUS FOR CHANGE

Why did the province of Ontario become concerned with the reform of legal aid? There is no simple answer to this question. Undoubtedly there was general dissatisfaction with the existing plan.[9] The social climate in the United States, and in particular the decision in *Gideon v. Wainwright,* gave considerable impetus to liberal thought in Ontario and, in fact, all parts of the country. Legal aid had been discussed in the press, magazines and on the national television network. Non-legal organizations also became interested.[10] Even legal education had its effect – partly due to a liberal influence permeating law schools which previously had been addicted to black-letter law teaching and practice-oriented curricula.[11] Extensive research programs in criminal law and criminology were also being established in the province at that time.[12]

One of the most interesting events in the expansion of social services had been the introduction of universal medical assistance, Medicare, in Saskatchewan in 1964.[13] No one can assess the effect these events, including the doctors' strike, had on the professions of Canada and the Canadian public. There is little doubt that the professions were in bad odor because many Canadians were shocked by the doctors' behaviour — even if they did not altogether sympathize with the Saskatchewan government's plan. It would be an exaggeration to say that the legal profession in Ontario (or anywhere in Canada) sought changes in legal aid because they were afraid of socialization. The government in power in Ontario hardly had the requisite political complexion to be interested in socializing the legal profession, particularly when so many legislators were lawyers. I think it fairly can be said, however,

Diefenbaker Government in 1960 but lack the force of a constitutional amendment as it is only an ordinary federal statute and is not an entrenched grundnorm. Only occasionally has a Canadian court recognized the due process of law and other fundamental freedoms supposedly legislated in the Bill of Rights. Regina v. O'Conner, 48 D.L.R.2d 110 (Ont. 1964), rev'd, O'Conner v. The Queen supra. See also Regina v. Gray, 132 Can. Crim. Cas. Ann. 337 (Victoria County Ct. 1962); Regina v. Drybones, 60 W.W.R. (n.s.) 321 (Nw. Terr. 1967). The Supreme Court of Canada has not recognized the Bill of Rights in any case although the latter decision is now on appeal to that court. A full recital of the constitutional problems facing Canada (including the status of the province of Quebec) cannot, however, be canvassed in this article.

[7] See Lockwood, A History of Royal Commissions, 5 Osgoode Hall L.J. 172 (1967).

[8] Province of Ontario, Report of the Joint Committee on Legal Aid, 1965. The major conclusions of the Committee are stated as follows:

[O]verwhelming opinion today is that legal aid should form part of the administration of justice in its broad sense. It is no longer a charity but a right. The voluntary plan in Ontario was conceived as a humanitarian gesture by the lawyers of Ontario and was viewed essentially as a charity. We believe from listening to those who have testified before the Committee, both lawyers and others, who represent a broad cross-section of responsible opinion throughout this province, that the stigma of charity should be removed from legal aid. . . . A person participating in the scheme, be he lawyer or a party to litigation or otherwise, in no way suffers from any suggestion that his cause is second-rate or that the matter is in any different category to that involving the relationship of private legal advisor and client.

Id. at 97.

If any system of legal aid is not to be regarded by the community as a charitable undertaking and where qualified applicants for legal aid are unable to pay for legal services, the question immediately arises who must pay the cost of a legal aid scheme including the remuneration of the members of the legal profession who participate in a plan which provides for such remuneration. The great body of opinion expressed in briefs and in oral submissions to the Committee was that the responsibility for the major cost of an extended legal aid scheme should be borne by Government.

Id. at 98.

[9] Id. at 19.

[10] Skatfield, Parker, Lyon & Fornataro, Report on Legal Aid in British Columbia, 7 Crim. L.Q. 72 (1965). This report was made on behalf of the John Howard Society of British Columbia, a penal reform and after-care group.

[11] See Parker, What You Should Know About Legal Education in Canada, 12 Student Lawyer J., No. 1, at 20 (Oct. 1966).

[12] E.g., The Criminal Law Program at Osgoode Hall Law School, the Centre of Criminology at the University of Toronto and the Sentencing Seminars at Queen's University.

[13] See Tollefson, Bitter Medicine: The Saskatchewan Medicare Feud (1963).

that the legal profession has never had the public respect accorded to medical doctors and that recent events accelerated the need for improved public relations. One must hastily add that the initiative for change, at least officially, came from the government. Leaders of the legal profession have taken pains to point out this fact to disabuse the public of any suspicion that lawyers were trying to line their own pockets.[14] All Canadian provinces have an advantage over the American states where reform within the legal profession is concerned. The bar is totally integrated on a province-wide basis so that there is no need to negotiate with various city, county and state bar associations. If there is a fault, it is the fact that the profession, in Ontario at least, is governed by a body which is too centralized and, some say, too autocratic. The Law Society of Upper Canada (the archaic name by which the governing body in Ontario is known) did an excellent job on this occasion of conducting a thorough survey and making good recommendations. The effect of the recent Medicare battles is evident on the very face of the new scheme which leaves control almost entirely in the hands of the profession.

Some statistics about Ontario should help American readers put into perspective the scope and relative importance of the Legal Aid Act. Ontario's 413,000 square miles makes it larger than Michigan, Illinois, Indiana, Minnesota, Ohio, Pennsylvania and Wisconsin combined. The province stretches from the Manitoba border (north of North Dakota) to the Thousand Islands and from Windsor to Hudson Bay.

The province is Canada's largest with a population of over seven million. Ontario's size and diversity create serious problems for the administration of any social institution including legal aid; these problems include hazardous weather conditions and the sparse population in the northern part of the province. At the same time, the southern part of the province has high density population along the lakefront from Windsor to Kingston, including the problems of metropolitan government in Toronto. The chosen form of legal aid had to embrace these contrasts. Any legal aid plan would have a good chance of succeeding in Toronto where there are more than 3,000 legal practitioners — just over fifty per cent of the province's lawyer population. The four other major urban centres, with populations ranging from 100,000 to 300,000, would be equally well provided for. On the other hand, there are jurisdictions in the north where lawyers are seldom seen or heard. So far there have been no reports of Canadian justice being dispensed by courts sitting on ice floes just south of the Arctic Circle. Similarly, there is no truth in the rumours that some adventurous young lawyers are donning fur parkas, buying teams of huskies and combining a trap line with a thriving practice in criminal law in the far north. Advocates of comprehensive legal aid hoped that Ontario lawyers would ensure not only that the Mounties would get their man, but also that he would be the right one. So much for the Canadian stereotype. No doubt the use of modern transport is ensuring that the most remote Ontario resident is able to obtain help.

II

PREVIOUS SYSTEMS OF LEGAL AID IN ONTARIO

In Canada there are no matters of exclusive federal jurisdiction which must be dealt with by a separate system of courts. In effect, all the superior courts are federal courts. The judges of these courts are appointed by the central government, but the everyday administration of justice is handled by the provincial government. Although the criminal law is embodied in a federal code,[15] it is administered provincially; so legal aid, as part of the machinery of justice, is a provincial responsibility. Until 1951 the provision for legal aid was very limited. On the civil side there was no aid for the indigent litigant. In criminal cases counsel was provided only for persons charged with capital offences. The provincial government paid a nominal *per diem* fee and provided transcripts and living and traveling expenses for appeals to the Court of Appeal or the Supreme Court of Canada. There had been some informal arrangements for free legal aid on other serious criminal charges, and the infrequently used practice of *in forma pauperis* appeals was available. No doubt there was a good deal of "charity" practised by lawyers, particularly in rural areas. But the official provision for legal aid was a mere token arrangement between the legal profession and the government.

The 1951 plan was instituted when the Law Society of Upper Canada recognized the need for wider coverage. This voluntary scheme was supervised by the Law Society and administered through local clinics and directors. The clinics received and screened all applications, applying a means test which was originally $1,200 for a single person or $1,800 for a married person (plus $200 for each dependent); these limits were later raised to $1,700 and $2,500 (plus $300 for each dependent). The director had discretion to grant legal aid in other deserving cases. Legal aid was unavailable for certain tort actions, including defamation and breach of promise, and for some proceedings in bankruptcy. In criminal cases summary conviction offences[16] were excluded, as were quasi-criminal offences such as those related to traffic and liquor. The most contro-

[14] See The Ontario Legal Aid Plan; a Symposium, 1 L. Soc'y Gazette 8 (1967) where Brendan O'Brien, Treasurer (i.e. President) of the Law Society said: [L]et me say to those who may still be hesitating about offering their services in legal aid matters, while it is true that the fees proposed are not overly generous, and no one is likely to get rich from legal aid clients, yet on the other hand there will be no write-off of bad debts at the end of the year in respect of legal aid work. If you do the work properly you get paid for it, and apart from the direct payment that you will receive you may find that the legal aid client of today will become a good private client tomorrow, or he may recommend you to others. In any event you will have had the satisfaction of having given your assistance to a fellow man who was in need.
Id. at 11.

[15] Criminal Code, 2 & 3 Eliz. II, c. 51 (Can. 1954).

[16] Id. at pt. XXIV; The Summary Convictions Act, Rev. Stat. Ont., c. 387 (1960)

versial exclusion on the criminal side was the denial of legal aid to those accused persons who previously had been convicted of criminal offences. This included of course the man who was in danger of being declared a "habitual criminal"[17] or a "dangerous sexual offender."[18] The legal aid plan of 1951 also provided for payment of witnesses and transcript fees. With this exception, the plan was truly voluntary as the *per diem* payments in capital cases ceased.

Given its obvious inadequacies, the 1951 voluntary plan worked reasonably well as a limited attempt to provide legal assistance to the indigent. The means test was much too stringent. The criminal side had placed undue burdens on the small criminal bar, particularly in the cities. The administration of the plan at the local level often placed heavy burdens on the director. The plan did not really provide adequate arrangements for advice and counselling situations where litigation was irrelevant or inadvisable. In other words, it was weak in terms of preventive law. It provided service on a "fire-fighting" basis. With the exception of neighbourhood law offices, any voluntary plan would suffer from this defect. Lawyers are more prepared to devote their time to litigation or even prelitigation negotiations rather than to extensive periods of counselling which do not provide ready, even if temporary or compromise, solutions. There is always a danger of this when a plan like the one existing in 1951 does not provide any remuneration. Office hours seem the most precious, and a lawyer who is willing to spend a whole morning in court to reach a conclusion in a legal aid client's case may balk at numerous office interviews which may have obviated the trial.

Even if inadequate, the voluntary plan established in 1951 had carried a heavy burden. In the County of York (where Toronto is situated) it was claimed that, on a *per capita* basis, twice as many criminal cases were handled by the county's lawyers as in Chicago under its public defender system.[19]

It is to the great credit of the legal profession in Ontario, its governing body, the Law Society of Upper Canada, and the provincial government that they recognized the public demand for change and expansion in legal aid. In addition to appointing a committee representing the bodies mentioned above, a law professor was retained to make a survey of legal aid.[20] His findings were startling. He estimated that over sixty per cent of accused persons in Ontario could not afford counsel, and yet only one in six was receiving aid. These findings were only estimates as reliable data was not available. This estimate may have been a little high, but the Committee agreed that at least one-half to two-thirds of accused persons were unrepresented and that the same proportion of people could not afford a lawyer and were first offenders.

The Committee made a full survey of all existing legal aid plans, including the public defender system (operating mostly in the United States), the semi-financed, semi-voluntary plans used in Australia and

British Columbia and the much more comprehensive plans operating in England and Scotland which are more socialized.[21]

When the Ontario Joint Committee on Legal Aid made its report, it recommended that the 1951 plan be discontinued. In its place, a system was suggested which would provide province-wide service, wholly financed by the provincial government and, hopefully, with the cooperation of the whole profession. The plan would be administered by the Law Society. The Committee also recommended that the proposed legal aid scheme would be as comprehensive as possible with a minimum number of exceptions. Perhaps the most surprising fact is that these recommendations, reported in March 1965, were accepted almost *in toto* in the Legal Aid Act of 1966. The plan came into operation in April 1967.

III

THE ONTARIO LEGAL AID PLAN

The Ontario plan, of course, borrowed from some plans and totally rejected others, but in a few important respects it is unique. The plan provides for a completely free choice of lawyers. The successful applicant for legal aid is given a legal aid certificate which simply entitles him to help under the Act and makes no mention of a specific lawyer. Legal Aid clients are urged to hire a lawyer of their own choosing. If they do not know the name of a lawyer, they are encouraged to get a recommendation from a friend or relative. Only after these enquiries have proved fruitless are they invited to choose a lawyer from a list of lawyers registered under the system. There is a clearly defined objective behind this policy decision on which administrators of the program place great emphasis. The drafters of the Legal Aid Act are

[17] Criminal Code, 2 & 3 Eliz. II, c. 51, § 660 (Can. 1954), as amended, Office Consolidation of the Criminal Code, c. 51, § 660 (Minister of Justice 1963).

[18] Criminal Code, 2 & 3 Eliz. II c. 51, § 661 (Can. 1954), as amended, Office Consolidation of the Criminal Code, c. 51, § 661 (Minister of Justice 1963).

[19] Of course, quantity is no substitute for quality. Furthermore, there may be something of a distortion because the Ontario report does not state what percentage of cases was defended. Another relevant factor is the high percentage, approximately 90 per cent of criminal cases, including many serious ones, which in Ontario are tried in the magistrates' courts. See Province of Ontario, Report of the Joint Committee on Legal Aid 16 (1965).

[20] Friedland, Legal Aid: Working Papers Prepared For The Joint Committee on Legal Aid (1964) (Mimeo, Osgoode Hall Law School Program in Criminal Studies).

[21] For a description of the British legal aid system see Matthews, The English System—A Native View, 22 Legal Aid Briefcase 71 (1963); Parker, C.J., Development of Legal Aid in England Since 1949, 48 A.B.A.J. 1029 (1962), and the Committee Report, supra note 8, at 30-34.

also very determined that the legislation foster the private practice of law rather than be an attempt to socialize the profession in any way. In the ideal case the client under the Act will initiate an entirely normal professional relationship with his lawyer rather than suffer any stigma of being a welfare recipient. This desire for preserving the private practice of law permeates the whole scheme; counsel on both sides are forbidden to inform the court that the case is a legal aid one.

The system is meant to provide just compensation for the legal profession. This does not mean that the profession should profiteer under the system but that the remuneration for legal aid lawyers will be sufficient to provide good service for the client. Despite protestations from the bar, the legal profession had been deluding itself in thinking that legal aid clients were being treated on an equal footing with the private client. This is no reflection on most of the profession but rather a facet of human nature.

Finally, the new plan is more comprehensive than any previously attempted. The plan provides not only representation at trial but also advice in a preventive law situation, full provision for free appeals and legal counsel from the very outset of any legal situation. This is particularly true of the criminal side where counsel are visiting the cells very early in the morning and advising, referring to counsel, arranging bail and adjournments so that the accused's legal rights are fully protected.

The official governing body of the legal profession, the Law Society of Upper Canada, is responsible for the administration of the new legal aid plan. The plan's chief executive is the Provincial Director. In addition to the legally-trained personnel, there are officers who supervise the financial aspects of the scheme. The Legal Aid Committee was established to assist and advise the Law Society, the Provincial Director and the Advisory Committee. It is comprised of three members of the judiciary — each representing a different stratum of the courts — two lawyers of the province and a senior public welfare officer. Each committee member will serve from one to three years, with the right of reappointment.

The originators of the plan were determined to hire a minimum headquarters staff while ensuring that men of the highest calibre could be provided. They wanted the scheme to be operated by private lawyers where possible at the local level wherever feasible. The province was divided into forty-six areas, and only one of those areas, namely that part which incorporated the metropolis of Toronto, has permanent full-time heads administering the area. The other forty-five areas have area directors assisted by area committees who are all lawyers in private practice. These directors and committees are responsible for the administration of the local program, including the maintenance of counsel panels within the area. Each area committee is comprised of five lawyers and other community members who help in administering the program.

The legal aid plan works on various levels. The recent decisions of the United States Supreme Court have shown that legal advice and assistance may be too late if it is only provided after the first court appearance.[22] The planners of the Ontario scheme were most concerned with providing legal aid as early as possible. Consequently the new plan has ensured that no administrative red tape robs the accused (or other litigants) of the legal help which he needs. Therefore, the accused's first contact with the legal aid plan is not with the lawyer who will necessarily take his case in court but with duty counsel. Early every morning in Toronto the police cells are visited by a supervising, *i.e.*, senior, duty counsel and a team of duty counsel (one for each court sitting) who offer their services to those in custody. All those desiring a lawyer are interviewed and preliminary advice is given as to plea, adjournment, bail or any other help. When the court convenes these duty counsel sit throughout the court session representing those who were in custody as well as any who appear on summons. Those who desire further advice (as to pleas in mitigation of sentence or to defend the charge against them) are then referred to the legal aid office where they are interviewed as to their financial position and, if eligible under the scheme, are provided with a legal aid certificate entitling them to the services of a lawyer. The most important aspect is that no one is initially deprived of legal aid at the crucial first appearance in court even if it is later determined that they can afford a lawyer from their own funds.

The duty counsel sits through the court hearings as a watchdog. He will sometimes intervene in cases even when the accused has decided to proceed without a lawyer. The magistrates will hear duty counsel at any time, and many parties' rights have been fully protected in this way.

The greatest weakness of the present system is that the duty counsel are not provided in the police station. This is not an oversight by the originators of the scheme who decided that intervention at that stage was ill-advised. This is not surprising because Canadian courts and, I think it is fair to say, Canadian lawyers are not as aware of the civil liberties issues which have attracted so much attention in the administration of criminal justice in the United States in recent years.[23] Even if the

[22] E.g., United States v. Wade, 288 U.S. 218 (1967); Miranda v. Arizona, 384 U.S. 436 (1966); Escobedo v. Illinois, 378 U.S. 478 (1946); Gideon v. Wainwright, 372 U.S. 335 (1963).

[23] One American survey has said of Canadian criminal procedure: "[T]here is probably little question that the police in Canada are less restricted than in many other common law countries." Developments in the Law: Confessions, 79 Harv. L. Rev. 935 1106 (1966). See also the leading case of Boudreau v. The King, 94 Can. Crim. Cas. Ann. 1 (1949). In Canada the exclusion of coerced confessions and illegally obtained evidence is discretionary in the trial court judge, although in practice fair play and a sense of justice usually prompts the judge to exclude the former and admit the latter. See also Parker, Recent Developments in the Law of Evidence, in Special Lectures of the Law Society of Upper Canada, Recent Developments in the Law (1966).

Ontario police would resent the presence of counsel at the interrogation stage, there seems little reason for not providing some assistance in arranging bail in the police station – particularly during the night when no duty counsel is provided.[24]

The other problem is that quite frequently the duty counsel has had insufficient time to be briefed by an accused who appears in court on summons and who did not see the duty counsel in the cells. Of course, to adjourn all such cases would place a great burden on the court calendar, and it is felt that any injustices can be remedied on appeal.

The Legal Aid Act has covered most legal matters. This, along with the abolition of any stringent means test, has made for a very comprehensive plan. Most plans in the British Commonwealth have had means tests which tended to be applied in a strict mechanical fashion with very little thought to the subjective situation of the applicant. The exclusions under the 1966 Legal Aid Act are very few and, in any event, most of the exclusions are not absolute but are subject to the discretion of the area directors and committees. On the criminal side, there are no outright exclusions. Section 12 of the Legal Aid Act of 1966 provides that a legal aid certificate is automatically issued in all cases in the Supreme Court and county courts (which have jurisdiction over jury trials), under the Extradition Act[25] or the Fugitive Offenders Act[26] and on any charge of indictable offence and any case where there is a possibility of preventive detention.

Although it is only discretionary, the practice has been to grant legal aid certificates "in any summary conviction proceeding under any Act of Parliament of Canada or of [the Ontario Legislature] if upon conviction there is likelihood of imprisonment or loss of means of earning a livelihood."[27] This gives a discretionary legal aid service in a very wide range of cases because it could include many traffic offenses where a driver's licence could be suspended or cancelled and any charge of quasi-criminal nature where a man's livelihood could be threatened by de-licensing or similar penalty. In addition, discretionary legal aid certificates could be issued in any proceeding in the juvenile and family court[28] and for hearings before a quasi-judicial or administrative board or commission.

The area committee also has authority to grant legal aid in appeals to the Supreme Court of Appeal of Ontario (the highest provincial tribunal) from summary convictions under the Criminal Code[29] or for appeals under the Ontario Summary Convictions Act[30] or on appeal to a quasi-judicial administrative body.

On the civil side, a clearer line is drawn between cases in which legal aid will be given (either as of right or by discretion) and those where no legal aid will be given under any circumstances. In the latter category, as laid down by section 15, no legal aid will be provided in cases of "defamation, breach of promise of marriage, loss of service of a female in consequence of rape or seduction, alienation of affection or criminal conversation," "in relator actions" and any proceeding relating to an election.[31] All civil actions in the Supreme Court, county or district courts (which are intermediate courts of limited jurisdiction)[32] surrogate courts and the Exchequer Court of Canada[33] are included in the scheme by section 12. The area director has a discretionary power to grant a legal aid certificate in any proceedings in the division (small claims) court, quasi-judicial or administrative board and bankruptcy proceedings.[34] Approval can be obtained from the legal clinics and, of course, police stations and cells, telling the public that legal assistance is available.[35] No improper motive is meant to be imputed to the Law Society in failing to have a more aggressive advertising campaign. The administrators of the scheme believed that they should start out in conservative fashion so that they could have a period of adjustment in the first year or so. They also believed that the scheme would attract more work than they could comfortably handle, and this has proved accurate. There are many backlogs in some areas of people who previously could not afford but who now want divorces, old debts collected, etc. The demand has been high; already the scheme has handled the work of 46,000 individual clients.[36] The most surprising

[24] See M. Friedland, Detention Before Trial (1966) for a description of the inequities of the bail system in Toronto's magistrates' courts. The plight of the prisoner in need of bail may be solved by the work of a group, sponsored by the Amicus Foundation and inspired by the Manhattan Bail Project, who are examining the bail system.

[25] Extradition Act, Can. Rev. Stat. c. 322 (1952).

[26] Fugitive Offenders Act, Can. Rev. Stat. c. 127 (1952).

[27] Legal Aid Act, 1966, c. 80, § 13 (Ont.).

[28] Id. at 487 & note 40 infra.

[29] Criminal Code, 2 & 3 Eliz. II, c. 51, pt. XXIV (Can. 1954), as amended, Office Consolidation of the Criminal Code, c. 51, § 13 (Minister of Justice 1963).

[30] The Summary Convictions Act, Rev. Stat. Ont., c. 387 (1960).

[31] Section 15(c) of the Legal Aid Act, 1966, c. 80, § 15 (Ont.). Section 15(c) debars a legal aid certificate "in proceedings for the recovery of a penalty where the proceedings may be taken by any person and the penalty in whole or in part may be payable to the person instituting the proceeding . . ."

[32] Depending upon the subject matter, the ceiling jurisdictional amount of the county court varies from $1,000 to $4,000. The County Courts Act, Rev. Stat. Ont., c. 76, § 19 (1960).

[33] See Exchequer Court Act, Can. Rev. Stat. c. 98 (1952).

[34] The Legal Aid Act, 1966, c. 80, § 13 (Ont.). In addition section 13(c) provides for drawing documents, negotiating settlements or giving legal advice wherever the subject-matter or nature thereof is properly or customarily within the scope of the professional duties of a barrister and solicitor.

[35] An advertising agency was retained by the Law Society to assist in publicizing the legal aid plan, within the guidelines described in the text. Globe and Mail (Toronto), June 15, 1967, p. 3, col. 7.

[36] This is only a rough estimate for the six months of operation ended September 20, 1967. Mr. Lawson, the Provincial Director, kindly supplied me with this information. More detailed statistics are instinctive. In brackets after the totals are the figures for the County of York (i.e. metropolitan Toronto) and a further breakdown into civil and criminal: Duty counsel have assisted 29,800 [13,600; 5,800; 24,000]; Applications received 28,000 [11,000; other breakdown not available]; Legal Aid Certificates issued 63,000 [4,800; 8,700; 7,600]; Provisional Certificates issued 6,600 [3,000; other breakdown not available].

thing is that the split between criminal and civil work has been roughly fifty per cent for each, although the latter includes all juvenile and family court work.

There have been few complaints concerning the operation of the scheme. Most have been related to administrative problems such as slow payments of accounts; but with experience and the computerization of the work in the office, this complaint should soon disappear. One of the most serious complaints has been that some young lawyers have been soliciting legal aid certificates from practitioners who were either unwilling or unable to fulfill their obligations on the legal aid certificate. This practice, which has been reported informally by some practitioners, is not as wickedly unethical as one would imagine. The problem could be solved by the administrative device of the legal aid certificate being transferred to the lawyer who is actually doing the work. The young lawyers have not been soliciting clients although some of their more senior colleagues consider that the "hustling" tactics are, at least, unseemly. These circumstances do raise some interesting peripheral issues or possibilities. Some observers of the legal aid scheme believe that one of the most severe tests which the plan will face is the period following the present "honeymoon" stage when there will be lawyers who do not wish to continue their names on the legal aid panels. The fear is that lawyers from the larger firms will begin to resent the time taken on the less lucrative legal aid work. There may be some merit in this fear because it would mean that senior, highly competent or experienced counsel would not make themselves available to the legal aid clients. The result might be that the Toronto equivalents of the Wall Street firms will, at best, limit their legal aid work to that done by the most junior lawyers on their staff whose time is less valuable than that of a lawyer engaged in commercial, corporate or tax practice. This can be remedied by a concerted effort by the legal aid administration and the Law Society to preach the gospel of professional responsibility. Perhaps these attempts will be as ineffectual as those to inculcate "proper" ethical standards among the profession at large.

The concomitant of this possible state of affairs is the establishment of a "legal aid bar." No one seems able to give any clear understanding of what this phrase means. Presumably, it would apply particularly to the criminal side of legal aid and would breed a group of lawyers who would specialize in legal aid cases. The fear raised by this specter is that the profession would degenerate into strata. One imagines that this is groundless and that two classes of practitioners have always existed[37] and if any professional trend were to emerge from the existence of legal aid, it would be a slight narrowing of the gaps between the graduations of the profession. The admittedly unsavory elements of the profession who had been the denizens of the police cells and corridors of the inferior courts would be less obvious. These lawyers, known in this hockey-conscious country as "rink-rats," who have exploited, frightened and confused defendants by demanding fifty dollars or more for pleading them guilty, obtaining adjournments or seeking bail, would disappear as the persons charged with offences would be advised and protected by duty counsel and their legal aid lawyers.

In any event, attempts to exploit the legal aid system have been avoided by the area directors who have rationed the issuance of legal aid certificates so that no lawyer is consistently doing work under the Act. This rationing process also obviates another way in which the legal aid scheme could become the domain of a particular segment of the profession. Furthermore, a practitioner cannot act both as duty counsel and legal aid lawyer in the same case. The administration of the plan does not encourage the establishment of private law offices in low-income areas solely to make legal aid more visible and available. This may seem strange to any American lawyer who has heard much in the United States of neighbourhood law offices[38] — the activists in the social reform struggle going on in troubled American cities. Of course, such control by the administrators, along with the discretion residing in the area director to refuse or restrict the issuance of legal aid certificates issued for a particular cause of action, *e.g.*, on landlord and tenant matters, or to a particular practitioner, can have a retarding effect on attempts to change the law in any particular field or area.

In recent years the law schools of Ontario, particularly Osgoode Hall Law School,[39] have carried out a heavy burden of legal aid — advising clients and appearing in all inferior courts in hundreds of cases every year. The Legal Aid Act does not make provision for full participation of law students. The reason is obvious: the new scheme provides for payment, which can only be made to the admitted practitioner. The law schools have been concerned with this deficiency because they have found that legal aid work has provided a valuable community service and a useful training device. The new system has accommodated the law student to some extent by allowing counsel to use the student as an interviewer, investigator and researcher. In addition, the law school's legal aid bureaus have been taking the cases of those who had been refused aid under the new Act. These cases have been mostly minor cases on summary jurisdiction.

I am unable to give an accurate and minute eye-witness account of how the legal aid system is operating because I am not an official of the scheme, a court officer or a private practitioner. I have done some field work. I visited the cells at eight o'clock one morning to see the duty counsel system in operation; I was impressed by the changes that had already occurred. The opportunities for a fast trial, adjournment or

[37] See J. Carlin, Lawyers on Their Own (passim) (1963).

[38] See Note, Neighborhood Law Offices: The New Wave in Legal Services for the Poor, 80 Harv. L. Rev. 805 (1967).

[39] For a description see Henderson, Students in Magistrates' Courts, 6 Obiter Dicta No. 4, pp. 1, 2 (1967).

bail have increased. The police realize that the lawyer will be seeing the accused very soon after arrest; this of course has a very salutary effect on police practices. The duty counsel, who is immediately available, also has had a therapeutic effect on those who are so upset by their experience that they otherwise might have made a precipitous decision about their plea or other personal matters. The whole system depends on having conscientious duty counsel who can exercise fast but responsible judgment in the cell interviews and who are prepared to do the same in the court-room even at the risk of incurring the wrath of judge or prosecutor. Some duty counsel have been inexperienced or unaggressive in the courtroom and have not carried out a watchdog role.

For one week I acted as duty counsel in the juvenile and family court. Under the Legal Aid Act the provision of legal aid in the jurisdiction is at the discretion of the area director.[40] Because few lawyers specialize in family law or have an interest in juvenile delinquency and are aware of the unique qualities of that court, special arrangements were made with the legal aid office for a pilot project in the Toronto Juvenile and Family Court. Duty counsel are now provided in all hearings in that court. In juvenile delinquency cases, which usually occupy the time of three courts every weekday morning, a duty counsel is provided in each courtroom. In the afternoons when three to five courts are hearing child welfare or family matters, one duty counsel is assigned, on a roving commission, to offer assistance where needed. To call the lawyers "duty counsel" is to negate the experimental nature of the project. By no means are all those interested in the juvenile court and who nevertheless support the legal aid program convinced that lawyers should appear in the juvenile and family court. Only a very small percentage of the juvenile delinquency cases or the child welfare applications, which are mostly concerned with custody, are contested. Most alleged delinquents admit the allegations, and parents of children in the wardship of child welfare organizations usually consent to the court's disposition of their children. Consequently, lawyers have been acting more as *amicus curiae* than as participants in an adversary system. Their role in the court's business has depended on their prior knowledge of the system, the personality of the judge and the type of case before the court. The panel of lawyers who have volunteered for service in that court either have had experience in the court or have been informed of its peculiar qualities. A special manual has been prepared which describes the philosophy and jurisdiction of the court. Very few legal aid certificates have been issued, but the lawyers have been making a valuable contribution. The legal aid lawyer has been able to correct procedural irregularities, object to inadmissible evidence and advise the parents as to the probable disposition of the case (which is more of a social counselling role than the giving of legal advice). These counsel have also checked the allegations against the child's story and had charges dropped in appropriate cases. The lawyer interferes in few cases, partly because the "guilt" and disposition are obvious — little Jimmy broke the window and his case is adjourned *sine die* after an admonition from the bench — or he feels so unfamiliar with the jurisdiction that he is unable to offer much constructive advice. Once again he fulfills a watchdog role, and although the cost of providing lawyers is high, the outlay is worthwhile. Not only are the juvenile's rights protected, but many unnecessary adjournments are avoided. The parents are often distraught and simply need a few minutes of consultation (while the court waits) for exaggerated fears to be assuaged. If legal aid were not readily available, the parent and child might seek an adjournment and an interview with a lawyer to obtain assistance very similar to that given by the *amicus curiae* counsel.

The greatest disadvantage in the present system arises in that minority of cases where the allegations are hotly disputed and in those where the disposition is a problem. There are very few of the former and they obviously require the issuance of a legal aid certificate. The latter cause the most difficulty because the lawyer knows no more than is in the child's file, and yet a legal aid certificate referral may not provide a satisfactory solution because the most relevant data may be social or psychological rather than legal. At the initial hearing it is too easy, in the friendly, "helping" atmosphere of the court, for the lawyer's usual pugnacity to be lulled by the seeming certitude of the social worker's diagnosis when the data collected in the social history may be inaccurate or incomplete. Even more important is the possibility that the recommendations concerning disposition may be inappropriate for the child and independent evidence from a behavioural scientist may be necessary. Yet few lawyers feel equipped to challenge the disposition process. Education of the lawyer is obviously required, and then the least that he can do is conduct an informed cross-examination of those recommending the disposition to an institution, foster care or other community resource.

V

SOME GENERAL OBSERVATIONS

What are the likely effects of legal aid? As stated earlier, it is really much too early to make an authoritative statement. The author's comments are not based on valid sociological observation but on hunch, vague rumour and conjecture. The system is likely to be as good as its administration and the men responsible for it. The legal profession and the Law Society are hoping that the plan does not become bogged down in officialese, the lassitude of the civil service and meaningless administrative difficulties. Every effort is being made to leave a maximum of autonomy in the hands of the profession. This will be achieved by

[40] The Legal Aid Act, 1966, c. 80 § 13 (b) (Ont.).

ensuring that the lawyer-client relationship is established (and left inviolate) at the earliest opportunity and by the very direct concern of the Law Society which is responsible for the program. The legal profession, at the present time, is proud of its achievement. There is a distinct feeling in the profession that its members are doing a worthwhile job and that they are now able to service a much larger segment of the population. The administrators of the program take pride in the fact that the provision of legal aid performs an *ombudsman* function in the community and that justice is now being done.

One can only hope that the aims of the Legal Aid Act do not prove to be too ambitious and that the high cost of providing private lawyers for all who fully or partially qualify for legal aid will not result in a curtailment of the coverage of the Act. Lawyers also hope that any complaints that they are being paid for "charity" work will be offset by the goodwill generated by their satisfied clients.

The fear of rising costs could most readily be felt in the criminal courts. The area director has discretion to refuse a legal aid certificate if he considers the matter frivolous. The solicitor who accepts the legal aid client is also under an obligation to deter his client from unnecessary litigation which would waste the time and money of the taxpayer.[41] These checks on the public will, no doubt, occur much more frequently in civil cases. The plight of the criminal legal aid client will probably result in few refusals, except on financial grounds, but the high costs of legal aid may well be felt in this area. As stated earlier there is no empirical data available at the present time, but fears have been expressed that there will be more adjournments, more jury trials, more "not guilty" pleas and more appeals in criminal cases which could disrupt the already overworked and inadequate criminal courts. There is, as yet, little evidence of these fears being realized. The duty counsel may well be able to expedite cases by giving advice to defendants with little chance of acquittal who might otherwise have had cases adjourned unnecessarily. Similarly, the state is saving money as well as preserving liberty when accused persons are granted bail where, under the old system, they have been kept in jail for longer periods.

There is little evidence that lawyers are using unfair delaying tactics in the courts. There may be some slow-down in the process of the magistrates' courts because the bench and bar are taking greater care in the disposition of cases, but this is a salutary effect and within the spirit of the Legal Aid Act.

Another interesting possible effect may be the use of pre-trial plea bargaining. This is very likely due to the mere presence of more lawyers in the system. Both inside and outside the system there should be improvements in the administration of criminal justice where few lawyers have been appearing and where legal arguments have been rare. In the last year, law schools have noticed that more students are attracted to the criminal law, partly because there has been an increased interest in this field of law throughout the whole of North America and partly because legal aid seems to make it possible for a young lawyer to specialize in defending accused persons. One experienced criminal lawyer has privately suggested that this fostering of expertise in criminal law is only ephemeral. Previously, the young man who had the courage to specialize in criminal law soon became either well known or discouraged and transferred to corporate law. This lawyer believes that the Legal Aid Act has attracted so many young lawyers to the field that few will become skilled specialists. There seems to be some merit in this argument because the Legal Aid administration is determined to avoid a "legal aid bar" and is ensuring that no lawyer learns his trade by means of legal aid clients. Some supporters of legal aid answer the criminal lawyer's observation by calling it sour grapes because he is losing clients to legal aid. As stated earlier, this may be true of the low-skilled, unethical criminal lawyer, but it is having no effect on the leaders of the criminal bar. The most experienced defence attorneys are making the greatest sacrifices under the present system of legal aid as was the case under the post- and pre-1951 plans. There are so few capable of defending a man charged with homicide, rape or a complicated fraud that these lawyers have always devoted a disproportionate amount of their time and talents to legal aid cases. If the legal aid defence of criminals is spread so thinly throughout the profession that it discourages specialization, then this burden will continue.

VI

CONCLUSION

Two commentators on legal aid, one American[42] and one Canadian,[43] have offered pessimistic prognoses on the effect of legal aid. Ironically, the Canadian, Professor Mewett, has attached greater significance to the liberty of the subject than shown in Professor Blumberg's argument. The latter is more persuasive because I agree that

[41] Reid in the Symposium, supra note 14, at 14 says:

I think there is a significant difference right at that point between the Ontario plan and the English plan, and it is worth dwelling on for just a moment. Under the English plan, as I understand it, the Legal Aid Committee in issuing a certificate expresses in effect an opinion that, let us say, a reasonable cause of action exists. That is not the case here. Whether an unreasonable cause of action exists is a matter for the solicitor who is confronted with the circumstances of the case. He must apply the rules which you apply to any ordinary situation, quite outside legal aid, such as those relating to an application to strike out an action as being frivolous.

Two judges in England have criticized the litigation of two cases which in their opinion were frivolous, and would not have been brought to court but for the existence of legal aid. See Note, News of Legal Aid in England, 1 L. Soc'y Gazette 38 (1967).

[42] Blumberg, Covert Contingencies in the Right to the Assistance of Counsel, 20 Vand. L. Rev. 581 (1967).

[43] Mewett, Legal Aid, 9 Crim. L.Q. 119 (1966).

the present preoccupation with "due process of law" sometimes leads only to notional increases in protection, and the effects are formalistic rather than substantive.[44] Professor Blumberg suggests that the wider use of legal counsel makes the adversary process more pervasive but that the adversary system itself is not conducive to greater protection as it simply perpetuates a system "compromised and modified [is] inappropriate in terms of the values of maximum production and efficiency that are being sought."[44] He believes that the

more libertarian rules will tend to produce the rather ironic end result of augmenting the existing *organizational arrangements, enriching court organizations with more personnel and elaborate structure, which in turn will serve to maximize organizational goals of "efficiency" and "production." Thus, many defendants will find that courts will possess an even more sophisticated apparatus for processing them toward a guilty plea!*[46]

Professor Blumberg believes that the eliciting of confessions, in the form of guilty pleas, has simply moved into the court arena because defence lawyers are only playing out the charade which is the criminal process. He describes this state of affairs in these terms:

The defense attorneys, therefore, whether of the legal-aid, public-defender variety, or privately retained, although operating in terms of pressures specific to their respective role and organizational obligations, ultimately are concerned with strategies which tend to lead to a guilty plea. It is the rational, impersonal elements involving economies of time, labor, expense, and a superior commitment of defense counsel to these rationalistic values of maximum production of court organization that prevail, rather than any particularistic, affective ties an accused may have reasonably expected to be the character of his relationship with his lawyer. The lawyer "regulars" are frequently former staff members of the prosecutor's office and utilize the charisma, "know-how," and contacts of their former affiliation as part of their stock in trade. But an accused and his kin, as with others outside the court community, are unable to apprehend the nature and dimensions of the close and continuing relations between the lawyer "regular" and his former colleagues in the prosecutor's office. Their continuing colleagueship is based on real professional and organizational needs of a quid pro quo, *which go beyond the limits of an accommodation or* modus vivendi *one might ordinarily expect under the circumstances of a seemingly adversary relationship. Indeed, the adversary features are for the most part muted, and exist even in their attenuated form largely for external consumption. The principals, lawyer and assistant district attorney, rely upon one another's cooperation for their continued professional existence, and so the bargaining between them usually tends to be "reasonable" rather than fierce.*[47]

We have insufficient evidence to know whether this is a fair assessment of any criminal court or of the Ontario scene in particular. Furthermore, we do not know whether there will be a significant change in the type of lawyer appearing in the Ontario criminal courts due to the operation of the Legal Aid Act – whether the young inexperienced lawyer is more or less susceptible to the pressures of Blumberg's supposed system. The Ontario lawyer would hope that there is less plea bargaining in his province than is found in the United States and therefore the Canadian system is "purer." One presumes that Blumberg includes the pre-court bargaining of pleas in his analysis; perhaps he underestimates the realism of the lawyer who is trying to get the best "deal" for his client while it appears to an observer of the process that he is selling out his client to the system. At the same time Blumberg have have highly romanticized ideas about the meaning of "due process" which could never operate in practice.

If the less experienced lawyers are taking legal aid cases, it may mean that the accused is not reaping the benefit of highly-developed bargaining skills, but this surely is fallacious because in the past the

[44] For some support for (and some disagreement with) this argument, see Parker, The United States Supreme Court and the Police, 9 Crim. L.Q. 54, 72 (1966). See also Interrogations in New Haven: The Impact of Miranda, 76 Yale L.J. 1519 (1967).

[45] Blumberg, supra note 42, at 605.

[46] Id. (emphasis in original).

[47] Id. at 589-90. Blumberg also states:

The virtually hostile attitude toward "outsiders" is in large measure engendered by a defensiveness produced by the inherent deficiencies of assembly-line justice so characteristic of our major criminal courts. Intolerably large caseloads of defendants, which must be disposed of in an organizational context of limited resources and personnel, potentially subject the participants in the court community to harsh scrutiny from appellate courts, and other public and private sources of condemnation. As a consequence, an almost irreconcilable conflict is posed in terms of intense pressures to process large numbers of cases on the one hand, and the stringent ideological and legal requirements of "due process of law" on the other. A rather tenuous resolution of the dilemma has emerged in the shape of a large variety of bureaucratically ordained and controlled short cuts, deviations, and outright rule violations on the part of court occupational incumbents, from judges to stenographers, in order to meet production norms. Fearfully anticipating criticism on ethical as well as legal grounds, all the significant participants in the court's social structure are bound into an organized system of complicity. This consists of a work arrangement in which the patterned, covert, informal breaches, and the evasion of "due process" are institutionalized, but are, nevertheless, denied to exist.

Id. at 588.

A wide variety of coercive devices are employed against an accused-client, couched in a depersonalized, instrumental, bureaucratic version of due process of law, and which are in reality a perfunctory obeisance to the ideology of due process. These include some very explicit pressures which are exerted in some measure by all court personnel, including judges, to plead guilty and avoid trial.

Id. at 589.

great majority of the accused persons who could not afford counsel were getting no help at all. In the past, eighty per cent of defendants were pleading guilty and a large proportion of them were unrepresented. If legal aid achieves nothing else, it at least means that the unrepresented accused is now advised by an attorney who may be able to bargain for a guilty plea to a lesser offence.

Professor Mewett, on the other hand, observes that our criminal law and procedure with protective and exclusionary rules of evidence, systems of defences and statutory checks and balances have been "geared to the concept of the criminal as the lone individual, not very intelligent, a member of a sub-group, pitted against the forces of the State."[48] He adds:

If we ever have a system whereby literally everyone is legally aided and properly defended, would not this change our attitude to the defenceless man on trial? There is no longer a "criminal class," if, indeed, there ever has been. Is it, indeed, possible that we shall have to take a long, close look at the whole adversary system and its applicability to criminal cases? I would be the last person to deny that if ever an innocent man is convicted justice has not been done to everyone. If, however, society ever reaches the point when too many persons are found not guilty in spite of their having committed a criminal act, justice is not being done to society. If mistakes are made in our present system, they are invariably (or as close to invariably as is significant) in favour of the accused, and, so long as this protects the accused without harming society, this is proper and desirable.[49]

I find these fears fanciful, and yet in many ways they have the same flavour as those of Blumberg. Mewett is suggesting that the system is just as unreal as that propounded by Blumberg but with the opposite results. The irony occurs in the fact that both commentators are pessimistic, the Canadian because civil liberties may run wild and the American because the protections of "due process" will have no more meaning than before. Both these views are too extreme. The result must be somewhere in between. Legal aid will do much good and very little harm. There will be no mass exodus from the prisons. The judiciary, at least in Canada, will not suddenly become addicted to acquittals. Of course Blumberg's complaint still remains; the system is far from perfect. If criminal justice is to improve, it will be achieved by the fresh approaches of young lawyers dedicated to worthwhile legal work who are only in criminal law because a legal aid system exists.

[48] Mewett, supra note 43, at 121.
[49] Id.

7. *Some Lessons of the U. S. War on Poverty*[*]

In his State of the Union Message for 1964, the President of the United States declared "all-out war – unconditional war" on poverty in America. The aim of this war was not to alleviate poverty but to eliminate it. Following this Message and the *Economic Report of the President,* the Administration sent a special message to Congress requesting passage of what became the Economic Opportunity Act of 1964.

This new effort was begun against the background of the system of social security which had grown up since the 1930's. The basis of this system is the Social Security Act of 1935, which provided a program of contributory old-age and disability pensions, along with state-administered programs of aid to families with dependent children. These were enlarged and extended in 1964 and 1965 with the addition of a "medicare" program for people over 65 years of age and further extensions of dependents' and survivors' benefits. In addition, there exists a complicated array of federal, state and local welfare assistance programs, food supplement programs, school lunch programs, etc., which vary widely in impact from state to state.

Supplementing the social security structure, the Economic Opportunity Act of 1964 established an Office of Economic Opportunity within the Office of the President, bearing responsibility for the operation of a number of programs. Initially these programs were:

1) a Job Corps for young men and women aged 16 to 21, providing education, work experience, and vocational training;

2) a program for Volunteers in Service to America (VISTA) to serve in a variety of federal, state and community anti-poverty programs;

3) a Community Action Program designed to provide services (legal assistance, health services, etc.), to co-ordinate all programs established at the community level and mainly by the community, and to encourage institutional development and change within communities; and

4) special programs for migrant workers.

* Reproduced with the permission of the Queen's Printer for Canada from the Economic Council of Canada *Fifth Annual Review,* (Ottawa: Queen's Printer, 1968), pp. 124-128 and 130-140.

In addition, the Office of Economic Opportunity (OEO) was to distribute funds to existing departments and agencies to operate other programs authorized by the Act. These included work training programs operated by the Labor Department, work study programs and adult education programs administered by the Department of Health, Education and Welfare; special rural anti-poverty programs operated by the Department of Agriculture; small business loans through the Small Business Administration; and community work and training projects for welfare recipients operated by the Department of Health, Education and Welfare.

The primary emphasis in all of these programs has been on self-help, self-development, and maximum participation and involvement of the poor themselves. This emphasis has been most marked in the youth programs with an educational purpose, and in the various Community Action Programs.

The programs of the war on poverty fall into four major categories: (1) manpower development, training and mobility programs; (2) individual improvement and/or educational programs; (3) community action and community change programs; and (4) income maintenance programs.

The main manpower programs under the Economic Opportunity Act are the Job Corps, the Neighborhood Youth Corps, the work experience program, and the new JOBS program. The Job Corps is a high-cost program, requiring about $7,500 per trainee-year. In terms of cost-benefit analysis, however, the Job Corps appears to be successful even if educational benefits alone are taken into account, and there are non-educational benefits as well. The Neighborhood Youth Corps, which does not provide for residential training centres, is a less costly program and apparently somewhat less successful. The work experience program is financed through the Department of Health, Education and Welfare and administered by the state welfare agencies. Its object is to provide maintenance grants, adult basic education, vocational instruction and other forms of training to adults with dependent children who are either actual or potential welfare recipients. The program appears to have been relatively unsuccessful, mainly because of low rates of course completions and job placements. The new JOBS program will provide federally subsidized job training programs to be administered by private businesses.

The chief educational programs are Head Start, for pre-school children; and Upward Bound, a pre-college program for secondary school students. There are also a number of additional programs administered under the Elementary and Secondary Education and Higher Education Acts of 1965 by the Department of Health, Education and Welfare. The Upward Bound program provides a full-time summer program together with other programs during the school year to high school students with college potential but who would otherwise not likely reach university. Tutoring, summer educational courses, and medical and dental care are supplemented by weekly stipends during the summer phase of the program.

The Community Action Programs have been evaluated as successful in the delivery of services, relatively unsuccessful in the co-ordination of programs, and fairly successful – though assessment is difficult – in bringing about institutional development and change. Direct services, such as the Legal Aid Services Program, have been highly successful in defending the poor before the courts, bringing suits on behalf of poor clients, and providing educational programs to acquaint the poor with their rights.

As co-ordinating bodies, the community action agencies which have been set up under the auspices of the Community Action Program have been relatively unsuccessful, partially because of the intensely complicated array of federal, state, and local programs which already exist. As instruments of institutional development, however, the community action agencies appear to be more successful in bringing together the people of poor communities to plan and implement measures at the community level. These centres are also experiencing considerable success in influencing the institutional environment – social welfare agencies, courts, police – in poor communities.

What are some of the lessons to be learned by Canada from recent U.S. experience in warring on poverty? Care must obviously be exercised in transferring these lessons, inasmuch as the U.S. poverty problem has certain characteristics not found to anything like the same extent in Canada – e.g., that part of the problem represented by large non-white populations living in urban ghettos. But the following principles, gleaned from the work of a number of American experts, would seem to have relevance for Canada:

1) High aggregate demand and strong labour markets are a highly necessary condition for achieving substantial reductions in poverty.

2) A full-scale war on poverty should embrace all of the four basic categories of anti-poverty programs mentioned earlier: manpower programs, individual improvement programs, community betterment programs, and income maintenance programs. Experience has shown that these categories are interrelated and mutually supporting.

3) The exercise of drawing statistical poverty lines, while bound to be somewhat arbitrary, is necessary for good social planning, because without it there is great danger that policy will take the easy way out and beam much of its program emphasis towards the moderately well-off.

4) Another danger is the political popularity of "trickle-down" approaches to poverty. Analysis has shown that spending money (e.g., on some kinds of economic development) in the general vicinity of poverty groups by no means guarantees that a substantial proportion of the benefits will in fact flow to the poor.

5) Individual anti-poverty programs should start with realistic expectations and the best possible built-in evaluation mechanisms, including notably mechanisms for data collection. Programs should normally

be held unchanged long enough for effective evaluation to take place, but beyond this there should be a frank willingness to experiment.

6) So-called "family structure effects" are an important consideration. The likelihood of success in programs for teen-agers is increased by success in programs for adults. For example, if one of the parents, previously unemployed, can be placed in employment, this will improve the prospect of lifting the children permanently out of poverty.

7) Education has certain limitations and difficulties as a specific anti-poverty weapon. The initial gains achieved in some educational programs for young children such as Head Start have shown a tendency to fade out later. High investment appears to be needed to overcome basic educational deficiencies. At the same time, educational programs have yielded valuable side-effects, such things as bringing children into contact with organized medical care for the first time in their lives. It has been observed that the over-all payoff from educational programs is increased if parents can be actively involved.

8) Substantial benefits have been noted from programs to improve family planning, the nutrition of expectant mothers, and the nutrition of infants up to three years of age.

9) There must be adequate recognition of the social adaptation involved in the absorption of the so-called "hard-core" poor into employment. Without such adaptation, there tends to be a high rate of drop-out from even good jobs. More needs to be known about the characteristics of the "hard-core" poor, and more done to elicit the co-operation of business in absorbing these people into productive employment. Partly, what is often involved is a process of job creation: not outright "make-work" schemes, but examination of growing labour requirements to see if these can be subdivided in ways that permit the absorption of trainees from among the "hard-core" poor.

* * *

CONCLUSIONS AND RECOMMENDATIONS

A more concerted and purposeful attack on poverty in Canada now is urgently required. Such an attack would not only benefit those low-income families whose needs now are inadequately met, but would also bring substantial benefits to all Canadians. The challenge, in the short run, is to alleviate the conditions which today thrust many Canadian families and individuals into involuntary poverty and hold them there. In the long run, the challenge is to prevent the development of those conditions. The aim must be to identify those measures that will meet this challenge effectively and economically, but also compassionately, taking care to preserve the human dignity and freedoms which our society cherishes.

The attack we envisage should be well prepared and conceived on a comprehensive scale. It should be presented to the public with a strong sense of commitment, but also realistically. False hopes of easy, short-run triumphs should be avoided, as should that brand of sentimentality which is satisfied to make gestures in the general direction of the poor, without enquiring closely into what such gestures actually accomplish. Compassion there must certainly be, but also a very hard-headed and up-to-date preoccupation with the measurement and evaluation of results. Far from being inconsistent, the two are indispensable elements of a sense of commitment that means to get somewhere.

There now are some important gaps in the information and analysis required to conduct a truly comprehensive attack on poverty in Canada. Filling some of these gaps will call for extensive research work by experts drawn from all the social sciences, and to some from the natural sciences as well. There are, however, many highly useful actions which need not wait upon time-consuming programs of data collection and research. An attack on poverty can be built up in stages, starting with the attainment of some obvious, short-run objectives, then gradually expanding to a broader advance as the more significant gaps in available knowledge and understanding are filled.

In both the short-run and the longer-run stages, the following general principles should play an important role:

1) The maintenance of high employment and strong and stable economic growth is crucial. No policies are more effective in helping to move families and individuals out of poverty than the combination of demand and supply policies required to sustain new job creation and the increasingly efficient use of manpower, capital and other productive resources. Without success on this front, other anti-poverty policies are unlikely to be of much avail.

2) No effort should be spared to generate a widespread sense of public commitment to and involvement in the elimination of poverty. This is especially necessary in Canada where responsibility for social policy is divided among three levels of government and a multitude of private agencies. A large proportion of the actual day-to-day work of fighting poverty has to be done at the local level, where policies conceived further up the line can often come to grief against various sorts of institutional barriers. A clear definition of goals and a strong sense of commitment and involvement are necessary to break down such barriers and engender the requisite spirit of intelligent co-operation between governments, private agencies, and the general public. It is of course particularly necessary to involve the poor themselves in the development of programs designed to help them. Their comments, when analyzed, may provide the most rapid available indications of gaps and weaknesses; yet this direct source of information has often been neglected in the past. Experience in the Gaspé and Lower St. Lawrence Region should be closely studied for indications of how techniques of "action research" and "social animation" can be used to foster a community-wide sense of involvement.

3) Apart from general employment and growth policies, anti-poverty policies should have a strong orientation towards people. This

may seem obvious, but a study done for the Economic Council on policies for rural adjustment has effectively shown how an excessive orientation towards physical resources rather than people can lead policy astray and cause it to be less helpful than it might otherwise have been in curing social distress.[1] Certainly, well-conceived anti-poverty policies will have many elements in common with policies to foster regional and area development and to accelerate national economic growth. In areas such as the Gaspé and Lower St. Lawrence Region, anti-poverty and regional development policies may to a considerable extent coincide. In other areas, however, where poverty occurs more in the form of pockets, anti-poverty policies should have a more distinct character of their own. The "trickle-down" effects of national and regional growth and development policies do not constitute an adequate solution to the problem of poverty.

4) Anti-poverty policies should also be strongly oriented towards poor people. Again, this may seem obvious, but it is too much taken for granted that almost any welfare or social development policy tends to have such orientation. The extent to which it actually has, can only be determined by carefully identifying poverty groups and evaluating the impact of policy on them.

5) The achievement of a correct blend of income-maintenance policies and other anti-poverty policies that seek rather to improve people's capacity to participate more effectively in Canadian economic life is extremely important. Where it can be effective, the second class of policy is greatly to be preferred. But for many people such as the old and disabled it cannot be effective, and in many other cases may need to be supplemented by income maintenance, temporarily or intermittently.

6) In fighting poverty, great emphasis should be placed on economic use of available funds and skills, and on the maximum development and employment of modern techniques of policy evaluation. This is not hard-heartedness but compassionate realism. In a society in which there are large, growing and competing claims on scarce resources, the resources available to fight poverty will always be limited, so that it will always be highly important to see that the greatest possible lasting benefit is achieved for each dollar spent. Moreover, we would add that the greater the certainty with which beneficial results can be predicted to flow from a well-planned structure of anti-poverty programs, the stronger will be the claims on total resources which can be voiced on behalf of those programs.

The Spectrum of Existing Policies

A Canadian attack on poverty does not of course start from scratch. Canada already has in operation, or on the statute books scheduled for implementation within the relatively near future, an impressive inventory of social legislation. There are important Canadian policies in all four of the major categories of anti-poverty programs mentioned in our brief survey of the U.S. war on poverty; manpower programs, individual improvement programs, community betterment programs, and income maintenance programs. In some areas, particularly income maintenance, the coverage of Canadian programs is superior to that of their U.S. counterparts.

It should be noted also that the comprehensiveness of this inventory has been significantly improved in recent years. Under the Canada Assistance Plan, for example, provinces may at their option combine four previously separated federal-provincial assistance programs (for the aged, the blind, the disabled, and the unemployed) into a single program. Assistance is based on a more comprehensive and flexible assessment of recipients' budgetary needs, and federal cost-sharing is extended for the first time to aid to needy mothers and their dependent children. In general, the Plan sets out to close previous gaps in the social security system. Some of its features are rehabilitative and preventive in character, designed to help people by their own efforts to rise and remain above poverty.

A selection of other relatively recent additions to the stock of social legislation and social policies would include the monthly guaranteed income supplement to certain Old Age Security pensions, major developments in manpower policy by both federal and provincial governments, and new training and other manpower initiatives sponsored by municipal governments and voluntary agencies.

But while the inventory is impressive, the means immediately available for assessing its impact on Canadians are not. Apart from a few illustrious exceptions, remarkably little has been done by way of systematic evaluation of these policies in operation, either separately or in combination.

One of the great uncertainties is the extent to which the existing structure of policies in fact constitutes an attack on poverty – the extent, that is, to which its benefits flow to those most in need. This uncertainty comes very much to the fore when proposals are made for major new anti-poverty measures such as the negative income tax or other income guarantees.[2] We do not wish to pass judgment one way or another on

[1] See Helen Buckley and Eva Tihanyi, *Canadian Policies for Rural Adjustment,* Special Study No. 7.

[2] Various forms of guaranteed minimum income have been proposed by different writers. The simplest form would be a minimum income grant paid by the government to all, regardless of means; if it were subject to income tax, part of it would be recouped in this fashion. Other forms of guarantee have been proposed that would operate more directly through the existing tax system. Under one form of "negative income tax," an official minimum income level would be established; all family heads and nonfamily individuals would be required to complete income tax returns; and where actual income fell below the official minimum, a "negative tax payment" by the government would make up the difference. Under another form, the payment would consist of "unused" income tax exemptions by those with incomes too low to be subject to tax. Many negative income tax proposals incorporate graduated incentives for recipients to seek work. The Guaranteed Income Supplement now payable to certain old age security pensioners is a type of negative income tax.

such proposals at the present time; we confine ourselves to noting that their adoption has been advocated by a number of distinguished figures, and to recommending that the possibility of their usefulness for Canada be subjected to serious and thorough study. But such a study must embrace, among other things, an examination of the costs and anti-poverty effects of a considerable range of existing policies which income guarantees would to some extent replace and to some extent supplement. Only in this way will it be possible to form a proper judgment as to whether some type of broader income guarantee might usefully be added to the Canadian armoury of weapons against poverty.

It will be clear that we have not ourselves been able to conduct at this stage a thorough and searching examination of the existing structure of Canadian social polices. Some very limited and preliminary enquiry has suggested, however, that both the coverage and efficacy of many parts of the structure leave much to be desired. Objectives are not always clearly defined, or have not been redefined in the light of changing circumstances. It is difficult, for example, to discover an authoritative statement of the fundamental objectives of the Family Allowances program in the circumstances of 1968. This is not to say that Family Allowances and other long-established programs are not continuing to serve some highly useful purposes but these purposes should surely be re-examined in the light of many important economic and social changes that have occurred over the last generation.

In some areas of policy, there appears to be an undue bias towards the mere alleviation rather than the eradication and prevention of poverty. Lack of co-ordination, not only between but within levels of government, is often apparent. In some places there is overlapping; in others, gaps. Objectives of policies and success in achieving objectives are rarely subjected to regular review. Often the data that would be required to do this are lacking. There is fairly strong evidence in some areas of high administrative overheads and inefficiencies.

The above must of course be regarded as a very limited and tentative assessment. Its main significance is that it appears enough to indicate the desirability of a much more thoroughgoing appraisal.

Near-Term Measures

As a first step in developing a more effective attack on poverty, all levels of government should immediately review, clarify and update the objectives of their existing social policies. This in itself may be enough to uncover many significant duplications, gaps and conflicts of objectives. It should also give some preliminary indication of the extent to which policies are really beamed at people living in poverty.

Secondly, consideration should be given to setting up organizations for achieving better co-ordination of social policies within and between governments, and between governments and the many voluntary agencies active in the social welfare field. Even if all that is achieved at the outset is a more systematic exchange of information and increased discussion of basic issues, these in themselves will be valuable. Several instances have been reported to us of different departments of the same government active in the field of anti-poverty policies proceeding in substantial ignorance of each other's activities, with little exchange of current operating information, let alone research results. At the federal level, the Special Planning Secretariat of the Privy Council Office, during the period when it was heavily concerned with anti-poverty matters, gave promise of being a useful co-ordinating and information-providing device. It should be revived or replaced in a more durable and effective form, with a clear responsibility to co-ordinate research interdepartmentally and organize regular assessments of federal social policies. It should also continue the very real asssitance which the Secretariat was able to provide to voluntary social agencies seeking guidance through the maze of federal programs.

Greater efforts should at once be made to exploit the considerable anti-poverty potential of the Canada Assistance Plan. This applies particularly to the preventive and rehabilitative aspects of the Plan, and its capabilities to aid those whose low income is due, not to a virtual absence of earnings, but to an insufficiency of earnings. As we noted earlier, this group accounts for a large proportion of the poor – a proportion not in the past well served by a program structure heavily weighted by "categorical" types of income maintenance.

There are indications also that the efficacy of the Canada Assistance Plan is being impeded by insufficient feedbacks of information from the provinces – information vitally needed for the effective exploitation of the Plan's full potential. This should surely be remedied. It seems intolerable that an absence of information should come between the poor and their needs.

The federal government should at an early date take the initiative of encouraging the development of a small number of pilot projects of intensive research into urban poverty. Suitable areas for study should be marked out in major metropolitan centres and carefully examined by interdisciplinary teams of researchers. As recommended earlier, action research and social animation should be among the techniques employed. Two major objects of these pilot studies should be: first, to develop effective research techniques for more general use later; and, second, to obtain a first critical assessment of the effectiveness of the various social policies for which the federal government is at present wholly or partly responsible.

The Senate of Canada might consider the advisability of creating a committee to enquire into the problem of poverty in Canada. An earlier Senate enquiry into the problem of land use in Canada helped to bring about the Agricultural Rehabilitation and Development Act (ARDA) in 1961. The enquiry we propose would deal with all aspects of poverty, urban and rural. Many excellent witnesses, both Canadian and foreign, would be available to appear before the committee, whose work could also be aided by a small but competent research staff. The work of such a committee could do much to define and elucidate the problem of poverty in Canada, and to build public support for a more effective structure of remedial measures.

A Longer-Term Strategy

The longer-term measures which we propose consist essentially of building up with all reasonable speed the knowledge and understanding necessary for the elimination of poverty in Canada. These measures would amount to a comprehensive evaluation and reappraisal of the structure of all policies, both governmental and private, having a major bearing on the problem of poverty, including a careful evaluation of the advantages and disadvantages of new proposals such as the negative income tax and other forms of minimum income guarantee. The work would draw on the skills of specialists in different social and behavioural sciences. It would have to be well co-ordinated under the direction of persons experienced both in research and in the assessment of the practicability and administrative efficiency of existing and proposed programs.

There would have to be common criteria of program evaluation. To be consistent without proposed emphasis on helping those most in need, this would involve the establishment of acceptable minimum standards of living for families and individuals in Canada. In terms of income, such standards would likely differ appreciably between regions, between urban and rural areas, and even between cities, reflecting differences in costs and other circumstances affecting family budgets. The establishment of such standards would be a difficult and controversial enterprise, but, we believe, essential. If social policies are to be assessed from the standpoint of what they are doing for those living in poverty, this group of people must be more precisely identifiable.

Anti-poverty programs should, however, be assessed not only by their actual or potential success in lifting people above poverty lines, but also by the way in which they bring this about. To the greatest extent possible, they should do so by fostering opportunities for independence and full participation in the Canadian economy and Canadian society. The availability of such opportunities is particularly important for the Indian, Eskimo, and Metis peoples.

The vicissitudes of life being what they are, the need for direct income maintenance programs will never disappear completely. There will always be some families and individuals unable to participate fully and independently in economic life because of age, disability, ill health, or other reasons. In addition to ensuring adequate standards of living, social assistance to such people should be provided in a way that fosters their full participation in other aspects of our common life. Assistance should be extended to them as a right rather than a privilege, with no stigma attached.

Very close attention should be given to the hazards of different anti-poverty programs working at cross-purposes. Instances have frequently been reported where attempts by members of families to increase earnings have resulted in abrupt declines in or even the termination of income maintenance or other social assistance. (For example, a family may be forced to move immediately out of subsidized housing into other accommodation at a substantial increase in rent which may exceed the increase in earnings.) In many such cases, the increased earnings have in effect been "taxed" at very high marginal rates, sometimes amounting to 100 per cent or more. This type of occurrence defeats the purpose of anti-poverty policies designed to encourage the development of income earning potential. It is of course no easy matter to devise policy mixes that ensure adequate minimum income but also incorporate incentives to seek earnings, but this is all the more reason for devoting much thought and effort to good policy co-ordination.

A searching appraisal of the most effective means of eliminating poverty should, of course, be deeply concerned with the costs of existing and proposed programs. It should make the maximum feasible use of the most up-to-date analytical methods. Cost-benefit analysis can be employed in some areas. Certain problems will no doubt be encountered, such as limitations of data and lack of a sufficient run of experience to give any reliable reading on what some programs are accomplishing. But strong efforts should be made to overcome data problems, to encourage the use of at least the cost-benefit type of framework to evaluate programs, and to build into new programs data feedback systems which will facilitate full-scale evaluation in due course.

Use of experimental methods should not be neglected. One particularly interesting experiment is under way in the United States: various forms of negative income tax will actually be paid to approximately 1,000 low-income family heads in the State of New Jersey over a three-year period. Among other things, this experiment will permit observation of the effects of a negative income tax on the incentive to seek paid work. This has always been a major concern in connection with the negative income tax and other minimum income guarantees.

While the appraisal we envisage would be much concerned with welfare and related social policies, it should look also at other policies having an important impact on low-income families. These include regional and other economic development programs, and policies affecting rates of growth and levels of aggregate demand in the economy. Attention should also be given to the impact of price increases and price levels on the poor. Some evidence is emerging from the United States that the urban poor, in particular, may pay more for identical consumer goods than other people do.

It would be highly desirable to assemble more adequate and up-to-date information than now exists concerning standards of nutrition and health among poor people in Canada. Such information might indicate groups in the population who could benefit from food aid and other interim measures.

Finally, tax considerations should not be exempted from an appraisal of policies relating to poverty. Among other things, it will be important to take into account the impact on low-income groups of sales and real property taxes. Some of the studies done for the Carter Royal Commission on taxation will be relevant in this connection.

In thus describing the kind of longer-term appraisal which we feel is required at this stage in order to develop more effective anti-poverty policies in Canada, it is important to keep clearly in mind the Canadian constitution and the fact that social policy is a field of concurrent jurisdiction in which all three levels of government are active on a large scale. Nor have we referred to the important discussions and decisions regarding social policy which lie ahead of the federal and provincial governments between now and the expiration in 1970 of agreements under the Established Programmes (Interim Arrangements) Act.[3] Important changes in the relative roles of the different levels of government in the field of social policy appear to be in prospect.

These impending discussions and changes would seem to make a fundamental appraisal of social policy in Canada very timely. They would also strongly argue for the desirability of making the appraisal a joint project, conducted on behalf of all three levels of government, with a view to producing a legacy of information, analysis and evaluative techniques that will permit governments and private agencies, each in their own spheres of responsibility, to work more effectively towards the elimination of poverty. Various kinds of inter-governmental arrangement are conceivable. Whatever arrangement is adopted should be one involving and eliciting the support of all levels of government, whose co-operation will be absolutely essential in the supply of information and many other respects.

For our own part, we intend to pursue further research into the problem of poverty in Canada, and will be reporting on it in subsequent Annual Reviews. Every effort will be made to dovetail this work effectively with the increased research which we hope will be undertaken by others.

The task of eliminating poverty is both complex and of high national priority. We believe that this is an urgent matter that warrants early consideration at the highest level of intergovernmental consultation.

[3] The Established Programmes (Interim Arrangements) Act of 1965 enabled the provinces to "contract out" of certain shared-cost programs on an interim basis, pending the development of more permanent arrangements. Only one province, Quebec, chose this option.

EDITOR'S NOTE: A Senate Committee on Poverty under the chairmanship of Senator David Croll was formed on November 26, 1968.

8. *Selectivity or Universality? Income Support Alternatives for Families with Children*[*]

James Cutt

In August, 1969, President Nixon sent to Congress a package of welfare reform proposals, the core of which was a negative income tax (NIT) scheme to be called the Family Assistance System (FAS). FAS is designed to replace the existing general welfare system referred to as Aid to Families with Dependent Children (AFDC), and would provide a guaranteed minimum income to all families with at least one child. The scheme is *selective* in two senses: first, by definition, the scheme is categorical, being limited to families with at least one child; and, second, families receiving payments must meet an income level eligibility criterion. It is with the latter type of selectivity — that involving an income test — that this paper is primarily concerned, since an income test places FAS in sharp contrast to an alternative proposal, specifically, the introduction of a system of family or children's allowances (CA) which would be *universal* with children regardless of family income. A CA scheme is, of course, also by definition selective in the first or categorical sense.

The Canadian welfare system is currently subject to critical examination, and the object of this paper is to offer a brief comparative evaluation of two rather modest options — the use of a selective NIT approach along the lines of the FAS proposal, as against the extension of the existing, universal, system of family and youth allowances. The approach taken will be, first, to provide a brief description and analysis of the FAS proposal, second, to treat similarly the universal CA approach with particular reference to the present Canadian scheme, and, third, to compare in terms of a broad set of evaluation criteria, economic, social, physchological and political, the FAS and CA approaches as options for Canada. The aspiration of the note is to establish a general

*A paper prepared for presentation at the Harrison Liberal Conference, Harrison Hot Springs, B.C., November 21-23, 1969. Printed with permission of the author.

framework for the universalism selectivity debate. The case for one or the other has generally been made in partial terms, the selectivists emphasizing the economic efficiency aspects of the comparison, the universalists stressing the social and psychological aspects.

THE PROPOSED FAMILY ASSISTANCE SYSTEM (FAS)

FAS takes a NIT approach, and, accordingly, has three variables — the actual minimum guarantee in the event of zero income from other sources, the negative tax rate by which payments under the scheme are reduced in relation to other income, and the third variable, determined in every case by the other two, the break-even level of income from other sources at which payments under the scheme drop to zero. The minimum guarantee is specified under the scheme as follows: $500 for each of the first two family members, and $300 for each subsequent family member. The basic floor payment — minimum income, in effect — for a family of four with no other income would thus be $1,600. Reflecting the Department of Labour's concern over work incentives, assistance payments would remain constant for the first $720 of annual work income (in effect, a NIT rate of zero), and would be reduced by 50 cents for each dollar of work income beyond $720 (a NIT rate of 50%). A family of four would thus be eligible for assistance payments up to an annual income of $3,920. The table illustrates this situation.

Benefit Schedule for a Family of Four

EARNED INCOME ($)	ASSISTANCE PAYMENT ($)	TOTAL INCOME ($)
0	1,600	1,600
720	1,600	2,320
1,000	1,460	2,400
1,500	1,210	2,710
2,000	960	2,960
2,500	710	3,210
3,000	460	3,460
3,500	210	3,710
3,920	0	3,920

USE OF A FAMILY ASSISTANCE SYSTEM IN CANADA

There are four major advantages of FAS which make the proposal an interesting one for consideration in the Canadian context. First, for a large segment of the poor (those with children FAS establishes a national floor under the poverty program, and, further, by *not* providing for regional deflation of payments according to cost-of-living differentials, provides for inter-regional income redistribution in addition to vertical redistribution of income between income groups. Second, payments under FAS are naturally concentrated among that population where adults have the highest labour force participation rates, and thus the greatest opportunity to respond to the work incentive aspects of the program. In short, the scheme may be said to focus on the working poor. Third, payment to families with children directs limited budgetary resources to that population (children in poor families) where income increases will have the highest probability of reducing the tendency for poverty to be transmitted between generations. FAS may indeed be viewed as a more comprehensive variant of a system of income-tested children's allowances, whereby payments would be geared to the number of children and total family income. Finally, a scheme such as FAS, unlike existing AFDC and Canadian general assistance payments, provides no incentive for families to split up in order to receive benefits.

FAS does nothing for the elderly poor or the poor without children, and, further, payment levels suggested in the U.S. are far below official poverty lines and may therefore be viewed as inadequate. The scheme must, however, be viewed as a "thin-end-of-the-wedge" or "foot-in-the-door" policy, and must be compared with similar strategies – a comprehensive but less generous scheme for all the poor, a scheme which concentrates on the elderly, or a program of children's allowances. The most interesting comparison would seem to be with a children's allowance program.

THE FAMILY ASSISTANCE SYSTEM (FAS) AND CHILDREN'S ALLOWANCE (CA): RELEVANCE FOR CANADA

[We shall attempt here to give] a brief comparative evaluation of two alternatives for Canada – first, a scheme such as FAS which would offer a negative income tax oriented guaranteed annual income of the order specified in the U.S. proposal to families with children, the *gross* cost of the scheme being of the order of $1 billion, the net cost working out to roughly $400 million – assuming that the scheme would replace present family and youth allowances (costing $600 million in 1967-1968), and, second, an improved children's and youth allowances program with allowances taxable costing gross $1.25 billion, an increase of $650 million which would permit increases in rates to $12 per month for each child aged 0-10 years, $14 per month for each child aged 10-16 years, and $16 per month as the Youth Allowance rate. The net cost would be as in the FAS scheme $400 million, given present Children's Allowances and Youth Allowances costs of $600 million, and assuming an average income tax rate on allowances of 20% which would recoup $250 of the gross cost of $1.25 billion.[1] It should be emphasized that these cost figures are

[1] It is assumed that present Canadian tax exemptions for children are retained. The redistributive impact of a CA scheme could be significantly increased by abolishing exemptions and using the increased tax revenue to increase CA payments. However, for a fair comparison, it would be necessary to abolish exemptions under the FAS scheme also, directing the increased revenue into higher income guarantees.

extremely crude, and are intended only to offer a rough basis for the comparison of two program alternatives – one selective, the other universal, costing the same amount.

The option of an income-tested children's scheme is not explored for two reasons: first, an income-tested children's allowance scheme using the same budgetary allotment as the two options above would really amount to a variation on the theme of FAS, with the available resources allocated simply according to the number of children, ignoring the adult or adults in the family; and, two, the issue of greatest interest is the choice between universality (in the CA scheme) and selectivity (in FAS).

CRITERIA FOR EVALUATION

I. Economic Efficiency

This criterion combines the two criteria of adequacy and economy, . . . and may be referred to as the "cost-effectiveness" of the programs. The cost level has been specified at a net figure of $400 million, and the problem becomes one of defining an index of effectiveness. Herein lies a problem. The usual procedure here is to define as the index of effectiveness the extent to which a dollar of resources raised to finance the scheme goes to diminish statistically defined poverty. For instance, the Economic Council defined particular income levels as constituting minimum acceptable levels – these levels being $1,500 for single persons and $2,500, $3,000, $3,500 and $4,000 for families of two three, four and five, respectively. Having specified minimum subsistence income levels for various family sizes, below which families are defined as living in poverty, the "poverty gap" or income deficit in an aggregate sense is then the difference between the sum of the incomes of poor families if these families in fact received the minimum specified subsistence income levels and the sum of the actual incomes received by these families. In the simplest sense, economic efficiency or cost-effectiveness could then be defined as 100 per cent if each dollar raised to finance the program in question found its way directly to reducing the poverty gap by one dollar.

How then do the two schemes measure up under this definition? FAS, which provides guaranteed minima considerably below specified minimum subsistence levels, may be considered 100 per cent efficient or cost-effective.[2] Clearly, a universal children's allowance scheme compares poorly in this sense. Although low-income families, where, on average, the number of children is larger than in higher-income families, would tend to receive higher payments than higher-income families, the percentage of the total allotment in the program going to those defined as statistically poor would be well below 50 per cent.

As one extends payments under a NIT scheme up to the "near-poor" through more generous NIT schemes with higher break-even points, (making, for purposes of comparison, appropriate adjustments in

CA payments) the efficiency gap between the two schemes diminishes – but almost entirely because of the decline in efficiency of the NIT approach at higher break-even points; the slight increase in efficiency of a (taxable) CA scheme as payments increase and are taxed at higher rates is not of great significance. The conclusion remains that for any feasible program alternatives in the NIT or CA framework, the economic efficiency of the NIT alternative will be considerably higher in every case.

The question is whether the definition of economic efficiency is adequate. If one chooses to define the objective of children-oriented programs as improving the lot of children in all income groups (on the defensible principle that families in virtually all income groups, certainly up to the top 10% could use payments under a universal CA scheme to improve the welfare of their children) then the criterion of efficiency has to be defined quite differently, and the selective approach of FAS may be seen as less efficient than the universal approach of CA. Clearly we are approaching a fundamental distinction between the two schemes – a distinction which will emerge more clearly after the discussion of broader social and political factors – that a NIT type of scheme is more efficient in a specific, "war on poverty," vertically redistributive sense, whereas a CA approach is more efficient in a broader, horizontally redistributive sense, redistributing income essentially from the childless to those with children. The CA approach, it emerged however, can only be one part of a poverty program, since it barely scratches the surface of satistically defined poverty.

II. Other Economic Effects

a) Effect on work incentives: A NIT scheme of the modest scale suggested in FAS would seem unlikely to cause serious effects on work incentives. The provisional evidence from New Jersey[3] suggests no significant labour withdrawal as a consequence of the various models in the experiment. Nevertheless, a selective scheme does have – according to the static theory – a double disincentive effect on work, one through the very fact of payment in a zero work/zero income situation, the second through the effect of a high tax rate on first earnings. A universal scheme has only the first of these effects, and in this static sense the CA approach is superior to FAS. There is now some support for the view that welfare schemes of any nature other than the traditional means-tested hand-outs may in fact exercise a positive effect on work effort, and the whole issue of work incentives is now receiving less emphasis than in the initial discussions on welfare programs.

[2] Note that more comprehensive and generous NIT schemes are less than 100 per cent efficient, many as low as 40 per cent or 50 per cent, in fact, because of the nature of a NIT scheme which, in the attempt to preserve work incentives, provides payments up to break-even points well in excess of specified poverty levels.

[3] See H. Watts, "Graduated Work Incentives: An experiment in negative taxation," *American Economic Review,* May 1969, 463-472.

b) Effect on Expenditure Patterns: In this case there seems little to choose between the schemes. The first evidence on the effect of NIT payments on expenditure patterns in New Jersey suggests that the increase in income of the lower income groups as a consequence of the scheme is spent in much the same fashion as increases in income among other income groups. The available evidence on the expenditure of children's allowances in Canada[4] suggests a wholly respectable expenditure pattern, and both proposals would appear free from attack on the grounds that the payments would be idly dissipated.

III. Stigma Effects

How the Options are Perceived: The first evidence from the New Jersey experiment suggests no stigma effect in payments made automatically through the NIT structure. There is, of course, an eligibility criterion in the form of a simple statement of income and family composition, and some recent commentators[5] have contended that something as simple as the income test preserves the distinction between the poor and the non-poor, and will come to define a particular social class who are recipients under the scheme. U.S. commentators, in particular, emphasize that the definition of two groups in this fashion may result in a stigma being attached to payments under the scheme. The case then follows for a universal scheme which does not use any test or declaration of any kind as a criterion of eligibility. In this sense the CA approach may be held to be superior since there is no possibility of any stigma effects under a universal scheme — but two caveats are necessary: first, there is the provisional evidence from New Jersey, cited above, and, second, and more important, there is the point that a CA program has a much smaller effect on the poverty gap than an FAS approach and therefore will require the retention of other assistance programs. If these other programs are of the traditional means-tested assistance nature, the aggregate amount of testing under a scheme which contains a CA system may be actually larger than under a scheme which relies substantially on a NIT (income-tested) approach, and the stigma effects of the two total schemes may well emerge as worse under the scheme containing, paradoxically, the completely untested universal CA system.

IV. Administrative Complexity

There can be little doubt that a selective NIT scheme such as FAS would be administratively more complex and more expensive (take a greater share of available resources for administrative purposes) than a universal CA scheme. Both for administrator and recipient, a universal scheme is clearly simpler than a selective scheme. In 1967, the total cost of administering the present Canadian CA program came to well below one per cent of total benefits paid. It is, however, likely that administrative costs under FAS or a broadly based NIT scheme would be sharply reduced over time as the initial problems, such as integration with the positive income tax, were overcome, and, with computer assistance, it would seem inappropriate to overstress the administrative difficulties of a NIT approach.

V. Social and Political Effects

A scheme such as FAS is by definition aimed only at those defined as statistically poor, say, the lowest 1/5th of the population. Particularly in the U.S. at present, the principal and rising source of opposition to new programs which benefit solely and specifically the poor, comes not from high income groups but from the great range of families in perhaps the next 2/5ths in terms of income, who find themselves in a position of financial stringency despite full and probably rather uninteresting employment, who feel caught by a variety of forces over which they have no control, such as inflation and rising taxes, and have come to resent program proposals in which they are represented as donors and not as recipients. FAS is just such a scheme.

The opposition of this large group can scarcely be overlooked. There is clearly the question of basic political acceptability, but the more important question relates to the social implications of the scheme. In the U.S. a scheme such as FAS could be described as follows: one group will receive it, another group will pay for it, and such groups are more than likely to be defined rather sharply by race and region. Such a scheme may then be considered to exacerbate social tensions and to emphasize division rather than the unities of the problem. As Scott Briar recently observed, "A broad program (such as CA, and as distinct from FAS) might help to create the conditions for greater harmony between the poor and the non-poor by blurring the arbitrarily and therefore erroneously sharp line dividing them and by focussing attention on the needs and discontents they hold in common."[6]

It is an interesting thought that most European welfare programs are viewed as a comprehensive package aimed at redistribution toward a socially tolerable and acceptable degree of inequality, and are not, and have never been, specifically directed to a particular income stratum defined arbitrarily as the statistically poor. As a consequence these European schemes have generally been multi-faceted, containing aspects which dealt with particular and specific privation, but in general emphasizing a broadly based approach to income redistribution rather than to poverty, however defined.

The racial issue is clearly not of as great consequence for Canada as for the U.S., but the broad argument holds. The unease which the

[4] See J. Vadakin, *Children, Poverty and Family Allowances* (New York: Basic books, Inc. 1968), Chapter 4.

[5] See, particularly, Scott Briar, "Why Children's Allowances," *Social Work*, January 1969, pp. 5-12.

[6] Briar, *op. cit.*, p. 9.

middle 2/5ths of the population will feel toward a program for which they are paying but which does not provide them with any benefits cannot and should not be neglected and it should be recorded that in terms of social consequences, and political acceptability, the universal approach of a CA scheme has much to commend it, certainly *as one part* of a comprehensive welfare program.

CONCLUSION

The separate components of the set of criteria which have been used to evaluate the FAS and CA alternatives clearly cannot be boiled down nearly into one simple decision criterion and the choice of an alternative depends on the weighting assigned each component part.

Defining economic efficiency in a strict but limited sense, it emerged that FAS was clearly superior to CA; defining economic efficiency in the broader sense of universal children's welfare, however, the CA approach was the better. The universal CA approach was seen as superior in terms of the effect on work incentives, but this whole issue was held to have been overstressed in any event. Neither approach seemed likely to have an undesirable effect on expenditure patterns. On the sensitive issue of stigma, the issue emerged as somewhat clouded; in terms of straight bald comparison, a universal CA scheme clearly carries no stigma whereas an income-tested FAS might be held at least to stigmatize in the indirect sense that it draws an arbitrary line between poor (recipients) and non-poor (donors); viewing the two alternatives in real, feasible policy terms, however, it was argued that the wider range of means- or needs-tested supplementary programs which would continue to be required with a CA scheme might make a program which included a CA scheme more tested, and therefore more stigmatized than a program such as FAS. The universal approach was held to be superior on grounds of administrative complexity, and in terms of political acceptability and social effects.

What has really emerged from the comparison is the rather interesting fact that FAS and CA are really different animals altogether, and may most effectively be seen as complements rather than as substitutes. While in this writer's view the long run orientation of a welfare program must be as part of an overall policy of redistribution to which many government programs contribute, there can clearly be no countenancing of absolute privation even in the short run. There is need therefore on economic, political and social grounds for a package or mix of programs which, on the one hand mitigate insofar as is possible absolute privation or poverty — this might be along the lines of a broadly based NIT scheme, or in the short run a categorical NIT scheme such as FAS — and, on the other hand, would offer the broadly based participatory sort of scheme of which a CA program is an excellent example. For a specified budgetary constraint, such a bi-faceted approach obviously involves diluting both programs to make possible the existence of the broader approach, but it is submitted here that such an explicit trade-off may be necessary on grounds of the set of comparative criteria set out above.

In any event, what is vital is that program alternatives of the sort examined above be subject to appraisal in terms of a broad set of evaluation criteria – in short, be subject to a general as distinct from partial analysis. The choice of a particular program depends on the weighting assigned each constituent evaluation criterion, and the least that can be expected from a general analysis is that the weighting assigned each criterion emerge explicitly in the ultimate choice of program design.

Bibliography

I. INTRODUCTORY ARTICLES

AGRICULTURAL ECONOMIC RESEARCH COUNCIL OF CANADA. *Rural Canada in Transition.* Marc-Adélard Tremblay and Walton J. Anderson (eds.). Ottawa: June 1966, 415 pp.

ANNUAL REVIEWS OF THE ECONOMIC COUNCIL OF CANADA. Selections from the Fifth (Ch. 6) and Sixth (pp. 107-114).

BAGDIKIAN, B. H., *In the Midst of Plenty.* Toronto: The New American Library of Canada, Ltd., 1964.

BARR, SHERMAN. "Budgeting and the Poor: A View from the Bottom," in *Public Welfare,* XXIII: 4 (October 1965), pp. 246-50, and pp. 293-94.

BERNSTEIN, SAUL. *Youth on the Streets.* Toronto: G. R. Welsh Co., Ltd., 1964.

BLISHEN, B. R. ET AL. (EDS.). *Canadian Society: Sociological perspectives.* Toronto: Macmillan of Canada, 1968.

CANADIAN ASSOCIATION FOR ADULT EDUCATION *What is Poverty and Who are the Poor?* Toronto: 1965.

CANADIAN CONFERENCE ON CHILDREN, 1965. *Background Papers:* Available from 52 St. Clair Avenue E., Toronto, Ontario. (1) Child Welfare Services (2) Social Bases of Education (3) Social Behaviour Surrounding Children's Health Problems (4) Social Bases of Maturity in Childhood.

CANADA, DEPT. OF FORESTRY. *Economic and Social Disadvantage in Canada.* ARDA. Ottawa: October 1964, 9 maps.

CANADA, DEPT. OF FORESTRY. *National Rural Manpower.* Ottawa: 1966, 11 pp. See under Bijer, G., National rural manpower.

CANADA, UNEMPLOYMENT INSURANCE COMMISSION. *The Amount and Nature of Unemployment in Canada.* Ottawa: 1965.

CAPLOVITZ, DAVID. *The Poor Pay More.* New York: The Free Press of Glencoe, 1963.

CMHC. *Urban Renewal.* Ottawa: 1965. See under Urban Renewal.

CANADIAN WELFARE COUNCIL. *Rural Need in Canada: The Background of Rural Poverty in Four Selected Areas.* Ottawa: 1965.

CANADIAN WELFARE COUNCIL. *Urban Need in Canada: A Case Report on the Problems of Families in Four Canadian Cities.* Ottawa: 1965, 443 pp.

CHARLES, K. J. "Automation: Problem and Opportunity," in *The Social Worker,* 33:2 (April 1965), pp. 95-102.

CRUTCHLEY, DAVID. "No Place for Youth," in *Canadian Welfare,* 42:1 (January/February 1966), pp. 15-18.

ECONOMIC COUNCIL OF CANADA. *Third Annual Review;* "Prices, Product, Employment." Ottawa: Queen's Printer, November 1966, 276 pp.

FRASER, SYMINGTON. *The Sixties: Rural Poverty – What Can ARDA do?* Canadian Association for Adult Education. Toronto: November 1964.

GODFREY, PATRICIA. *The Sixties: Poverty in Our Society*. Canadian Association for Adult Education. Toronto: 1965, 19 pp.

GOFFMAN, I. J. *Some Fiscal Aspects of Public Welfare in Canada*. Canadian Tax Foundation. Toronto: 1965.

GUILLEMETTE, ANDRE M. "Welfare in French Canada," in *Canadian Welfare,* 42:1 (January/February 1966), pp. 8-13. (Historical.)

HEATLEY, R. B. AND GIL SCHONNING. Dept. of Labour. "Impact of Winter on the Canadian Worker," summarized in *Labour Gazette* (November 1965), pp. 1040-43.

INDIAN AFFAIRS AND NORTHERN DEVELOPMENT. *Northwest Territories Today*. Ottawa: Queen's Printer, 1965. See under *Canada, Northern Affairs and National Resources, Northwest Territories Today.*

KUMOVE, LEON. "Nobody Starves," in *Canadian Welfare,* 42:5 (September/October 1966), pp. 198-206.

Labour Gazette. "A Profile of Poverty in Canada" (May 1966), pp. 220-21. (Summary of papers presented at the Federal-Provincial Conference on Poverty and Employment.)

Labour Gazette. "Canada's First National Conference on the Problems of Aging" (April 1966), pp. 166-68.

Labour Gazette. "The Aging Worker in the Canadian Economy" (November 31, 1965), 242 pp.

LYONS, WALTER. "Services to the Aged Beyond the Institutional Setting – What is our Responsibility?" *Canadian Welfare,* 42:1 (January/February), pp. 2-7.

MADDEN, JOHN J. "Some Aspects of Poverty." Paper presented at the Canadian Conference on Social Welfare, Hamilton, Ontario (June 2-5, 1964).

MALTHUS, T. R. *First Essay on Population*. London: Macmillan & Co., 1926.

MENZIES, M. W. *The Report of the Economic Canada Farm Survey*. Department of Forestry, ARDA. Ottawa: 1965.

MILLER, HERMAN P. *Rich Man, Poor Man*. New York: Thomas Y. Crowell, 1964.

MOORE, J. O. "People – Liability or Resource?" in *Canadian Welfare,* 42:3 & 4 (July/August 1966), pp. 112-21.

NOVA SCOTIA DEPARTMENT OF PUBLIC WELFARE. Papers prepared for Conference on Poverty. Halifax: December, 1965.

ONTARIO DEPARTMENT OF LABOUR. *Poverty in Ontario, 1964*. Toronto: 1964.

OSTRY, SYLVIA AND JENNY PODOLUK. *The Economic Status of Aging*. Ottawa: Queen's Printer, 1966.

PEGREY, CHARLES. "Destitution and Poverty," in *Alienation: The Cultural Climate of Our Times*. G. Sykes (ed.). New York: G. Braziller, 1964.

PODOLUK, J. R. *Earnings and Education*. DBS. Ottawa: 1965.

——— *Identification of Low Income Families*. DBS. Ottawa: November 1965.

SCHLESINGER, B. *Poverty in Canada and the U.S.; Overview and Annotated Bibliography*. Toronto: University of Toronto Press, 1966, 211 pp.

SCHORR, ALVIN L. "The Family Cycle and Income Development," in *Social Security Bulletin,* 29:2 (February 1966), pp. 14-25, and p. 47.

SIMMEL, GEORG. "The Poor," in *Social Problems,* 2 (Fall, 1965), pp. 118-40.

SPINLEY, B. M. *The Deprived and the Privileged*. London: Routledge and Kegan Paul, 1953.

WHYTE, D. R. "Sociological Aspects of Poverty: A Conceptual Analysis," in *Canadian Review of Sociology and Anthropology,* 4 (November 1965), pp. 175-89.

——— "Social Determinants of the Inter-Community Mobility: An Inventory of Findings," in *Canadian Review of Sociology and Anthropology,* 4 (1) (February, 1967), pp. 1-23.

WOODSWORTH, D. E. "An Approach to the Understanding of Poverty," in *The Social Worker,* XXXIII (July 1965), pp. 152-57.

II. SOCIOLOGICAL PERSPECTIVES ON POVERTY

BAETZ, REUBEN C. "Economic Boom or Social Bust?" in *Canadian Welfare* (September/October 1965), pp. 236-42.

BESNER, A. "Economic Deprivation and Family Patterns," in *Welfare in Review*, III:9 (September 1965).

BLODIN, MICHEL. "L'animation sociale en milieu urbain: une solution," in *Recherches Sociographiques*, VI (Septembre/décembre 1965), pp. 283-304.

CHANCE, N. A. *Poverty and Social Disorganization: A Survey of the Literature*. Manuscript Report 219, Sterling County Study, Ithaca, New York.

CONNOR, DESMOND. "Understanding Your Community." Antigonish, Nova Scotia: St. Francis Xavier University, 1964, 35 pp.

COOLEY, C. H. "Poverty," in *Social Organization*. New York: Schocken Books, 1962, pp. 292-300.

HEFFERMAN, JOSEPH. "Social Animation and the Poverty Problem," in *The Social Worker*, XXXIII (July 1965), pp. 169-75.

HONIGMANN, JOHN J. "Social Disintegration in five North Canadian Communities," in *Canadian Review of Sociology and Anthropology*, 2:4 (November 1965), pp. 199-214.

Labour Gazette. "Change Skill and Technological Change" (September 1966).

LINDECKER, FRED W. "Poverty's Second Generation," in *The Nation* (September 1964), pp. 163-65.

MCDONALD, J. C. *Impact and Implications of Office Automation*. Ottawa: Queen's Printer, 1964.

MELTZ, NOAH H. *Changes in the Occupational Composition of the Canadian Labour Force, 1931-61*. Ottawa: Queen's Printer, 1965.

METZGER, P. L. AND T. V. PHILBROOK. "Sociological Factors Influencing Labour Mobility: A Pilot Study of Two Sub-Regions of New Brunswick." Fredericton: Dept. of Labour, 1964, 70 pp.

MILLER, S. M. "Poverty," in *Transactions of the 6th World Congress of Sociology*. Geneva: International Sociological Association, 1965, pp. 173-185.

ORNATI, OSCAR. "Affluence and the Risk of Poverty," in *Social Research*, 31:3 (Autumn 1964), pp. 333-46.

SCHLESINGER, B. "Le service social, les services sociaux et les pauvres," in *Service Social*, XIV (January/June 1965), pp. 66-79.

RIENDEAU, ROBERT. "Poverty in Canada in 1964." Paper presented at the Canadian Conference on Social Welfare, Hamilton, Ontario (June 2-5, 1964).

ROSE, A. *Regent Park: A Study in Slum Clearance*. Toronto: University of Toronto Press, 1958.

ROWNTREE, B. S. *Poverty and the Welfare State*. London: Longmans, Green, 1951.

SAUNDERS, GEORGE. Department of Labour. "Wage Determination in Canada," in *Occasional Paper #3*. Ottawa: Queen's Printer (April 1965), 44 pp .

SHENE, DORA L. *The 'Culturally Deprived' in School and Society: Selected Approaches*. Board of Education, City of Toronto, 1966.

SHOSTAK, A. B. AND W. GOMBERG (EDS.). *New Perspectives on Poverty*. Englewood Cliffs, New Jersey: Prentice-Hall, Inc., 1965.

TITMUSS, R. M. *Income Distribution and Social Change*. London: George Allen & Urwin, Ltd., 1962.

WEISS, D. "Who is the Enemy in the War against Poverty?" in *The Social Worker*, XXXIV (February 1966), pp. 52-53.

WILL, R. E. AND H. G. VATTER (EDS.). *Poverty in Affluence*. New York: Harcourt, Brace and World, 1965.

WOOD, W. D. AND R. S. THOMAS (EDS.). *Conference on Areas of Economic Stress in Canada*. Kingston: Queen's University, International Relations Centre, 1965.

III. OPPORTUNITY STRUCTURES AND THE CULTURE OF POVERTY
A. SOURCES OF VARIATION

(i) Regional

ATLANTIC DEVELOPMENT BOARD. *Regional Economic Planning*. Ottawa: 6 pp.

ATLANTIC PROVINCES ECONOMIC COUNCIL. *Productivity, The Use of Human Resources, and the Income Gap*. Halifax, Nova Scotia: July 1967, 33 pp.

BREWIS, T. N. *Regional Economic Policies in Canada*. Toronto: Macmillan of Canada, 1969.

BREWIS, T. N. "Regional Development, The Need for a Federal Policy," in *Business Quarterly*, 27 (Fall 1962), pp. 41-45.

BUCKLEY, HELEN AND EVA TIHANYI. *Canadian Policies for Rural Adjustment: A Study of the Economic Impact of ARDA, PFRA and MMRA*. Ottawa: Queen's Printer, 1967, 268 pp.

CANADA, DEPARTMENT OF AGRICULTURE; ARDA; AND PROVINCE OF NEWFOUNDLAND. *Educational Needs to Equip Rural People for Employment within a Changing Environment*. Ottawa: ARDA Project #1024, 1965.

CANADA, NORTHERN COORDINATION AND RESEARCH CENTER. *Social Science Research Abstracts, 1959-65*. Ottawa: 1966, 64 pp.

CHERNICK, S. E. *Disparités Interrégionales du Revenu*. Ottawa: Imprimeur de la Reine, 1966, 98 pp.
English ed. only — *Interregional Disparities in Income*.

CONNOR, D. N. ET D. W. MAGILL. *Instruction et Développement Rural*. Ottawa: Imprimeur de la Reine, 1967, 127 pp.

DEHEM, ROGER. "Concepts of Regional Planning," in *Canadian Public Administration*, IX:2 (June 1966), pp. 158-63.

DENTON, FRANK. *Analysis of Interregional Differences in Manpower Utilization and Earnings*. Ottawa: Queen's Printer, 1966, 65 pp.

FOGARTY, P. J. "Poverty in Rural Areas: With Particular Reference to Saskatchewan." Paper presented at the Canadian Conference on Social Welfare, Hamilton, Ontario (June 2-5, 1964).

HLADY, W. M. AND F. E. PRICE AND ASSOCIATES, LTD. *A Sociological Study of the Saskatchewan River Delta*. Ottawa: Federal Department of Forestry and Rural Development, 1967, 90 pp.

HODGE, G. "Do Villages Grow? Some Perspectives and Predictions," in *Rural Sociology*. 31:2 (June 1966), pp. 183-96.

LOTZ, J. R. "The Squatters of Whitehorse: A Study of the Problems of New Northern Settlements," in *Arctic* 13:3 (September 1965), pp. 172-88.

MACKAY, W. A. *Regional Interests and Policy in the Federal Structure*. Paper given at Conference of the Learned Societies, CPSA, Vancouver, 1965, 17 pp.

PARR, JOHN B. "Outmigration and the Depressed Area Problem," in *Land Economics*, XLII:2 (May 1966), pp. 149-59.

PEPIN, PIERRE-YVES. "Life and Poverty in the Maritimes," in *ARDA Research Reports*. Ottawa: Federal Department of Forestry and Rural Development, RE-3, 1968, 230 pp.

RICHARDS, J. HOWARD. "Perspectives on Regional Planning," in *Community Planning Review*, 17:1 (*Spring* 1967), pp. 18-19, and pp. 22-24.

SAUVE, MAURICE. *Politics of Rehabilitation and Development*. Notes of a speech delivered by the Hon. Maurice Sauvé, September 1966, 8 pp.
Comment on speech and ARDA, October 15, 1966, "Making Canada Work," 6 pp.

ST. FRANCIS XAVIER UNIVERSITY. *Review of the Work of the Extension Department, 1963-1964*. Antigonish, Nova Scotia: 1963, 16 pp.

WILSON, THOMAS. *Financial Assistance With Regional Development*. Report prepared for the Atlantic Provinces Research Board. Fredericton, New Brunswick: 1964, 72 pp.

VANDERKAMP, J. "Interregional Mobility in Canada: A Study of the Time Pattern of Migration," in the *Canadian Journal of Economics*, 1:3 (August 1968), pp. 595-608.

(ii) Age

THE AGING IN CANADA, *1966*. Ottawa: Canadian Welfare Council Committee on Aging, 1966.

The Canadian Conference on Aging—Proceedings. Ottawa: 1966, 150 pp.

CANADIAN CONFERENCE ON CHILDREN. *Background Papers.* Toronto: 1965, incl. "The Social Bases of Education" (F. Jones).

Canadian Labour. "CLC Brief on Aging," 11:6 (June 1966), pp. 14-17.

MILLER, E. AND G. MUNROE. "Children and Extreme Poverty," in *Canadian Welfare,* 41:2 (March/April 1965), pp. 68-72.

ONTARIO. *Report of the Ontario Legislature's Select Committee on Youth.* Kingston, Ontario: Hanson and Edgar Ltd., 1967, 408 pp.
See under *Ontario Legislative Assembly, Select Committee On Youth.*

(iii) Education

CARD, B. Y. *Professional Teachers' Perceptions of Social Factors Influencing Learning.* Edmonton: University of Alberta, Department of Sociology, 30 pp.

CONNOR, D. M. AND D. W. MAGILL. *The Role of Education in Rural Development.* ARDA Research Report #RE-1. Ottawa: Queen's Printer, December 1965, 131 pp.

ECONOMIC COUNCIL OF CANADA. *Sixth Annual Review;* "Trends and Regional Differences in Education."

FARINA, MARGARET. *A Report on the School Completion Project Conducted by the Central Neighborhood House, Toronto.* Toronto: Central Neighborhood House, 1964, 119 pp.

JONES, F. E. *The Social Bases of Education.* Toronto: Canadian Conference on Children, 1965, 92 pp.

LANDSBERG, MICHELE. "How our Middle-Class Schools Create Dropouts," in *Chatelaine,* October 1965, pp. 62-68.

LINTON, T. E. "Social and Cultural Factors in Deviant Classroom Behavior," in *Canada's Mental Health Supplement,* #52 (July/August 1966).

MALIK, M. A. *School Performance of Children in Families Receiving Public Assistance in Canada.* Ottawa: Canadian Welfare Council, September 1966, 245 pp.

NEW BRUNSWICK, DEPARTMENT OF LABOR. *Curriculum Research Study,* Fredericton, New Brunswick: 1964.

QUICK, E. J (ED.). *New Opportunities for the Culturally Disadvantaged.* Toronto: Canadian Education Association, 106 pp.

REID, T. E. "Education: The Key to Freedom in an Automated Society," in *Labour Gazette,* LXV:10 (October 1965), pp. 887-96.

WHITWORTH, F. E. ET R. MARTINEAU. *La Publication de la Recherche en Education au Canada.* Ottawa: Conseil Canadien pour la Recherche en Education, 1967, 26 pp.

WILKINSON, B. W. Department of Labour, Economics and Research Branch. *Studies in the Economics of Education.* Ottawa: Queen's Printer, 1966, 148 pp.

(iv) Social Class

DAVIS, ALLISON. *Social Class Influence Upon Learning.* Cambridge: Harvard University Press, 1948.

FRYER, JOHN L. "Technological Change and White Collar Workers," in *Canadian Labour,* 11:7 (August 1966).

GOW, KATHLEEN M. "Social Work and Social Class," in *The Social Worker,* XXXII (October 1965), pp. 218-225.

PARKS, ARTHUR C. *Productivity, the Use of Human Resources, and the Income Gap,* for the Atlantic Provinces Economic Council, 1967, #11, 32 pp.

PORTER, JOHN. *The Vertical Mosaic.* Toronto: University of Toronto Press, 1965.

(v) Ethnic Diversity

BEN-DOR, SHMUEL. *Makkovik: Eskimos and Settlers in a Labrador Community.* St. John's: Institute of Social and Economic Research, Memorial University of Newfoundland, 1966, 208 pp.

BOROVOY, A. A. "Indian Poverty in Canada," in *Canadian Labour,* 11:12 (December 1966), pp. 13-15.

BROWN, J. F. "New Housing for the Eskimos, Rehabilitation for Real," in *Urban Renewal and Public Housing in Canada,* 3:2, 2nd quarter, 1967, pp. 12-15.

BUCKLEY, HELEN, J. KEW AND J. B. HAWLEY. *The Indians and Metis of Northern Saskatchewan.* Saskatoon: Center for Community Studies, University of Saskatchewan, 1963, 114 pp.

CALDWELL, GEORGE. *Indian Residential Schools.* Ottawa: Canadian Welfare Council, 1967, 202 pp.

CANADA, INDIAN AFFAIRS BRANCH. *Survey of the Contemporary Indians of Canada: Economic, Political, Educational Needs and Policies, Part I,* October, 1966. Ottawa: Queen's Printer, 1967, 409 pp.

CANADIAN CORRECTIONS ASSOCIATION. *Indians and the Law.* Ottawa: Queen's Printer, August 1967, 67 pp.

CARD, B. Y., G. HIRABAYASHI, AND C. FRENCH. *The Metis in Alberta Society with Special Reference to Social, Economic and Cultural Factors Associated with Persistently High Tuberculosis Incidence.* Edmonton: University of Alberta, 1963.

CARNEY, R. J. AND W. O. FERGUSON. *A Selected and Annotated Bibliography on the Sociology of Eskimo Education.* Edmonton: University of Alberta, 1965, 59 pp.

CHANCE, NORMAN A. (ED.). *A Culture in Crisis: The Problems of Developmental Change Among the Cree, for McGill-Cree Project.* Ottawa: Federal Department of Forestry and Rural Development, 1968, 200 pp.

———, *The McGill-Cree Project,* Project Report. Montreal: McGill University, Department of Sociology and Anthropology, November 1966, 23 pp.

DALHOUSIE UNIVERSITY. *The Condition of Negroes of Halifax City, N.S.* Halifax: Institute of Public Affairs, 1962.

DAMAS, D. "Diversity in White-Eskimo Leadership Interaction," in *Anthropologica,* VIII:1 (1966), pp. 45-52.

ELEEN, JOHN. "The Poverty of Canadian Indians," in *Canadian Labour,* 10:7-8 (July/August 1965), 25 pp.

FERGUSON, E. *Newcomers in Transition: A Project of the International Institute of Metropolitan Toronto, 1962-64.* Toronto: The Institute. See under *International Institute of Metropolitan Toronto.*

FRANSEN, J. J. *Employment Experience and Economic Position of a Selected Group of Indians in Metro Toronto.* Toronto: University of Toronto School of Social Work, 1964, 105 pp.

HAGAN, WILLIAM T. *Indian Policy and Judges: Experiments in Acculturation and Control.* New Haven and London: Yale University Press; Montreal: McGill University Press, 1966.

HAWTHORN, H. B. ET AL. *The Indians of British Columbia.* Toronto: University of Toronto Press, 1958.

INGLANDER, EDITH. *The New People: The Eskimo's Journey Into our Time.* Garden City, N.Y.: Doubleday and Co., Inc., 1966, 205 pp.

JENNESS, D. *Eskimo Administration III: Labrador.* Montreal: Arctic Institute of North America, 1965, 94 pp.

LAGASSE, J. H. ET AL. *The People of Indian Ancestry.* Winnipeg: Queen's Printer, 1959, Vol. 1, 179 pp.; Vol. 2, 132 pp.; Vol. 3, 134 pp. See under *Manitoba, Department of Agriculture & Immigration, Social & Economic Research Office.*

LOTZ, JIM. "Human Rights of Indians and Eskimos," in *Canadian Labour,* 12:12 (December 1967), pp. 12-13 and p. 33.

MELLING, JOHN. *Right to a Future: The Native People of Canada.* Toronto: The Anglican Church of Canada and the United Church of Canada, 1967, 150 pp.

MORTIMORE, G. E. "Poverty, Separateness Indian's Major Problems, But Integration Won't Help at All," in *The Globe and Mail,* Toronto: May 27, 1965.

———, Series on the Indians of Canada in *The Globe and Mail,* Toronto: October 1967:

"Our Neglected Super-Citizens." October 21, pp. 16-20.

"Just Outside of Town are the Indians." October 21, pp. 20-21.

"The Hunting Days are Gone." October 28, pp. 7-9.

"What Next?" October 29, pp. 10-11.

ONTARIO HUMAN RIGHTS COMMISSION. "Special Issue on Indians." Toronto: Department of Labour, 1967. Available from 1260 Bay St., Toronto.

OSWALT, WENDELL H. *This Land Was Theirs. A Study of the North American Indian.* New York: John Wiley & Sons, Inc., 1966, 560 pp.

PLATIEL, RUDY. "Self-rule Produces Confidence," in *Indian Record,* XXX:3 (March 1967), pp. 14-15.

PODHORECKY, Z. S. *Ethnic Identity of the Metis in Saskatchewan.* Saskatchewan: University of Saskatchewan, 1965, 6 pp.

PRICE, BALCHEN AND ASSOCIATES. *White Bear Indian Reserve: Recreation Potential.* Ottawa: Federal Department of Forestry and Rural Development, 1967, 233 pp.

ROGERS, E. S. "Leadership Among the Indians of Eastern Subarctic Canada," in *Anthropologica,* VII:2, 1965, pp. 263-84.

SHAND, G. U. *Adult Education Among the Negroes of Nova Scotia.* Halifax: Dalhousie Institute of Public Affairs, 1961.

SHIMPO, M. AND R. WILLIAMSON. *Socio-Cultural Disintegration Among the Fringe Salteaux.* Saskatoon: Centre for Community Studies, April 1965, 291 pp.

SLOBODIN, RICHARD. *Metis of the MacKenzie District.* Ottawa: Canadian Research Centre for Anthropology, 1966, 175 pp.

SMITH, A. J. "The Environment of the Canadian Indian," in *Habitat* (July/August 1965), pp. 2-9.

TREMBLAY, M. A. *Social Dynamics and Patterns of Education.* Paper presented at the Canadian Welfare Council Annual Meeting, May 1963. Ottawa: Canadian Welfare Council, 1963.

WAX, ROSALIE H. "The Warrior Dropouts," in *Trans-action,* 4:6 (May 1967), pp. 40-46.

III. OPPORTUNITY STRUCTURES AND THE CULTURE OF POVERTY

B. THE CULTURE OF POVERTY

ANDERSON, ISABEL. *Internal Migration in Canada, 1921-1961.* Study #13 of the Economic Council. Ottawa: Queen's Printer, 1966, 90 pp.

ANDERSON, R. K. "World Trends in Population Control," in *Canadian Journal of Public Health,* 57:2 (February 1966), pp. 51-54.

ASIMAKOPULOS, A. "The Income Distribution of Canadian Urban Family Saving, 1959," in *Canadian Journal of Economics and Political Science,* XXXII:1 (February 1966), pp. 15-26.

AYRES, B. *Caseload Analyses Vancouver.* Community Chests and Councils of the Greater Vancouver Area, September 1965.

BLOOM, BENJAMIN S., ALLISON DAVIS AND ROBERT HESS. *Compensatory Education for Cultural Deprivation.* Department of Education, University of Chicago, 1965.

Current Anthropology. Vol. 10 (April/June 1969), pp. 181-201.

FAMILY SERVICE ASSOCIATION OF METROPOLITAN TORONTO. "FSA Looks at the Low-Income Earner," in *On Record* (March/April 1965).

———, "FSA Looks at Housing," in *On Record* (June/July 1966).

FARIS, JAMES C. *Cat Harbour: A Newfoundland Fishing Settlement.* St. John's: Memorial University, Insitute of Social and Economic Research, 1966, 249 pp.

LOTZ, J. R. "The Dawson Area: A Regional Monograph." Ottawa: Northern Corridor and Resource Centre, Dept. of Northern Affairs and National Resources, 1965, Yukon Project #2.

ONTARIO FEDERATION OF LABOUR. *The Automated Society: Good or Bad?* Toronto: 1965, 39 pp.

Ontario Housing. 12:2 (1966). Issue devoted to the aging and their problems.

RIESSMAN, F. *The Culturally Deprived Child*. New York: Harper, 1962.

ROACH, JACK L. AND ORVILLE GURSTIN. "An Evaluation of the Concept: Culture of Poverty," in *Social Forces,* 45 (March 1967), pp. 383-92.

SCHMEISER, D. A. *Civil Liberties in Canada*. Toronto: Oxford University Press, 1964, 302 pp.

SOCIAL PLANNING COUNCIL OF METROPOLITAN TORONTO. *Guide for Family Budgeting*. Toronto: 1964, 64 pp.

TITMUSS, RICHARD. "Poverty and Social Security," in *Canadian Welfare,* 41:3 (May/June 1965).

VALLEE, FRANCIS G. "The Coop Hut in the Arctic," in *North,* 13:3 (May/June 1966).

VALENTINE, CHARLES A. *Culture and Poverty: Critique and Counter Proposals*. Chicago: University of Chicago Press, 1968.

YERBY, ALONZO. "The Disadvantaged and Health Care," in *Public Welfare,* XXIV:1 (January 1966), pp. 73-77.

IV. PROGRAMS AND STRATEGIES

(a) Regional and Community Planning

BERGEVIN, J. B. "Gaspé: A Case Study in Regional Planning," in *Canadian Public Administration,* IX:I (March 1966), pp. 86-95.

CARVER, H. "Community Renewal Programming," in *Habitat* (May/June 1965), pp. 6-10.

CITY OF OTTAWA, PLANNING BRANCH, PLANNING AND WORKS (SEPTEMBER). *Lower Town East Neighborhood Study*. Ottawa: March, 1966. See under *Ottawa, Department of Planning and Works, Planning Branch, Lower Town.*

COMMUNITY PLANNING ASSOCIATION OF CANADA. "The Citizen's Role in Community Planning." Ottawa: 1966.

CONNOR, DESMOND M. "Diagnosing Community Problems." Antigonish, Nova Scotia: St. Francis Xavier University, September 1966.

FRIEDMANN, J. AND M. ALONSO (EDS.). *Regional Development and Planning: A Reader*. Cambridge: The MIT Press, 1964.

GANS, HERBERT J. "The Failure of Urban Renewal," in *Commentary,* 39:4 (April 1965), pp. 29-31.

GOODENOUGH, N. H. *Cooperation in Change: An Anthropological Approach to Community Development*. New York: Russell Sage Foundation, 1963.

HODGE, G. "Urban Systems and Regional Policy," in *Canadian Public Administration,* IX:2 (June 1966), pp. 181-93. (Nature and role of urban systems.)

JONES, MURRAY V. "Urban Focus and Regional Planning," in *Canadian Public Administration,* IX:2 (June 1966), pp. 171-180.

Labour Gazette. "Plant Relocation and Its Consequences." (August 1965).

MACDONALD, A. A. AND M. B. CLARE. *A Survey of Human Resources and Their Rural Environment*. ARDA Res. 32012, Antigonish, Nova Scotia: St. Francis Xavier University, 1966.

———. "Rural South Inverness Resource Survey." ARDA Res. 22002, Antigonish, Nova Scotia: St. Francis Xavier University, 1966, 205 pp.

NELSON, THOMAS. *Policies for Regional Development*. Toronto: Clarke Irwin and Co., Ltd., 1964, 93 pp.

(b) Health and Welfare

BOURQUE, G. AND R. BROWN. *Federal Legislation Related to Social Welfare, 1908-65.* Ottawa: Department of National Health and Welfare, 1966.

CANADIAN WELFARE COUNCIL. *Health Services for Canada.* Ottawa: 1965.

GELPER, SYLVIA M. "The Path to Health Insurance," in *Canadian Public Administration,* IX:2 (June 1966).

GRANT, V. B. *Health Care for the Community.* Baltimore: The Johns Hopkins Press, 1963, 194 pp.

GRIPTON, JAMES. "Blueprint for Revision in Public Welfare in Quebec: An Essay Review," in *Social Service Review,* XXXIX:3 (September 1964), pp. 320-32.

KATZ, A. H. "Application of Self-Help Concepts in Current Social Welfare," in *Social Work,* 10:3 (July 1965).

LAYCOCK, J. E. "A Blueprint for Health Services in Canada: An Essay Review," in *Social Service Review,* XXXIX:1 (March 1965), pp. 72-82.

MATHEWS, V. L. "The Public Health Implications of Population Trends," in *Canadian Journal of Public Health,* 57:2 (February 1966), pp. 60-64.

MENNIE, W. A. "Health and Poverty," in *Medical Services Journal,* XXI:11 (December 1965), pp. 787-84.

MILLER JAMES R. "Human Genetics in Public Health Research and Programming," in *Canadian Journal of Public Health,* 57:1.

MORGAN, J. S. *The Prospect of Welfare.* Ottawa: Canadian Welfare Council, August, 1965.

———, (ED.). *Welfare and Wisdom.* Toronto: University of Toronto Press, 1960. See under *University of Toronto, School of Social Work, "Welfare & Wisdom."*

———, AND A. ROSE. "The Unfinished Business of Social Security: Part I and Part II," in *The Social Worker,* 33:3 and 33:4 (July 1965 and October 1965).

OSBORNE, JONES E. "Canada Combats Poverty Through Social Policy," in *Public Welfare,* XXIV:2 (April 1966).

OWEN, JOHN E. "Some Basic Assumptions of Welfare Work," in *Canadian Welfare,* 42:5 (September/October 1966). (Principles which guide social welfare workers.)

PALTIEL, FREDA L. "Welfare Research in Canada — A Review," in *Canadian Welfare,* 42:5 (September/October 1966), pp. 172-83.

PHILLIPS, R. A. J. "Poverty and Health," in *Medical Service Journal,* 21:11 (December 1965), pp. 820-22.

STUBBENS, HENRY. "Public Attitudes Toward Welfare," in *Canadian Welfare,* 41:4 (July/August 1965).

TOLLEFSON, E. A. *Bitter Medicine: The Saskatchewan Medicare Feud.* Saskatoon: Modern Press, 1964, 236 pp.

(c) Housing Programs

ADAMSON, R. T. "National Housing Measures and Their Relation to Work and Opportunity Programmes." Ottawa: CMHC (November 1965), 33 pp.

Canadian Labour. 11:3 (March 1966). (Issue on Housing.)

GILLIES, JOHN. "From Shacks to Modern Towns." *The Globe and Mail,* Toronto. (November 10, 1966), p. 9.

GOLDBLATT, SYLVIA. "Integration or Isolation," in *Habitat* (January 1966), pp. 14-23.

MACDONALD, A. A., A. D. MACHEAN AND W. B. CLARE. *Eastern Counties Co-op Housing Survey.* Antigonish, Nova Scotia: St Francis Xavier University Extension Dept., June, 1965.

MURRAY, JAMES A. *Good Housing for Canadians.* Toronto: Ontario Association of Housing Authorities. See under *Ontario Association of Housing Authorities.*

RINGER, P. "Housing and the Poor," in *Ontario Housing,* 12:1 (February 1966).

ROSE, A. *Rehabilitation of Housing in Central Toronto.* Toronto: City of Toronto Planning Board, September 1966, 96 pp.

Social Planning Council of Metropolitan Toronto.
- "A Statement on Housing and Urban Renewal" (September 1965), 6 pp.
- "A Background Statement on Social Services in Public Housing" (March 1966), 3 pp.
- "Further Steps in Housing Improvement" (June 1966), 10 pp.
- "A Preliminary Study of Social Implications of High Density Living Conditions," 1966, 35 pp.

(d) Economics

FRYER, J. L. "Poverty: Can We Afford It?" in *Information,* XIV (April 1966), pp. 25-28.

SCHULTZ, T. W. "Investing in Poor People: An Economist's View," in *American Economic Review,* LV:2 (May 1965), pp. 510-20.

THEOBALD, R. "Jobs for All or Incomes for All: An Urgent Choice," in *Public Welfare,* XVIV:1 (January 1966), pp. 43-49.

WAISGLASS, HARRY J. *Toward Equitable Income Disribution.* Toronto: United Steelworkers of America, 1966.

WOODSWORTH, DAVID. "Community Funds and the War on Poverty," in *Canadian Welfare,* 42:2 (March/April 1966), pp. 54-62.

(e) Legal Aspects

DOVERMAN, MAX. "Today's Legal Revolution: The Reformation of Social Welfare Practice," in *Social Service Review,* XL:2 (June 1966).

GROSSER, C. F. AND E. V. SPARER. "Legal Services for the Poor: Social Work and Social Justice," in *Social Work,* vl:1 (January 1966), pp. 81-87.

(f) Opportunity Programs (Employment)

ABRAMSON, J. "The Power of an Image to Affect Commitment to Social Action," ARDA. Ottawa: 1968.

ADAMS, V. F. *Counselling and Guidance.* Toronto: Collier Macmillan, Canada Ltd., 1965.

BROWN, R. I. *Public Assistance Programmes in Canada: A Brief Analysis.* Ottawa: Department of National Health and Welfare, 1965.

CANADIAN COUNCIL FOR RESEARCH IN EDUCATION. *Fourth Canadian Conference on Educational Research.* Ottawa: 1966.

Canadian Labour. 11:1 (January 1966). *(Issue devoted to "Manpower Policy in Canada.")*

CWC Poverty Supplement. November 1967. Privy Council, Special Planning Secretariat, "Meeting Poverty," (33 issues). See under *Canada Privy Council, Special Planning Secretariat.*

CYC. *A Report on Community Organizing Projects, Summer 1965.* Ottawa: 1965.

DENAULT, HAYDA. "La pauvreté et le service en Amérique Au Nord," in *Service Social* IX (November/December 1960), pp. 50-81. (Historical survey from the 1800's.)

HILL, W. G. "The Family as a Treatment Unit: Differential Techniques and Procedures," in *Social Work,* 11:2 (April 1966).

KEPPEL, F. "Education and Welfare: Allies Against Poverty," in *Public Welfare,* XXIII:4 (October 1965).

Labour Gazette. "Accelerated Vocational Training for Adults," LXV:8 (August 1965), pp. 704-05.

______, "Blaheney House for the Handicapped" (September 1966), p. 519.

"The War on Poverty" (September 1965), pp. 794-98. (Summary of Programs: ARDA, CYC, The Canadian Assistance Plan, etc.).

______, "Work and Opportunity Programs" (October 1965).

LAMPMAN, ROBERT J. "Approaches to the Reduction of Poverty," in *American Economic Review,* LV:2 (May 1965), pp. 521-29.

LANCTOT, JEAN-B. *The ARDA Programmes of Community Development.* Ottawa: Department of Forestry, ARDA (November 1965), 33 pp. and appendices.

MENZIES, M. W. *Poverty in Canada: Its Nature, Significance and Implications for Public Policy.* Winnipeg: Manitoba Pool Elevators, 1965.

MOGULD, M. B. "Involving Low-Income Neighbourhoods in Anti-Delinquency Programs," in *Social Work,* 10, No. 4 (October 1965), pp. 51-57.

MORGAN, J. S. "The Real Issues in A War on Poverty," in *Information,* XIV (April 1966), pp. 28-32.

(g) General

MACLEAN, D. F., AND T. M. JONES. *Feasibility Studies of Centres for Residential Adult Education in the Maritime Provinces.* Halifax: Institute of Public Affairs, 1965, 153 pp.

MCGANN, DAVID. "More in Sorrow. Social Action and the Indian Boarding Home Program", in *Canadian Welfare,* 43:4 (July/August 1967), pp. 24-29.

MESSNER, J. A. "Day Care – Right or Remedy?" in *Canadian Welfare,* 42:2 (March/April 1966), pp. 63-7.

OTTAWA WELFARE COUNCIL, CENTRAL VOLUNTEER BUREAU. *After-Four Center, A Pilot Project, 1965-1966.* Ottawa: 1966, 28 pp.

PAUKERT, FELIX. "Sécurité sociale et redistribution du revenu: étude comparée," in *Revues inter-nationale du Travail,* 98:5 (November 1968), pp. 467-95.

SOCIAL PLANNING COUNCIL OF CALGARY. *An Area Approach to Services for Low-Income Families,* 1965, 10 pp.

VALLEE, F. G. *Povugnetuk and its Cooperative: A Case Study in Community Change.* Ottawa: Northern Coordination and Research Center, Department of Indian Affairs and Northern Development, 1967, 57 pp.

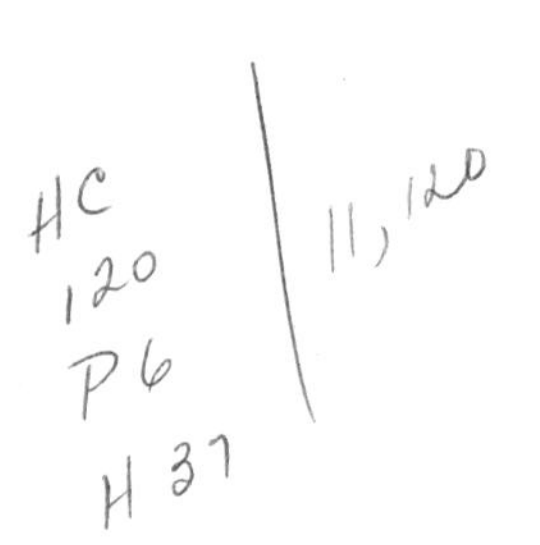

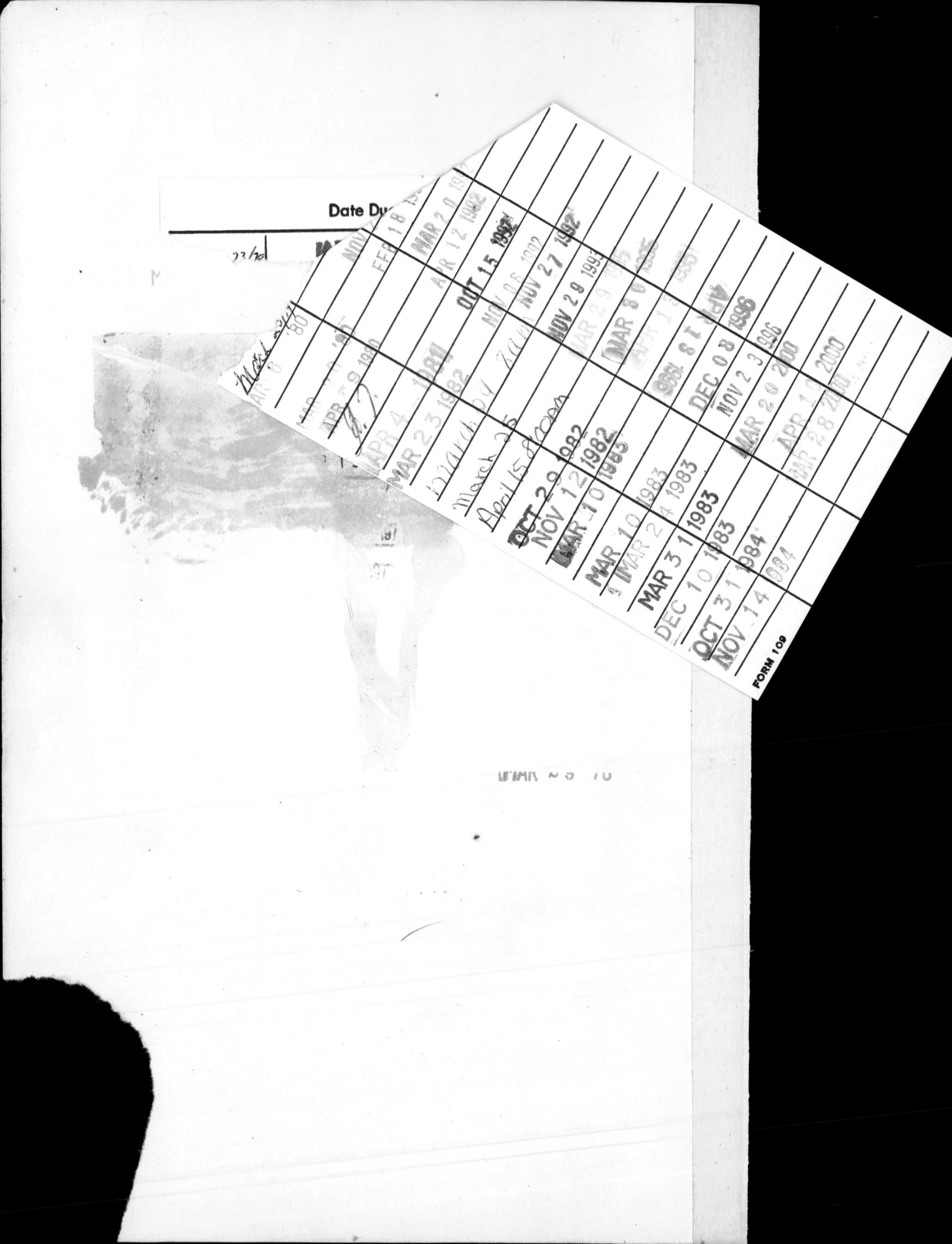